✳ THE KANSAS COOKBOOK

THE KANSAS COOKBOOK

Recipes from the Heartland

FRANK CAREY & JAYNI NAAS

ILLUSTRATED BY ROBIN M. NANCE

UNIVERSITY PRESS OF KANSAS

© 1989 by Frank Carey and Jayni Naas
Illustrations © 1989 by the University Press of Kansas
All rights reserved

Published by the University Press of Kansas (Lawrence, Kansas 66045),
which was organized by the Kansas Board of Regents and is operated and
funded by Emporia State University, Fort Hays State University, Kansas
State University, Pittsburg State University, the University of Kansas,
and Wichita State University

Library of Congress Catalog Card Number: 89-51768

Printed in the United States of America
10   9   8   7   6   5   4   3   2

✳ Contents

Preface vii

Acknowledgments ix

Appetizers 1

Soups and Stews 30

Beef and Red Meats 61

Pork 125

Poultry and Game 155

Fish 198

Pastas, Grains, and Casseroles 216

Vegetables 246

Salads 288

Breads and Breadstuffs 319

Relishes and Preserves 364

Desserts 384

Kansas Menus 455

Contributors 459

Index 463

✳ Preface

In May of 1988, we stirred up a hornet's nest with a press release soliciting recipes for our forthcoming Kansas cookbook. The release quoted a *Dateline America* article in which Charles Kuralt put out a traveler's advisory for those heading west from Kansas City. Stock up on peanut-butter sandwiches, he warned, because there is "nothing to eat until one reaches Denver. Kansas is the gastronomic wasteland of America."

Proud Kansas cooks were spurred into action. Recipes began pouring in from all over the state. We were sent recipes that had been handed down through generations, complete with charming stories and family histories. Recipes came in from people of nearly every ethnic group that had settled in Kansas. There were recipes that showcased Kansas ingredients and recipes that cooks sent simply in the spirit of sharing their family favorites. Every one of them sounded deliciously Midwestern, with names like Lou Belle's Best-Ever Meat Loaf, Catfish Grilled in Corn Husks, Sand Hill Plum Butter, and Poor Man's Soup with a Rich Man's Flavor. We never expected such a warm and supportive response from so many people.

Throughout the summer, we cooked and tested, sorting through the recipes to find the ones that fit our criteria for the cookbook. Our research into the historical foodways of Kansas described a foundation of simple cooking based on the farm tradition of the people who settled in this region. Ethnic cuisines remain undiluted for a state populated by such diversity, creating strong undercurrents that still influence the way Kansans choose to cook. Kansas cooking is honest and sincere; its ingredients are fresh and real. Meals have lasting integrity without trendy affectation. In short, wholesome ingredients are prepared straightforwardly and presented as a celebration of themselves.

We also created our own recipes, possessed by the notion that simple ingredients and good techniques would

produce a meal worthy of Kansas' heritage. Traveling
throughout the state, learning more about its people,
agriculture, and history, inspired more recipes. We modernized historic dishes and created contemporary recipes
befitting today's trend toward Heartland cooking. All
were inspired by the many excellent Kansas ingredients
available to us. Kansas is a major source for foods that
feed the nation and the world; it should be known as well
as a source for inspired cooking.

The result is over four hundred well-tested recipes.
We avoided cryptic instructions, choosing instead de-
scriptive phrasing that truly instructs and reassures the
cook. To show how each recipe is sewn into the quilt
of Kansas foodways, each contains a historical note, a
personal comment, or a serving suggestion. Providing a
backdrop to the recipes are personal anecdotes and short
accounts of ethnic settlement and historic events.

Throughout this experience we have learned as much
about people as we have about food. From our press
release, we solicited recipes "to find out what Kansans
really cook." That we did. What we received in those
letters and conversations as well was a sense of family
and heritage. Foods evoke memories of good times and
hard times. In the past, food melted away barriers to a
stranger approaching a campfire or between immigrants
on neighboring homesteads. Today, food brings people
together for the harvest, the church social, or the family
reunion. The "breaking of bread" is a tradition that will
be lost if not practiced. Folks throughout America are
looking to the Heartland as a source of wholesome inspiration. For the greatest gift in dining is not the fanfare
and panache of a glitzy restaurant but a more costly in-
vestment: the gift of your time and the sharing of a meal.

✳ Acknowledgments

We would like to express our sincere thanks to the many Kansas cooks who sent us their special recipes and stories. Though they could not all be published, each submission provided an accurate feeling for what Kansans like to cook.

A special thanks to the following people: Wilma Ackerman, whose contagious enthusiasm spurred our first wave of contributors; Lorraine Kaufman, who introduced us to the Swiss and German Mennonite cooking of central Kansas; and Jay Pruiett, our resource on game cookery. For the delicious Swedish recipes from the community of Lindsborg our thanks to Alice Brax and to Anna Marie Krusic, who sparked the interest of good cooks in southeast Kansas. In difficult times, the support and encouragement of our friends Kelly Kindscher and Sandy Strand proved invaluable, as did their information on foods—wild and domestic. Also, we give our thanks to the staff of the University Press of Kansas for their guidance and support throughout this project.

✳ APPETIZERS

Appetizers include an unlimited variety of foods and beverages served as a preview to the dishes to come. At their best, they create anticipation for what is to follow without giving an actual sample of the main event. To achieve their purpose of sparking the appetite, they must be attractive and temptingly flavored.

Today's preference for honest and simple meals often presents the diner with a tasteful array of crisp vegetables accompanied by a highly seasoned dipping sauce. In Kansas, hors d'oeuvres and canapés are only as common as the formal dinner that would follow such appetizers. The pervasiveness of casual entertaining in Kansas lends itself to more familiar appetizers such as snacks and cocktail food.

Some ethnic groups, however, traditionally serve appetizers before holiday meals. The most dazzling array of appetizers, including deliciously decorated canapés, would be found at a traditional Swedish smorgasbord. The generous variety offered usually includes tiny Swedish Meatballs. Sweet Macaroni served with homemade wine is a Christmas tradition in southeast Kansas homes with an Italian influence. Those with an English heritage might toast the holiday season with a glass of Wassail. On Strawberry Hill, the Croatians serve Nadjev, a ham dressing stuffed in sausage casings.

Wild delicacies, too, are often served as appetizers. Venison Mincemeat Pie or Fried Morel Mushrooms, offered as a starter, give guests the opportunity to savor those unique flavors without competition from other dishes.

Snacks make great starters for dining and are essential for other kinds of entertaining. Kansas is one of the top ten producers of popcorn, an ever-popular snack. Garlic Popcorn, Oven Caramel Corn, and Cinnamon Popcorn are three variations offered here for the jaded snacker. Soy Nuts and Granola are suggested as tasty snacks made of common Kansas ingredients.

✳ Fresh Asparagus Spears with Dip

Karen Pendleton, Lawrence

The origin of asparagus is not well documented, but it is considered to be a plant of the Old World. It grows best in regions where the ground freezes several inches deep in the winter; thus when brought to Kansas it flourished. Karen Pendleton, whose farm produces many acres of asparagus, counsels, "The key to good asparagus is eating it fresh, minutes from the garden."

2 pounds fresh asparagus spears
assortment of fresh vegetables (optional)

ASPARAGUS DIP
2 cups asparagus, cooked
½ cup sour cream
¼ teaspoon hot pepper sauce
½ teaspoon dill
½ teaspoon salt

Wash the asparagus to remove sand. Trim the bottoms to the tender part of the stalk and arrange the spears on a large platter. You may include other fresh vegetables such as cherry tomatoes, cucumber sticks, broccoli tops, snow peas, zucchini, and carrots. Serve with Asparagus Dip.

Asparagus Dip: Cook the asparagus in a small amount of water until tender. Drain. Put the asparagus, sour cream, hot sauce, dill, and salt in a blender or food processor. Blend until smooth. Cover and chill for 1 hour.

Serves 8 or more.

Option: If you don't care for raw asparagus, blanch the asparagus in boiling water for 20 seconds. Remove and place in a pan of ice water to cool. Drain and chill. This will remove the "grassy" taste but leave the spears firm for dipping.

✳ Corn Puffs

Edna McGhee, Madison

Kansas corn, fresh from the field or a backyard garden, makes these fritters a

2 eggs
1 cup mashed potatoes
½ cup all-purpose flour
1 teaspoon baking powder

favorite. Serve Corn Puffs as an appetizer or with cold sliced meats and fresh tomatoes.

½ teaspoon salt
⅛ teaspoon pepper
2 tablespoons milk
1 cup fresh or canned whole kernel corn
2 tablespoons onion, finely chopped
2 tablespoons green pepper, finely chopped
vegetable oil or shortening for deep-fat frying

In a large mixing bowl, beat the eggs. Add the mashed potatoes and beat until well blended.

Sift the flour into a small bowl. Stir in the baking powder, salt, and pepper. Add the dry ingredients to the potato mixture, mixing well. Blend in the milk. Fold in the corn, onion, and green pepper.

In a heavy-bottomed pan, heat the oil or shortening over high heat until hot enough to sizzle. Drop the batter by tablespoonfuls into the oil and fry until golden brown, turning once. Drain on paper towels and serve immediately.

Makes 18.

✳ Baked Artichoke Hearts

Artichoke hearts, dipped in garlic butter, rolled in a cheese-and-bread-crumb mixture, and baked to a golden brown, make a delicious first course for an elegant meal. Artichoke recipes such as this one have roots in Italian cookery and may appear on the tables of Italian families in southeast Kansas.

1 13-ounce can artichoke hearts
¼ cup butter
1 garlic clove, minced
¼ cup Parmesan cheese, grated
¼ cup fresh white bread crumbs

Drain the artichokes well by pressing out the excess moisture. Slice in half. Melt the butter over low heat and stir in the minced garlic. Combine the Parmesan cheese and bread crumbs in a small bowl. Dip the sliced artichoke hearts into the garlic butter and roll them in the cheese-and-bread-crumb mixture. Place them in a small baking dish and drizzle with the remaining garlic butter.

Bake uncovered at 425 degrees for 15 to 20 minutes, until lightly browned.

Serves 4.

✳ Marinated Peppers

Marinated peppers can dress up an appetizer plate or brighten salads in late summer and early fall, when homegrown peppers abound. For a colorful array, use a variety of hot and mild, including bell peppers, green chilies, banana peppers, and jalapeños.

3 pounds mixed peppers

MARINADE
½ cup olive oil
3 tablespoons lemon juice
½ teaspoon salt
3 whole garlic cloves, peeled

Arrange the peppers on a foil-covered baking sheet. Broil, turning frequently, until the peppers are wrinkled and charred on all sides. Place the peppers in a sealed paper bag for 1 hour for easier peeling.

Peel and remove stems, seeds, and pith, rinsing under cold water. Drain well and pat dry with paper towels. Slice the peppers into 1-inch-wide strips.

Marinade: Combine all the ingredients for the marinade in a large bowl, mixing well. Add the pepper slices to the bowl and stir gently to combine. Cover and chill for at least 24 hours before using.

Makes 2 to 3 cups.

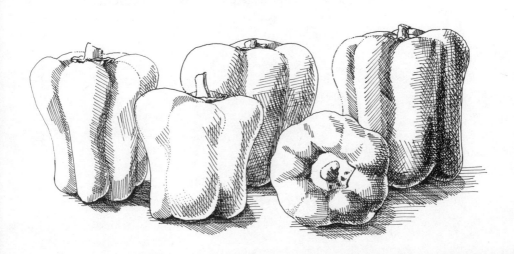

✳ Guacamole Quesadillas

More than any other ethnic food in Kansas, Mexican cuisine seems to be the most popular. Kansans have practically adopted it as their own. These simple avocado- and cheese-filled tortillas are quickly fried, then topped with lettuce and salsa. A tasty appetizer, they can also be served as a vegetarian entree.

3 ripe avocados
1 tablespoon lemon juice
4 garlic cloves, minced
¼ teaspoon salt
¼ teaspoon pepper
1 package 8-inch flour tortillas
½ cup Monterey jack cheese, shredded
2 tablespoons vegetable oil or shortening
shredded lettuce
salsa

Peel the avocados, remove the seeds, and coarsely chop. In a large bowl, mash the avocados with a potato masher or a fork. Add the lemon juice, garlic, salt, and pepper. Mix well and add more seasonings to taste.

Place 2 tablespoons of the guacamole on the center of each tortilla and sprinkle with about 1 tablespoon of the cheese. Fold each tortilla in half and secure with 3 toothpicks. Heat the oil or shortening in a medium-sized frying pan over medium-high heat. When hot enough to sizzle, place 2 quesadillas at a time in the frying pan and fry each side for about 30 seconds, or until lightly browned. Drain on paper towels. Add more oil to the pan if necessary and continue cooking the quesadillas. Remove the toothpicks and serve immediately with the shredded lettuce and salsa.

Makes 8 to 10.

✳ Fried Morel Mushrooms

In the early spring, wild morel mushrooms grow abundantly in Kansas. Indian tribes and early settlers sought them as food, as do mushroom enthusiasts today. Perhaps the best description of where to find them is found in these words of folklore:

When the bracken
    fern is still rolled
    up like a fiddlehead
And the buds on
    the oak trees are
    the size of
    squirrels' ears
And if the nights are
    warm, the spring
wet and the white
    violets bloom,
Go and search
    beneath a dying
    elm . . .

This recipe is the most popular way to cook morels and to savor their delicious, nutty flavor.

butter or vegetable oil
fresh morel mushrooms*, sliced lengthwise
all-purpose flour
salt and pepper, to taste

Rinse the sliced morels in several changes of salt water, about 1 teaspoon of salt to 1 quart of cold water. Rinse in plain water and drain on paper towels.

Over medium-high heat, melt the butter or oil in a frying pan until hot enough to sizzle. Dredge the sliced morels in the flour. Shake off excess flour and place the mushrooms in the frying pan. Fry until golden brown, turning once. Drain the mushrooms on paper towels. Add salt and pepper to taste.

Servings: Never enough!

* Never eat wild mushrooms you cannot positively identify.

✳ Morel Mushroom Turnovers

If you're lucky enough to have a secret morel patch, the following recipe will turn this coveted mushroom into a gourmet appetizer. If you're not inclined to hunt for morels, you may substitute fresh button mushrooms.

8 ounces morel mushrooms*, sliced lengthwise
1 small onion, finely chopped
6 tablespoons butter, divided
¼ teaspoon marjoram
¼ teaspoon thyme
¼ teaspoon salt
⅛ teaspoon pepper
½ cup cream

PASTRY
8 ounces cream cheese, softened
½ cup butter, chilled
1½ cups all-purpose flour

Rinse the sliced morels in several changes of salt water, about 1 teaspoon of salt to 1 quart of cold water. Rinse in plain water and drain on paper towels. Finely chop the morels and set aside.

In a large frying pan, melt 3 tablespoons of the butter over medium-low heat. Add the onion and cook until soft and transparent. Add the remaining 3 tablespoons of butter and the chopped morels and cook until tender. Stir in the marjoram, thyme, salt, and pepper. Turn the heat to medium-high and add the cream. Cook and stir until the mixture is thick and bubbly, about 3 to 5 minutes. Remove the pan from the heat and cool the mixture to room temperature. Meanwhile, make the pastry.

Pastry: Using a pastry blender or a fork, cut the cream cheese and butter into the flour. Knead lightly on a floured surface until smooth. If you are not using the pastry immediately, wrap it in waxed paper and refrigerate.

To assemble, roll the pastry out to ¹⁄₁₆-inch thickness on a lightly floured surface. Cut into 2- to 3-inch rounds with a cookie cutter. Place 1 teaspoon of the mushroom filling on the center of each round. Fold in half, sealing the edges firmly with your fingertips. Prick each turnover with a fork and bake on an ungreased cookie sheet

*Never eat wild mushrooms you cannot positively identify.

at 350 degrees for 18 to 20 minutes, or until edges of the turnovers begin to brown.

Makes 5 dozen.

✳ Grilled Mushrooms

Grilling mushrooms is an enterprising way to keep hungry guests at bay when cooking outdoors. The smoky flavor of mushrooms cooked on the backyard barbecue makes a delicious appetizer or side dish for grilled meats. Put them on first once the coals are ready.

1 pound button mushrooms
¼ cup butter, melted
2 teaspoons soy sauce
2 teaspoons lemon juice
1 teaspoon tarragon

Rinse the mushrooms and drain on paper towels. Place the mushrooms on a large piece of heavy aluminum foil, turning up the edges to form the shape of a bowl.

Melt the butter in a small pan and stir in the soy sauce, lemon juice, and tarragon. Pour over the mushrooms. Close the foil over the mushrooms, leaving the top slightly open. Place directly over hot coals on a covered grill and cook for 30 minutes.

Serves 6.

✳ Broiled Mushrooms with Herb Butter Stuffing

Herbs grow well in the Midwest and provide gardeners with an array of fresh flavors for cooking. These mushroom appetizers are filled with a fresh herb stuffing that complements their natural savory flavor.

1 pound large button mushrooms (about 12 mushrooms)
¼ cup butter, slightly softened
1 green onion, finely chopped
½ teaspoon fresh parsley, finely chopped
½ teaspoon fresh marjoram, finely chopped
½ teaspoon fresh thyme, finely chopped

Rinse the mushrooms and drain on paper towels. Carefully remove the stems from the mushrooms and set aside. Refrigerate the caps until ready to use.

In a mixing bowl, cream the butter until light and fluffy. Add the green onion and the chopped herbs. Mix well.

Finely chop enough of the reserved mushroom stems to make ¼ cup and add to the herb butter. Cover and refrigerate for 30 minutes.

Place a large piece of aluminum foil on a cookie sheet. Turn up the edges slightly, to catch the juices. Place the mushroom caps top side down on the cookie sheet. Fill each cap with the herb butter stuffing.

Preheat the oven broiler. Place the cookie sheet 6 inches from the broiler. Broil for 4 to 6 minutes, until the mushrooms and herb butter stuffing begin to brown. Serve warm.

Serves 4 to 6.

✳ Venison Mincemeat Pie

Harry W. Kroeger, Jr., Lawrence

Before the pioneers settled on the prairies, buffalo, antelope, and elk roamed Kansas in large numbers, while deer populated the state's eastern woodlands. Zebulon Pike reported seeing deer in the wooded areas of east-central Kansas in 1806 and herds of mule deer were a common sight along the Smoky Hill, Saline, and Solomon rivers in 1866. By 1890,

the deer were rapidly disappearing from Kansas due to drought and encroaching civilization, and by 1933, deer were considered absent from Kansas.

In the late 1930s and early 1940s, the Kansas Fish and Game Commission stocked deer in various parts of the state, and consequently the population has steadily increased. Today, white tailed deer and

Rocky Mountain mule deer are once again commonly seen in wooded areas near dawn or dusk.

This recipe for a mincemeat pie made with venison and Jonathan apples makes a perfect fall treat for the Kansas deer hunter. Harry Kroeger likes to serve this aromatic pie as an appetizer, but it also makes a good side dish or dessert.

½ pound venison
3 ounces beef suet
1 pound Jonathan apples, cored and quartered
½ pound raisins, or ¼ pound each currants and raisins
½ teaspoon cinnamon
½ teaspoon ginger

½ teaspoon ground cloves
½ teaspoon allspice
¼ teaspoon nutmeg
¼ teaspoon salt
½ cup apple cider
¼ cup brandy
½ cup sugar
1 tablespoon cornstarch
2 unbaked 9-inch double-crust pie shells

Trim the fat from the venison and cut into 1-inch cubes. Place the venison in a large saucepan and add enough water to cover. Simmer over low heat for 35 minutes. Do not boil, as the venison will become tough and stringy. Leaving the venison in the broth, cool slightly. Cover and refrigerate overnight. When well chilled, remove the fat from the broth and discard. Remove the meat and reserve the broth for another use.

Grind the venison, beef suet, and half of the apples together using the coarse blade of a meat grinder. Place the meat mixture in a large bowl. Coarsely chop the remaining apples and combine with the meat mixture. Add the raisins, spices, and salt and set aside.

In a small saucepan, combine the cider, brandy, and sugar. Warm over low heat, stirring until the sugar is dissolved. Add the cornstarch and stir to combine. Pour the cider mixture into the meat mixture, mixing well. Pour into 2 unbaked pie shells. Adjust the top crusts and crimp the edges. Cut slits for the steam to escape.

Bake at 450 degrees for 30 minutes, or until the crust is golden.

Serves 16.

✳ Buffalo Chicken Wings with Blue Cheese Dip

Merle Bird, Rossville

This recipe comes not from Kansas, but from New York. A bar in Buffalo was out of nearly everything for making hors d'oeuvres, but out of desperation was born inspiration. From a few simple ingredients emerged a nationally famous recipe.

So how did it get in this book? There were two reasons. The contributor is certainly a hundred percent Kansan—Merle Bird, a Topeka-based food writer, who champions simple food pleasures and good humor. And secondly, as we're sure Merle would agree, it's only fair that if New Yorkers can lay claim to "buffalo," then Kansans can claim their chicken wings.

16 chicken wings (about 3 pounds)
vegetable shortening
¼ cup butter or margarine, melted
hot pepper sauce, to taste
3 celery stalks, halved and cut into 3-inch lengths

BLUE CHEESE DIP
2 to 4 ounces blue cheese, crumbled
½ cup mayonnaise
½ cup sour cream

Separate each chicken wing into thirds at the joints. Reserve the wing tip portion for stock or discard.

In a deep skillet, melt shortening to a 1-inch depth. Heat the oil to almost smoking, about 375 degrees, and deep-fry a few chicken wings at a time until lightly browned. Drain them on paper towels. Arrange the chicken wings on a serving dish.

Combine the melted butter or margarine and hot pepper sauce. Baste the cooked wings and serve with celery sticks and Blue Cheese Dip.

Blue Cheese Dip: Combine all ingredients for the dip in a blender or a food processor. Place in a small bowl, cover, and refrigerate if made in advance.

Makes 32 appetizers.

✳ Vietnamese Spring Rolls

When the Vietnamese migrated to this country after the Vietnam War, they brought along their traditional recipes. The Vietnamese people serve spring rolls for all occasions, and the rolls are becoming increasingly familiar to Kansans as well.

These gourmet delights are crispy golden brown on the outside, with imaginative ingredients on the inside. The recipes are numerous, and the ingredients vary according to what is available and preferred by the cook. When served, crisp vegetables accompany the spring rolls, and Nuoc Mam, a fish sauce, is served for dipping.

Judith Paisley-Brown, director of the Dodge City Refugee Program, says, "I have had spring rolls dozens of times and have yet to eat the same thing twice. Also, while each woman's is distinc-

½ pound boneless pork loin or boneless pork chops
¼ pound shrimp
¼ cup fresh button mushrooms, finely chopped
2 green onions, finely chopped
1 garlic clove, minced
⅛ teaspoon salt
⅛ teaspoon pepper
1 package dried rice papers or spring roll wrappers*
1 egg yolk, beaten
vegetable oil for deep-fat frying

NUOC MAM
3 tablespoons lime juice
½ cup fish sauce*
½ cup cold water
2 to 3 tablespoons sugar, to taste
2 garlic cloves, minced
½ teaspoon red pepper flakes

lettuce leaves
shredded carrot
cucumber slices
fresh mint leaves

Cut excess fat from the edges of the pork and grind it in a meat grinder. Shell and devein the shrimp and grind or finely chop. Place the ground pork and shrimp in a bowl. Stir in the chopped mushrooms, green onion, garlic, salt, and pepper.

With scissors, cut the rice papers or spring roll wrappers into small triangles or squares. Brush lightly with water to dampen. After a few seconds, the square or triangle will become flexible and ready to fill. Place about 1 teaspoon of the mixture on the rice paper or wrapper and roll up, tucking in the edges. Seal with a small amount of egg yolk. Repeat until all the filling is used.

*Rice papers or spring roll wrappers and fish sauce can be found in Asian or Oriental grocery stores.

tively her own, even those vary from one time to the next—sort of like the American meat loaf."

Cover and refrigerate until ready to use. (The rolls may be made several hours in advance.)

Pour vegetable oil 2 to 3 inches deep in a heavy-bottomed pan. Heat until the oil is hot enough to sizzle (375 degrees). Deep-fry the spring rolls, 5 or 6 at a time, until golden brown, about 1 to 2 minutes. Drain on paper towels.

Nuoc Mam: In a small bowl, combine all the ingredients and let stand for 1 hour before serving.

To serve, place several spring rolls, accompanied by small bowls of Nuoc Mam, on individual plates garnished with lettuce leaves, shredded carrot, cucumber slices, and mint leaves.

Makes about 3 dozen.

Strawberry Hill

Before the Civil War most immigrants to the United States came from northern and western Europe. During the 1880s immigrants began arriving from southern and eastern Europe. As with many before them, they left to escape religious and political oppression, military obligations, and poverty in the old country. Among this later group were Croatians, Slovenians, Serbians, and Bulgarians. These southern Slavs, along with Germans, Russians, Poles, Irish, and Swedes, came to the region to work in the meat-packing houses and settled in Kansas City, Kansas, in the area known as Strawberry Hill. Named for the wild strawberries that once grew there, this ethnic community is located on the bluffs overlooking the confluence of the Kansas and Missouri rivers. Originally, most immigrants settled in the west bottoms, known as the "patch," but as they prospered, they began to move out of the patch and up the "hill."

Each group brought to the hill its unique ethnic traditions, a source of group identity and pride. An example is the art of wine-making, practiced by nearly everyone in earlier times. In *Images of Strawberry Hill*, edited by Jennie A. Chinn (Topeka: Kansas State Historical Society, 1985), Marijana Grisnik offers this description of her painting *Making Wine:* "Fall is coming because the leaves on the trees are turning to orange and this is the time to make the wine. In the old country wine is served with every meal, so that's the way it is here. The wine was stored in big bottles and in barrels. They made enough wine for the whole year." Many families raised hogs and chickens in their backyards, and smokehouses were a common sight. When neighbors came to help with the butchering, a good-natured argument would usually develop over who made the best wine.

The women in the community often gathered to prepare traditional foods for holidays and festivals. The Croatian women would make specialties such as Nadjev, a ham dressing stuffed in casings that is baked, thinly sliced, and served as an appetizer. Another popular recipe is a delicious holiday nut bread referred to as Polish Nut Bread by the Poles and *povotica* by the Croatians—usually made in large quantities!

The colorful community of Strawberry Hill still exists today, though its population has dwindled in recent years. However, church groups, lodges, and ethnic organizations, working to maintain the area's cultural heritage, hold annual dinners, ethnic dances, and festivals.

 # Nadjev

(Ham Dressing Stuffed in Casings)

Marijana Grisnik, Kansas City

Marijana Grisnik, known as the "Strawberry Hill Painter," captures the traditions, customs, foodways, and everyday life of her people on Strawberry Hill in Kansas City, Kansas. Marijana tells us that

this unusual recipe (pronounced nah-DAV) was brought to Strawberry Hill by immigrants from Croatia, a region of Yugoslavia.

Nadjev is served chilled, most often as an appetizer, but it can

also be used as a side dish and is best when prepared a day in advance. "When family and friends gather for Easter, Christmas, and weddings, they enjoy this Croatian delicacy," says Marijana.

1½ loaves sliced white bread (day-old dry bread is best)
2 cups cooked (smoked) ham
6 to 8 green onions
1 teaspoon pepper
12 eggs, lightly beaten
1 casing, cut in half and soaked in water
vegetable oil
¼ cup of water

Cut the bread into cubes and place in a large bowl. Dice the ham and include some fat. Chop the green onions, using only the green tops. Add the ham, onion tops, and pepper to the bowl. Add the beaten eggs and toss lightly, just until the bread is moistened.

Tie one end of a casing with string. Stuff with the dressing and tie to close. (Do not stuff tightly.) Repeat with the remaining casing.

Brush the stuffed casings with a small amount of vegetable oil and prick all over with a needle. Place them in a shallow baking dish. Add ¼ cup of water and bake uncovered at 300 degrees for 45 minutes. Remove from the pan and drain. Cool and refrigerate.

Slice Nadjev into ¼- to ½-inch slices and serve chilled. Serves 12 or more.

✳ Swedish Meatballs
(Köttbullar)

Gladys Peterson, Lindsborg

You will always find Swedish meatballs on a smorgasbord, as well as on American buffets, for it is the dish that endeared Swedish cooking to Americans. This traditional dish is very popular in the Swedish community of

1 pound lean ground beef or ground chuck
1 medium potato, peeled
½ medium onion, peeled
1 teaspoon salt
½ teaspoon ground allspice
1 14-ounce can beef broth or consommé
1 soup can (14 ounces) water

Put the meat in a large mixing bowl. Grate the potato and the onion over the meat. Add the salt and the allspice.

Lindsborg in central Kansas.

The following recipe, contributed by Gladys Peterson, has been adapted from an old recipe once used in a cooking school at the royal palace in Sweden.

Mix well and form into balls the size of walnuts, about 1½ inches in diameter.

Pour the beef broth and water into a 2-quart saucepan and bring to a boil. Carefully drop in all the meatballs, one at a time. Simmer for 20 minutes over low heat.

Remove the meatballs with a slotted spoon and place in a large saucepan or a baking dish. Skim the fat off the broth. Add the broth to the meatballs and cover. Heat on top of the range over low heat, or bake at 350 degrees for 30 minutes.

Serves 4 to 6.

✳ Super Crunch Muffins

Judith Bird, Dodge City

Kansans love college sports. Highlight a "game day" brunch with these crunchy muffins. They won't go unnoticed by the spectators.

2 cups all-purpose flour, sifted
1 tablespoon sugar (optional)
½ teaspoon salt
2 teaspoons baking powder
1 10-ounce can cream of chicken soup, undiluted
1 egg, beaten
¼ cup vegetable oil
1 3-ounce can French-fried onion rings, crumbled
½ cup potato chips, crumbled
½ cup cheddar cheese, grated

In a large bowl, combine the flour, sugar if desired, salt, and baking powder.

In a separate bowl, combine the soup, egg, and oil. Add the liquid mixture to the dry ingredients and stir until moistened. Stir in the crumbled onion rings and fill greased muffin tins two-thirds full. Combine the chips and cheese and sprinkle on top of each muffin.

Bake at 400 degrees for 18 to 20 minutes, or until browned. Immediately remove from the pan and serve hot.

Makes 12.

✳ Sweet Macaroni

Norman and Anna Marie Krusic, Frontenac

This sweet Italian dish was traditionally served with home-made wine on Christmas Eve by Norman Krusic's grandmother, who came to southeast Kansas from Fossato, Italy. The colorful dish makes an attractive addition to parties and family gatherings during the holiday season.

1 pound curly macaroni
1 tablespoon butter
1 lemon
1 orange
½ cup honey
1½ cups fresh bread crumbs
1 cup sugar
1 cup raisins
1 teaspoon nutmeg
1 pound English walnuts
¼ cup Parmesan cheese
1 6-ounce jar maraschino cherries

Boil the macaroni in a large pot of water until tender, adding the butter to keep it from sticking. Drain well and rinse in cold water. Drain the macaroni again and place it in a large bowl.

Grate the lemon and orange and reserve the grated rind, about 1 teaspoon each. Squeeze the juices from the fruits into a small bowl. Stir in the honey. Pour the juice mixture over the macaroni, mix well, and set aside.

Combine the bread crumbs, sugar, raisins, nutmeg, and grated lemon and orange rind in a large bowl. Finely grind the walnuts and place in a bowl. Grate the Parmesan cheese into another small bowl.

Place half of the macaroni on a large platter. Sprinkle half of the bread-crumb-and-sugar mixture over the macaroni. Top with half of the walnuts and half of the Parmesan cheese. Repeat with the remaining ingredients. Slice the maraschino cherries and place on top.

Serves 12.

✳ Soy Nuts

Agnes Gladden, Dodge City

Agnes Gladden's family raises 480 acres of soybeans. Agnes tells us, "We plant them with a planter after all the frost is gone in the spring. Here in western Kansas where we have very little rainfall, we water them twenty-four hours a day by circle irrigation. We harvest them at the end of September or the first part of October.

You can cook soybeans like navy beans. Let them soak overnight and cook them with ham hocks. They are more solid and crunchy than navy beans."

Soybeans are highly nutritious and make a delicious fried snack. They also make a crunchy topping for green salads and can be substituted for the peanuts in chocolate peanut clusters and other candies.

2 cups soybeans
½ teaspoon salt
vegetable shortening or oil for deep-fat frying
salt, to taste

Wash the soybeans 3 times in warm water and drain well after each washing. Place them in a large bowl, add the salt, and cover with water. Soak the soybeans for 12 to 16 hours, adding more water when needed to keep the beans covered.

When ready to fry, drain the soybeans well. Heat the shortening or oil to about 375 degrees in a large, heavy-bottomed pan. Deep fry the soybeans until they rise to the top of the oil and turn golden brown. Remove them with a slotted spoon and drain on paper towels. Sprinkle with salt to taste.

Makes 2 cups.

✳ Garlic Popcorn with Toasted Almonds

Kansas ranks among the top ten states in

½ cup sliced almonds
8 cups freshly popped corn

popcorn production. Here's an Italian twist on this all-American snack.

6 tablespoons butter
3 garlic cloves, minced
salt, to taste

Toast the almonds by placing them on a baking sheet in a 300-degree oven for 5 to 10 minutes, turning frequently, until golden. Combine the almonds with the freshly popped corn in a large bowl.

Melt the butter in a small pan over low heat. Add the minced garlic to the butter and heat for 1 minute. Pour the garlic butter over the popped corn and almonds, tossing to coat. Add salt to taste.

Serves 4 to 8.

✳ Oven Caramel Corn

Marilyn Eck, Bartlett

Sorghum, used in many of the sweet treats of bygone years, has always been regarded as healthful and even as a remedy for various ailments.

15 to 20 cups popped corn (1½ cups unpopped)
2 cups peanuts (optional)
2 cups brown sugar
1 cup butter or margarine
½ cup sorghum
½ teaspoon salt
1 teaspoon vanilla extract

In the nineteenth century, it was called "the sugar of the Plains." Today we know it as a very nutritious food —a good source of potassium, calcium, and iron.

"This recipe for caramel corn is an old family standby," says Marilyn Eck. "It always goes over well with children and adults alike."

½ teaspoon soda
⅛ teaspoon cream of tartar

Pour the popped corn into a large bowl or roasting pan. Add the peanuts and mix well.

In a large, heavy-bottomed pan, combine the brown sugar, butter or margarine, sorghum, and salt. Cook over low heat, stirring frequently, until the sugar dissolves and the mixture comes to a boil. Remove from heat and stir in the vanilla, soda, and cream of tartar. Mix well and pour the mixture over the popped corn and peanuts. Stir to coat thoroughly.

Turn the mixture into shallow pans or cookie sheets. Bake at 250 degrees for 45 to 60 minutes, turning every 15 minutes. Cool and store in airtight containers.

Makes 15 to 20 cups.

✳ Cinnamon Popcorn

A bowl of pink Cinnamon Popcorn makes a tasty holiday party snack.

3 tablespoons butter
6 tablespoons sugar
2 tablespoons corn syrup
¼ teaspoon baking soda
3 to 5 drops cinnamon oil, to taste
red food coloring
8 cups freshly popped corn

Place the butter, sugar, and corn syrup in a small pan over low heat. Stir frequently, until the butter melts and the sugar dissolves. When the mixture begins to boil, remove from heat. Add the baking soda and mix well. Add the cinnamon oil to taste and 2 to 4 drops of red food coloring. The color should be medium pink.

Place the popped corn in a large bowl. Pour the mixture over the popped corn and gently stir to coat. Turn the corn onto 2 baking sheets. Bake at 250 degrees for 45 to 60 minutes, turning the mixture every 15 minutes.

Remove the cinnamon popcorn from the baking sheets to cool and store in an airtight container.

Makes 8 cups.

✳ Granola

This versatile, all-natural treat has been a Midwestern favorite since the 1960s. It is chock-full of the many good foods Kansas has to offer. Eat it as a snack, as a topping for fresh fruit, or as a cereal.

1½ cups wheat flakes
1½ cups rolled oats
½ cup wheat germ
½ cup unsweetened shredded coconut
1 cup pecans, broken
½ cup almonds, slivered or sliced
½ cup raw sunflower seeds
¼ cup vegetable or safflower oil
6 tablespoons honey
1 teaspoon vanilla extract
½ teaspoon cinnamon
¾ cup dried apricots, coarsely chopped, or ½ cup raisins

In a large bowl, combine the wheat flakes, rolled oats, wheat germ, coconut, pecans, almonds, and sunflower seeds. Set aside.

In a small pan, warm the oil and honey. Remove from heat and add the vanilla and cinnamon, mixing well. Pour the mixture over the granola, stirring until well combined.

Spread the granola on a large baking sheet and bake at 350 degrees. After 10 minutes, remove the pan from the oven and turn the granola over. Repeat twice at 10-

minute intervals. Bake the granola for a total of 35 to 40 minutes, until lightly browned. Remove from the oven and turn several times while mixture is cooling. Add the dried apricots or raisins. Store in an airtight container.

Makes about 6 cups.

✳ Prairie Fire Dip

Teresa Morgan, Roeland Park

Pray for rain.

1 16-ounce can refried beans
1 cup provolone cheese, shredded
2 tablespoons butter or margarine
1 cup beer or water
2 tablespoons onion, finely chopped
2 garlic cloves, minced
3 to 4 tablespoons chili powder, to taste
¼ to ½ teaspoon crushed red pepper flakes, to taste
hot pepper sauce, to taste

tortilla chips

Combine all dip ingredients in a large saucepan. Stir over medium heat until all ingredients are heated thoroughly and the cheese is melted. Serve the dip warm, in a large bowl surrounded with tortilla chips.

Serves 8 or more.

Victoria: A Bit of Old England

The village of Victoria in Ellis County was settled by English aristocrats and gentry in 1873. Accustomed to a leisurely lifestyle in England, this group, led by Sir George Grant, brought their wealth and culture with them to Victoria.

The contrast of aristocratic and pioneer life on the prairie is well described by Mary Carrick Havemann in *Pioneer Women: Voices from the Kansas Frontier*, edited by Joanna L. Stratton (New York: Simon & Schuster, 1982): "Out in the 'short grass country' of western Kansas, when the pioneer days of the early seventies are mentioned, we think of covered wagons, meager homestead fare, parched fields, sunbonneted women who dared hardships, and bronzed, square-jawed Yankee men, who wrote history with the plow.

Then of those towns—outposts of civilization, yet filled to the brim with such humanity as knew no law or civilization. There were many of them—Abilene, Dodge, Hays—frontier cowboy towns where history was written with the gun—and written quickly. . . .

But close your eyes on this rough hard history of the plains, forget the roughneck cowboys. . . , the saloon brawls, the death-dealing gunmen who fattened Boot Hill, and that floating and often broken brushwood washed out of the main stream of American civilization into pioneer outposts. Forget time and distance—let yourself be transported to a spot in Kansas, twelve miles southeast of Hays, along the Union Pacific Railway. . . .

Open your eyes on Victoria, with all that name implies of British culture and traditions. It was 1872, and Victoria, Kansas, was a bit of old England transplanted in full bloom to the raw prairies of the middle west."

As it turned out, the wealthy English did not take to farming and preferred fox hunts, cricket games, and social engagements over farm chores. Eventually discouraged by poor crop yields and the hardships, most of the settlers returned to England or moved to Hays in 1876. By 1878, the community was completely deserted.

Pioneer Women includes Catherine Cavender's description of the lavish parties held by the Victoria settlers. "The English gave wonderful entertainment; dinners with long tables, laden with baked buffalo, antelope and quail, mince pies, plum puddings, and tipsy cake, and after the dinner a dance that lasted till morning and there were Lords and Lairds to dance with, too!"

Though these aristocrats of Victoria contributed little in the way of agriculture, Kansas is richer for the traditional recipes they left behind.

✳ Wassail

Nancy Vogel, Hays

The most successful English settlement in Kansas was Wakefield. The town was established in 1872 by the Reverend Richard Wake who purchased one hundred thousand acres of land in north-central Kansas from the Union Pacific Railroad for investors in Wakefield, England. Due to the lack of any language barrier, the English were quickly absorbed into Kansas life, and little of their national identity remains. However, their most famous holiday drink, Wassail, is still a favorite of Kansans.

The English custom of serving Wassail dates back to the Saxons, whose toast, was-hael! meant "health to you!"—the reply being drinc-hael!

Nancy Vogel, a professor of English, writes, "A toast of this traditional drink, known around the world as a herald of the Christmas holiday season, opens the evening festivities at the annual Madrigal Dinner at Fort Hays State University."

2½ cups sugar
5 cups water
¼ teaspoon whole cloves
5 cinnamon sticks
5 allspice berries
2½ tablespoons crystallized ginger, chopped
4 cups orange juice
2½ cups lemon juice
10 cups apple cider

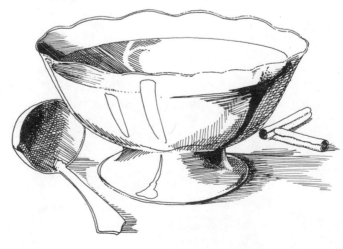

In a 2-gallon pot, boil the sugar, water, cloves, cinnamon sticks, allspice berries, and ginger for 10 minutes. Cover and let stand for 1 hour in a warm place. Strain the liquid and add the orange juice, lemon juice, and cider. Strain once more. Heat to serve, or chill to store.

Makes 28 6-ounce servings.

Variation: Spirits, such as brandy, sherry, or ale, may be added to taste.

✳ Swedish Coffee

Mrs. Alice Brax, Lindsborg

Alice Brax shares this recipe from a Swedish cookbook from Lindsborg. According to Measure for Pleasure, by Bethany Teachers' Wives (Lindsborg: Bethany Press, 1961), Scandinavians hold the undisputed claim of being the greatest coffee drinkers in the world. It is little wonder that they have perfected the very best methods of brewing their favorite beverage.

A pot of steaming coffee is always on hand in a Swedish home in Lindsborg. A true Swede prepares coffee by the steeping method and prefers it stronger than the way it is usually served.

coffee, regular grind
1 egg, slightly beaten
cold water

Measure 1 level tablespoon of ground coffee per person and place it in a small bowl. Add 1 teaspoon of the beaten egg for every 2 tablespoons of coffee. (The egg clarifies the coffee by absorbing the fine particles that make it appear cloudy.) Mix in a little cold water (1 to 2 tablespoons) and set aside.

Bring fresh water to a boil, 1 cup per person. Add the coffee mixture to the kettle. Simmer slowly for 2 to 3 minutes, stirring occasionally. Pour a little cold water (about 1 tablespoon) into the spout to settle the grounds. Strain the coffee through a very fine strainer into a preheated server.

Swedish Coffee for 50: Use 3 rounded cups of ground coffee. Mix 2 slightly beaten eggs and ½ cup of cold water with the ground coffee. Follow the instructions above.

✳ Aunt Ida Weaver's Eggnog

Shelley White, Lawrence

"Although of German, Welsh, and English ancestry, my father's family has made their homes in Kansas for several generations," says Shelley White. *"My grandparents lived in Osage City where I remember Grandma Lillian tending a vast garden of day lilies and Grandpa Roscoe sharing alfalfa pills at dusk with his tame rabbits.*

Long before I was born, Christmas in Osage City meant preparing Aunt Ida Weaver's Eggnog. For years it was Grandpa's task to make the nog, and only he knew just exactly how much whisky was added. It must have been quite a bit, for the children were only allowed a half cup! While Roscoe and Lillian are both gone now, on Christmas morning you will still find my family enjoying this fine concoction and remembering those special people."

9 large egg yolks
2 cups sugar
⅛ teaspoon nutmeg
2 cups whisky (bourbon or Scotch)
9 egg whites, whipped
1 quart milk

1 quart heavy or whipping cream, whipped
nutmeg, freshly ground

Place the egg yolks in a very large bowl. Beat with an electric mixer at high speed until the yolks are creamy and lemon colored. Gradually add the sugar and nutmeg, beating constantly. Pour in the whisky, beating well.

In a separate large bowl, beat the egg whites until soft peaks form. Beat the milk into the egg whites. Pour the milk mixture into the yolk mixture, beating constantly at high speed. Cover the eggnog and chill until ready to serve.

Shortly before serving time, whip the cream until soft peaks form. Fold into the chilled eggnog. Serve with a sprinkle of nutmeg.

Makes 40 ½-cup servings.

✳ Frosted Punch

Ruby Kessler, Sawyer

This refreshing, old-fashioned punch can be served at weddings and showers or for

1½ cups sugar
1 cup water
3 6-ounce cans frozen orange juice concentrate
3 6-ounce cans frozen pineapple juice concentrate

friends on a warm
day. Be prepared to
make a second batch.

¼ cup lemon juice
1 quart ginger ale
1 gallon lime sherbet

In a saucepan, boil the sugar and water together for
2 full minutes. Remove from the heat and pour into a
large bowl. Add the frozen orange and pineapple juice
concentrates and dilute with water according to manufacturer's directions. Add the lemon juice and mix well. Chill
1 hour.

Just before serving the punch, stir in the ginger ale and
top with large scoops of lime sherbet.

Makes 32 6-ounce servings.

✳ SOUPS AND STEWS

I n nineteenth-century cookbooks, there were few directions for making soups and stews. Because a stockpot simmered constantly on the stoves of early kitchens, cookbook authors considered it more beneficial to devise rules rather than recipes. Even today, these guidelines for making soup stock are the foundation for a flavorful soup or stew. They wisely recommended that fresh meats make better stock than leftovers and that, for rich stock, one quart of water should be used for each pound of meat. Since the simmering stock is always reducing and therefore concentrating its flavors, the good cook should add salt only near the end of cooking.

Soups and stews continue to be personal concoctions, and nearly everyone who cooks has a special combination of vegetables, meat, and stock he or she likes to prepare, especially for wintry days. Such personal triumphs are often handed down and bring to life memories of loved

ones and thoughts of better days. These foods that nourish the soul as well as the body are often referred to as comfort foods. Soups, more so than other foods, seem to have the ability to soothe us when we want to retreat from the day's frenzy.

It is not surprising that most cultures have a soup or stew identified with their nationality and way of life. Swedes make a soup of rich stock into which they dip their hearty rye bread; the French slowly sauté onions to extract their sweetness before adding a meat stock for onion soup; and the Russians simmer cabbage or beets in hearty broth to make their borscht. However, available ingredients as well as heritage determined the soups and stews of Kansas kitchens.

In the following pages, the hearty Swedish Dopp I Grytan and the Czech Christmas Soup are holiday traditions. Earlier times are recalled in the recipes for Classic Beef Stew and Black Walnut Soup. For delicious starters, try the Swedish Fruit Soup or the Parsley-Parsnip Soup.

✳ Classic Beef Stew

A pot of simmering beef stew has meant a hearty meal to many generations of Kansans, harking back to the days when buffalo stews were cooked on the prairies by the Plains Indians and early settlers. Since then, stews have comforted many a Kansas homesteader during a blizzard, fed cowboys on the cattle trail, stretched meals for the hungry during the Great Depression, and today remind us of home and family on a wintry evening.

3 pounds beef chuck or shoulder roast
3 tablespoons butter
2 tablespoons vegetable oil
1 cup all-purpose flour
1 onion, diced
1 15-ounce can beef broth
2 cups water
½ teaspoon thyme
½ teaspoon basil
½ teaspoon tarragon
½ teaspoon rosemary
1 bay leaf
1 teaspoon salt
4 large carrots, peeled and cut into 1-inch pieces
2 sticks celery, cut into 1-inch pieces
4 large potatoes, peeled and quartered
¼ cup butter
¼ cup all-purpose flour
1 10-ounce can corn, drained

Trim the meat into lean 1-inch pieces. Melt the butter and oil in a large skillet over medium-high heat. Dip the meat in the flour, shake off the excess, and add to the skillet. Cook until well browned, turning often, about 15 minutes.

Place the meat and the onion in a large pan or stockpot. Add ¼ cup of the beef broth to the hot skillet, stirring up the caramelized drippings. Add the drippings to the stockpot. Add the remaining broth, water, and seasonings. Cover and simmer over low heat. After 1 hour, add the carrots and celery. Cover and simmer until tender, about 30 to 40 minutes more.

Meanwhile, boil the potatoes until they can be easily pierced with a knife.

Cut the butter into ¼ cup of flour and knead just until it becomes a smooth paste. Five minutes before serving, bring the stew to a boil and thicken by whisking in small bits of the butter and flour mixture with a wire whip. Add the corn to the thickened stew and return to boiling.

To serve, place the potatoes in individual bowls and ladle the stew on top.

Serves 6 to 8.

✳ Dopp i Grytan
(Dip into Kettle)

Mrs. Albertha Sundstrom, Lindsborg

On Christmas Eve, the unique Swedish custom of Dopp I Grytan—literally, "the dipping of bread in the pot"—is still observed by many families in Lindsborg. This ancient rite commemorates famines in Sweden, when the only available food was dark bread and broth. At the holidays, a kettle of this rich broth was kept on the back of the stove, and members of the family would help themselves to bread and dip it into the hot broth whenever they became hungry. This relieved the busy mother from preparing a noon meal as she completed the final preparations for Christmas Eve dinner.

Some Swedes butter hearty rye bread to go with their soup, while others prefer to pour the meat and broth right over the bread. Pickles, coffee, and cookies often accompany this meal. This recipe, from the Bethany Teachers' Wives Measure for Pleasure (Lindsborg: Bethany Press, 1961), was sent to us by Albertha Sundstrom.

3 pounds veal or lean beef
3 pounds lean pork
salt, to taste
1 bay leaf
allspice, to taste
salt and pepper, to taste
Swedish Rye Bread

Trim any excess fat from the meat. Salt it generously and place it in a large bowl. Cover and refrigerate for several hours or overnight.

Put the meat in a large soup kettle or Dutch oven. Cover with water. Add the bay leaf. Add the allspice, salt, and pepper to taste. Bring to a boil, then reduce heat to low. Simmer, partially covered, for several hours,

until the meat is tender. Remove from heat and cool.
Cover and refrigerate overnight.

In the morning, skim the fat from the broth. Remove
the meat and cut into serving pieces. Return the meat to
the broth and simmer over low heat until ready to serve.
Serve with Swedish Rye Bread.

Serves 15.

✳ Steak Soup

Caroline Wittman, Topeka

*The popularity of this
soup can be attributed
to the intensity of its
beef flavor. Served
in small amounts, it
makes a great start to
a hearty meal.*

1½ pounds round or chuck steak
¼ cup butter
6 cups water
1 teaspoon salt
1 teaspoon pepper
1 16-ounce can whole tomatoes, chopped
1 10-ounce package frozen mixed vegetables
1 cup carrots, peeled and chopped
1 cup celery, chopped
1 cup onion, chopped
½ cup butter or margarine
1¼ cups all-purpose flour

Trim the round or chuck steak and chop it into bite-size
pieces. Melt ¼ cup of butter in a soup pot or Dutch oven
and brown the meat over medium heat. Add the water,
salt, pepper, and tomatoes and bring to a boil. Reduce
the heat to low and simmer for 30 minutes.

Add the remaining vegetables and return the soup to a
boil. Reduce heat to low and simmer for an additional 30
minutes.

Knead the butter and flour together to make a paste.
Thicken the soup as it simmers by adding the paste bit by
bit, stirring with a wire whip, until the desired thickness
is achieved.

Serves 6 to 8.

The New Immigrants

Vietnamese refugees began to settle in Kansas in 1975, after the Vietnam War. The largest group, more than three thousand, settled in Wichita; others moved to Garden City, Liberal, Dodge City, Salina, and Kansas City. Many of these Vietnamese were "boat people"; others came by air immediately following the fall of South Vietnam. They came from all walks of life and all types of communities.

Ken C. Erickson, refugee services coordinator in Garden City for the Kansas Department of Social and Rehabilitation Services, writes: "The refugees here are the lucky few who were accepted for resettlement in the United States. No tax breaks, no job guarantees, no additional welfare or special benefits. They are here, in Garden City, Dodge City, and Liberal, to work in the packing industry, just like the immigrants of a century ago. . . . Like other new arrivals in Garden City, they work long strenuous hours."

Judith Paisley-Brown, director of the Dodge City refugee program writes, "Most of the interesting stories I've heard about migration relate to their experiences during their escapes from Vietnam. I have a feeling that coming to Kansas is somewhat anti-climactic after that! The recounts I've heard are quite long and always heartbreaking. People can accomplish some pretty remarkable things when they are running for their lives to a place they know little or nothing about."

As the Vietnamese settle in, restaurants featuring the cuisine of Vietnam are springing up in the areas where they live, giving Kansans the opportunity to enjoy some of their traditional foods. Spring rolls, soups, and a variety of enticing dishes appear on the menus. Shallots, scallions, and fresh coriander are often utilized in Vietnamese cooking. Lemon grass, with its lemon-scented flavor, accents many dishes. Raw vegetables and salads are a part of most meals. Lettuce, cucumbers, carrots, coriander, and mint accompany most dishes. Erickson describes Vietnamese food: "I have found a cuisine that is at once continental in its elegance . . . yet almost American in its hearty simplicity—hearty meals that include a heady mixture of continental, Southeast Asian, and Chinese elements in one cuisine. Good eats."

✳ Vietnamese Beef and Noodle Soup
(Pho Tai)

This beautiful soup is typical of the many versions of a beef and noodle soup that is very popular in Vietnam. It is now well known to those who dine in the Vietnamese restaurants that have been established in Kansas by the Vietnamese refugees who settled here after the Vietnam War.

The presentation of Pho Tai is dramatic. Boiling broth is poured into large bowls filled with raw beef, noodles, and onions, cooking the thinly sliced ingredients instantly. A platter of fresh mint, basil, lime wedges, and several other ingredients is passed at the table as condiments for the soup.

8 ounces rice sticks or Oriental egg noodles*
3 14-ounce cans beef broth
1 14-ounce can chicken broth
1 teaspoon five-spice powder
½ teaspoon Hoisin sauce*
1 small mild onion
¼- to ½-pound flank steak
3 green onions, sliced diagonally
2 tablespoons fresh cilantro, chopped
fresh basil leaves
fresh mint leaves
8 ounces fresh bean sprouts
Hoisin sauce
6 to 8 lime wedges

Boil the rice sticks or egg noodles in a large pot until tender. Rinse and drain well and divide into 6 to 8 large soup bowls.

Slice the onion as thinly as possible into rings and place them on top of the noodles. Slice the raw flank steak very thinly and add to the bowls. (For easy slicing, put the meat in the freezer until partially frozen. Slice and allow to thaw completely before using.) Sprinkle the sliced green onion and chopped cilantro over all.

In a large pot, combine the beef broth, chicken broth, five-spice powder, and Hoisin sauce. Simmer over low

---

* Rice sticks or Oriental egg noodles and Hoisin sauce are available in Oriental grocery stores.

heat for 5 minutes. Raise the heat to high and bring the broth to a rolling boil. Pour the boiling broth over the ingredients in the soup bowls.

Place the basil and mint leaves, bean sprouts, Hoisin sauce, and fresh lime wedges on a large platter. Let each person top the Pho Tai with the selections to taste.

Serves 6 to 8.

✳ Beef and Cheese Chowder

Dorothy Geier, Girard

Rich and savory, this soup makes a tasty meal-in-one.

3 large potatoes, peeled and diced
3 carrots, peeled and diced
3 sticks celery, diced
1 onion, diced
1 pound ground beef
¼ teaspoon garlic salt
¼ teaspoon onion salt
1 11-ounce can cheddar cheese soup

Place the potatoes, carrots, celery, and onion in a large pot. Add just enough water to cover. Bring to boil, reduce heat to low, and simmer for 10 minutes.

Meanwhile, brown the ground beef in a skillet over

medium heat. Season it with the garlic and onion salts.
Pour off any excess fat and add the meat to the pot of
vegetables and the remaining water. Stir in the cheddar
cheese soup. Cover and simmer for 30 minutes.

Serves 6.

✳ "Cure-all" Chicken Soup

Recent scientific evidence has proven what aunts and grandmothers have known all along—chicken soup is good medicine. As a meal that stirs up memories of warmth and security, it most certainly fits the definition of comfort food.

1 whole chicken
1 onion, studded with 2 whole cloves
1 stalk celery, with leaves
1 cup onion, chopped
1 cup carrot, peeled and sliced into ¼-inch rounds
½ cup celery, thinly sliced
3 whole garlic cloves, peeled
1 bay leaf
⅛ teaspoon thyme
¼ teaspoon dill
⅛ teaspoon red pepper flakes
pinch of saffron (optional)
1 teaspoon salt
¼ teaspoon pepper
1 14-ounce can chicken broth, or chicken bouillon, to taste
   (optional)
1 cup fresh or frozen peas
½ cup uncooked white rice, or 1 cup uncooked pasta

Place the chicken in a large stock pot or Dutch oven. Add
the onion, studded with cloves, and celery stalk. Cover
the chicken with water and bring to a boil over high heat.
Reduce heat to low and simmer for 1 hour, or until the
chicken is tender. Skim off any residue that forms on top.

Discard the onion and celery stalk. Remove the chicken
from the broth and cool slightly. Discard the skin and
bones and cut the meat into bite-size pieces. Pour the
broth into a container and skim off the excess fat.

Wash the stock pot or Dutch oven and return the
skimmed broth to the pot. Add the chicken pieces and
remaining ingredients, except the peas and rice or pasta.
For more intense flavor, add a can of chicken broth or

chicken bouillon to taste. Simmer, partially covered, for about 20 minutes. Add the peas and rice or pasta and simmer for 20 minutes more.

Serves 6 to 8.

✳ Chicken Borscht

Georgina Johnson, Hillsboro

Georgina Johnson tells us that borscht is a Russian vegetable soup, made with a hearty meat stock and often enriched with sour cream just before serving. This soup is a traditional favorite of the German Mennonites who came to Kansas from Russia. There are many variations for borscht— this one is made with chicken.

1 whole chicken, about 3 pounds
1 can tomato soup
1 medium head of cabbage, chopped
1 large onion, chopped
1 small sweet red pepper, seeded and chopped
2 tablespoons fresh parsley, chopped
1 head fresh dill, or dried dill to taste
1 bay leaf
salt, to taste
1 cup sour cream

Cut the chicken into pieces and trim away the excess fat. Place the chicken pieces in a large pot, add 3 quarts of water, and bring to a boil. Reduce heat to low and simmer until the chicken pieces are tender. Remove the meat, discarding the skin and bones. Cut the meat into bite-size pieces and return it to the broth. Skim any excess fat from the broth. Add the remaining ingredients, except the sour cream. Simmer until the vegetables are tender, about 1 hour. Stir in the sour cream just before serving.

Serves 4 to 6.

✳ Catfish Stew

This stew of catfish, corn, and potatoes makes a hearty and healthful down-home meal. Homemade corn

3 bacon strips
1 cup onion, chopped
¼ cup celery, chopped
2 medium red potatoes, peeled and cut into 1-inch cubes
1 16-ounce can tomatoes, undrained

bread is the perfect
accompaniment.

1 14-ounce can chicken broth
1 bay leaf
½ teaspoon salt
¼ teaspoon pepper
hot pepper sauce, to taste
1 cup freshly shelled corn, or 1 8-ounce can corn, drained
1 pound catfish fillets, cut into 1-inch cubes
1 tablespoon all-purpose flour
1 tablespoon butter

Fry the bacon over medium-low heat in a stock pot or
Dutch oven until golden brown. Remove the bacon and
drain on paper towels. Crumble and reserve. Add the
onion and celery to the bacon drippings and cook until
tender.

Add the potatoes, tomatoes, chicken broth, and seasonings. Bring to a boil, then reduce heat to low. Cover
and simmer for 15 minutes.

Add the corn and catfish and simmer uncovered for
about 10 minutes more, or until the catfish flakes easily
with a fork.

In a small cup, combine the flour and butter. Drop
the mixture a teaspoon at a time into the stew, stirring
constantly until it thickens slightly. Stir in the crumbled
bacon and serve immediately.

Serves 4 to 6.

✳ Czech Christmas Soup (?)

Mrs. Frank G. (Marie) Vopat, Wilson

Marie Vopat and others of Czechoslovakian descent in Wilson enjoy preparing the traditional dishes passed down from their ancestors who settled the area in the 1870s. She serves this Czech soup to her family on Christmas Eve, accompanied by Houska, a braided holiday bread.

Carp in Black Sauce

6 pitted prunes
½ cup raisins
6 pearl onions, skinned
4 cups water
1 pound fresh fish fillets
1 sugar cookie, crushed
1 gingersnap, crushed
1 tablespoon vinegar
1 tablespoon butter
1 tablespoon all-purpose flour
salt, to taste

Place the prunes, raisins, pearl onions, and water in a large pan or soup kettle. Simmer over low heat until the onions are tender.

Cut the fish fillets into 1-inch pieces and add to the soup. Simmer until tender, 5 to 10 minutes. Add the crushed cookies and vinegar, stirring gently to combine.

In a small pan, melt the butter. Add the flour and mix until smooth. Slowly stir this mixture into the soup until it thickens slightly. Add salt to taste. Serve hot.

Serves 4 to 6.

Salt Pork

Before the days of refrigeration, salt pork was a mainstay in the American diet. Salt-curing the pork preserved the meat for winter provisions and for long journeys. According to Sam Arnold in *Fryingpans West* (Denver: Arnold and Company, 1985), so strong was the belief in the reliability of this meat that pamphlets (written by enterprising but inexperienced authors) instructed pioneers crossing Kansas to stock their wagons with hundreds of pounds of salt pork per person. Their advice resulted in a glut of salt pork each time the wagon trains arrived at Fort Laramie.

As one of the few meats available to Southern slaves, salt pork also figured as an important flavoring to the Southern-style dishes brought by the Exodusters to Kansas. Recipes with European heritage flavored their stews and casseroles with it as well. And a chuck wagon never hit the trail without a provision of salt pork for bean dishes.

Today, one can find salt pork in almost any supermarket. Its appearance is quite similar to that of bacon but its use is restricted more to braising meats, flavoring potage, and barding game birds. Look for a streak of lean in good quality salt pork. Rinse or bring it to a boil in cold water if the pork is too salty for the dish it will be flavoring.

Though its popularity has diminished over the years due to cholesterol-conscious cooking, the flavor of salt pork is unmatched in soups, bean dishes, and stews. Even with today's emphasis on crisp vegetables, there is never a protest over green beans slowly cooked with a piece of salt pork.

✳ Grampa's Favorite Soup

Josephine Caput, Frontenac

This recipe for a savory ham and rice soup may become your favorite as well. Its simple ingredients turn a holiday ham into a convenient and hearty meal.

½ pound ham or salt pork, diced
½ cup onion, chopped
4 quarts water
1 6-ounce can tomato paste
2 cups rice, uncooked
2 potatoes, peeled and diced
1 teaspoon salt

In a Dutch oven or stock pot, brown the diced ham or salt pork with the onion over medium heat. Add the water and tomato paste. Adjust the heat so the soup remains at a simmer. Add the rice, diced potatoes, and salt.

Continue to cook slowly until the rice is cooked and the potatoes are tender, about 30 minutes.

Serves 6 to 8.

✳ Cream of Country Ham Soup

This old-fashioned soup combines the classic flavors of ham and white sauce and makes good use of leftover ham.

2 slices bacon, diced
1 cup onion, diced
1 teaspoon brown sugar
3 tablespoons all-purpose flour
4 cups water
1 celery stalk, finely chopped
1 carrot, finely chopped
½ cup green pepper, diced
1 cup ham, finely diced
3 to 4 cups milk
salt and pepper, to taste

Fry the bacon pieces and the onion in a stock pot over medium heat. After a few minutes, add the brown sugar.

Cook, turning occasionally, until the onion is soft and brown. Stir in the flour and cook for 2 minutes more.

Slowly add the water to the pan, stirring constantly to avoid lumps. Add the celery, carrot, green pepper, and ham. Simmer over low heat until the vegetables are tender, about 1 hour.

Add the milk a little at a time, diluting the soup to the desired thickness. Add salt and pepper to taste and simmer 15 minutes more.

Serves 8 to 10.

✳ Beans with Ham Hocks

In earlier times, beans were considered convenience food and were cooked routinely, at least once a week for most families. Joan Carey, of Topeka, recalls that her mother, Grace Pattie, would always cook beans on Mondays, her wash day. "Mom would put on a large pot of beans with ham hocks or salt pork in the morning. She could then tend to the laundry (which took all day back then) and, by dinner time, the beans would be ready. All that was required to complete the meal was a pan of skillet corn bread."

1 pound Great Northern or pinto beans
2 to 3 smoked ham hocks
1 large onion, chopped
1 carrot, peeled
1 celery stalk, with leaves
3 whole cloves
¼ teaspoon thyme
1 whole garlic clove, peeled
1 bay leaf
1 teaspoon salt
¼ teaspoon pepper

Wash the beans and place them in a large bowl. Cover with cold water and soak overnight.

Drain the beans and put them in a large stock pot or Dutch oven. Cover generously with cold water. Add the ham hocks and the remaining ingredients. Bring to a boil, reduce heat to low, and simmer partially covered for about 3 hours, or until the beans are tender.

Discard the celery, whole cloves, garlic clove, and bay leaf. Remove the ham hocks and carrot and cool slightly. Take the meat off the bones, chop the carrot into small pieces, and return both to the pan. Skim the excess fat from the soup and reheat before serving.

Serves 6.

✳ Cassoulet

(Cassoulet du Languedoc)

Simone Johnson, Topeka

Cassoulet is a specialty of the southwestern part of France. It is a bean-and-meat, stew-like casserole, and the recipe varies according to the locale.

"When I first came to Kansas," Simone Johnson tells us, *"I stopped at a farm on the way to Eskridge to buy a goose, hoping to make a good* cassoulet de Castelnaudary. *It is prepared with the meat from a goose which has been force-fed with corn to produce the famous* foie gras. *The meat used to be kept in crocks, covered with the fat rendered by a slow cooking of the meat. Now it is canned commercially and sold under the name* confit d'oie. *My Eskridge goose was a skinny barnyard variety that did not justify the amount of work involved (plucking, cleaning, cooking) as it did not furnish any fat. Now I am happy making a Cas-*

2 pounds dry white beans (navy or Great Northern)
5 quarts boiling water
1 pound salt pork, cut into 3 slices
half of a fresh pork rind (optional)

BOUQUET GARNI
6 sprigs fresh parsley
3 leafy tops of celery
4 sprigs fresh thyme
2 bay leaves
4 black peppercorns
2 garlic cloves, whole

2 carrots, cut into chunks
2 whole onions, each studded with 2 whole cloves
1 pound fresh pork sausage or garlic sausage links
¼ cup oil, bacon fat, or lard
1½ pounds lamb shoulder or leg, cubed
2 pounds pork loin, cubed
2 cups onion, finely chopped
1 16-ounce can tomatoes, drained and chopped
2 garlic cloves, minced
1 cup beef broth
salt and pepper, to taste
½ cup coarse bread crumbs
butter or bacon fat

Wash the beans and place them in a large bowl. Cover with water and soak overnight. (Or add the washed beans to boiling water, boil for 2 minutes, and let stand for 1 hour.)

Drain the beans and place in a large stock pot or Dutch oven. Cover with 5 quarts of boiling water. Add the sliced salt pork and, if desired, the pork rind.

Bouquet Garni: Place all the ingredients for the bouquet on a piece of cheesecloth and tie securely.

soulet du Languedoc which substitutes lamb for the goose meat."

Add the bouquet garni, carrots, and the whole onions to the pot of beans. Cover and simmer over low heat for 1½ hours, adding water if needed. Skim, if necessary.

While the beans are cooking, prick the sausages and cook in a large pan of boiling water for 10 minutes. Remove from the pan and drain well. Heat the oil in a large Dutch oven over medium heat. Brown the cubes of lamb and pork and the boiled sausages, turning often. Add the chopped onion, tomatoes, garlic, and beef broth. Add salt and pepper to taste. Cook slowly over low heat for 1 hour, adding additional beef stock, if needed.

When the beans are cooked, discard the carrots, onions, and bouquet garni. Cut the salt pork into cubes. Discard the rind or cut it into cubes. Strain the beans and reserve the liquid.

Place half of the cubed salt pork in the bottom of a large casserole. Alternate the beans with the meat mixture, ending with the remaining salt pork and rind. Add enough of the reserved liquid to cover. Sprinkle the bread crumbs on top and dot with butter or bacon fat. Bake at 300 degrees for 1½ hours.

Serves 8 to 10.

✳ Kansas Corn Chowder

Maize, which we now call corn, was a staple in the diet of the Plains Indians. Thomas Say, a scientist exploring Kansas, wrote of a soup made with corn that was prepared by Indians in 1819. "They commonly placed before us a sort of soup, composed of maize of the present season . . . appropriately named sweet corn, boiled in water, and enriched with a few slices of bison meat, grease, and some beans, and to suit our palates, it was generally seasoned with rock salt, which is procured near the Arkansas River."

The following recipe for corn chowder, though dissimilar to the stew described above, nevertheless showcases corn as a nourishing grain. It is an unusual grain at that. So sweet and plump when fresh-picked, it is typically eaten as a vegetable.

6 tablespoons butter
1 onion, chopped
2 stalks celery, thinly sliced
1 sweet red pepper, diced
6 tablespoons all-purpose flour
2 14-ounce cans chicken broth
2 cups fresh corn or 1 17-ounce can corn, drained
½ teaspoon dry mustard
½ cup milk
salt, to taste

Melt the butter in a large saucepan. Add the onion, celery, and red pepper. Cook over medium heat until the vegetables are soft.

Add the flour and cook for about 2 minutes, stirring frequently. Stir in the chicken broth slowly, using a wire whip to break up any lumps.

Add the corn and dry mustard. Bring the soup to a boil, add the milk, and reduce heat to low. Simmer for 20 minutes, stirring occasionally. Add salt to taste.

Serves 4.

✳ Fresh Asparagus Soup

Karen Pendleton, Lawrence

John and Karen Pendleton of Lawrence grow asparagus on

1 pound fresh asparagus, chopped
½ cup onion, chopped
1 14-ounce can chicken broth

*their farm just east
of town. In May, it
is quite a sight to see
acres of asparagus
spears shooting up
from the ground. John
explains that you must
pick only those spears
that are at least eight
inches tall, snapping
them off at the base.
Karen has many as-
paragus recipes, but
this is John's all-time
favorite.*

2 tablespoons butter or margarine
2 tablespoons all-purpose flour
1 teaspoon salt
⅛ teaspoon pepper
1 cup milk
½ cup sour cream
1 teaspoon lemon juice
fresh chives, chopped (optional)

Cook the asparagus in a covered saucepan with the onion and ½ cup of the chicken broth for 8 to 10 minutes over medium heat, until the asparagus is tender. Press the asparagus mixture through a food mill, or blend in an electric blender or food processor until smooth. Set aside.

In a large pan, melt the butter or margarine over medium heat. Blend in the flour, salt, and pepper. Slowly stir in the remaining chicken broth. Cook, stirring constantly, until the mixture reaches boiling point. Stir in the asparagus puree and the milk. Add a little of the hot mixture to the sour cream, then stir the sour cream into the hot mixture. Add the lemon juice.

Heat just to serving temperature, stirring frequently. Serve with a sprinkle of fresh chives, if desired.

Serves 4.

✳ Spinach Soup

Julia Egnatic, Kansas City

*Julia Egnatic tells us
the secret to being a
good cook is tasting
the food as you cook it.
"I never really follow
a recipe," she says. "I
just taste the food while
it's cooking and add
whatever seasonings
I think it needs. You*

½ cup salt pork or 4 bacon strips, diced
1 cup onion, chopped
4 cups pork or chicken broth
1 15-ounce can spinach
3 tablespoons white vinegar
1 teaspoon salt
2 teaspoons pepper
2 tablespoons all-purpose flour
1 egg
1 cup sour cream

just have to have cour-
age and good cooking
instincts."

3 cups milk
1 teaspoon prepared horseradish
pinch of sugar

Fry the salt pork in a large frying pan over low heat.
When there are enough drippings, add the chopped onion
and cook until soft and transparent.

Transfer the salt pork and onion to a soup pot or Dutch
oven. Add the broth, spinach, vinegar, salt, and pepper.
Simmer uncovered over low heat for 30 minutes.

In a large bowl, beat the flour and egg together. Add
the sour cream, milk, horseradish, and sugar. Beat until
well combined. Slowly add this mixture to the soup,
stirring constantly over medium heat. Beat with an egg
beater or a wire whip until smooth. Continue beating
while bringing the soup to a boil. Remove from heat
and cover until ready to serve. Serve warm or at room
temperature.

Serves 6 to 8.

✳ European Vegetable Soup

*This simple, country-
style soup uses mostly
aromatic vegetables
and has only a pinch
of seasoning. It is truly*

3 small leeks
2 tablespoons butter
6 green onions, chopped
2 sticks celery, chopped
1 carrot, peeled and finely chopped

a celebration of the garden. Putting soup through a food mill, as this recipe recommends, is common practice for Europeans, and it is often mentioned by Kansas cooks with European ancestry as a way of making simple soups fancy. Pureeing blends the flavors and makes a beautiful and sophisticated presentation. A simple dot of butter can be substituted for the more elaborate enrichment of sour cream and chives in this recipe.

1 turnip, peeled and finely chopped
1 16-ounce can butter beans, drained
3 cups chicken broth
¼ teaspoon thyme
salt and pepper, to taste
sour cream and chopped chives, to garnish

Peel away the outer leaves of the leeks and discard. Cut off the green tops 1 inch above the white section. Discard the tops. Cut the leeks lengthwise, rinse under running water to remove any sand particles, and dice.

Melt the butter over medium heat in a large saucepan until foaming. Add the vegetables to the saucepan and sauté until tender, about 5 minutes. Add the butter beans and chicken broth. Bring the soup to a boil, reduce heat, and simmer for 25 minutes. Remove the soup from heat and add the thyme. Puree in a food mill, blender, or food processor.

Reheat the soup to a simmer over low heat and season with salt and pepper. Serve with a dollop of sour cream and chives.

Serves 4 to 6.

✳ Vegetable Soup

Hildred Schmidt, Walton

The classic vegetable soup is difficult to define. It may begin with a chicken or a meaty beef bone, or with just the stock of aromatic vegetables alone. Sharing a soup made to your personal taste becomes a gift from the heart.

This soup, colorful and robust, has a telling character.

4 carrots, peeled and thinly sliced
4 potatoes, peeled and cubed
1 onion, chopped
4 whole garlic cloves
1 tablespoon fresh parsley
⅛ teaspoon salt
1 cup beef broth
¼ cup celery, chopped
½ cup broccoli flowerets
1 16-ounce can green beans, undrained (home-grown preferred)
dash of cayenne pepper or red pepper flakes

In a soup pot, combine the carrots, potatoes, onion, garlic, parsley, and salt. Add water to cover generously and bring the mixture to a boil. Reduce heat to low and simmer until vegetables are tender-crisp, about 10 minutes.

Add the beef broth, celery, broccoli, green beans and a dash of cayenne pepper or red pepper flakes. Bring the mixture to a boil, reduce heat to low, and simmer another 10 minutes, or until the second set of vegetables is tender. Remove the garlic cloves before serving.

Serves 4 to 6.

✳ French Onion Soup

(Soupe à l'Oignon)

The French settlers brought this flavorful soup to the United States more than a century ago, when it seemed to turn up everywhere, including Kansas. With its hearty ingredients— broth, onions, cheese, and bread—it was readily adopted by all who tasted it. Just before serving, the

¼ cup butter
¼ cup olive oil
7 to 8 cups onion, chopped
¼ cup all-purpose flour
3 14-ounce cans chicken broth
3 14-ounce cans beef broth
salt and pepper, to taste

CROÛTES
16 ½-inch slices of French bread
1 tablespoon olive oil
2 whole garlic cloves, peeled

1 cup gruyère cheese, shredded

soup is topped with a large Croûte (a slice of toasted French bread) and cheese and placed under the broiler.

Melt the butter and olive oil in a large pan or Dutch oven over medium heat. Add the chopped onion and cook until tender and lightly browned, about 30 minutes.

Sprinkle the flour over the onions, stirring for 2 minutes. Slowly add one can of the broth, stirring until well blended. Add the remaining cans of broth and simmer the soup, partially covered, for 1 hour. Add salt and pepper to taste. Skim off the excess fat if necessary.

Croûtes: Arrange the slices of French bread in a single layer on a baking sheet. Bake at 325 degrees for 15 minutes. With a pastry brush, coat both sides of the bread slices with olive oil. Turn the slices over and bake for an additional 15 minutes, or until the bread is dry and the edges are golden. Rub each slice with a garlic clove and set aside.

To serve, pour the soup into individual bowls. Top each with 2 croûtes and sprinkle with 2 tablespoons of the shredded cheese. Put the bowls on a baking sheet and broil for 1 to 2 minutes, until the cheese has melted and is lightly browned.

Serves 8.

✳ Parsley-Parsnip Soup

Diana Matthews, Lawrence

This uniquely flavored soup can be served hot or cold and makes a delicious all-weather appetizer.

8 parsnips
4 green onions, chopped
1 cup fresh parsley, snipped
4 cups water
1 14-ounce can chicken broth
1 teaspoon dried chives
⅓ teaspoon tarragon
salt and pepper, to taste
sour cream
parsley sprigs

Peel the parsnips and cut into strips. Combine in a large pot with the green onion and parsley. Add the water and boil until the vegetables are tender, about 10 to 15 minutes.

Drain the vegetables and parsley, reserving the cooking water. Blend the vegetables and parsley in a blender or food processor. Add the chicken broth, chives, and tarragon and continue blending until smooth. If the soup appears too thick, gradually add as much of the reserved cooking water as needed, blending until the desired consistency is reached. Season with salt and pepper to taste.

Serve hot or cold. Top each serving with a dollop of sour cream and a sprig of fresh parsley.

Serves 4.

Homestead Fever

When Congress passed the Kansas-Nebraska Act of 1854, Kansas was officially opened to settlement, and homesteading fever swept across the country.

The largest number of early homesteaders came from the Old Northwest Territory—Ohio, Illinois, Indiana, Michigan, and Wisconsin. Many of these people had previous pioneering experience and already knew how to break land and build log cabins. Some left comfortable homes, good jobs, and an easier life in search of land and opportunity.

Lillie Marcks described her family's departure from Tiffin, Ohio, in May 1869. "Some cried and talked of Indians and bears. I was seven years old, had been staying with friends in Tiffin three weeks and they felt so badly about my going west and had me so beautifully dressed that even my father and mother scarcely knew me. . . . I recall my mother's headaches on the trip, and many children dirty and cross, and how we longed for the journey's end" (in *Pioneer Women: Voices from the Kansas Frontier*, edited by Joanna L. Stratton [New York: Simon & Schuster, 1982]).

Starting in the 1860s, thousands of acres of land were transferred by treaty from Indians to the government. Most of it then passed into the hands of railroad companies, town promoters, and land speculators. The Homestead Act of 1862 enticed many people to pull up stakes, and when the Civil War ended, a large influx of settlers began moving into Kansas.

Freed blacks were a special group of homesteaders who came from the South to Kansas in search of better lives and a plot of ground they could call their own. Many settled in river towns such as Wyandotte, Leavenworth, Atchison, and Topeka. The most enterprising of the black settlements was Nicodemus, which was once a thriving community of several hundred farmers and businessmen in western Kansas.

Although some Europeans had migrated to Kansas at the opening of the territory, the major wave came in the late 1860s. Most of these immigrants were Germans, but the French, Swedes, Czechs, Italians, and many other foreigners were encouraged to come by promoters or relatives in the United States for the opportunity of acquiring land and escaping political and religious oppression.

Homesteading land was a dream come true for many settlers, but they were often faced with some unwelcome surprises from Mother Nature. The immigrant's perspective is aptly described in *Cather's Kitchens: Foodways in Literature and Life*, by Roger L. and Linda K. Welsch (Lincoln: University of Nebraska Press, 1987): "Imagine, for example, the dilemma of the migrant Norwegian family arriving in America . . . they face hazards and problems they never imagined in their worst dreams in the Old Country: prairie fires moving faster than a man could ride on horseback, Indian raids, grasshopper storms, murderous hail that could drop livestock in the pastures, heat and cold beyond their experience, and half the rainfall they would have expected at home. Everything had changed, in field and town, house and barn."

✳ Poor Man's Soup with a Rich Man's Flavor

Kittie Furbeck Dale, Ellis

"In 1878, my grandparents came from Illinois, to homestead land in Kansas. They came part way to Ellis in a covered wagon, and finished the journey in a railroad immigrant car," writes Kittie Furbeck Dale. *"Their young son Frank declared he would fight the Indians for only one thing, his red fiddle. A natural musician, he played his rollicking fiddle symphonies for over 50 years, much to the delight of despairing settlers.*

My mother, Sophia Elizabeth Egger, and Frank, the fiddling man, were married in 1893 and reared thirteen children, living part of the time in a sod house on the plains. In those days, you made do with what you had. My mother remembers, as a child, that the cast iron soup kettle on the back of the cookstove was seldom without this homemade nourishing soup. I was number seven in the family and inherited my grandmother's original soup recipe."

3 potatoes
1 onion
1 rounded tablespoon lard or shortening
1 rounded tablespoon all-purpose flour

DUMPLINGS
1 or more eggs, beaten
all-purpose flour

salt and pepper, to taste

Peel and dice the potatoes and onion. Place in a large pan or stock pot and cover with at least 1 quart of water. Bring to a boil, reduce heat to low, and simmer until the potatoes are tender-crisp.

In a small skillet, melt the lard or shortening over medium heat. Add the flour and stir constantly, until the mixture reaches a rich caramel color. Stir the mixture into the soup and continue simmering.

Dumplings: In a medium-sized bowl, beat 1 egg or more until fluffy. Stir in enough flour (about ¼ cup to each egg) to make a stiff dough. Drop from the tip of a spoon into the soup. Cover the pan and allow the dumplings to steam at a simmer for 6 to 8 minutes. The dumplings are done when an inserted toothpick comes out clean. Add salt and pepper to taste.

Serves 4.

✳ Butter Balls in Chicken Broth
(Butter Glase)

Esther Reilly, Dorrance

Butter Glase are dumplings seasoned with allspice and cooked in chicken broth or chicken soup. This recipe is a favorite of Esther Reilly's family, of Volga German heritage. The Volga Germans were descendants of Germans who had settled in the Volga region of Russia in the eighteenth century.

4 cups bread crumbs
2 eggs
1 teaspoon allspice
½ cup butter, melted
¼ cup chicken broth or milk, if needed
6 cups chicken broth or chicken soup

To make the bread crumbs, use about 8 slices of day-old, dry bread. Broil the bread on a baking sheet until browned lightly on both sides. Cool and crush finely. Measure 4 cups of crumbs.

Put the bread crumbs in a large bowl. Add the eggs, allspice, and the melted butter. Mix well. If the mixture appears too dry to form into balls, add up to ¼ cup of chicken broth or milk. Form the mixture into balls about 1 inch in diameter. Place the balls on a baking sheet and chill for at least 1 hour.

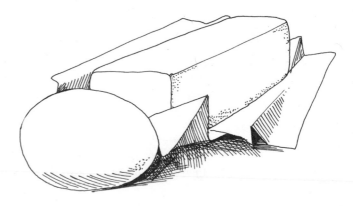

Bring the chicken broth or chicken soup to a boil over high heat in a stock pot or Dutch oven. Add some of the butter balls as the broth continues to boil. They will rise to the top when done, about 10 minutes. Remove them with a slotted spoon and place them in a bowl. Add more of the butter balls and repeat the procedure.

Return the cooked butter balls to the soup, heat, and serve.

Serves 4 to 6.

✳ Black Walnut Soup

Black walnut trees flourish along the creeks and rivers of eastern Kansas. Because the walnuts are rich in protein and fat, the pioneers sometimes made them into soup when there was a shortage of meat.

This contemporary version makes a distinctive and flavorful first course to an elegant meal.

¼ cup butter
2 tablespoons all-purpose flour
1 14-ounce can chicken broth
1 14-ounce can beef broth
¼ teaspoon red pepper flakes
1 bay leaf
¼ teaspoon marjoram
¼ teaspoon pepper
½ cup black walnuts, chopped
2 tablespoons all-purpose flour
3 tablespoons sour cream

Melt the butter in a large pan or Dutch oven. Add the flour and cook over medium-low heat, stirring for 1 minute. Slowly add the chicken and beef broth, stirring constantly. Add the red pepper flakes, bay leaf, marjoram, pepper, and black walnuts. Simmer for 15 minutes over low heat.

Beat the flour and sour cream together in a small bowl until a smooth paste is formed. Add a small amount of the hot soup, about ¼ cup, to the sour cream mixture. Stir until smooth, then add the mixture slowly to the soup, stirring with a large wire whip to combine. Cook for 1 minute more without boiling and remove from heat. To serve, cool the soup to lukewarm.

Serves 4.

✳ Rose Hip Soup

(Nyponsoppa)

Lorraine J. Kaufman, Moundridge

One of the loveliest wildflowers, the wild rose, was used by early settlers for a healthful soup made from its seed pods. Lorraine Kaufman informs us that "the red seed pods or rose hips become succulent as they mature and after a frost they can be gathered and dried. The rose hips can then be made into a distinctive dessert with a tart flavor that is rich in vitamin C. Considered a real delicacy among Swedish people, Nyponsoppa, or Rose Hip Soup, is served with whipped cream and topped with slivered almonds.

Dried rose hips, an instantly prepared mix, and tinned Nyponsoppa are available in Swedish import food stores. For those who want the adventure of gathering and drying their own rose hips, they can prepare them according to the following recipe."

⅔ cup dried rose hips
4 cups cold water
½ cup sugar
3 tablespoons cornstarch
¼ cup whipping cream, whipped
slivered almonds

Wash the rose hips thoroughly and drain well. Place them in a large pan or stock pot and add the cold water. Cover tightly and simmer gently over low heat for 2 hours, stirring occasionally.

Pour the cooked rose hip mixture into a strainer and drain off the liquid into a saucepan, reserving ½ cup. Press the rose hips through the strainer to make a puree. Measure 3 tablespoons of the puree and add it to the saucepan. Return the saucepan to the heat. Add the sugar and stir until dissolved, allowing the liquid to come to a boil.

Mix the cornstarch with the reserved ½ cup of liquid. Pour the mixture slowly into the boiling liquid, stirring constantly until it thickens. Reduce the heat to very low and cook for 10 minutes. Remove from heat and cover. Cool by placing the saucepan in cold water.

Top each serving with a dollop of whipped cream and sprinkle with slivered almonds.

Serves 6.

✳ Swedish Fruit Soup

(Frukt Soppa)

Addie Johnson, Hutchinson

This versatile Swedish soup can be served hot or cold, as a first course or a dessert.

½ *pound pitted prunes*
¼ *pound dried apricots*
1 *cup raisins*
4 *tablespoons large tapioca*
3 *apples, peeled and diced*
1 *lemon, sliced*
1 *orange, sliced*
1 *cup sugar*
¼ *teaspoon salt*
1 *cinnamon stick*
2 *quarts water*
½ *cup maraschino cherries*

Place the prunes, apricots, raisins, and tapioca in a large bowl. Add just enough water to cover and soak for 8 hours or overnight.

Place the soaked fruit mixture in a large pan or Dutch

oven. Add the apples, lemon, orange, sugar, salt, and cinnamon stick. Pour in 2 quarts of water and stir to combine.

Simmer the mixture over low heat, stirring occasionally until the fruits are soft, 10 to 15 minutes. If the soup seems too thick, add more water. Add the cherries and serve hot or cold.

Serves 6 to 8.

❋ BEEF AND RED MEATS

I n 1854, *Harper's Weekly* reported that the most common meal from coast to coast was steak. Although most beef had been raised in Georgia and the Carolinas, that year Texas longhorns arrived in New York City. However, their exotic appearance may have caused more excitement than their taste. "Texas cattle were tough to handle," cattle drivers would say a few years later, "but tougher to eat."

Beef has always been abundant, but not always easily available. Once the railroads met the Texas longhorns in Kansas, the beef industry began to develop. The Texas cattle ranchers responded to the eastern demand for beef after the Civil War by moving their cattle north to Kansas railheads as the railroads extended west. The industry boomed in 1867 when Joseph G. McCoy, an Illinois cattleman, envisioned the town of Abilene as a major shipping point. He built cattle pens large enough to hold three thousand head on the outskirts of a town scarcely more than a few blocks long.

For the next two decades, as the railhead moved to Ellsworth, to Newton and Wichita, and eventually to Caldwell, the history of cattle and cowboys captured the imagination of a nation and the world. The most famous of the cattle towns, Dodge

City is synonymous with the riotous lawlessness of the
rugged cowpoke "kicking up a little dust" after the arduous journey from Texas along the Western Cattle Trail.

"Texans shipped up the horns and we put the bodies
under them," old Kansas cattlemen used to say because
the rich grassland of the Kansas Flint Hills fattened the
cattle before they were loaded on the trains and sent
east.

By the 1880s, the beef industry had spread across
Kansas. The 1879 quarantine line on southern cattle
stopped all cattle drives at the state line, preventing the
spread of "Texas fever" to the susceptible "blooded"
stock raised in Kansas. As more Kansans made claim
to the land the proliferation of fencing put an end to the
open range and, without the free grass, driving cattle
became economically infeasible. Kansans began to raise
their own cattle instead of processing and shipping Texas
herds. Soon the practice of fattening beef over the summer established Kansas as the primary region for cattle
raising.

Cattle profits brought wealth to the state, but hard lessons were yet to be learned. By the end of the century,
many ranchers had failed due to drought, blizzards, over-
stocking, disease, and competition for water and grazing
land. Out of these hard times modern ranching techniques developed, with less reliance on nature and more
advancement in scientifically formulated feed rations,
grassland maintenance, and veterinary care.

Today, about 700,000 cattle are pasture-fed in Kansas
annually. With another 4 million cattle raised on feed,
Kansas now holds the position of being the number one
meat-packing state in the nation, raising and processing
the cattle on the same prairie where the industry was
born. Exotic breeds from Europe and Asia now share the
plains along with other well-established American breeds
where once only buffalo roamed.

Kansans enjoy red meats other than beef. Though
the buffalo were hunted to the point of extinction, a few
ranchers kept small herds for nostalgic reasons as well
as out of admiration for their hardiness. From these buffalo herds, crossbreeding produced the first cattalo and,

later, the more successful beefalo. Both beefalo and buffalo may be purchased from the rancher, and buffalo is
sometimes found in larger grocery stores. Sheep ranching developed in Kansas along with the cattle industry,
but they were raised more for their wool than for food.
Today, lamb is raised commercially in Kansas. Feed lots
and a processing plant now exist in Harper. The production of veal is not a commercial industry in Kansas,
but can be found in grocery stores wherever cultural or
cosmopolitan tastes create a demand.

The meats that Kansas ranchers produce are the envy
of the world. In the recipes that follow, there are the
favorite roasts and chilies of cattlemen, past and present,
along with recipes featuring beefalo and buffalo. Recipes
of lamb and veal indicate the Italian influence in our state,
while recipes using lean cuts of beef and lamb for the grill
make a contemporary statement.

✳ Welcome Pot Roast

Mariellen Appleby, Sedan

On Sunday, there are two traditions in the Midwest—church and pot roast. The family attends Sunday morning services while at home the pot roast slowly braises. A heavenly aroma that promises a delicious dinner greets the family upon their return.

Mariellen Appleby named this recipe Welcome Pot Roast because it was the standard menu served by her mother when special guests were invited for dinner. Recalling bygone days of courting, she says it could have just as easily been called "Beau's Pot Roast."

1 large bay leaf
3 to 5 pounds beef roast (arm, blade, or chuck)
1 cup all-purpose flour
1 teaspoon salt
¼ teaspoon pepper
¼ cup vegetable oil or bacon drippings
½ teaspoon Worcestershire sauce
1 medium onion, thinly sliced
½ cup water
6 medium potatoes, peeled
4 carrots, peeled
6 small onions, peeled

GRAVY
reserved juices
2 tablespoons all-purpose flour
½ cup water

Break the bay leaf into 4 pieces. Cut 4 small slits in the beef roast and insert the bay leaf pieces.

Combine the flour, salt, and pepper in a wide pan. Dredge the roast in the flour and shake off the excess.

Heat the oil or the bacon fat over medium heat in a Dutch oven or a pan large enough to hold the roast. Slowly brown the roast on all sides. Drain off all but 2 tablespoons of the fat. Sprinkle the roast with the Worcestershire sauce and top with the sliced onion. Add the water to the pan. Cover and braise over low heat for 2 to 3 hours.

After 1 to 1½ hours (depending on the size of the roast), add the potatoes, carrots, and onions. Cover and continue cooking for about 1 hour more, or until the vegetables and meat are tender. Remove the roast and the vegetables to a serving platter.

Gravy: Pour the pan juices into a saucepan. Skim off excess fat. Heat to simmering over medium heat. Combine the flour and water in a small covered container. Shake vigorously to blend. Pour the flour and water mixture slowly into the simmering juices, stirring constantly until the desired thickness is achieved. Let the gravy simmer over low heat for 1 to 2 minutes, stirring occasionally. Pour into a serving bowl.

Serves 6.

✳ Gnocchi with Meat Sauce

(Gnocchi con Salsa di Carne)

Kristine Leann Turner, Chanute

This delicious Italian recipe for gnocchi (pronounced NYOK-kee), or potato dumplings, served with a rich meat sauce, arrived with a comment that seems to exemplify the sentiment of many Kansas cooks. "This recipe," writes Kristine Leann Turner, "has been handed down from my great-grandmother, Ezelena Mendici Farneti, who came from Gubio, Italy, at the same age as I am now—fourteen. She and I would roll the gnocchi and talk. This is the way I learned about my heritage. Each time I help my mother make the gnocchi, I think about my Nona."

MEAT SAUCE
4 to 5 pounds boneless beef roast
¼ cup olive oil
2 garlic cloves, minced
½ cup fresh button mushrooms, sliced
1 carrot, peeled and chopped
1 10-ounce can tomato puree
3 cups water
2 tablespoons fresh parsley, chopped
1 teaspoon basil
1 teaspoon salt
¼ teaspoon pepper

GNOCCHI
2 pounds red potatoes, peeled and boiled
1 egg, beaten
2 to 2½ cups all-purpose flour
1 teaspoon salt
Romano cheese, grated

Meat Sauce: Cut the roast into 4 or 5 large chunks, trimming off any excess fat. Heat the olive oil in a large heavy-bottomed pan or Dutch oven over medium-high heat. Brown the meat and garlic, turning often. Remove the meat chunks from the pan and set aside.

Add the mushrooms and carrot to the pan and sauté over medium-high heat until tender, 5 to 10 minutes. Return the meat to the pan and stir in the tomato puree, water, parsley, basil, salt, and pepper. Bring the mixture to a boil over medium-high heat. Reduce heat to low and simmer, partially covered, for about 4 hours. Check the sauce after 3 hours; if it appears thick, cover the pan completely for the last hour. Stir occasionally to avoid sticking. When the meat is tender, remove it from the pan, reserving the sauce. Skim any excess fat from the sauce. Cut the beef roast into bite-size pieces and keep warm until ready to serve.

Gnocchi: Boil the potatoes in a large pot of water until tender. Drain and press through a potato ricer, or mash thoroughly. Cool to room temperature.

Place the potatoes in a large bowl and stir in the egg. Gradually add the flour, mixing well until it forms a manageable soft dough. Roll the dough onto a lightly floured surface to ¾-inch thickness. Cut into ¾-inch squares. Dust the gnocchi lightly with flour and drop them into a large pot of salted boiling water. Cook until they rise to the top, 2 to 3 minutes. (They will become tough if overcooked.) Drain and serve immediately.

To serve, place the gnocchi on a platter. Sprinkle with grated cheese and cover with the meat sauce. Garnish with additional grated cheese. Serve with the beef roast on the side.

Serves 6 to 8.

Variation: Substitute 1 pound of spaghetti for the gnocchi.

✳ Barbecued Chuck Roast

Elizabeth W. Carlson, Topeka

Grilling this economical cut of beef produces a surprisingly tender and flavorful entree. Serve as you would any large steak, carving it at the table, hot from the grill.

3½ to 4 pounds chuck roast, 2½ to 3 inches thick

MARINADE
¼ cup olive oil
¼ cup red wine vinegar
¼ cup dry sherry
2 teaspoons soy sauce
1 teaspoon rosemary

½ teaspoon dry mustard
4 garlic cloves, minced

2 tablespoons catsup
1½ teaspoons steak sauce
½ teaspoon Worcestershire sauce

Place the chuck roast in a wide bowl.

Marinade: Combine all the ingredients and pour over the roast. Cover and refrigerate for a full 24 hours, turning the meat several times.

Remove the meat and drain. Add the catsup, steak sauce, and Worcestershire sauce to the marinade. Stir well and baste the meat with the marinade before grilling.

Grill over hot coals, turning frequently and basting with the marinade every 5 to 10 minutes. Grill for about 30 to 40 minutes, or until desired doneness is achieved. (Internal temperature of 155 degrees for medium-rare.)

Serves 6.

✳ Braised Beef Burgundy

Barbara Holzmark, Leawood

Serve this hearty beef dish with freshly cooked noodles or steamed rice. For the best flavor, use lean meat and a good quality red wine.

2 pounds beef stew meat
1½ cups all-purpose flour
1 teaspoon salt
¼ teaspoon pepper
3 tablespoons vegetable oil
1 large onion, chopped
1 8-ounce can tomato sauce
1 cup dry red wine
1 4-ounce jar sliced mushrooms with liquid
2 tablespoons fresh parsley, chopped, or 1 tablespoon dried parsley
1 bay leaf
¼ teaspoon thyme
¼ teaspoon salt
⅛ teaspoon pepper

Cut the stew meat into cubes, trimming off excess fat. Place the flour, salt, and pepper in a bag. Drop the meat cubes into the bag and shake.

In a Dutch oven or large pan, heat the oil over medium heat. Cook the chopped onion until lightly browned, turning often. Add the floured meat to the pan and brown, turning occasionally.

Stir in the remaining ingredients. Bring the mixture to a boil. Reduce the heat to low, cover, and simmer for 1½ to 2 hours, or until the meat is fork-tender, stirring occasionally. Add ½ cup of water during the last hour of cooking if the sauce becomes too thick.

Serves 6.

Harvest Honeymoon

"It is strange to think this happened 80 years ago," writes Mrs. Jean Schmelzla of Fulton. "Charlie and Maud were my grandparents and this is the story of their honeymoon taken from my grandmother's diary."

On August 20, 1908, the newlyweds, Charlie and Maud Strain, left Alton, Missouri, in a covered wagon with a span of young mules. They stopped in Bourbon County, Kansas, and worked for a sawmill man named Sam Strawby. After Maud's sister Nell joined them, they headed on toward Wichita and joined a threshing crew near Bainsville.

Charlie used his mules to haul water for the thresher, earning three dollars a day. Maud and Nell ran the cook shack for two dollars a day with board.

The cook shack was ten feet wide and twenty feet long. It was on wheels and was pulled behind the threshing machine. There was a big cast-iron stove at the front end with a big iron pot for cooking meats and vegetables, and a three-gallon coffee pot. A table sat halfway in the middle. The women baked their own breads, pies, and cakes, and once a week they made biscuits for breakfast.

Once, with the meat and vegetables cooking, pies baking, and bread rising, the boss announced that they were heading on. With Maud and Nell finishing the meal, they were moved to the next farm, and by the time they had arrived and the men had washed up, the meal was ready to eat.

With such nomadic beginnings, home life could only become more stable for the young couple.

✳ # Home-Style Steak with Butter Crumb Dumplings

Patricia Habiger, Spearville

Patricia Habiger considers this dish a "man's meal" and takes it out to the field workers at harvest. The dumplings replace potatoes in this hearty dish.

2 pounds round steak
⅔ cup all-purpose flour
1 teaspoon salt
¼ teaspoon pepper
¼ cup vegetable oil or shortening
1 10-ounce can cream of chicken soup

BUTTER CRUMB DUMPLINGS
2 cups all-purpose flour
3 teaspoons baking powder
1 teaspoon poultry seasoning
½ teaspoon salt
1 cup milk
½ cup melted butter, divided
1 cup fine dry bread crumbs

Trim the fat from the edges of the round steak and cut the meat into 6 individual servings. Combine the flour, salt, and pepper in a shallow bowl. Dredge the meat in the flour mixture.

Heat the oil or shortening in a large skillet over medium-high heat. Brown the meat quickly on both sides, then transfer to a 13 x 9–inch baking dish. Add the soup, plus a can of water, to the skillet and stir to combine. Bring the mixture to a boil and pour over the meat. Cover with foil and bake at 350 degrees. After 30 minutes, add the dumplings.

Butter Crumb Dumplings: In a large bowl, combine the flour, baking powder, poultry seasoning, and salt. Add the milk and ¼ cup of the melted butter. Stir just until the dry ingredients are moistened. The mixture will not be smooth. In a separate bowl, combine the remaining ¼ cup of melted butter with the bread crumbs. Drop the dumplings by rounded spoonfuls into the buttered crumbs and roll until well coated.

Place the dumplings on top of the meat and bake uncovered at 425 degrees for 20 to 30 minutes more.

Serves 6.

✳ Mother's Oven Steak

Mrs. George (Wilma) Ackerman, Sabetha

Cooking often stirs up memories, and this recipe reminds Wilma Ackerman of her mother Ollie Marthaler Bauman, a soft-spoken and talented homemaker of Swiss and German descent. Though the recipe was simple, it was one of the family's favorite meals.

2 pounds beef chuck or round, tenderized
2 eggs
1 cup cracker crumbs
¼ cup vegetable oil or fat
salt and black pepper, to taste
1 large onion, sliced
6 tablespoons catsup

Cut the meat into 6 portions. In a wide bowl, beat the eggs slightly. Dip the meat in the egg and coat with the cracker crumbs. In a skillet, preheat the oil to hot but not smoking, and brown the steaks.

Salt and pepper the steaks and place them in a 13 x 9–inch pan. On each steak, put a tablespoon of catsup and a slice of onion. Cover the pan with foil and bake at 350 degrees for 1 to 1½ hours, or until tender.

Serves 6.

✳ Swiss Steak

Baking meats was a favorite technique of pioneer cooks because

2 pounds round steak, tenderized
2 whole garlic cloves
¾ cup all-purpose flour

it did not require con-
stant attention and
slow cooking made
the tougher cuts more
tender. Swiss Steak—
hearty and nourishing
—was one such dish.

1½ teaspoons salt
½ teaspoon pepper
¼ cup bacon drippings
1 cup onion, chopped
⅓ cup carrot, finely chopped
⅓ cup celery, finely chopped
⅓ cup green pepper, finely chopped
1 16-ounce can tomatoes, undrained and chopped
1 cup beef broth

Trim the fat from the edges of the meat and cut into 6 servings. Rub each piece with garlic cloves. Combine the flour, salt, and pepper in a small bowl. Rub or pound as much of the flour mixture into the meat as possible.

Heat the bacon drippings over medium-high heat. Add the meat and sear quickly on both sides. Place the meat in a 13 x 9–inch baking dish.

Add the onion, carrot, celery, and green pepper to the drippings. Cook over low heat for 5 minutes. Pour in the tomatoes and beef broth. Bring the mixture to a boil and pour over the meat. Cover the baking dish with foil and bake at 300 degrees for about 2 hours, or until the meat is tender. Skim any excess fat from the dish and serve.

Serves 6.

✳ Chicken-Fried Steak with Gravy

As the name implies,
round steak in this
recipe is cooked like
fried chicken but with
less oil. In recent
times, soda crack-
ers have become the
preferred breading
instead of flour. Rice
or mashed potatoes
should accompany
this family favorite,

1½ pounds tenderized top round steak, ½ inch thick
garlic salt and pepper, to taste
1 egg
1 tablespoon milk
1 cup soda cracker crumbs, finely crushed
¼ cup olive oil

G R A V Y
2 tablespoons all-purpose flour
1 cup chicken broth
½ cup milk
salt and pepper, to taste

because a wonderful gravy is made from the drippings.

Remove any excess fat from the edges of the round steak and cut the meat into individual serving pieces. Sprinkle lightly with garlic salt and add pepper to taste, rubbing the seasonings into the meat.

In a bowl, combine the egg and milk and beat well. Place the crushed cracker crumbs in a separate bowl. Dip the steaks into the egg mixture and coat with the cracker crumbs.

Heat the oil over medium-low heat. Add the steaks and brown slowly, about 5 to 8 minutes. Turn and brown 5 to 8 minutes more. Cover the pan, reduce the heat to low, and cook for 20 to 30 minutes, until the steaks are tender. Remove the steaks from the pan and keep warm.

Gravy: Add the flour to the pan drippings, stirring over medium-low heat until the flour begins to color. Combine the chicken broth and milk and add slowly, stirring until the gravy begins to boil. Continue stirring and cook for 2 to 3 minutes more. Pour the gravy into a bowl and serve immediately with the steak.

Serves 4.

✳ Round Steak with Green Peppercorn Gravy

This recipe makes an elegant meal with an inexpensive cut of meat.

1½ pounds top round steak, tenderized
salt and pepper, to taste
1 cup all-purpose flour
2 tablespoons butter

2 tablespoons olive oil
1 cup whipping cream
½ teaspoon Dijon mustard
1 tablespoon green peppercorns*

Remove any excess fat from the edges of the round steak. Cut the meat into individual servings. Sprinkle each piece with salt and pepper. Coat the meat with flour, shaking off excess.

Heat the butter and olive oil in a large skillet over medium-high heat. Brown the meat in the skillet until golden, about 5 minutes on each side. Reduce heat to low, cover the pan, and simmer for 10 to 15 minutes, or until tender. Remove the meat from the drippings and keep warm.

Add the whipping cream, mustard, and green peppercorns to the pan drippings. Raise heat to medium-high and bring to a boil, stirring frequently until the cream turns golden and thickens slightly, 3 to 5 minutes.

To serve, arrange the steak pieces on a platter or on individual plates and top with the green peppercorn sauce.

Serves 4.

*Green peppercorns packed in water or brine can be found in gourmet stores. Simply rinse in cold water and drain well before using.

✳ Italian Meat Roll

Norman and Anna Marie Krusic, Frontenac

This recipe was handed down to Norman and Anna Marie Krusic from Norman's grandmother, Zelinda Massine, who came from Italy to

2 pounds tenderized boneless round steak, ½ inch thick
salt and pepper, to taste
1 medium onion, finely chopped
2 garlic cloves, minced
1 green pepper, seeded and finely chopped
2 tablespoons parsley, chopped
½ cup Romano cheese, grated

live in Frontenac over
one hundred years
ago with her parents.
After her father was
killed in a mine ex-
plosion, Zelinda and
her mother took in
boarders. This meat
roll served with pasta
was a favorite meal of
the boarders. Zelinda
Massine lived 104
years, becoming Fron-
tenac's oldest resident.

½ cup fresh mushrooms, sliced, or 1 2-ounce jar sliced
   mushrooms, drained
1 cup dried bread crumbs
¼ cup olive oil
2 garlic cloves, coarsely chopped
1 6-ounce can tomato paste
1 cup water
⅛ teaspoon allspice
¼ teaspoon salt
⅛ teaspoon pepper
1 pound spaghetti, cooked

Place the steak on a cutting board. Sprinkle the meat
with salt and pepper to taste. Sprinkle the onion, garlic,
green pepper, parsley, grated cheese, and sliced mushrooms evenly over the meat. Top with the dried bread
crumbs. Starting at one end, roll the meat up tightly
and tie with string. Set aside.

Heat the olive oil over medium heat in a Dutch oven
or a large, heavy-bottomed pan. Add the chopped garlic
cloves and brown lightly. Add the meat roll and brown
on all sides.

Stir the tomato paste, water, allspice, salt, and pepper
into the pan. Cover and simmer over very low heat for
about 1 hour, or until tender.

Remove the meat roll from the tomato sauce and slice
into 1-inch rounds to serve. Arrange the spaghetti on the
side and top with the tomato sauce.

Serves 6.

✳ Barbecue Beef Brisket

Mrs. George (Wilma) Ackerman, Sabetha

*Beef brisket wasn't
always popular in
northeastern Kansas.
Thanks to Wilma
Ackerman's favorite*

4 to 10 pounds beef brisket
½ teaspoon onion salt
½ teaspoon garlic salt
½ teaspoon celery salt
¼ cup liquid smoke

family recipe, the good name of barbecued brisket was spread throughout the state. Mrs. Ackerman was the first president of the Nemaha County CowBelles (now called the CattleWomen), and she used this recipe to promote beef sales in Sabetha, Seneca, Topeka, and Atchison.

It is easy to see why this easy-to-prepare dish became a "standard" recipe for brisket. Slice leftovers and freeze them in family-sized portions for quick and versatile meals.

salt and pepper, to taste
2 tablespoons Worcestershire sauce

BARBECUE SAUCE
1 cup catsup
1 tablespoon Worcestershire sauce
3 dashes Tabasco sauce
1 cup water
¼ cup vinegar
1 tablespoon sugar
1 teaspoon salt
1 teaspoon celery salt

Place the brisket in a large roasting pan. Sprinkle with the onion, garlic, and celery salts and the liquid smoke. Cover and refrigerate overnight.

Discard the marinade and sprinkle the brisket with salt, pepper, and Worcestershire sauce. Cover with aluminum foil and bake at 275 degrees for 4 hours for small to medium-sized briskets or 5 hours for larger briskets.

Barbecue Sauce: In a large bowl, combine all the ingredients for the barbecue sauce, mixing well. (You may substitute 2½ cups of your favorite commercial barbecue sauce.)

Drain the liquid from the roasting pan and coat the brisket with the Barbecue Sauce. Cover and bake for 1 hour more. After cooking, let the brisket stand for at least 10 minutes. Slice against the grain to serve. Serves 10 or more.

✳ Cattlemen's Prime Rib Special

A Kansas cattleman's cookout or family gathering on the ranch

1 8-pound boneless rib roast
garlic-flavored olive oil*
black pepper, coarsely ground

*To make garlic-flavored olive oil, place 2 whole peeled garlic cloves in ¼ cup high-quality olive oil. Cover and let sit for at least 24 hours.

is celebrated with a
fine cut of beef, often
spit-roasted over a fire
pit. A cut of beef like
prime rib is usually
roasted with very little
seasoning, since its
natural flavor stands
on its own.

This oven-roasted
version seasons the
prime rib with only
garlic-flavored olive oil
and coarsely ground
black pepper.

Baste the rib roast with garlic-flavored olive oil and coat
generously with black pepper. Position the meat, fat side
up, on a rack in a shallow roasting pan. Roast the meat
uncovered at 425 degrees for 15 minutes. Reduce heat to
325 degrees and roast for approximately 20 minutes per
pound. (For medium rare, total cooking time is 2 hours to
2 hours 40 minutes, or until the internal temperature is
155 degrees. Check the temperature by inserting a meat
thermometer into the center of the meat.)

Let the roast stand for 15 minutes before slicing. Skim
the fat from the drippings and serve the drippings with
the meat.

Serves 8 to 10.

Variation: To grill, prepare the meat as directed above
and brown on all sides (about 3 minutes per side) directly over the hot coals. Continue cooking the meat over
indirect heat. For this method, divide the hot coals, banking them on each side of a drip pan. Place the meat on
the grid directly over the drip pan for indirect cooking.
Cover the grill.

The cooking time should be about the same, but check
with a meat thermometer. Add more hot coals as necessary after the first hour of cooking for even heat. Hickory
chips may be added to the hot coals for hickory flavor.

✳ Beef Tenderloin Fillets with Sweet Red Pepper Stuffing

*The beautiful, rolling
Flint Hills of Kansas
have provided perfect
grazing land for cattle,
and beef tenderloin is
perhaps the finest cut
of beef that Kansas
has to offer. In this
elegant recipe, beef
tenderloin fillets are
stuffed with sweet red*

SWEET RED PEPPER STUFFING
3 tablespoons butter
1 cup sweet red pepper, seeded and chopped
¼ cup onion, chopped
2 garlic cloves, minced
3 tablespoons Romano cheese, grated

4 beef tenderloin fillets, about 1½ inches thick
2 teaspoons pepper, coarsely ground
1 cup cherry wood chips (optional)
salt, to taste

pepper, onion, garlic, and Romano cheese and grilled over hot coals with cherry wood chips.

Sweet Red Pepper Stuffing: Melt the butter over low heat in a large frying pan. Add the chopped red pepper and onion. Cook slowly, stirring frequently, until the vegetables are tender, about 10 to 15 minutes. Add the garlic during the last few minutes of cooking. Remove mixture from the heat and cool slightly. Stir in the Romano cheese and set aside.

Make a deep horizontal slice in the side of each tenderloin fillet to form a pocket for stuffing. Do not cut completely through the meat. Fill each pocket with the stuffing mixture, about 2 to 4 tablespoons each. Close the openings with toothpicks to hold the stuffing in. Rub about ½ teaspoon of the pepper into both sides of each fillet.

Place the cherry wood chips on a piece of aluminum foil. Seal tightly to make a foil packet. Poke a few holes in the foil to allow the smoke to escape.

Place the foil packet directly on very hot coals. Replace the grid, arrange the tenderloin fillets over the hot coals, and cover the grill. Cook for 5 minutes. Turn the fillets and salt the top sides. Continue cooking for 3 to 5 minutes more, or until desired doneness is achieved. Remove the toothpicks before serving.

Serves 4.

Variation: Pan-fry the stuffed fillets in 2 tablespoons of olive oil over medium heat for 3 to 5 minutes each side, or until desired doneness is achieved.

✳ Beef Tenderloin Fillets with Shallot and Parsley Butter

This recipe calls for pan-frying beef tenderloin fillets and topping them with Shallot and Parsley Butter for an impressive presentation. For best results, prepare the butter a few hours ahead, to allow a blending of flavors.

SHALLOT AND PARSLEY BUTTER
¼ cup butter, slightly softened
1 tablespoon shallot, finely chopped
2 teaspoons fresh parsley, finely chopped

4 beef tenderloin fillets
pepper, to taste
2 tablespoons olive oil
salt, to taste

Shallot and Parsley Butter: In a mixing bowl, cream the butter until light and fluffy. Add the chopped shallot and parsley and mix well. Place the mixture in a small bowl. Cover and chill until firm, about 30 minutes. Remove from the refrigerator about 5 minutes before serving to soften slightly.

Rub pepper into both sides of each tenderloin fillet. Heat the olive oil in a frying pan over medium heat. Place the fillets in the pan and cook for 5 minutes. Turn the fillets over and salt the top sides. Cook for 3 to 5 minutes more, or until desired doneness is achieved. Remove the fillets from the pan and top each with a dollop of Shallot and Parsley Butter to serve.

Serves 4.

Variation: Grill the fillets over a hot charcoal fire, cooking for 3 to 5 minutes on each side, or until desired doneness is achieved. Top with Shallot and Parsley Butter to serve.

✳ Freight Train Fillets

Bob Schaffer, Lawrence

Bob Schaffer's recipe for Freight Train Fillets took second place at the 1988 Douglas County Fair Barbe-

6 beef tenderloin fillets, 1½ inches thick
¾ cup olive oil
¾ cup soy sauce
2 garlic cloves, minced
6 lean bacon strips

cue Cook-Off. The beef tenderloin fillets are marinated in a soy sauce and garlic mixture, wrapped with bacon strips, and grilled over medium-hot coals. They're good enough to stop a freight train on its tracks!

Place the tenderloin fillets in a baking dish. Combine the olive oil, soy sauce, and garlic. Pour over the fillets. Cover and refrigerate for 24 hours, turning occasionally.

Remove the fillets from the marinade and drain. Wrap 1 strip of bacon around each fillet and secure with a toothpick.

Grill, covered, over medium-hot coals for about 5 minutes each side, or until desired doneness is achieved.

Serves 6.

✳ Steaks on a Hickory Log

Mark Creamer, Lawrence

Mark Creamer cooks these steaks on family outings or at home on a homemade barbecue fire pit. For the coals, Mark advises, "Use natural logs and stay away from treated lumber. While you are making the coals, you may want to bake a potato to go with your steak. Just wrap the washed potatoes in aluminum foil and toss them right into the fire."

Once ready, the intense heat of the coals will immediately sear the outsides of the steaks, producing a juicy and flavorful steak unique to this practical outdoor method. Mark suggests one additional technique: "Have plenty of beer on hand in case the fire flares up while the steaks are cooking."

6 to 8 hickory logs, 3 to 4 inches in diameter, split or whole
4 rib-eye or T-bone steaks, cut 1 inch thick
salt and pepper, to taste

Build a fire with kindling and paper in a safe area. Let it burn until there is an adequate fire to ignite the logs. Place the logs on the fire and let them burn down completely into coals, breaking them into small pieces. Make an even, flat bed of glowing coals upon which to place the steaks. This may take about 3 hours.

Place the steaks directly on the coals. Cook them as you would on a grill, turning once with long-handled tongs, until desired doneness is achieved. Medium-rare steaks take about 4 to 6 minutes each side. Remove the steaks from the hot coals using tongs and mittens. Carefully brush off any ashes or hot coals that may cling to the meat before serving. Add salt and pepper to taste.

Serves 4.

✳ Pioneer Coffee Steaks

A pot of steaming hot coffee was always within reach in a pioneer kitchen and was the natural choice when looking for something to deglaze a pan after frying a steak. An 1874 recipe entitled "A Delicious Beef Steak," by Mrs. J. S. Rice in The Kansas Home Cookbook (The Ladies of Leavenworth, Leavenworth, 1874), *suggests topping a pan-fried steak with the pan juices flavored with coffee and butter.*

4 rib-eye steaks
pepper, to taste
1 tablespoon butter
1 tablespoon olive oil
salt, to taste
½ cup brewed coffee
½ teaspoon beef bouillon
2 tablespoons whipping cream (optional)
1 tablespoon butter

Trim excess fat from the edges of the steaks. Rub pepper into both sides of each steak. Melt the butter and olive oil in a large frying pan over medium-high heat, until hot enough to sizzle. Place the steaks in the pan and cook for 5 minutes. Turn over, salt the top sides, and cook for 3 to 5 minutes more, or until desired doneness is achieved.

Remove the steaks from the pan. Add the coffee and beef bouillon to the remaining juices. If a richer flavor is

This modern version recommends succulent rib-eye steaks and adds a little beef bouillon with the coffee when reducing the pan juices for the sauce.

desired, add the cream. Boil the mixture over medium-high heat, stirring occasionally until the juices reduce to about half. Remove the pan from the heat and swirl in 1 tablespoon of butter (unless the cream has been added) until melted. Pour the sauce over the steaks and serve immediately.

Serves 4.

✳ London Broil in Red Wine Marinade

Until recent years, flank steak was used almost entirely for braising and stewing. It is now considered a choice cut of meat for grilling or oven broiling. This recipe calls for London broil, a flank or skirt steak cut into strips and rolled into individual steaks. They can be found in most supermarkets.

4 London broil steaks

RED WINE MARINADE
1/4 cup olive oil
2 tablespoons red wine vinegar
2 garlic cloves, minced
1 bay leaf
1/4 teaspoon salt
1 teaspoon pepper, coarsely ground

Place the steaks in an 8-inch baking dish.

Red Wine Marinade: Combine all the ingredients for the marinade in a small bowl, mixing well.

Pour the marinade over the steaks. Cover and refrigerate for 3 hours, turning occasionally in the marinade.

Drain the steaks and arrange on a foil-lined baking sheet. Place them about 3 inches under the oven broiler and broil for 3 to 5 minutes each side, or until desired doneness is achieved.

Serves 4.

Variation: The steaks may be grilled directly over hot coals on a covered grill for 3 to 5 minutes each side, or until desired doneness is achieved.

❋ Flank Steak Mexicana

In 1987, Frank won first place in the outdoor grilling category of the Kansas Beef Cook-Off, sponsored by the Kansas Beef Council and the Kansas CattleWomen. He then won the competition for the Upper Plains Region and went on to represent Kansas in the 1987 National Beef Cook-Off in Sun Valley, Idaho.

Frank comments, "This recipe makes a great impression when it is served. Everyone loves the presentation of grilled beef on a colorful bed of lettuce and vegetables. It's perfect for outdoor entertaining."

1½ pounds beef flank steak, trimmed of excess fat
½ teaspoon ground cumin

MARINADE
½ cup olive oil
2 tablespoons lime juice
2 garlic cloves, minced
½ teaspoon crushed red pepper
1 teaspoon salt
¼ teaspoon pepper

1 head Boston lettuce
1 avocado, cut into wedges
2 medium tomatoes, cut into wedges
6 flour tortillas, warmed

Rub the cumin into both sides of the flank steak and place in a large pan or a plastic bag.

Marinade: Combine all the ingredients for the marinade. Pour the marinade over the meat, turning to coat. Cover the pan, or tie the bag securely, and refrigerate for 1 hour (or overnight), turning occasionally.

Remove the meat from the marinade. Grill over medium coals, turning once, about 5 to 6 minutes each side, or until desired doneness is achieved. Let the steak stand for 5 minutes before carving.

Carve the steak against the grain into thin slices. Place the lettuce leaves on a platter and arrange the steak slices on top. Garnish with the avocado and tomato wedges. Serve with warmed flour tortillas on the side.

Serves 4 to 6.

❋ Flank Steak with Onions and Red Wine Glaze

Flank steak is a flavorful cut of beef and works well for pan-

1½ pounds flank steak
1 teaspoon pepper, coarsely ground
2 tablespoons butter

*frying. This version is
topped with fried onion
wedges and glazed
with red wine.*

1 tablespoon olive oil
salt, to taste
1 large onion
½ cup dry red wine
1 tablespoon soy sauce
½ teaspoon Dijon mustard

Trim the flank steak to remove all surface fat. Rub the pepper into both sides of the meat.

Heat the butter and olive oil in a large frying pan over medium heat. When hot, cook the flank steak until the first side is browned, 5 to 10 minutes. Turn the steak over and salt the top side. Cook for 5 to 10 minutes more, or until desired doneness is achieved. Remove the steak from the pan and keep warm.

Peel the onion and slice it into wedges. Add the onion wedges to the pan drippings and cook over medium heat, stirring frequently, until tender-crisp. (Add a little more butter if necessary.)

Combine the red wine, soy sauce, and mustard in a small bowl, mixing well. Add the mixture to the onion and pan drippings. Raise the heat to medium-high and cook, stirring frequently, for about 3 minutes, or until the liquid reduces slightly.

To serve, slice the meat against the grain into thin strips. Spoon the onions and wine glaze on top.

Serves 4.

✳ Sirloin Steak with Midwest Marinade

*From the chuck wagon
on the trail drives
to the turn-of-the-
century Midwestern
kitchen, coffee and beef
have been two flavors
often served together.
This recipe makes a
marinade of coffee,*

2 ½ pounds top sirloin steak, 1½ inches thick

MIDWEST MARINADE
¾ cup very strong hot coffee
1 teaspoon beef bouillon
1 teaspoon brown sugar
2 tablespoons brandy
1 teaspoon Worcestershire sauce
1 ice cube

producing a savory glaze on the meat as it is grilled.

Trim any excess fat from the steak.

Midwest Marinade: In a small bowl, combine all the ingredients for the marinade except the ice cube. Stir until the beef bouillon and brown sugar are dissolved. Add the ice cube to cool the marinade.

Place the steak in a sealable plastic bag and pour the marinade over the steak. Seal the bag tightly. Cover and refrigerate for 3 hours, turning the bag occasionally.

Remove the steak from the marinade and place in a covered grill directly over hot coals. Cook, occasionally basting with the marinade, for 7 to 8 minutes each side, or until desired doneness is achieved. Let the steak stand for 5 minutes before cutting into serving size portions.

Serves 4 to 6.

✳ Country Steak Kabobs

Teresa Morgan, Roeland Park

Outdoor grilling is a passion for many Kansas cooks. Combining fresh garden vegetables with tender

1 pound sirloin or top round steak

MARINADE
1 5-ounce can tomato juice
¼ cup catsup

cuts of beef makes this recipe a great summer combination.

¼ cup white vinegar
2 to 3 tablespoons prepared mustard
1 tablespoon brown sugar
salt and pepper, to taste

8 to 10 whole mushrooms
8 to 10 pineapple chunks
1 large sweet red pepper, cut in 1-inch chunks
2 small zucchini, cut in thick slices
8 to 10 small whole onions, or wedges
8 to 10 cherry tomatoes

Cut and trim the steak into lean, 1½-inch cubes.

Marinade: Combine the ingredients for the marinade in a shallow pan.

Add the steak cubes and stir to coat. Refrigerate for 1 to 2 hours, stirring occasionally.

Drain the meat and reserve the marinade. Thread the meat and the remaining ingredients alternately onto skewers. Grill directly over hot coals, turning and basting frequently with the marinade, for 5 to 10 minutes, or until desired doneness is achieved.

Serves 4.

✳ Beefiesta Kabobs

Louise Berning-Wendler, Scott City

To promote the beef industry in western Kansas, the Scott City Chamber of Commerce sponsors an annual August event called The Beefiesta. Area businesses that are active in the beef industry set up tasting booths and give out samples of their best beef recipes.

3 pounds sirloin steak

MARINADE
1 tablespoon meat tenderizer
3 tablespoons liquid smoke
½ cup brown sugar
¼ teaspoon nutmeg
½ teaspoon paprika
½ teaspoon celery salt
½ teaspoon onion salt
½ teaspoon garlic salt
1 teaspoon salt
¼ teaspoon pepper

Louise Berning-Wendler of the Security State Bank writes, "The employees of our bank are eager to help each year in the preparation and serving of our outstanding recipe! The late John L. Meyers originated this recipe for the bank's booth."

16 to 20 whole mushrooms
16 to 20 whole cherry tomatoes
2 green peppers, cut into 1-inch chunks
1 large onion, cut into wedges
1 8-ounce can pineapple chunks
vegetable oil

Trim the fat from the sirloin and cut into cubes. Place the meat in a large bowl.

Marinade: Combine the ingredients for the marinade in a small bowl. Pour over the meat, cover, and refrigerate overnight.

Wash and prepare the vegetables and fruit. Drain the meat and place on barbecue skewers, alternating it with the vegetables and fruit. Brush the vegetable and fruit pieces lightly with vegetable oil.

Place the kabobs on a grill over hot coals, or broil in the oven for 5 to 10 minutes, or until desired doneness is achieved. Turn the kabobs frequently while cooking.

Serves 8 to 10.

Chuck Wagons

The chuck wagon was a necessity for the crews who drove cattle across the state of Kansas. In the lexicon of the cowboy, "chuck" was slang for food. Cowboys working from dawn till dusk had little time to eat until the herd was bedded down for the night. The cook usually drove the wagon several miles ahead of the outfit to set up camp and feed the hungry cowboys when they arrived. Dutch ovens, a wash tub, dried fruit, coffee, flour, beans, and lard were just a few of the items the cook carried in his wagon. His "chuck box" included spices, soap and towels, knives, and dish pans.

Beef, of course, was the staple food along the trail and with it the cook concocted many slow-simmering stews. A favorite meal among the cowboys was a stew made with the heart of a steer called "Son-of-a-Gun Stew" or, in more polite company, "A Gentleman From Texas."

(On the trail, it was known by coarser names and probably included "good" in the phrase as a compliment to the cook!) A more typical meal, breakfast or supper, might be a large T-bone steak fried in tallow and served with biscuits and coffee. For a change of pace and flavoring, a side of bacon was almost always brought along to be added to beans and stews.

A cowpoke could spend two months on the trail before he reached a railhead like Abilene. A bath, a shot of "something to wash down the trail dust," and a decent meal were in order. Sometimes the hotels and restaurants could not accommodate the sudden influx of customers—the many cowboys who had been paid off simultaneously and were ready to spend. To fill the need, the chuck wagons from the various outfits came into town to feed their crews. Chuck wagons, or lunch wagons, as they were later known, would set up in front of saloons to sell foods to passers-by. The lunch wagons of the western cowtown became a custom that prevailed in the Midwest and continued into the automobile age.

The following recipes for chilies and beef and bean meals recall those hearty and flavorful chuck wagon meals of the days of cattle drives.

✳ Roundup Chili

The following recipe spruces up a typical meal prepared by the chuck wagon cook for the cowboys on the cattle trail.

MARINADE
2 tablespoons olive oil
3 tablespoons lime juice
4 garlic cloves, minced
2 teaspoons ground cumin
2 tablespoons chili powder
1 teaspoon salt

2 pounds boneless beef stew meat
1 14-ounce can tomatoes, undrained and chopped
½ cup onion, finely chopped
1 teaspoon beef bouillon
¼ teaspoon red pepper flakes

½ cup water
½ cup beer or water
1 16-ounce can pinto beans, drained

Marinade: Combine the ingredients for the marinade. Mix well with a wire whip.

Place the beef in a large bowl. Pour the marinade over the beef and mix to coat. Cover and refrigerate for 24 hours, stirring twice.

In a Dutch oven or a large heat-proof baking dish, combine the tomatoes, chopped onion, beef bouillon, red pepper flakes, water, and beer. Add the beef, with the marinade.

Bring the mixture to a boil over medium-high heat. Cover and bake in the oven at 350 degrees for 30 minutes. Uncover and cook for an additional 30 to 45 minutes, until the meat is tender. Remove the meat from the pan and place in a separate bowl, reserving the pan drippings.

Skim the fat from the pan drippings and simmer over medium heat, reducing the mixture by about half. Return the meat to the pan and add the drained beans. Mix well and heat thoroughly, about 5 minutes.

Serves 4.

✳ Dodge City Chili

Warren A. Bird, Dodge City

What does a hungry stagecoach driver like to eat? We found the answer from Warren Bird, who developed his chili recipe while working long, hot summers as a stagecoach driver at Boot Hill in Dodge City.

Some cooks like

4 pounds lean chuck roast
3 tablespoons lard or kidney suet
⅓ cup Roberto's hot Mexican chili powder
⅓ cup mild chili powder
¼ cup ground cumin
2 15-ounce cans beef consommé
salt, to taste
corn chips
salsa
fresh cilantro

to add peppers, garlic, and onions, but Warren sticks to the basics of chili powder, broth, and beef. As an alternative, he suggests using venison for half of the meat. "It is really a wonderful dish, milder than you might think," he adds, "and fixed just the way a hungry cowpoke would want it to be— just plain good!"

Trim the chuck roast into lean ½-inch cubes and set aside. In an iron skillet over medium heat, melt the lard or suet. Lightly brown the beef and remove the skillet from the heat. Do not drain. Combine the chili powders and the cumin in a small bowl. Sprinkle the seasoning over the meat while gently stirring until each piece is well coated. Slowly stir in the consommé.

Begin to heat the chili at a low temperature. Do not boil. Continue to simmer for 3 to 4 hours, depending on the consistency desired. (The longer it cooks, the thicker it will be.) Refrigerate overnight to enhance the flavor, but do not remove the fat when reheating to serve. Add salt to taste.

Serve very warm with corn chips and salsa. Garnish each bowl with a dollop of salsa and a sprig of cilantro.

Serves 6 to 8.

✱ Country Chunky Chili

Lou Belle Meyer, Sylvan Grove

Lou Belle Meyer's spicy chili recipe has been a favorite of the Meyer family for thirty years. Serve this chili with corn tortillas, rice, or garlic bread.

2 tablespoons vegetable oil
3 pounds beef round or chuck, cut into cubes
1 large onion, chopped
1 green pepper, chopped
2 tablespoons chili powder
½ teaspoon cayenne pepper
½ teaspoon ground cumin
1 teaspoon oregano
1 tablespoon paprika
2 garlic cloves, minced
1½ teaspoons salt
1 15-ounce can tomato sauce
1 15-ounce can stewed tomatoes
2 15-ounce cans kidney beans, drained

Heat the oil in a large pan or Dutch oven. Brown the beef over medium-high heat. Lower heat to medium and add the onion and green pepper. Cook, stirring until the vegetables are tender.

Transfer the mixture to a large casserole. Stir in the remaining ingredients. Cover and bake at 325 degrees for 2 hours, or until the beef is tender. After 1½ hours, remove the lid to allow the chili to thicken. If the chili seems too thick, add a small amount of warm water to the pan.

Serves 6 to 8.

✱ Cinnamon Chili

This recipe won Frank the honor of being a finalist in the 1986 Kansas Beef Cook-Off, sponsored by the Kansas Beef Council and the Kansas Cattle-

1 pound ground beef
1 yellow onion, chopped
2 cloves garlic, minced, or ¼ teaspoon garlic powder
1 4-ounce can chopped green chilies
1 8-ounce can tomato sauce
1 16-ounce can whole tomatoes
1 15-ounce can Mexican-style chili beans

Women. The addition of ground cinnamon and cloves gives this chili a unique flavor and spicy aroma.

2 tablespoons chili powder
½ teaspoon salt
½ teaspoon cumin
1 teaspoon cinnamon
½ teaspoon ground cloves
1 jalapeño pepper, seeded and finely chopped (optional)

In a large skillet, brown the ground beef with the onion and garlic. Drain off all but 3 tablespoons of the pan drippings and add the remaining ingredients, mixing well. Let the chili simmer over low heat, stirring occasionally, for 20 minutes or more to enhance the flavor.

   Serves 4.

✳ Cinnamon Chili Mac

Tex-Mex flavors have influenced Kansas

1 16-ounce bag medium shell macaroni
1½ pounds ground beef

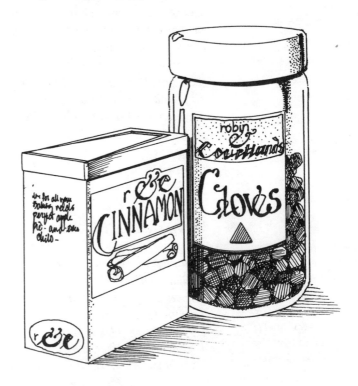

cooks since the days of the trail drives. This hearty casserole of ground beef, macaroni, and Monterey jack cheese is spiced with chili powder and cinnamon.

1 onion, chopped
1 green pepper, seeded and chopped
1 16-ounce can tomatoes
1 15-ounce can tomato sauce
2 garlic cloves, minced
1 tablespoon chili powder
1 teaspoon cinnamon
1 teaspoon sugar
1 teaspoon salt
1 cup Monterey jack cheese, shredded

Cook the macaroni in a large pot of boiling water, rinse, and drain. Set aside.

Brown the ground beef with the onion and green pepper over medium heat. Drain off all but 2 to 3 tablespoons of the drippings. Add the tomatoes, tomato sauce, garlic, chili powder, cinnamon, sugar, and salt. Stir in the cooked macaroni and ¾ cup of the cheese. Pour the mixture into a 13 x 9–inch baking dish. Top with the remaining ¼ cup of cheese. Cover with foil and bake for 20 minutes at 350 degrees. Uncover and bake for an additional 10 minutes or until hot and bubbly.

Serves 8.

✳ Chuck Wagon Bean Pot

Joyce Shafer, Ada

Hungry cowboys on the long drives from Texas to the cattle towns of Kansas consumed many hearty meals that featured beef and beans. These dishes are easy to prepare and can serve as an entire meal for a large number of people.

Joyce Shafer feeds not only her family but also a crew of cattle- men year-round. Her recipe, served with oven-fresh corn bread, is a favorite of the ranch crew, especially in the winter.

1½ to 2 pounds ground beef
1 cup onion, chopped
1 cup celery, chopped
1 8-ounce can tomato sauce, or 1 cup catsup

2 cups water
1 10-ounce package frozen mixed vegetables
2 16-ounce cans ranch-style beans
salt and pepper, to taste

In a large pot or Dutch oven, brown the ground beef with the onion and celery over medium heat. Add the remaining ingredients and mix well. Simmer over low heat for 1 hour.

Serves 8.

✳ Burger Bean Bake

Marilyn Eck, Bartlett

This recipe is a tasty variation of the traditional bean-and-beef meals that remain popular in many Kansas kitchens today.

2 bacon strips, cut into small pieces
1 medium onion, chopped
1 pound lean ground beef chuck
2 16-ounce cans pork and beans
½ cup catsup
½ cup sorghum
½ teaspoon dry mustard
1 tablespoon Worcestershire sauce
¼ teaspoon liquid smoke (optional)

In a large frying pan or Dutch oven, fry the bacon pieces over medium heat. Remove the bacon pieces, reserving the drippings. Cook the chopped onion in the drippings until tender. Add the ground beef and cook until browned.

Add the pork and beans and the bacon pieces to the beef mixture. Stir in the catsup, sorghum, dry mustard, Worcestershire sauce, and liquid smoke. Pour the mixture into a large baking dish and bake uncovered at 375 degrees for 30 minutes.

Serves 4 (or 8 as a side dish).

✳ Beef and Bean Dinner

Mariellen Appleby, Sedan

Mariellen Appleby's recipe for Beef and Bean Dinner has been enjoyed by her family and friends for many years. This hearty meal can be assembled in the morning, placed in a slow cooker, and served at dinner for a family on the go. A quick stove-top version may be cooked in a Dutch oven.

Complement the meal with just a salad and hot sourdough bread.

1 pound ground beef
6 bacon strips, cut into small pieces
1 cup onion, chopped
¼ cup brown sugar
1 cup catsup
1 tablespoon liquid smoke (optional)
3 tablespoons white vinegar
1 15-ounce can butter lima beans, drained
1 15-ounce can kidney beans, drained
1 16-ounce can pork and beans, undrained
1 teaspoon salt
¼ teaspoon pepper

Brown the ground beef in a large frying pan over medium heat. Drain off excess fat. Put the beef in a 3½-quart slow cooker, for all-day cooking, or in a Dutch oven, for a quick stove-top version.

In the same pan, fry the bacon pieces and onion over medium-low heat, until the bacon is cooked and the onion is tender. Add to the ground beef and mix well. Add the remaining ingredients to the cooker or Dutch oven and stir to combine.

Cover the slow cooker and cook on low for a minimum of 4 hours and a maximum of 9 hours. If using a Dutch oven, partially cover and simmer over low heat for 30 minutes, stirring occasionally.

Serves 6.

✳ Lou Belle's Best-Ever Meat Loaf

Lou Belle Meyer, Sylvan Grove

Ground beef became popular in American cookery in the early

2 eggs
⅔ cup milk
1½ teaspoons salt

part of the twentieth century, and culinary creations such as the meat loaf quickly emerged. Its roots are in European cooking, where ground meats are formed into loaves called pâtés.

Meat loaf is comfort food in the Heartland, and Kansans are proud of their family recipes. This recipe has been a longtime family favorite. The Meyer family is still in the cattle business on their original homestead now over a hundred years old.

¼ teaspoon pepper
3 slices bread, crumbled
1 onion, finely chopped
½ cup carrot, shredded
1 cup cheddar cheese, shredded
1½ to 2 pounds lean ground beef

TOPPING
¼ cup brown sugar
¼ cup catsup
2 to 3 teaspoons prepared mustard, to taste

In a large bowl, lightly beat the eggs. Add the milk, salt, pepper, and bread. Beat the mixture with a fork until the bread has disintegrated. Add the onion, carrot, cheese, and beef. Mix well and form into a loaf. Place the meat loaf in a loaf pan.

Topping: In a small bowl, combine the brown sugar, catsup, and mustard, to taste. Spread over the meat loaf. Bake at 350 degrees for 1¼ to 1½ hours.

Serves 6 to 8.

✳ Vegetable Meat Loaf

Mrs. Larry G. (Deb) Martin, Redfield

This excellent meat loaf appeals to contemporary tastes because it uses less meat and more vegetables. It is cooked in an electric skillet or a frying pan and is truly a no-fuss recipe. As with all meat loaves, the leftovers make excellent sandwiches.

1 pound ground beef
1 egg
1 onion, chopped
¼ cup green pepper, chopped
1 carrot, grated
¼ head of cabbage, grated
½ cup dry bread crumbs or crackers
salt and pepper to taste
¼ cup tomato sauce or catsup

In a large bowl, combine all the ingredients except the tomato sauce, mixing well. Shape the meat mixture into a loaf and place in an electric skillet or a frying pan. Top with the tomato sauce or catsup.

Cover and cook at 350 degrees for 10 minutes in an electric skillet, or for 10 minutes over medium heat in a frying pan. Reduce heat to simmer, or low, and continue cooking for 40 minutes longer.

Serves 6 to 8.

✳ Papa Joe's Italian Meatballs and Spaghetti

Olga Saia, Frontenac

The heritage of fine Italian meals is very much alive in southeast Kansas. Many Italians came to Crawford and Cherokee counties in the 1870s to work in the coal, lead, and zinc mines, and they brought the recipes of their homeland. The Italian

SAUCE
2 tablespoons olive oil
½ cup onion, chopped
1 or more garlic cloves, minced
2 cups canned Italian tomatoes or fresh tomatoes
1 6-ounce can tomato paste
2 to 3 tablespoons fresh parsley, chopped
2 or 3 fresh basil leaves
1 to 3 teaspoons sugar, to taste
½ teaspoon salt
pepper, to taste

cultural tradition of good food and social gatherings is reflected in the numerous holiday celebrations and group events held in these communities.

This Italian meatball recipe from Olga Saia uses an Old World method to obtain more tender meatballs by poaching them in tomato sauce.

MEATBALLS

1½ pounds lean ground beef
½ pound ground pork
5 to 6 eggs, beaten
1 cup fine fresh bread crumbs
½ cup Romano cheese, finely grated
1 teaspoon salt
½ teaspoon pepper
1 or 2 garlic cloves, minced
2 to 3 tablespoons fresh parsley, finely chopped
2 fresh basil leaves, finely chopped
¼ cup water

1 16-ounce package spaghetti
¼ cup Romano cheese, finely grated

Sauce: Heat the olive oil in a large skillet over medium heat. Add the onion and garlic and cook for about 8 minutes, until they are soft and transparent. Add the toma-

toes, tomato paste, parsley, basil, sugar to taste, salt, and pepper. Reduce heat to low and simmer for about 40 minutes, stirring occasionally. While the sauce is simmering, make the meatballs.

Meatballs: With your hands, thoroughly combine the ground beef, pork, and 5 of the eggs. Add the remaining ingredients, mixing well. If the meat seems stiff, add the remaining egg.

Shape the meat mixture into walnut-size balls (approximately 1½ inches in diameter). Drop the meatballs into the simmering sauce, cover, and cook over low heat for 1 hour. To keep the meatballs from sticking to the pan, check them after 20 minutes and stir gently if needed. Skim any excess fat from the sauce.

Boil the spaghetti in a large pot of water until tender, about 10 minutes. Drain and place it in a large serving bowl. Pour the meatballs and sauce over the spaghetti and toss gently. Sprinkle with Romano cheese.

Serves 6 to 8.

✳ Risotto Milanese

Josephine Caput, Frontenac

Risotto, in its classic Italian form, is a method of cooking rice by gently sautéing it, then adding broth a little at a time. This allows the rice to plump up by absorbing the liquid slowly. Contemporary cooks have elaborated on tradition by making a one-pan meal of this classic side dish. Josephine's grandmother, the creator of this recipe, recommends using the

¼ cup olive oil
½ cup onion, chopped
1 garlic clove, minced
1 pound ground beef chuck
1 6-ounce can tomato paste
4 ounces fresh button mushrooms, sliced, or 1 4-ounce jar
    sliced button mushrooms, drained
1½ cups uncooked rice
6 cups chicken broth
salt and pepper, to taste
½ cup Parmesan cheese, grated

In a Dutch oven, heat the olive oil over medium heat and sauté the onion, garlic, and ground beef until lightly browned. Stir in the tomato paste, sliced mushrooms, and rice.

broth from a freshly boiled chicken for best results.

In a large pot, bring the chicken broth to a boil and season with salt and pepper to taste. Add the broth to the meat mixture a little at a time, stirring constantly until all the broth is added.

Simmer uncovered over low heat, stirring occasionally, for about 30 minutes, or until rice is tender and moist but not mushy. Stir in the cheese just before serving.

Serves 6 to 8.

✳ Bierocks

Esther Reilly, Dorrance

Recipes for Bierocks, or "cabbage pockets," were brought to Kansas by the Volga Germans who emigrated from Russia. Well known in the south-central and western parts of the state, Bierocks are yeast pastries filled with beef and cabbage and baked to a golden brown.

This recipe was a favorite of Esther Reilly's family when she was growing up in Kansas. "My father never spoke much about his life in Russia," she said. "He would say, 'I am an American now.' He had served in the Russian army before coming to America in 1912 and his life was very hard."

FILLING
1 pound ground beef
½ cup vegetable shortening or oil
3 medium onions, chopped
1 medium head cabbage, shredded
salt and pepper, to taste

YEAST DOUGH
1 cup milk, scalded
½ cup sugar
1 teaspoon salt
½ cup shortening
1 package dry yeast
1 cup warm water
1 egg, beaten
6 cups all-purpose flour

Filling: In a large frying pan, fry the ground beef over medium heat. Drain off the excess fat and set aside.

In a large pan or Dutch oven, heat the shortening or oil over medium heat. Add the onion and cabbage and cover. Reduce the heat to medium-low and cook, stirring occasionally, until tender. Stir in the ground beef and add salt and pepper to taste. Cool to lukewarm before assembling the Bierocks.

Yeast Dough: To scald the milk, pour it into a saucepan and heat over medium heat until it is hot but not boil-

*Esther's mother,
however, always re-
called the love and
fellowship within their
home in Russia de-
spite the hard times,
and she brought those
values to her new home
in Kansas.*

ing. Remove it from heat and add the sugar, salt, and shortening. Cool to lukewarm.

Dissolve the yeast in the warm water. Add to the milk mixture. Stir in the beaten egg. Add 3 cups of flour and mix until smooth. Work in the remaining flour as needed, until the dough can be easily handled.

Turn the dough onto a lightly floured surface and knead until smooth and elastic, about 10 minutes. Place it in a lightly greased bowl and cover. Let the dough rise in a warm place until doubled in size, about 1 hour.

To assemble, roll out the dough on a floured surface to about ⅛-inch thickness. Cut the dough into 5-inch squares. Place some of the filling on each square and pinch the edges together to form a rectangle or triangle.

Place the Bierocks on greased cookie sheets. Let them rise in a warm place for 15 to 20 minutes. Bake at 350 degrees for 20 to 30 minutes, or until golden brown.

Makes 18 to 20 Bierocks.

✳ Indian Tacos with Hot Sauce

David A. Gaddy Cox, Kansas City

At almost any Kansas fair, the booth with the longest line is the one that serves Indian Tacos—usually run by a fund-raising orga- nization for the local Native American com- munity. The fry bread is cooked fresh to order and makes a natural platter for the meat fill- ing and the garnish of garden-ripe vegetables.

HOT SAUCE

1 quart stewed tomatoes, chopped
3 medium onions, chopped
2 green peppers, seeded and chopped
3 celery sticks, chopped
4 to 8 ounces jalapeños, seeded and finely chopped (to taste)
1 to 2 tablespoons crushed red pepper flakes (to taste)

FILLING

2 pounds ground beef
2 onions, chopped
2 green peppers, seeded and chopped
2 to 3 ounces jalapeños, seeded and finely chopped (optional)
¾ cup catsup
¼ cup chili powder
1 tablespoon crushed red pepper flakes (to taste)

1½ teaspoons salt
1 tablespoon pepper

6 to 8 Indian Fry Bread rounds

TOPPINGS
shredded lettuce
chopped tomato
shredded cheddar cheese
chopped black olives
sour cream

Hot Sauce: Place all the ingredients in a large pot and bring to a boil over high heat. Reduce heat to low, cover, and simmer for 3 to 4 hours. The sauce should be thick when done. During the last hour of cooking prepare the filling.

Makes about 1 quart of sauce.

Filling: In a large skillet, brown the meat with the onion and green pepper. Drain any excess fat from the meat and stir in the jalapeños. Add the catsup, chili powder, red pepper flakes, salt, and pepper. Simmer for 10 minutes over low heat, stirring occasionally.

Serve open face by spooning some of the filling on the fry bread. Add shredded lettuce, tomato, cheese, black olives, and sour cream. Top with Hot Sauce.

Serves 6 to 8.

✳ The Great Stuffed Pumpkin Recipe

Nancy Vogel, Hays

The explorers Lewis and Clark were the first to record that the Sioux Indians used seed meal in their dishes. This festive pumpkin, stuffed with

1 pie pumpkin, about 10 inches in diameter, well washed
1 to 2 tablespoons butter, softened
salt and pepper, to taste
1 pound ground beef
2 onions, chopped
1 16-ounce can tomatoes, undrained
1 10-ounce package frozen corn

sunflower seed meal as well as ground beef, vegetables, and fruit, makes a dramatic presentation at the table and is perfect fun for a Halloween dinner. Nancy Vogel suggests using mini pumpkins, for marvelous individual servings.

1 10-ounce package frozen green beans
1 cup green pepper, chopped
2 fresh peaches, peeled and cut into chunks, or 1 cup frozen
    peaches, thawed
1 cup cooked chicken meat
1 cup sunflower seed meal or sunflower kernels
1 teaspoon salt
½ teaspoon pepper

As if making a jack-o'-lantern, cut a fairly wide lid out of the pumpkin and remove all the seeds from the inside down to the pulp with a large spoon. Reserve the lid. Spread the butter inside the pumpkin and sprinkle with salt and pepper. Place the pumpkin in a lightly greased baking dish, with the lid on but ajar at least 1 inch so that the steam can escape. Bake at 350 degrees for about 40 minutes. As the pumpkin bakes, check the inside for an accumulation of juice. Using a ladle, empty it, or the pumpkin will collapse.

While the pumpkin is baking, brown the ground beef and chopped onion together in a large pot over medium heat. Add the remaining ingredients and cook for 1 hour over low heat, stirring occasionally.

To serve, put the stew inside the pumpkin. Spoon out the cooked walls of the pumpkin as you ladle each serving.

Serves 6 to 8.

✳ Mexican Beef Pasties

Barclay J. Brumley, Manhattan

Barclay Brumley was the Kansas winner of the 1988 Kansas Beef Cook-Off, sponsored by the Kansas Beef Council and Kansas CattleWomen, with his recipe for Mexican Beef Pasties. As part of his prize, Barclay represented Kansas in the 1988 National Beef Cook-Off in Jackson, Mississippi.

1½ pounds lean ground beef
¾ cup onion, chopped
2 tablespoons green pepper, chopped
1½ cups taco sauce
6 tablespoons catsup
2 tablespoons brown sugar
1½ teaspoons basil
1½ teaspoons oregano
1 teaspoon ground cumin
1 teaspoon seasoned pepper
¾ teaspoon garlic salt
2 9-ounce packages refrigerated pastry pockets*
red, yellow, and/or green peppers, cut into rings (optional)
red, yellow, or green chili peppers (optional)
sour cream
taco sauce

Brown the ground beef with the onion and green pepper in a large frying pan over medium heat for 8 to 12 minutes, breaking the beef into small pieces. Pour the beef mixture into a colander to drain off excess fat and return to the frying pan.

Stir in the taco sauce, catsup, brown sugar, basil, oregano, cumin, seasoned pepper, and garlic salt. Cook the mixture, stirring frequently, over low heat for 8 to 10

*Pastry pockets can be found in the refrigerated food section of grocery stores. Keep the pastry pockets refrigerated until ready to use and work with one package at a time. Shaping is difficult if the dough becomes warm.

minutes, or until almost all of the liquid has evaporated. Remove from the heat.

Unroll 1 package of pastry pocket dough. Separate into 4 squares and place them on an ungreased baking sheet, stretching the squares slightly. Spoon 6 tablespoons of the beef filling in the center of each square, packing the filling tightly. Fold the dough over the filling to form a rectangle, stretching slightly to make the sides meet. Press edges with a fork to seal. Cut 3 slits, each ½ inch long, in the top of each pasty. Repeat with the remaining package of dough and filling, forming 4 more pasties on a second cookie sheet.

Bake at 375 degrees for 12 to 17 minutes, or until golden brown. Serve warm and garnish with pepper rings and chili peppers, if desired. Top the pasties with sour cream and taco sauce to serve.

Serves 4.

✳ Shepherd Pie

Shepherd Pie is a great way to use leftover roast beef, pork, or lamb. This contemporary version, however, is freshly made with lean ground beef.

1 pound lean ground beef
½ cup onion, chopped
¼ cup green pepper, seeded and chopped
1 15-ounce can tomatoes, undrained and coarsely chopped
1 teaspoon beef bouillon
2 teaspoons basil
½ teaspoon oregano
½ teaspoon salt
¼ teaspoon pepper
2 cups boiled potatoes (about 2 large potatoes)
2 egg yolks
½ teaspoon salt
¼ teaspoon white pepper
2 to 4 tablespoons milk
2 egg whites
2 tablespoons butter

In a large pan or Dutch oven, brown the ground beef over medium heat with the onion and green pepper. Add the tomatoes, beef bouillon, basil, oregano, salt, and pepper. Simmer over low heat for 20 minutes to blend the flavors. Remove from the heat and set aside.

Place the boiled potatoes in a large bowl and mash. Measure 2 cups. With an electric mixer, blend in the egg yolks, salt, and white pepper. Add the milk, a tablespoon at a time, until the potatoes are smooth and thick.

In a separate bowl, beat the egg whites until stiff peaks form. Gently fold them into the mashed potatoes. Spread half of this mixture into a lightly greased 9-inch baking dish. Pour in the meat mixture and top with the remaining potato mixture. Dot with butter and bake at 400 degrees for 15 minutes or until the top is golden brown.

Serves 6.

✳ Polenta with Meat Sauce

Cornmeal mush is known by many names in different cultures. The Plains Indians made a ground maize porridge and fried or baked it on hot rocks near a fire. The pioneers prepared a similar fried version. The Italians, one of the few European cultures to accept corn into their diet, call it Polenta and serve it with a savory meat sauce.

POLENTA
3 cups water
1 cup cold water
1 cup yellow cornmeal
1 teaspoon salt

MEAT SAUCE
1 pound ground beef
½ cup onion, finely chopped
¼ cup carrot, finely chopped
¼ cup celery, finely chopped
2 garlic cloves, minced
¼ cup tomato paste
1 16-ounce can tomatoes, undrained and coarsely chopped
1 teaspoon salt
¼ teaspoon pepper
½ cup dry red wine
¼ cup water
¼ cup half and half
½ cup Parmesan cheese, grated

Polenta: Bring 3 cups of water to boil in a large saucepan or Dutch oven. Meanwhile, pour 1 cup of cold water into a large bowl and stir in the cornmeal and salt. Slowly pour the cornmeal mixture into the boiling water, stirring constantly with a wire whip. When the mixture comes to a full boil, reduce heat to low and continue stirring with a large spoon for 10 to 15 minutes, or until mixture becomes thick.

Spread the mixture evenly into a greased 13 x 9–inch baking dish. Set the polenta aside while preparing the meat sauce.

Meat Sauce: In a large saucepan or Dutch oven, brown the ground beef and drain off the excess fat. Add the onion, carrot, celery, and garlic. Stir in the tomato paste, tomatoes, salt, pepper, red wine, and water.

Bring the mixture to a boil. Partially cover the pan and reduce the heat to low. Simmer for about 1 hour, stirring occasionally, until the vegetables are tender. Stir in the half and half and simmer for 10 minutes more.

To assemble, pour the meat mixture over the Polenta and sprinkle with grated Parmesan cheese. Bake uncovered at 350 degrees for 10 to 15 minutes, or until hot. Let stand for 10 minutes. Cut into wedges and serve.

Serves 4 to 6.

✳ Steakburgers Deluxe

"From the 1920s on, the hamburger began

1½ *pounds extra-lean ground beef*
6 *bacon strips*

its reign as America's most popular form of meat," writes James Beard in James Beard's American Cookery *(Boston and Toronto: Little, Brown and Company, 1972). Almost everyone loves hamburgers, and the variations are endless. This elegant version of the economical burger has become a standard in its own right.*

barbecue sauce
salt and pepper, to taste
6 onion buns

Form the ground beef into 6 patties about 1 inch thick. Wrap a strip of bacon around the edges of each patty and secure with toothpicks. Sprinkle with salt and pepper to taste. Brush lightly with barbecue sauce.

Place the steakburgers on the grill over medium-hot coals. Cover and cook for about 5 minutes each side, or until desired doneness is achieved. Remove the toothpicks and serve the steakburgers on onion buns.

Serve 6.

✳ Diner-Style Burgers

Have you ever been lucky enough to find one of those great diners that serves up delicious little hamburgers complete with mustard, pickle, and onion? In the 1950s, they were on every corner in Kansas towns. They made burgers "their way" and you loved it.

Well, don't lose your cool! Now you can serve up your own diner-style burgers at home. The secret is in the cooking method, so follow the instructions carefully. To get the full effect, wrap the cooked burgers in deli paper, place them in a small white paper bag, and roll down the top to close. Let each person open the bag and take a whiff!

Go all the way and serve these with French fries and a chocolate malt.

1 pound ground beef
salt and pepper, to taste
1 medium onion, thinly sliced
prepared mustard
small hamburger buns
dill pickle slices

Form the hamburger into 6 to 8 small hamburger patties, about ½ inch thick. Sprinkle with salt and pepper to taste.

Preheat a large skillet over medium heat until hot. Fry

the burgers in the skillet for about 1 minute, pressing them lightly with a spatula. Place the sliced onion around the burgers. Turn the burgers and the onion after 3 to 5 minutes of cooking. Press down lightly and fry 3 minutes more, or until the burgers are nearly done. Drain off most of the accumulated fat.

Spread mustard on the bottom halves of the buns. Place them on top of the burgers. Piggyback the top half of the bun on the bottom half. Place the lid on the skillet and turn the heat to low. Cook for about 2 minutes to steam the buns.

To remove from the pan, slide the spatula under each burger. Lift off the top half of the bun and place under the burger as you slide it off the spatula onto a plate. Turn the burger over, lift the top, and add a scoop of the fried onion. Lift the burger and place 3 dill pickle slices between the burger and bun on the mustard side.

Makes 6 to 8 burgers.

✳ Oven Barbecued Burgers

Theodora Dixon, Caney

Theodora Dixon says this is a good emergency recipe that stretches a pound of hamburger to feed a crowd.

1 pound very lean ground beef
½ cup onion, diced
¼ cup Worcestershire sauce
3 tablespoons prepared horseradish
1 tablespoon prepared mustard
½ cup catsup
dash of hot pepper sauce

hamburger buns or bread

Combine all of the ingredients in a large bowl. Spread the mixture on hamburger buns or bread to cover completely. Place the burgers on a cookie sheet and oven-broil until nicely browned.

Serves 8 to 10.

✳ Sloppy Joes

Joyce Shafer, Ada

"We are a farm family," writes Joyce Shafer, "so I am always feeding hungry harvesters, cattlemen, and field workers year-round. This recipe has gone to the harvest field since 1970."

These savory "loose meat" burgers are a tasty alternative to the standard hamburger patty.

2 tablespoons fat (bacon drippings, shortening, or vegetable oil)
1 pound ground beef
½ cup onion, chopped
½ cup celery, chopped
¼ cup green pepper, chopped
6 tablespoons catsup
1 cup water
1 tablespoon Worcestershire sauce
2 tablespoons vinegar
2 tablespoons brown sugar
½ teaspoon chili powder
¼ teaspoon garlic powder
1 teaspoon dry mustard
½ teaspoon paprika
1 teaspoon salt
¼ teaspoon pepper
1 tablespoon chopped parsley

6 hamburger buns

Heat the fat in a large pot or Dutch oven over medium heat. Brown the ground beef with the onions, celery, and green pepper. Drain off the fat and add the remaining ingredients, mixing well. Simmer over low heat until the vegetables are tender and the mixture thickens, 30 to 45 minutes. Serve on hamburger buns.

Serves 6.

✳ Kibba

Beulah Farha, Wichita

*Each September, St.
George's Orthodox
Church in Wichita
holds an annual
dinner featuring tra-
ditional Lebanese spe-
cialties. Beulah Farha
tells us that Kibba
is a Middle Eastern
delicacy. Ground beef
(or lamb) is combined
with bulgur wheat and
spices, formed into pat-
ties, and grilled over
hot coals or pan-fried.*

*1 cup fine bulgur wheat
1 pound very lean ground beef (sirloin or round)
1 medium onion, grated
½ teaspoon cinnamon
½ teaspoon nutmeg
1 to 2 teaspoons salt, to taste
¼ teaspoon pepper
melted butter*

Rinse the bulgur wheat in cold water and drain well.
Place it in a small bowl, cover, and refrigerate until ready
to use.

Place the ground beef in a large bowl. Add the onion,
cinnamon, nutmeg, salt, and pepper. Mix thoroughly and
add the bulgur wheat. Mix by hand or in a food processor
until well combined. Keep a bowl of ice water nearby in
case the mixture becomes stiff. Dip your hands into the
ice water and sprinkle it on the meat as needed. Shape
the meat mixture into patties.

Brush with melted butter if grilling, or pan-fry in a
small amount of melted butter. Cook for about 4 to 5
minutes each side.

Serves 6.

✳ Calf's Liver with Sour Cream Sauce

Mrs. Robert Jandera, Hanover

*Few dishes are held
in as high esteem as
calf's liver—or as
equally disdained. A
true delicacy, calf's
liver is superb when
prepared with careful*

*3 tablespoons butter or margarine
2 tablespoons onion, finely chopped
1½ to 2 pounds calf's liver
1 6-ounce can sliced mushrooms
½ cup dry red wine
1 cup celery, thinly sliced
¼ teaspoon tarragon*

attention. This recipe
is similar to the classic
recipe for beef stroga-
noff and provides a
delicious alterna-
tive to the standard
liver-and-onions.

¾ teaspoon sugar
¾ teaspoon salt
⅛ teaspoon pepper
dash of nutmeg
3 tablespoons fresh parsley, chopped
1½ tablespoons all-purpose flour
¼ cup water
¾ cup sour cream
2 cups cooked white rice

Melt the butter or margarine in a large frying pan over low heat. Add the onion and cook until soft but not brown. Cut the liver into ½-inch strips. Raise the heat to medium and brown the liver strips in the pan, turning often.

Drain the mushrooms, reserving the liquid. Add the sliced mushrooms to the pan and brown lightly. Add the reserved mushroom liquid, red wine, celery, tarragon, sugar, salt, pepper, nutmeg, and parsley. Cover, reduce heat to low, and simmer for 5 minutes.

In a small bowl, blend the flour and water together to form a smooth paste. Slowly add the mixture to the pan, stirring constantly until the sauce thickens and comes to a boil. Remove the pan from heat and blend in the sour cream. Serve immediately over hot rice.

Serves 4.

The Noble Buffalo

George Catlin, who in the 1830s captured in words and paint images of life on the plains before white settlement, wrote: "The buffalo herds, which graze in almost countless numbers on these beautiful prairies, afford an abundance of meat. So much is it preferred to all other, that the deer, the elk, and the antelope sport upon the prairies in herds in the greatest security. The Indians seldom kill them, unless they want their skins for a dress.

The buffalo is a noble animal that roams over the vast prairies, from the borders of Mexico on the south to

Hudson's Bay on the north. Their size is somewhat above that of our common bullock, and their flesh of a delicious flavor, resembling and equalling that of fat beef" (*George Catlin: Letters & Notes on the North American Indians*, edited by Michael M. Mooney [New York: Clarkson N. Potter, 1975]).

Though large numbers of the American buffalo once roamed throughout Kansas, their numbers were drastically decreased in the 1870s. Thousands were slaughtered by white hunters for their hides, and thousands more were shot from passenger train windows simply for sport. The New York *Tribune* reported that in the winter of 1874 as much as 2 million pounds of buffalo meat was sent east from Kansas. However, so extensive was the slaughter that most carcasses were left to the wolves, providing another source of income for the settlers— "bone-picking"—the sale of buffalo bones for fertilizer. At the turn of the century, there were less than a thousand buffalo in the United States. Because a few ranchers (among them Charles Goodnight of Oklahoma, namesake of the cattle trail) admired the hardiness of this docile "monarch of the plains," the buffalo were left unfettered on their ranches. Gradually these herds increased in numbers.

In the 1970s, an interest in raising buffalo commercially developed throughout the country and especially in Kansas. Ray O. Smith of Ottawa County has been raising buffalo on his central Kansas ranch near Longford since April 1962. He says that at one time he had over six hundred head of buffalo, but now he keeps a smaller herd. "Buffalo are hardy and can tolerate very cold weather," says Ray. "They have a thick hide on their head and shoulders which allows them to face the wind, unlike domestic cattle. I've seen them lie on the ground unconcerned with a wind chill of fifty degrees below zero."

When asked for a favorite buffalo recipe, Ray tells us that he prefers the natural flavor of buffalo meat. "When I cook buffalo, I want to *taste* buffalo," he says. "I don't put anything on it but salt and pepper."

In recent years, buffalo meat has been advocated because of its low fat content and low cholesterol. Buffalo roasts, burgers, and steaks (with T-bones the favorite) are all delicious and available to consumers. Buffalo can be purchased from the producers, as well as at some grocery stores and restaurants in Kansas. When cooking buffalo, Ray recommends cooking it more slowly and over lower heat than beef.

✳ Buffalo Barbecue

David Dary, Lawrence

David Dary, past president of Western Writers of America and Westerners International and author of The Buffalo Book *(New York: Avon, 1983), submitted this recipe for barbecuing buffalo. In his book he writes, "For those readers who have tasted a good buffalo steak or ribs or stew, or enjoyed a chunk of buffalo hump cooked in coffee, or bitten into a large slice of buffalo barbecue, the following recipes may cause you to drool. If you have never tasted buffalo, you are missing a treat."*

This recipe is not for a backyard barbecue. It should only be attempted by the experienced outdoor cook.

100 pounds or more of buffalo meat
5 pounds salt
½ pound pepper
3 3-ounce bottles of celery salt

Dig the barbecue pit 3 feet wide, 4 to 5 feet deep, and 2 to 3 feet long for each 100 pounds of buffalo meat. Use cottonwood or box elder wood for the fire. (Do not use any wood containing pitch, as pitch may flavor the meat.) Place the wood in the pit and set aflame. Let the wood burn down in the pit until there are 18 to 20 inches of coals (this may take a few hours).

Cut the buffalo meat into 10-pound chunks. Combine the salt, pepper, and celery salt in a large pan or tub. Rub this mixture on dampened chunks of meat. Wrap each chunk of meat in cheesecloth and cover with aluminum foil.

When the coals are ready, sprinkle a little dry sand on them and place the foil packages of meat on top. Cover with steel posts and roofing tin and enough dirt to seal the pit.

Let the buffalo meat cook for 8 to 12 hours.

Serves 200 to 250.

✳ Buffalo Burgundy

David Dary, Lawrence

This recipe substitutes lean, rich-tasting buffalo steak in the traditional recipe of beef and red wine. For greater success, use a full-bodied wine identical in quality to what you would serve with it.

1 pound buffalo steak
salt and pepper, to taste
1 cup all-purpose flour
¼ cup vegetable shortening
2 carrots, peeled and grated
1 celery stick, finely sliced
1 small onion, finely chopped
1 garlic clove, minced
½ cup dry red wine
1½ cups water
¼ teaspoon rosemary
2 cups hot cooked white rice

Cut the buffalo meat into strips about ¼ inch wide and 2 inches long. Season with salt and pepper to taste and dredge the meat strips in the flour.

Heat the shortening in a large frying pan over medium-high heat. Brown the meat strips quickly and drain them briefly on paper towels.

Place the meat in a 1½-quart casserole. Add the carrot, celery, onion, and garlic and mix lightly. Add the wine, water, and rosemary and stir.

Cover and bake at 350 degrees for 1½ to 2 hours, adding a little water periodically as needed to prevent dryness. Serve with the cooked rice.

Serves 4.

Beefalo

Cattalo is the hybrid produced by crossing the American buffalo with domestic cattle. In the 1880s, C. J. "Buffalo" Jones, who coined the name, claimed to be the first to cross-breed the animals. The purpose was to exploit the hardiness of the buffalo, but many problems arose during early experimentations—such as sterility, breeding difficulties, and birthing complications.

In 1973, D. C. "Bud" Basolo, a California rancher, came up with a sturdy hybrid of the domestic cow and buffalo, which he named "Basolo Hybrid Beefalo." Basalo refused to share his secret but sold the bull semen throughout the country, as ranchers took an interest in raising beefalo. In the mid-1970s Kansans began raising beefalo, with most herds coming from Basolo's stock.

Beefalo are three-eighths bison and five-eighths beef and resemble cattle in appearance. Ralph Leonhard, president of the Kansas chapter of The American Beefalo World Registry, says that beefalo is considered a hardy breed that calve easily and can withstand weather extremes. They produce more meat, with more protein and less fat, than domestic cattle, and those who raise beefalo claim the meat is richer in flavor than beef. Better as foragers than cattle, they are therefore cheaper to feed. Though beefalo is not yet commercially available, it is a growing industry, and the meat can be purchased from many breeders in Kansas.

The taste of beefalo is so similar to that of beef that you may not notice the difference. Because of less fat marbling in the muscle tissue, shorter cooking times produce better results. Steaks should be cooked to rare or medium-rare only, as they can become tough if overcooked. Meat loaves and stews should be cooked at a lower temperature and for less time than beef.

✳ Beefaloaf

Gloria Leonhard, Berryton

Ralph and Gloria Leonhard raise beefalo on their ranch in Berryton. Gloria uses beefalo in place of beef in this meat loaf recipe, preferring its fine flavor and lean quality.

3 pounds ground beefalo
1½ cups quick oatmeal
½ cup onion, chopped
2 eggs, beaten
1½ cups milk
3 teaspoons salt
½ teaspoon pepper

TOPPING
⅔ cup catsup
2 tablespoons brown sugar
2 tablespoons mustard

Combine the beefalo, oatmeal, and onion in a large bowl. Add the beaten egg, milk, salt, and pepper. Mix well and pack the mixture into a 13 x 9–inch baking dish. Or shape the mixture into 2 loaves and place in loaf pans.

Topping: In a small bowl, combine the catsup, brown sugar, and mustard. Mix well and pour over the beefaloaf.
   Bake uncovered at 325 degrees for 45 to 60 minutes. Serves 8 to 10.

✳ Speedy Beefalo Chili

Gloria Leonhard, Berryton

Because it is so lean, beefalo makes a de-lightful chili without the discouraging greasy layer of many such dishes. This ver-sion has the additional contemporary appeal of being quick and easy.

2 pounds ground beefalo
1 cup onion, chopped
½ cup green pepper, chopped
2 16-ounce cans tomato sauce
2 teaspoons salt
½ teaspoon pepper
2 to 3 teaspoons chili powder, to taste
2 16-ounce cans kidney beans, drained

Brown the ground beefalo with the onion and green pepper in a large pan or Dutch oven over medium heat.

Stir in the tomato sauce, salt, pepper, and chili powder to taste. Simmer uncovered over low heat for 15 minutes, stirring occasionally. Add the kidney beans and simmer for 5 minutes more.

Serves 6 to 8.

✳ Beefalo Stew

The following recipe calls for ground beefalo and is an easy recipe that the kids can help make. If you can't find beefalo, you may substitute very lean ground beef.

1 pound ground beefalo
1 medium onion, chopped
1 small green pepper, seeded and chopped
1 16-ounce can tomatoes, chopped and undrained
½ cup uncooked white rice, rinsed and drained
1 cup water
1 teaspoon beef bouillon
1 7-ounce can corn, drained
3 garlic cloves, minced
1 teaspoon salt
¼ teaspoon pepper

Brown the ground beefalo with the chopped onion and green pepper in a large pan or Dutch oven over medium heat.

Add the remaining ingredients and stir to combine. Bring the stew to a boil, stir, and cover. Reduce heat to low and simmer for 15 minutes. Remove from heat and serve immediately.

Serves 4 to 6.

✳ Veal Scallops with Tarragon Sauce

With more concern for leaner cuts of meat, cooks are looking to veal as a popular choice. Since veal is

8 veal scallops
1 tablespoon butter
1 tablespoon olive oil
salt and pepper, to taste
2 green onions, chopped

*favored by the Italians,
the increased interest
in veal has naturally
produced an interest in
Italian veal dishes.*

½ teaspoon tarragon
¼ cup dry vermouth
½ cup beef broth
1½ teaspoons cornstarch

Place the veal scallops between 2 sheets of waxed paper
and pound gently with a meat mallet to ⅛-inch thickness.

Heat the butter and olive oil in a large frying pan over
medium-high heat. When hot enough to sizzle, add the
veal scallops (do not crowd) and cook quickly, turning
once, 2 to 3 minutes each side. Remove the scallops to a
warm platter and sprinkle with salt and pepper to taste.

Reduce heat to medium and add the green onion to
the drippings. Sauté for 1 minute. Add the tarragon and
vermouth and simmer until the liquid reduces by half, 2
to 3 minutes.

In a small bowl, combine the beef broth and cornstarch. Add the mixture slowly to the pan, stirring until
thick and bubbly. Pour the sauce over the veal scallops
and serve immediately.

Serves 4.

Variation: You may substitute 4 skinned and boned
chicken breast halves in place of the veal. Pound them
to ¼-inch thickness and proceed as directed.

✴ Veal Scallops with Mushrooms and Onion

*The subtle flavor of
veal is the secret to its
versatility. Because it
absorbs other flavors
well, it lends itself to
delicately seasoned
sauces—as in this
recipe.*

1 pound veal scallops, pounded
salt and pepper, to taste
2 tablespoons butter
1 tablespoon olive oil
1 tablespoon butter
4 ounces button mushrooms, sliced
1 small onion, finely chopped
1 garlic clove, minced
¼ teaspoon tarragon
½ cup dry white wine

Place the veal scallops between two sheets of waxed paper and pound gently with a meat mallet to ⅛-inch thickness. Sprinkle with salt and pepper to taste.

Heat the butter and olive oil in a large frying pan over medium-high heat. When hot enough to sizzle, place the veal scallops in the pan. Cook, turning once, until lightly browned, 2 to 3 minutes each side. Remove the veal from the pan.

Add 1 tablespoon of butter to the remaining drippings. Add the mushrooms, onion, and garlic. Cook, turning frequently, until the mushrooms and onion are tender, about 5 minutes. Sprinkle the mixture with the tarragon and pour in the white wine. Simmer the mixture until the liquid is reduced by about half. Return the veal to the pan and heat throughout. Place the veal on a platter. Spoon the mushrooms and onion mixture on top.

Serves 4.

✳ Italian Leg of Lamb

Thomas Alexios, Lawrence

In the late 1800s, sheep ranching rivaled the cattle industry in Kansas. The number of range sheep

1 5- to 6-pound leg of lamb
3 garlic cloves
3 to 4 tablespoons olive oil
5 tablespoons Romano cheese, grated
1 pinch oregano

1 pinch parsley
1 pinch rosemary
1 pinch basil
3 tablespoons Italian-style dried bread crumbs
4 garlic cloves, each cut into 2 to 3 slivers
4 ounces Romano cheese, cut into small slivers
½ cup water
1 fresh basil leaf (optional)

SAUCE
¼ to ½ cup chicken broth
⅛ cup red wine

Then was about three times greater than today. Raised mainly to meet the demand for wool from mills in England, little of the flock was used for food. The sheep industry declined in Kansas due to overproduction and competition from other countries. A second growth period prior to World War II began to decline after the war from a shortage of labor and the attraction to more profitable agricultural endeavors.

Today, spring lamb is often raised by Kansas farmers from small flocks solely for personal consumption. But increasingly, lamb can be found in the meat sections of the stores that cater to more cosmopolitan tastes.

Lamb has been a traditional dish of cultures that border the Mediterranean. This recipe of Italian heritage originated two generations earlier and is a delight for garlic lovers.

Prepare the leg of lamb, if necessary, by removing the papery outer layer of meat. Mince the 3 garlic cloves, add them to the olive oil, and let stand for at least 30 minutes.

In a small bowl, combine the grated Romano cheese, the herbs, and the bread crumbs and set aside.

With a sharp pointed knife, puncture the fat side of the lamb at 1-inch intervals. Using the knife to hold the puncture open, pack each opening with a sliver of garlic and a sliver of Romano cheese. Rub the lamb with the garlic and olive oil mixture, then sprinkle the bread crumb and herb mixture generously over the meat.

Preheat the oven to 450 degrees. Place the meat on a rack in a large baking dish with ½ cup of water and a fresh leaf of basil. Put the lamb in the oven, reduce the temperature to 325 degrees, and bake until the internal temperature reaches 160 degrees (approximately 30 to 35 minutes per pound). Remove the lamb from the oven and let it stand while you make the sauce.

Sauce: Skim any excess fat from the pan drippings. Pour the drippings into a saucepan and add the chicken broth and wine. Bring the sauce to a boil, then lower the heat and simmer for about 5 minutes.

Carve the leg of lamb and drizzle some of the sauce over each serving.

Serves 6.

✳ Marinated Grilled Lamb

Niki Schneider, Lawrence

For a gourmet grilling experience, cook a leg of lamb outdoors. Serve this succulent grilled lamb with fried potatoes and a green vegetable.

1 5- to 6-pound leg of lamb (small end)
3 garlic cloves, sliced in half lengthwise

MARINADE
¾ cup olive oil
⅓ cup dry red wine
6 sprigs fresh thyme, or 1 tablespoon dried thyme
1 teaspoon rosemary
1 garlic clove, minced (optional)

Bone the leg of lamb (or ask your butcher to do it) with a sharp knife following close to the bone and along the muscle so as not to disturb the center of the meat. You should have a flat, steaklike piece of meat. With a small knife, pierce 6 holes in different parts of the meat and insert a piece of garlic.

Marinade: In a bowl, combine all ingredients, adding more garlic if desired.

Place the lamb in a large pan. Pour the marinade over the lamb. Cover and refrigerate for at least 4 hours, or all day if possible. Turn the meat 4 times in the marinade during this time.

Remove the meat from the refrigerator about 1 hour before grilling to return it to room temperature. Lift the meat from the marinade and drain briefly before grilling.

Grill the lamb directly over hot coals in a covered grill. Cook for 10 to 15 minutes each side. Check the temperature with a meat thermometer inserted into the thickest part of the meat. The temperature should be 145 to 150 degrees for rare, or 155 to 160 degrees for medium. Do not overcook.

Let the lamb stand for 5 to 10 minutes before cutting. Slice across the grain to serve.

Serves 8.

✳ Lamb Hash

Hash is a part of the American food tradition. It has always meant a hardy, quickly prepared meal made of leftover meats, broth or gravy, and potatoes.

3 tablespoons olive oil
3 cups potatoes, diced into ½-inch cubes (about 2 large potatoes)
1 medium onion, finely chopped
3 garlic cloves, minced
salt and pepper, to taste
3 tablespoons all-purpose flour
1½ cups chicken broth
3 cups cold roast lamb, diced into ½-inch cubes

Heat the olive oil in a large skillet over medium heat. Add the cubed potatoes and onion and fry for about 20 minutes, or until golden, turning occasionally. During the last few minutes, add the garlic and salt and pepper to taste.

Sprinkle the flour over the potatoes and mix well. Continue cooking for 1 to 2 minutes, turning often. Raise the heat to medium-high and slowly add the chicken broth, stirring until the mixture is thick and bubbly. Reduce heat to low and add the cubed lamb. Simmer, stirring occasionally, for 5 minutes.

Serves 4.

Variation: Cold roast beef may be substituted for lamb, using beef broth instead of chicken broth. Prepare as directed.

✳ Lamb Chops with Garlic and Rosemary

Lamb Chops are a good choice for a fast but elegant main course. In this recipe, they are quickly browned, then simmered in white wine with rosemary.

8 loin lamb chops, 1¼ inches thick
2 garlic cloves, peeled
salt and pepper, to taste
1 tablespoon butter
1 tablespoon olive oil
½ cup dry white wine
¼ teaspoon rosemary, crushed

Remove excess fat from the lamb chops. Rub the chops on both sides with the garlic cloves. Sprinkle each with salt and pepper.

Heat the butter and olive oil over medium-high heat in a large frying pan. Brown the chops, about 2 minutes on each side. Add the white wine and crushed rosemary to the pan. Reduce the heat to low, cover and simmer for 3 to 5 minutes, or until desired doneness is achieved.

Remove the lamb chops from the pan and top with the pan juices to serve.

Serves 4.

✳ PORK

The first pigs to enter Kansas arrived with Coronado in 1540. Swine continued to be a mainstay in the diet of explorers and pioneers, who brought them either on the hoof or as smoked or salted provisions. Immigrants to the United States came with their own special recipes for pork. In fact, the influence of the Pennsylvania Dutch and German immigrants was so great in the 1830s and 1840s that the city of Cincinnati was dubbed "Porkopolis."

In the late nineteenth century, Europeans from pork-consuming countries of southern and eastern Europe settled in the Strawberry Hill area of Kansas City. A second generation of Pennsylvania Dutch and a wave of German Mennonites from Russia brought a heritage of sausage-making to the state. Even today, it is easy to find excellent sausage in the family-owned shops in the towns they founded—Wilson, Hillsboro, Hesston, and Kansas City, to name a few.

Pork production was revolution-

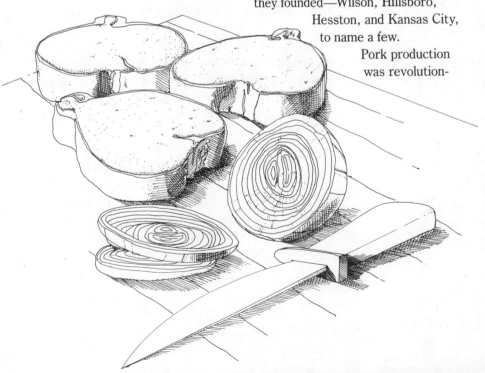

ized when Indian corn, or maize, was adopted as feed. That changed swine from the pastured and "swill-fed" animal of the Old World to the penned and corn-fed hog of today. Throughout the Corn Belt, the number of hogs increased. Soon, hogs were no longer driven to market in small herds along the backroads but shipped on the railways to the region's two major slaughter centers— St. Joseph and Kansas City. Today, Kansas has several processing plants, with the largest located in Arkansas City.

In the early days, most farmers and more than a few city dwellers kept a pig for butchering. Not only did it supply versatile meat products, but its lard, second in quality only to butter, was of equal importance for baking, general cooking, and preserving of other meats. "The most important butcher's meat in the world is, and always has been, pork," writes Waverly Root, author of the encyclopedic work *Food* (New York: Simon & Schuster, 1986). The entire animal, from head to hoof, was used for such cuts as spareribs, bacon, roasts, hams, jowls, head cheese, pig's feet, and liver. The pork meats were either roasted or "fried down," placed in earthenware jars, and covered with lard. Some of the lard was ground and rendered for cooking oil. Pork hocks and feet were either smoked or pickled and put by. The remainder of the animal—the head, heart, liver, tongue, and ears— was ground and stuffed into sausage casings made out of the intestine.

In the recipes that follow, Pork Tenderloin with Poached Apples and Ribs 'n Kraut display pork with German flavoring, while the Czechoslovakian influence is present in Czech Sausage, or Jaternice. Of contemporary interest are Breaded Fresh Pork Tenderloin, Coriander Pork Chops with Red Wine, and a sparerib recipe for any time of the year called Indoor/Outdoor Ribs.

✳ Roast Pork with Vegetables and Gravy

Kansas ranks among the top ten pork-producing states, with more than eleven thousand farm operations, so it's no wonder pork roast is a Heartland favorite. A succulent pork roast, oven-roasted with vegetables, makes a fine meal for the family or for special occasions.

1 3½- to 4-pound pork loin roast
4 whole garlic cloves, peeled
1 teaspoon tarragon
½ teaspoon pepper, coarsely ground
salt, to taste
¾ cup beef broth, divided
3 potatoes, peeled and quartered
8 thin carrots, peeled
12 whole pearl onions, peeled

GRAVY
pan juices
beef broth
2 tablespoons all-purpose flour
salt and pepper, to taste

Cut 4 slits in the pork roast and insert the garlic cloves. Rub the tarragon and pepper on all sides of the roast. Sprinkle lightly with salt. Place the roast, fat side up, on a rack in a large roasting pan. Add ½ cup of the beef broth to the pan.

Place the roast uncovered in an oven preheated to 450 degrees and immediately reduce heat to 350 degrees. Roast for 45 minutes.

Place the potatoes, carrots, and onions around the roast and add the remaining ¼ cup of beef broth to the pan. Cover the pan and continue cooking for about

1¼ hours more, or until the internal temperature reaches 170 to 175 degrees and the vegetables are tender. (The total roasting time should be approximately 30 to 40 minutes per pound.) Remove the pork roast and vegetables from the pan. Let the roast stand for 10 minutes before carving.

Gravy: Pour the pan juices into a measuring cup. Skim 2 tablespoons of fat from the pan juices and place in a saucepan. Skim the remaining fat from the juices and discard. Add enough beef broth to the pan juices to make 1 cup. Set aside.

Place the saucepan with the fat over medium heat. Add the flour and stir for about 1 minute. Slowly add the pan juices, stirring, until the gravy thickens slightly and begins to boil. Let the gravy boil over low heat, stirring frequently for about 1 minute. Add salt and pepper to taste.

Carve the roast and serve with the vegetables. Pass the gravy.

Serves 4.

✳ Pork Roast with Apple-Ginger Sauce

When it comes to pork, the great Midwestern hobby of backyard barbecuing includes more than just spareribs. A pork sirloin roast is a delicious choice for grilling. In this recipe, the roast is rubbed with cinnamon for extra flavor. The drippings are added to the baste to make a flavorful sauce.

1 2- to 2½-pound pork sirloin roast, boned and tied
½ teaspoon cinnamon
salt and pepper, to taste

BASTE
1 cup unsweetened apple juice
1 tablespoon soy sauce
1 tablespoon butter
1 garlic clove, minced
¼ teaspoon ground ginger

Rub the outside of the pork roast with the cinnamon. Add salt and pepper to taste.

Baste: In a small saucepan, combine the ingredients for the baste and simmer over low heat for 5 minutes.

To grill, divide the hot coals, banking them on each side of a drip pan. Place the pork roast on the grid directly over the drip pan to catch the drippings. Cover the grill and cook the roast for 1½ to 2 hours, or until an inserted meat thermometer reads 170 degrees. If needed, add a few extra coals to the grill after 1 hour. Brush the roast with the baste 3 to 4 times during the last 45 minutes of cooking. When done, remove the roast from the grill and keep warm.

Apple-Ginger Sauce: Skim the fat from the juices collected in the drip pan. Pour the juices in a small saucepan and add the remaining baste. Bring the mixture to a boil, reduce heat to low, and simmer for 10 minutes.

Remove string and slice the pork roast into ½-inch slices. To serve, top each serving with a generous spoonful of the Apple-Ginger Sauce.

Serves 4.

✳ Spinach Salad with Pork and Pears

This recipe works wonders with the Sunday pork roast leftovers, but you may find yourself roasting pork just to make this beautiful salad meal.

1 pound fresh spinach, rinsed and stemmed
8 to 10 ounces cold cooked pork roast, thinly sliced
2 pears, cored and sliced
1 red onion, thinly sliced

SOY VINAIGRETTE
1 cup olive oil
⅓ cup red wine vinegar
1 tablespoon soy sauce
3 garlic cloves, minced

Divide the spinach leaves among 4 dinner plates. Slice the pork roast and place 3 to 4 slices in the center of each salad. Arrange the sliced pears and onion around the pork.

Soy Vinaigrette: Combine the ingredients for the vinaigrette in a small bowl. Mix well and pour over the salads.

Serves 4.

The Good Old Days

The chores of homemaking on the farm tugged at
the housewife's attention like children at her apron.
Eunice M. Pittman of Bloom describes cooking in the
early 1900s and the concerns that accompanied the hard
work.

"The 'good old days' of threshing machines were
very different from today's combine harvests, especially
where food was concerned.

Remember, in the early 1900s, only the very lucky
town dwellers even had an ice box. In the country, there
was no way to keep any kind of fresh meat, so you prepared meat in the cold months for summer use. Pork, the
most common, became home-cured hams and bacon. The
rest, like sausage and tenderloin, were fried-down by
cooking them in a skillet, placing them in a deep crockery
2-gallon jar, and covering them immediately with fresh
hot rendered lard. Yes, they were sealed very well, well
enough to keep for summer use by storing the crocks in
a cool place. Beef was cut up and canned in glass jars and
cooked in a hot water bath for several hours, as there
were no pressure cookers in those days.

Most everything was homegrown. All sorts of vegetables were planted in the garden. Fruit grown in a
nearby orchard was canned when it was in season for
later use. The housewife raised a flock of young frying
chickens, which were butchered fresh, to be changed off
with the preserved meats.

Cooking for the men helping in the fields was a very
hard job for the housewife. She cooked on a coal- or
wood-burning stove in the stifling summer heat, usually
in August. There were no bakeries for breads, cakes, or
pies out in the country. Bread was one of the major foods
hard to prepare in the summer because of its lengthy
time of preparation."

Although life was difficult in "the good old days,"
hard-working families enjoyed the satisfaction of self-
sufficiency—being able to produce the food and nearly
every necessity on the farm. Proudly, they carved out a
life for themselves and future generations.

✳ Apple-Stuffed Pork Tenderloin

*The pork tenderloin
is considered one of
the most tender and
versatile cuts of pork
available. This recipe
fills the tenderloin with
an apple stuffing, the
perfect choice being
Kansas's Jonathan
apple. When served,
the meat is sliced
into rounds for an
attractive presentation.*

2 whole pork tenderloins, about 1½ pounds
salt, to taste
6 tablespoons butter
1 medium onion, finely chopped
1 large tart apple, chopped into ½-inch pieces
¼ cup pecans, coarsely chopped
1½ cups corn bread stuffing
¼ teaspoon marjoram
1 tablespoon fresh parsley, chopped
4 to 6 tablespoons chicken broth
4 bacon strips
2 teaspoons pepper, coarsely ground

Trim the pork tenderloins of excess fat. Make 3 lengthwise cuts, without cutting through the meat, and pound
to ⅜-inch thickness. Salt lightly and set aside.

Melt the butter in a large pan over low heat. Add the
onion and cook for 5 to 8 minutes, or until tender. Add
the apple and pecans and continue cooking, turning often,
for 3 to 5 minutes more, or until the apples are tender-
crisp.

Remove the pan from heat and stir in the marjoram,
parsley, and corn bread stuffing. Moisten the mixture
with the chicken broth.

Spread half the stuffing on each tenderloin and roll up.
Crisscross 2 strips of bacon and wrap around each tenderloin. Secure with toothpicks and rub each tenderloin
with 1 teaspoon of pepper.

Place the tenderloins on a roasting rack over a large
baking dish or on a foil-lined baking sheet. Oven-roast at
350 degrees for 25 to 30 minutes. Baste the tenderloins
with the pan drippings or melted butter after 15 minutes.
To serve, slice into 1-inch rounds.

Serves 6.

Variation: To grill over indirect heat, divide the hot coals,
banking them on each side of a drip pan. Place the stuffed
tenderloins on the grid directly over the drip pan. Cover
the grill and cook for 25 to 30 minutes. Move the ten-

derloins directly over the hot coals for about 1 minute
on each side to brown the bacon.

✳ Pork Tenderloin with Poached Apples

*With autumn comes
apple season in
the eastern part of
Kansas, and pork
tenderloin served
with apples is a fall
favorite. The apples,
poached in a sauce
made of the drippings,
vinegar, and sugar,
are reminiscent of the
sweet-sour flavoring
used in the cuisine
of the German com-
munities in central
and western Kansas.
Potato pancakes and
steamed broccoli make
good side dishes.*

2 whole pork tenderloins, about 1½ pounds
salt and pepper, to taste
3 bacon strips
¼ cup applejack
½ cup apple-cider vinegar
½ cup water
¼ cup sugar
1 medium Jonathan apple, cored and sliced into wedges

Trim the pork tenderloins of excess fat. Salt and pepper
to taste. Set aside.

In a large frying pan, cook the bacon over medium heat
until brown and crispy. Remove the bacon from the pan
and drain on paper towels. Crumble and reserve.

Reduce the heat to medium-low and add the pork tenderloins to the bacon drippings. Cook slowly, turning
often, until the tenderloins are tender and dark golden-
brown on all sides, 20 to 30 minutes. Remove the frying
pan from the heat. Pour the applejack over the tenderloins and immediately set aflame. Gently shake the pan
until the flame dies. Remove the tenderloins from the pan
and place on a platter.

Combine the vinegar, water, and sugar in a small bowl.
Pour the mixture into the drippings and return the frying pan to the heat. Add the apple slices and bring to a
boil over high heat. Boil rapidly, stirring occasionally,
until the apples are tender and the mixture reduces and
becomes syrupy, about 5 to 7 minutes.

Return the tenderloins to the pan and add the crumbled
bacon. Cook for 1 minute, turning the tenderloins once
to coat with the apple syrup. Place the pork tenderloins
on a serving platter and slice diagonally. Spoon apples
and syrup over the tenderloin slices.

Serves 4 to 6.

✸ Breaded Fresh Pork Tenderloin

Back in the 1950s,
Highway 40 was dotted
with roadside diners
where you could get
a good "fresh pork
tender." Now you can
make your own, going
one step further with
fresh bread crumbs,
garlic salt, and marjo-
ram. It's so good, you
can throw away the
bun!

1 pound whole pork tenderloin
1 egg
2 cups fresh white bread crumbs (about 4 slices of bread)
½ teaspoon marjoram
½ teaspoon garlic salt
½ teaspoon pepper
2 tablespoons olive oil
1 tablespoon butter

Slice the tenderloin into ¾-inch rounds. Place each round between two sheets of waxed paper and gently pound with a smooth-faced mallet to ¼-inch thickness.

In a shallow bowl, beat the egg well with a fork. Tear the bread into several pieces and place it in a food processor. Whirl until you have fine crumbs. Measure 2 cups of crumbs and pour them into a large bowl. Add the marjoram, garlic salt, and pepper, mixing to combine.

Heat the olive oil and butter in a large frying pan over medium-high heat. Dip half of the pork tenderloins in the beaten egg and coat with the bread crumb mixture. Place the tenderloins in the pan and fry for 3 minutes, then turn over and fry for about 3 minutes more, until the topping is golden. Repeat the procedure with the remaining tenderloins, adding more oil and butter if necessary.

Serves 4.

✸ Pork with Sweet and Sour Sauce

Marilyn Eck, Bartlett

Homesteaders raised
mostly hogs before
cattle ranching came to
the plains. Neighbors
often gathered to share
the butchering task
and made use of every

3 pounds lean pork, diced
3 tablespoons bacon fat
4 tablespoons cornstarch
½ cup water
2 tablespoons soy sauce
½ cup apple-cider vinegar
½ cup sorghum

bit of the animal. The
trimmings would be
used for sausage or
perhaps fried up and
added to a sauce, as in
this recipe. Though a
sweet and sour sauce
in those days would be
based on the apple, this
contemporary version
calls for pineapple.

1 teaspoon salt
2 cups unsweetened pineapple juice
1 15-ounce can pineapple chunks, drained
4 cups cooked white rice

In a large frying pan, brown the pork in the bacon fat
over medium-high heat. Set aside.

In a small bowl, combine the cornstarch and water,
mixing until smooth. Pour the mixture into a large pan or
Dutch oven. Add the soy sauce, vinegar, sorghum, salt,
and pineapple juice.

Simmer over medium heat, stirring until the mixture is
clear and thick. Add the pork with the pan drippings and
cover. Cook over low heat for 1 hour.

Add the pineapple during the last 5 minutes of cooking.
Serve on a bed of white rice.

Serves 8 to 10.

✳ Peppered Pork Chops

*Recipes for fried pork
chops made their way
into Kansas kitchens
in the early days of
settlement. Easy to
prepare, pork chops
could be quickly fried
in a skillet of hot
lard and served with
gravy on the side. This
contemporary recipe
updates an old-time
favorite by frying the
peppered pork chops
in butter and deglaz-
ing the pan with white
wine.*

4 center-cut pork loin chops, ½ inch thick
1 teaspoon pepper, coarsely ground
salt, to taste
2 tablespoons butter
⅓ cup dry white wine
2 tablespoons butter, chilled

Trim the pork chops of excess fat. Rub about ¼ teaspoon
of pepper into each pork chop and add salt to taste.

Melt the butter over medium-high heat in a large frying pan until hot. Add the pork chops and fry for 3 to 5
minutes on each side. (If the butter begins to burn, lower
heat to medium.) Remove the chops from the pan and
keep warm.

Pour the white wine into the pan drippings and raise
heat to high. Boil rapidly until the liquid is reduced by
about half. Remove the pan from heat and whisk in the
butter until melted. Pour over the pork chops and serve
immediately.

Serves 4.

✳ Cowboy Pork Chops

Cowboys consumed primarily beef on the cattle trail, but occasionally the cook fried pork for a welcome change of pace. Since cornmeal, flour, and chili powder were always in the cook's chuck box, these ingredients provided a tasty coating for pork chops.

4 butterflied center-cut pork loin chops, ½ inch thick
1 egg
2 tablespoons milk
¼ cup yellow cornmeal
¼ cup all-purpose flour
1 teaspoon chili powder
¼ teaspoon salt
⅛ teaspoon pepper
1 tablespoon butter
1 tablespoon vegetable oil

Trim any excess fat from the pork chops. Combine the egg and milk in a bowl. Combine the cornmeal, flour, chili powder, salt, and pepper in a separate bowl. Dip each pork chop in the egg-and-milk mixture, then coat with the cornmeal mixture.

Heat the butter and oil in a large frying pan over medium heat. Add the pork chops and fry for 3 to 5 minutes on each side, or until golden.

Serves 4.

✳ Coriander Pork Chops with Red Wine

The flavor of coriander has been introduced to Kansas through many cultures. Its leaves, resembling parsley, are used in salads and sauces of Mexican origin. Coriander seed, when freshly crushed, imparts its distinctive aroma to Danish pastry and Swedish coffee cake. In this recipe, ground coriander, traditionally used in

4 center-cut pork loin chops, ½ inch thick
1 teaspoon ground coriander
salt and pepper, to taste
1 tablespoon butter
1 tablespoon olive oil
½ cup dry red wine

Trim the excess fat from the pork chops. Rub ¼ teaspoon of the ground coriander into both sides of each pork chop. Sprinkle with salt and pepper to taste.

Heat the butter and olive oil in a large frying pan over medium-high heat. Add the pork chops and fry for 3 to 5 minutes each side. Remove the pork chops from the pan and keep warm.

sausage recipes, as-
serts itself in a tasty
sautéed dish.

Pour the red wine into the pan drippings and raise heat to high. Boil rapidly until the liquid is reduced by half, about 2 to 3 minutes. Pour the wine sauce over the pork chops and serve.

Serves 4.

✳ Pork Smothered with Onions

These thick-cut pork
chops are browned,
then simmered with
sliced onion in dry
vermouth and herbs
for a quickly prepared
but impressive dish.

4 butterflied center-cut pork chops, 1¼ inches thick
salt and pepper, to taste
4 tablespoons butter, divided
1 large onion, thinly sliced into rings
½ cup dry white vermouth
¼ teaspoon rosemary
¼ teaspoon marjoram
¼ teaspoon thyme

Trim the pork chops of excess fat. Sprinkle with salt and pepper to taste. Melt 2 tablespoons of the butter in a

large frying pan over medium-high heat. Place the chops in the pan and brown quickly, about 2 to 3 minutes each side. Remove the chops from the pan and set aside.

Add the remaining butter and the onion to the pan drippings. Reduce heat to medium-low and cook the onion until tender, stirring occasionally, 5 to 8 minutes.

Return the chops to the pan and add the vermouth, rosemary, marjoram, and thyme. Bring the mixture to a boil. Cover, reduce heat to low, and simmer for about 15 minutes, or until the pork chops are tender.

Remove the pork chops to a serving platter. Continue simmering the juices uncovered until slightly reduced, about 1 to 2 minutes. Pour the onion and juices over the pork chops and serve immediately.

Serves 4.

✳ Baked Pork Chops with Vegetables

In this recipe, thick pork chops are baked with carrots and onion and topped with a light gravy made from the drippings.

4 butterflied center-cut pork chops, 1¼ inches thick
salt and pepper, to taste
1 tablespoon butter
1 tablespoon vegetable oil
3 to 4 medium carrots
1 large onion
1 tablespoon butter
2 garlic cloves, minced
¼ cup water
2 tablespoons all-purpose flour
¼ cup chicken broth or water

Trim the fat from the pork chops and sprinkle each with salt and pepper to taste.

Heat the butter and oil in a large frying pan over medium-high heat. Add the pork chops and brown, about 2 to 3 minutes each side. Remove the pork chops from the pan, reserving the drippings, and place chops in a 9-inch baking dish.

Peel the carrots and cut in half crosswise. Slice each

half into 3 or 4 thin strips. Chop the onion into 1-inch pieces. Add 1 tablespoon of butter to the pan drippings. Add the vegetables and cook over medium heat, turning frequently until they are tender-crisp. Add the minced garlic and cook for 1 minute more. Pour the vegetables and drippings over the pork chops. Add ¼ cup of water to the baking dish and cover tightly with foil.

Bake at 350 degrees for 30 to 40 minutes, until the pork chops and vegetables are tender.

Remove the pork chops and vegetables from the baking dish. Pour the juices into a small pan and simmer over medium heat. In a cup or small bowl, mix the flour into ¼ cup of chicken broth or water. Slowly stir in just enough of the mixture to thicken the simmering juices slightly. Simmer the gravy for a few seconds and pour over the pork chops and vegetables to serve.

Serves 4.

✳ Indoor/Outdoor Ribs

There are as many ways to cook ribs as there are backyards, but the secret is long, slow cooking. This method is for those

2 slabs baby back ribs or spareribs
½ teaspoon cinnamon
½ teaspoon ground cloves
¼ teaspoon pepper
1 cup hickory wood chips
barbecue sauce (optional)

*backyard chefs who
don't have smokers
for slower cooking or
prefer a more conve-
nient method. Included
is a variation called
Rainy Day Ribs, for
days when you crave
the taste of ribs but
the weather won't
cooperate.*

Remove the membrane from the back of each slab of ribs. Rub the cinnamon, clove, and pepper into both sides of each slab.

In a large baking pan, place the ribs on a wire rack, which should be high enough so that the ribs will not touch their drippings. Add 1 cup of water to the pan. If the pan has no lid, cover with aluminum foil and seal the edges well. Bake at 300 degrees for 3 hours.

To finish and smoke the ribs, divide the hot charcoals in a grill, banking them on each side of a drip pan. Put the hickory wood chips on a large square of aluminum foil, seal tightly, and pierce the packet several times to release the smoke. Place the wood chip packet directly on the hot coals and replace the grid. Put the ribs in the center of the grid and baste with your favorite barbecue sauce, if desired. Cover the grill and cook for about 10 minutes. Turn the ribs over, baste the other side, and cook for an additional 10 minutes, or until the ribs are glazed but still moist.

Serves 4.

Variation: For Rainy Day Ribs, bake as directed. To finish, place the ribs on a broiler rack under the oven broiler (with or without barbecue sauce) and brown for several minutes, turning once.

✳ Country-Style Ribs with Willer Barbecue Sauce

David Willer, Lawrence

*Meaty and flavorful,
country-style ribs are
a favorite of outdoor
cooks. Because David
Willer's homemade
barbecue sauce im-
proves with age, it
should be made a day
or two in advance.*

WILLER BARBECUE SAUCE
*2 15-ounce cans tomato sauce
½ cup molasses
10 to 12 garlic cloves, whole
2 tablespoons dry mustard
2 tablespoons ground cumin
1 teaspoon pepper
½ teaspoon cinnamon*

¼ teaspoon anise seed
½ teaspoon crushed red pepper
½ to 1 cup red wine vinegar, to taste

12 country-style pork ribs
salt and pepper, to taste

Willer Barbecue Sauce: In a large pan, combine all the ingredients except the wine vinegar. Simmer slowly, partially covered, over low heat for 1 hour. Stir occasionally. After 1 hour, add the wine vinegar to taste and continue to simmer for 15 minutes more. Cool, cover, and refrigerate until ready to use.

Makes 1 quart.

Sprinkle the ribs with salt and pepper to taste. Brush the ribs lightly with Willer Barbecue Sauce.

In a covered grill, divide the hot charcoals, banking them on each side of a drip pan. Cook the ribs over indirect heat by placing them directly over the drip pan. Cover the grill and cook for a total of 45 to 60 minutes, turning once. When the ribs are tender, place them directly over the hot coals and baste with the barbecue sauce, turning often, for 10 to 15 minutes.

Serves 4.

✳ Ribs 'n' Kraut

Barbara Holzmark, Leawood

One of the oldest methods of preparing pork ribs is boiling them with sauerkraut. Farm folk, especially those of European descent, often cooked ribs this way during the time of slaughtering and smoking.

Barbara Holzmark's recipe for Ribs 'n Kraut is topped

2½ to 3 pounds country-style pork ribs
salt and pepper, to taste
1 32-ounce can sauerkraut with liquid
1 24-ounce can tomato or vegetable juice
2 tablespoons brown sugar
2 teaspoons caraway seeds
1 large onion, quartered
2 to 3 carrots, peeled and cut into 2-inch pieces
4 medium potatoes, peeled and sliced in half

Place the ribs, meaty side up, in a large pan or Dutch oven. Season with salt and pepper, to taste.

with vegetables for a complete meal-in-one.

In a large bowl, combine the sauerkraut with liquid, tomato or vegetable juice, brown sugar, and caraway seeds. Place the mixture on top of the ribs. Top with onion, carrots, and potatoes.

Cover and bake at 350 degrees for 2½ to 3 hours, or until the ribs are tender. Baste the vegetables and sauerkraut with the accumulated drippings during the last hour of cooking. If dry, add ½ cup of water.

Serves 6.

✳ Scrapple

Doris R. Loganbill, Moundridge

Scrapple (also known as panhaus) was a filling staple for many Kansans in earlier times. Doris Loganbill recalls that this meat-filled and crisply fried mush was made by her parents during the 1930s depression years. "They would purchase a young pig and fatten it until winter, then butcher it," says Doris. "The head, scraps, and liver were cooked and made into scrapple. This provided for busy-day dinners and, as a treat, was made into sandwiches for school lunches."

2 pounds pork shoulder
1 beef bouillon cube
2 teaspoons salt
2 quarts water
2¼ ounces pork liver
2 cups cold water
1½ cups cornmeal
1 teaspoon pepper
vegetable oil for frying
butter and maple syrup (optional)

Place the pork shoulder, beef bouillon, and salt in a large pot and add 2 quarts of water. Bring the mixture to a boil over high heat. Reduce heat to low and simmer partially covered for 30 minutes. Add the pork liver and cook for an additional 30 minutes, or until the meat is very tender. Remove and cool the meat and liver, reserving 1 quart of the stock. Remove the meat from the bone, keeping 2 tablespoons of the fat. Finely chop the meat, liver, and reserved fat in a food processor, or grind in a meat grinder. Set aside.

In a mixing bowl, slowly stir the cornmeal into the cold water. Pour the reserved meat stock into a large pan. Bring it to a boil over high heat and slowly add the cornmeal mixture. Reduce heat to medium and cook, stirring constantly, until the mixture is thick. Add the pepper and the chopped meat. Continue cooking for 5 minutes more.

Pour the scrapple into a buttered loaf pan or baking dish. Cool to room temperature, then cover and chill until firm.

To serve, remove the scrapple from the loaf pan and slice into ⅜-inch slices. Fry in hot oil over medium-high heat until brown, about 10 to 15 minutes. Serve plain or with butter and maple syrup.

Serves 6 to 8.

Variation: For a different flavor, add ¼ teaspoon of summer savory and ¼ teaspoon of sage to the cornmeal mixture.

✳ Cabbage Rolls with Creamed Sauerkraut

In the 1880s, many southern and eastern Europeans settled on Strawberry Hill in Kansas City, Kansas. Well into the 1930s, nearly all of the households raised hogs and chickens in their backyards. Some folks even had smokehouses for curing meats. Other Slavic families established farms nearby in the western part of Wyandotte County and provided such produce as cabbage and turnips to the market, allowing the Strawberry Hill residents to make sauerkraut and other traditional dishes of their homeland.

1 large head cabbage
½ teaspoon salt
2 16-ounce cans sauerkraut
4 bacon strips
1 onion, chopped
3 garlic cloves, minced
½ pound ground pork
½ pound ground fresh ham
½ cup cooked rice
1 egg, slightly beaten
1 tablespoon sweet Hungarian paprika
¼ teaspoon marjoram
1 teaspoon salt
¼ teaspoon pepper
1 8-ounce can tomato sauce
1 cup water
3 tablespoons butter
2 tablespoons all-purpose flour
1 cup sour cream

Boil water in a pan large enough to hold the cabbage. Add the cabbage and salt and bring to a second boil. Reduce heat to low and simmer for 8 minutes. Remove the cabbage and rinse in cold water. Carefully peel off the large leaves and drain them on paper towels.

Drain the sauerkraut and soak it in cold water for 10 minutes. Drain well, pressing out the water. Set aside.

Fry the bacon in a frying pan over medium heat. Drain and crumble. Set aside. Cook the onion and garlic in the pan drippings over low heat until tender.

In a large bowl, combine the ground pork and ham. Add the cooked onion mixture, crumbled bacon, rice, egg, paprika, marjoram, salt, and pepper. Mix well.

Place 2 to 3 tablespoons of the meat mixture in the center of each cabbage leaf. Beginning with the thick end of the leaf, roll up tightly, folding in the sides. Repeat until all the meat mixture is used.

Spread the sauerkraut in the bottom of a 5-quart pan or Dutch oven. Arrange the cabbage rolls on top, seam-side down. Combine the tomato sauce and water in a small bowl and pour over the cabbage rolls. Bring the liquids to a boil, then reduce heat to low. Cover and simmer for 1 hour. Remove the pan from heat and carefully take out the cabbage rolls, leaving the sauerkraut and juices in the pan. Keep rolls warm.

Creamed Sauerkraut: In a small pan, melt the butter over low heat. Add the flour and stir constantly until it begins to color. Stir in the sour cream and cook for 2 to 3 minutes, until bubbly. Pour this mixture into the sauerkraut, mixing well. Cook over medium heat for about 5 minutes, until bubbly. Spoon the creamed sauerkraut onto a large platter. Arrange the cabbage rolls on top.

Serves 4 to 6. Makes 16 to 18 cabbage rolls.

✳ Ham Loaf with Mustard Sauce

Mrs. Harold Johnson, Dwight

2 pounds fresh ham, ground
1 pound smoked ham, ground
1 cup milk

*farmer, ham loaves
have been a popular
food in rural commu-
nities in the past as
well as the present.
Ham loaves are rich
and filling and very
easy to prepare.*

1 teaspoon prepared mustard
2 eggs
3 cups cornflakes
½ teaspoon salt
¼ teaspoon pepper

MUSTARD SAUCE
6 tablespoons brown sugar
2 tablespoons all-purpose flour
1 tablespoon prepared mustard
⅓ cup vinegar
⅓ cup hot water
1 egg
1 tablespoon butter

Mix the fresh ham and the smoked ham together in a
large bowl. Add the milk, mustard, eggs, cornflakes, salt,
and pepper, mixing well.

Form the mixture into a loaf and place in a large baking
dish or on a foil-lined baking sheet. Bake at 350 degrees
for 1¼ hours.

Mustard Sauce: Combine the brown sugar and flour in
a medium-sized saucepan. Add the mustard, vinegar,
and hot water, mixing well. Cook over low heat, stirring
constantly, until the mixture thickens. Remove it from
heat.

In a medium-sized bowl beat the egg well. Pour the
mustard sauce slowly over the egg, stirring constantly
with a wire whip. Add the butter and mix well. Spoon the
mustard sauce over the top of the ham loaf during the last
10 minutes of baking, or serve on the side.

Serves 6 to 8.

✳ Baked Ham Loaf

Mrs. C. H. (Maxine) Liming, Dearing

*"This was the original
recipe of my mother,
Maud Savage Hast-*

1 egg
1 cup buttermilk
2 cups soft bread crumbs

ings," writes Maxine Liming. "She used to make it when I was a child back in the late 20s and early 30s."

1½ teaspoons prepared horseradish
1 teaspoon salt
1 pound cured ham, ground
1 pound ground pork
½ pound ground beef

In a large bowl, beat the egg with a fork or a wire whip. Add the buttermilk, bread crumbs, horseradish, and salt, mixing well. Add the ground ham, pork, and beef, mixing well.

Shape the mixture into a loaf and place in a large baking dish or on a foil-lined baking sheet. Bake at 350 degrees for about 1 hour.

Serves 6.

✳ Charcoal-Grilled Ham Steak with Hot Mustard Sauce

During the early days of settlement in Kansas, the homesteaders often built smokehouses to aid in the cooking and preparation of meats. These tiny, windowless structures were usually made of stone and had a small area for fire and ashes, a chimney, and oven space.

Hams were soaked in brine or rubbed with salt, then brushed with sorghum molasses or coated with sugar. Next, they were wrapped in muslin and brushed again with molasses. A small fire was then built in the smokehouse to smoke the hams. Maple, apple, and hickory logs were sometimes used, but on the plains, corncobs were more common.

In this recipe, smoked ham steaks are basted with Hot Mustard Sauce and grilled over hot coals. The sauce must be started the day before to allow the mustard and vinegar mixture to mellow overnight. The leftover mustard is delicious on sandwiches or as a baste for grilled chicken.

2 1-pound slices smoked center-cut ham steaks, ½ inch thick

HOT MUSTARD SAUCE
½ cup white vinegar
5 tablespoons dry ground mustard

1 egg
½ cup sugar
½ teaspoon salt

Hot Mustard Sauce: In a small bowl, combine the vinegar
and dry mustard, mixing well. Cover and let stand unre-
frigerated for at least 10 hours, or preferably overnight.

In a saucepan, beat the egg well with a wire whip. Add
the sugar and salt, mixing well. Stir in the mustard mixture. Cook over medium heat, stirring constantly until
the mixture thickens, 5 to 10 minutes. Do not let the
mixture boil. Remove from heat and strain the mustard
into a small bowl or jar. Cool to room temperature. Cover
and refrigerate until ready to use.

Makes 1 cup.

Baste the ham steaks on both sides with some of the
Hot Mustard Sauce. Place them on the grill, directly
over hot coals. Grill for 3 to 5 minutes each side, or until
golden brown, basting with more mustard when turning.

Cut each ham steak into 2 or 3 servings and pass the
remaining Hot Mustard Sauce.

Serves 4 to 6.

Variation: The flavor of the mustard sauce may be varied
by adding fresh or dried herbs to the vinegar and mustard
mixture.

✳ Ham Steak with Apricot Nectar

*In this recipe, smoked
ham steak is fried,
then glazed with a
sauce made with apri-
cot nectar for a quick
and easy entree. Serve
with baked potatoes
and sweet corn.*

1½ pounds smoked center-cut ham steak, sliced thick
1 tablespoon butter
⅓ cup apricot nectar

Heat the butter in a large frying pan over medium-high
heat. Add the ham steak and fry until browned, 5 to 8
minutes on each side.

Remove the ham and keep warm. Add the apricot
nectar to the pan drippings. Bring to a boil, stirring frequently until the sauce reduces slightly and becomes

syrupy, 2 to 3 minutes. Pour the sauce over the ham and serve.

Serves 4.

✳ Hazel's Delicious Quiche

Hazel E. Fenske, Wichita

Though this quiche, filled with ham and cheese, is welcome at any meal, Hazel Fenske likes to present it in the morning to overnight guests by slicing it in small pieces and serving it with cinnamon rolls and fresh fruit. You may also undercook it by 10 minutes and warm it in the oven the next morning for a "hurry up" breakfast.

3 eggs, beaten
1½ cups evaporated milk
½ teaspoon salt
dash pepper
⅛ teaspoon basil
dash of nutmeg
1 cup Swiss cheese, grated
1 cup ham, chopped
1 unbaked 9-inch pie shell

In a large bowl, beat the eggs well. Beat in the milk, salt, pepper, basil, and nutmeg. Fold in the grated cheese and ham. Pour the mixture into the pie shell and bake at 350 degrees for 40 to 45 minutes.

Serves 6 to 8.

The French Influence

In 1869, a Frenchman, Ernest Valeton de Boissiere, came to Kansas to found a socialistic colony which he established in Franklin County, twenty miles southwest of Ottawa. To support itself, the colony raised silkworms and made the delicate silk fabric. Soon it acquired the name Silkville.

Mulberry trees, upon which the silkworms thrive, were planted, and the silkworms were imported from California. French workers with experience in the silk industry were recruited to come to Kansas. At its peak, Silkville's products were ranked with the best from France, Italy, and Japan at the 1876 Centennial Exposition in Philadelphia.

The French colony also raised cattle and planted a fruit orchard. For several years they kept up a prosperous dairy industry that produced fine cheeses. According to *Harvest of American Cooking* by Mary Margaret McBride (New York: Putnam, 1957), the women of the colony quickly gained a reputation for cooking some of the finest food in Kansas. They concocted such gourmet delights as "garlic-spiced sauces for native quail" and filled their kettles with "black bean soup and stews of wild turkey and little new potatoes."

De Boissiere believed in the possibility of a self-sufficient community, but the attraction of owning their own land lured many French families away and the colony was abandoned in 1886 when the settlers left in search of better opportunities in Kansas.

✳ Pork and Sauerkraut Casserole

(Choucroute Garnie)

Simone Johnson, Topeka

The accessibility of the ingredients allowed the French settlers to

1½ *pounds salt pork*
4 *pounds sauerkraut*
1 *bay leaf*

*re-create in Kansas
this traditional casse-
role of pork sausage
and sauerkraut. Most
any pork sausage will
do—Polish, Italian,
smoked, or fresh.*

*Simone Johnson
enjoys preparing this
dish from her home-
land. Simone moved to
Kansas after serving
in the French Army
during World War II.
A former professor of
French at Washburn
University in Topeka,
she is now retired.*

*4 sprigs fresh parsley
6 black peppercorns
6 juniper berries
2 onions, each studded with 2 whole cloves
2 carrots, cut into chunks
1 teaspoon thyme
3 garlic cloves, minced
2 cups dry white wine
2 cups chicken broth
salt and pepper, to taste
1½ pounds pork sausages, cut into 2-inch pieces
6 frankfurters
6 smoked pork chops or ham slices
6 potatoes, peeled*

Slice the salt pork into 3 slices and blanch in 2 quarts of boiling water for 20 minutes. Drain well and place in the bottom of a 4-quart casserole or Dutch oven.

Rinse the sauerkraut several times and drain well. Squeeze out as much water as possible. Put the sauerkraut in the casserole over the salt pork slices.

Place the bay leaf, parsley sprigs, black peppercorns, and juniper berries in a piece of cheesecloth. Tie and put in the middle of the sauerkraut.

Arrange the onions, carrots, thyme, and garlic on the sauerkraut. Cover with wine and chicken broth. (Add additional chicken broth if more liquid is needed to cover the ingredients.) Season with salt and pepper to taste.

Bring the mixture to a boil on top of the stove. Cover and cook at 325 degrees for 3 hours.

Meanwhile, brown the sausages in a large skillet over medium heat. Remove from the pan and drain on paper towels. Boil the frankfurters in a large pan for 5 minutes and drain.

Remove the casserole from the oven and place the sausages, frankfurters, and the smoked pork chops or ham slices on top. Cover and return to the oven for an additional 30 minutes.

Meanwhile, boil the potatoes until tender.

To serve, discard the herb bag. Mound the sauerkraut in the center of a large heated platter. Chop the cooked salt pork into bite-size pieces and place on the platter. Arrange the sausages, frankfurters, pork, and potatoes over and around the sauerkraut. Serve with a variety of mustards.

Serves 6 to 10.

✳ Black Beans, Smoked Sausage, and Rice

Beans, sausage, and rice were staples in the diets of cattlemen and early settlers. Here's an easy-to-prepare dish using all three ingredients.

3 bacon strips
1 onion, chopped
2 15-ounce cans black beans, rinsed and drained
1 cup uncooked white rice
2½ cups water
2 garlic cloves, minced
½ teaspoon oregano
½ teaspoon cumin
¼ teaspoon salt
¼ teaspoon pepper
1 bay leaf
1 pound smoked pork sausages

In a large pan or Dutch oven, cook the bacon strips over medium-low heat. Remove bacon and crumble. Set aside. Add the chopped onion to the pan drippings and cook, stirring occasionally, until the onion is tender but not browned.

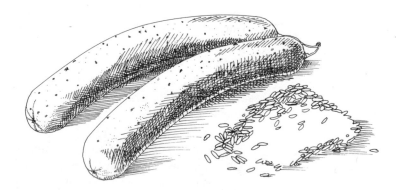

Add the black beans, rice, water, garlic, oregano, cumin, salt, pepper, and bay leaf. Stir in the crumbled bacon. Bring the mixture to a boil and cover the pan. Reduce heat to low and cook for 20 minutes, or until rice is tender.

While the beans and rice are cooking, prepare the smoked sausage. Slice the sausages into 1-inch pieces and place them in a skillet. Cover with a lid and cook over medium-low heat for 5 minutes. Remove the lid, drain the excess fat, and brown the sausage for 5 to 8 minutes. Remove the sausage from the pan and add it to the cooked beans and rice. Serve at once.

Serves 4 to 6.

✳ Country Pork Sausage

Doris R. Loganbill, Moundridge

"Sometime in December, when cold weather had set in, the butchering of hogs would begin," recalls Doris Loganbill. "Activities would start early, about sun up, or as the help arrived. The large kettles of water were put on the fires that were started outside. The hogs were slaughtered and the hard work began. This was also a day of visiting and fellowship with the extended family members—grandparents, aunts, uncles, and cousins."

This simple recipe makes plenty of sausage to freeze for later use. Serve it grilled, broiled, or pan-fried, with fried potatoes and sauerkraut, or coleslaw.

10 pounds fresh lean pork roast
½ cup brown sugar
5 tablespoons salt
2 teaspoons pepper
¼ teaspoon sage

Grind the pork in a meat grinder to a coarse texture. (Coarse ground pork makes better sausage than if it is ground too fine.) Place the meat in a very large bowl or plastic tub. Add the remaining ingredients and mix well. Stuff the sausage loosely into well-washed casings and tie links at 1 foot intervals, or store in bulk in covered containers. Freeze sausage for longer storage.

To cook: If the sausage is in casings, cut into 2-inch pieces and pan-fry. Whole links of sausage may be boiled for 5 minutes, then browned in a skillet or on the grill or under the broiler. Form bulk sausage into patties and pan-fry.

Makes 10 pounds.

The Czech Capital of Kansas

Immigrants from the Austro-Hungarian province of Bohemia, which later became part of Czechoslovakia, began arriving in the United States in the 1870s, seeking refuge from economic and political oppression. After arriving in New York and earning enough money to head west, many came to Kansas in the hope of acquiring land for farming.

The first Czech settlements in Kansas were in Republic County near Cuba and Munden, but settlements sprang up later in other counties as well, including Ellsworth. Some have maintained that the Wilson area in Ellsworth was chosen because the landscape reminded the Czechs of their homeland.

In 1967, Wilson was proclaimed by the state as the "Czech Capital of Kansas." Every July thousands of people descend on the little central Kansas town to attend the After Harvest Czech Festival when Wilson proudly sponsors one of the largest small-town parades in the state. It is a time of reunion for families who come to dance the polka and feast on Jaternice, a Czech sausage, and Kolaches, the popular fruit-filled pastries. Many residents don traditional Czech costumes and speak Czech to one another while trading stories of visits to ancestral homes in the old country. Outsiders are welcomed and are encouraged to sample the Czech dishes at the local church, where one can feast on a menu of these ethnic delights.

✳ Czech Sausage
(Jaternice)

Mrs. Anna Benyshek, Cuba

Today, butcher shops in central Kansas, around Wilson and Cuba, are proud of their unique versions of Jaternice (pronounced YEE-ter-neet-zah). It is a traditional food of the Czech culture and is usually served in casings or as a stew. The flavor can be a strong "acquired" taste or mild as a veal sausage, depending on the cook's preference.

1 hog head
1 pork heart
1 tongue, scalded and skin removed
2 ears, scalded and skin removed
1 pork liver
3 tablespoons salt
1 large loaf stale bread
6 garlic cloves, minced
1 large onion, finely chopped
1 tablespoon marjoram
1 tablespoon pepper
1 teaspoon allspice
1 teaspoon ginger
1 teaspoon ground cloves

In a large pot, boil all the meats together with the salt until tender. Remove the meat from the pot and reserve the broth. Remove any bones and put the meat through a meat grinder.

Soak the bread in water, squeeze it dry, and crumble it into a large bowl. Add the ground meat and the spices and mix thoroughly.

Stuff the mixture into well-washed sausage casings and tie into sausage links. Bring the broth to a boil and add the sausages. Reduce heat and simmer for 10 minutes. Rinse the sausages in cold water and cool. To serve, fry them slowly in butter or oil until brown.

✳ Mexican Sausage
(Chorizo)

Susie Bermudez, Lawrence

Chorizo is a Mexican-style sausage flavored

1 pound pork sausage
1 pound ground beef

with the traditional seasonings of oregano, peppers, and cumin. It can be found in Mexican food stores in Topeka and the Kansas City area, or wherever the desire for Mexican flavors has created a demand. Regardless, this versatile sausage is easily made at home.

Chorizo can be fried and mixed with cooked pinto beans or combined with scrambled eggs and topped with hot sauce. It is also a delicious filling for enchiladas and bean burritos.

4 dried chile anchos
4 garlic cloves, minced
2 bay leaves
2 whole cloves
1 teaspoon oregano
½ teaspoon cumin
1 teaspoon salt
1 teaspoon pepper, coarsely ground
½ cup vinegar

Combine the pork sausage and ground beef in a large bowl. Cover and refrigerate until ready to use.

To prepare the chile anchos, open the chilies and rinse out the seeds. Place the chilies in a pot of boiling water and boil for 5 minutes. Remove the pot from heat, cover, and let stand for 15 minutes.

Drain the chilies and place them, along with the garlic, spices, and vinegar, in a blender or food processor and blend until smooth. Pour into the meat mixture and stir until well combined.

Place the sausage in a colander or a strainer. Put the colander or strainer in a large bowl, cover, and refrigerate overnight to allow the liquids to drain from the meat. Pour off any accumulated juices before using, as the sausage should be fairly dry.

Store the sausage in airtight containers in the refrigerator, or freeze for longer storage. The sausage may also be put into casings.

Chorizo may be fried in a skillet over medium heat and used in traditional Mexican dishes.

Makes 2 pounds.

* POULTRY AND GAME

Cooking poultry has always been a Midwestern standard by which to measure a cook's abilities. Whether stuffed and roasted, fricasseed, or delicately sautéed, it is always well received at the table. Judged by the moistness of the meat, the crispness of the skin, and the quality of its gravy, roast turkey and batter-fried chicken are often the flagships of a good cook's repertoire. Made with few ingredients, these marvelous dishes depend almost entirely on the cook's meticulous technique and fussy attention.

Henhouses were common on the early homestead and even in town. Chickens were raised for the eggs as well as their meat. In hard times, "egg money" bought many niceties that couldn't be made on the farm. A freshly butchered chicken was considered a special meal, sparked perhaps by a surprise visit from the parson.

Getting the bird from the chicken coop to the dinner table, however, was no easy task and was definitely "women's work"—as Charley O'Kieffe points out: "While the young man in the family was taking his lessons in butchering and other branches of animal husbandry, his sister or girl friend was getting used to, and learning the knack of, chopping off the head of some ancient rooster or an old biddy hen who had signed her own death

warrant by falling down on egg-laying, her real mission
in life" (in Kay Graber, *Nebraska Pioneer Cookbook* [Lin-
coln, University of Nebraska Press, 1974]).

Even in modern days of store-bought poultry, chicken
remains the universal fare when company comes for
dinner because it pleases any palate, young or old.
Chicken is a versatile meat that lends itself to casseroles,
pot pies, and various one-pan dishes using the popular
chicken breast fillet. When choosing the best-quality
chicken, look for a fresh bird that has not been previ-
ously frozen. White moist skin and white bones indicate
freshness, while brown bones indicate that the chicken
has been frozen. Select a bird with a minimum amount
of fat and a large breast, if white meat is preferred. Fresh
chickens are available at specialty meat shops and at
some farmer's markets.

Though roast turkey is an institution, especially at holiday time, the following pages include Kansas recipes for
capon (a large neutered rooster), which many believe
surpasses the turkey in flavor. Both birds fit nicely on a
covered grill, and if trends toward outdoor cooking continue, grilled poultry will remain a popular way to bring
out the flavor of the bird with less fuss—regardless of
the season.

Some of the chicken recipes, like the tasty shortcut
version of Hunter's Chicken, evolved from early game
recipes. Ironically, modern cookbooks now refer the cook
to chicken recipes when cooking game. Wild fowl are
abundant in Kansas and, considering the effort expended
to bag the bird, an equal culinary effort is a deserving
homage to the local delicacy.

Hunters in Kansas will find good populations of quail,
pheasant, duck, dove, wild turkey, prairie chicken, deer,
and rabbit—and in response, this section includes recipes
for Baked Prairie Chicken with Corn Bread Dressing,
Hunter's Pheasant with Red Wine Sauce, Smothered
Quail, and Perfect Deer Steaks. Also, for the adventurous hunter, is a recipe for Bar-B-Q Beaver. Each recipe
displays its Kansas heritage and is exotic enough to be
worthy of the hunter's prize.

✳ Parson's Pan-Fried Chicken

According to Kay Graber, author of Nebraska Pioneer Cookbook (Lincoln: University of Nebraska Press, 1974), "Fried chicken—'parson food,' as it was called, because it was inevitably served when the preacher came to dinner—remained company fare until well after the turn of the century."

The always-popular fried chicken is often featured as the main course of a harvest dinner and remains a "must" for potlucks and family picnics. One of the great pleasures of the American palate, Kansas cooks are enthusiastic about their own special methods of frying chicken, as seen in the following recipes.

1 whole frying chicken

MARINADE
1½ cups water
3 tablespoons lemon juice
1 garlic clove, minced
¼ teaspoon salt

1 cup buttermilk
1 cup all-purpose flour
2 teaspoons basil
1 teaspoon marjoram
1 teaspoon thyme
½ teaspoon celery salt
½ teaspoon pepper
vegetable shortening for frying

CHICKEN GRAVY
3 tablespoons fried chicken drippings
2 tablespoons all-purpose flour
1 to 1½ cups milk
salt and pepper, to taste

Cut the chicken into serving pieces. Rinse, drain well, and place in a large bowl.

Marinade: Combine the water, lemon juice, garlic, and salt in a small bowl. Pour over the chicken, cover, and refrigerate for 1 to 2 hours, turning the chicken pieces 2 or 3 times.

When ready to cook, drain the chicken pieces. Pour the buttermilk in a wide shallow bowl. Combine the flour, basil, marjoram, thyme, celery salt, and pepper in a paper or plastic bag. Dip the chicken pieces in the buttermilk and place 2 to 3 pieces at a time in the bag. Shake to coat.

Melt the vegetable shortening in a large frying pan over medium-high heat to about ¼-inch depth. Heat until hot enough to sizzle. Place the coated chicken pieces in the pan, skin-side down, being careful not to crowd them. Brown, uncovered, for 5 to 10 minutes. Turn the pieces over and brown the other side, about 5 to 7 minutes. Pour off all but about ¼ cup of the drippings and cover the pan with a lid. Turn heat to low and cook for 30 to 40 minutes, until tender. Remove the chicken pieces from the pan and drain on paper towels.

Chicken Gravy: Pour off all but 3 tablespoons of the drippings. Add the flour and brown, stirring over medium heat. Slowly add as much milk as needed, stirring until the gravy is thick and bubbly. Add salt and pepper to taste.

Serves 4.

✳ Jefferson County Fried Chicken

Aletha Hensleigh, Winchester

Aletha Hensleigh, food columnist for The Free Spirit *(a Jefferson County advertising paper), says that fried chicken is as American as hamburgers and is a good choice for picnics as well as company dinners.*

In her column called "Have Fun In Your Kitchen," she writes, "When we came to the farm in the early forties there was a definite fried chicken season, from early May until August. Fried chicken is no longer a seasonal treat, with the year-round availability of fryers in any food store, or from our home freezers. . . . I've tried every method or hint I've come onto to achieve that crisp golden crust with tender well-cooked meat inside that spells the best in fried chicken. Our sons have said, 'Write down just how you fry chicken!' and it has not always been the same. It is a little hard to be definite about either method or seasoning, but this is how I fry chicken most successfully."

1 whole frying chicken
1 egg, beaten
dash of paprika
dash of chili powder
garlic salt or powder, to taste
salt and pepper, to taste
1½ cups all-purpose flour
vegetable oil or shortening for frying

Cut the chicken into serving pieces, rinse well, and pat
dry with paper towels.

In a shallow bowl, combine the beaten egg, paprika,
chili powder, garlic salt or powder, salt, and pepper. Roll
the chicken pieces in the mixture to coat. Pour the flour
into a heavy brown paper bag and drop the chicken pieces
in, 2 to 3 pieces at a time, shaking to coat.

In an electric skillet, heat the vegetable oil or shortening to 350 degrees and to a depth of at least ½ inch. If
using a frying pan, heat over medium-high heat. Add the
chicken pieces without crowding, cover, and cook until
the undersides are golden brown, 10 to 12 minutes. Turn
over and cook for 10 to 12 minutes more, or until completely browned and tender and the juices run clear when
pierced with a knife. Drain on paper towels.

Serves 4.

Harvest Meals

The old-fashioned threshing machines of the early days of
harvesting required the help of a crew of men to cut, bun-
dle, shock, rack, haul, and thresh the wheat. As many
men and horses as possible were recruited to bring in the
harvest. Children carried water for the men and animals.
Older boys, anxious to prove themselves, found opportunities to take over the reins, as the young girls and
women prepared two or more meals a day for the entire
group. In the rural communities of Kansas, neighbors
pitched in to help one another because it was understood
that someday the help might be needed in return.

The harvest was then, as it still is now, a time of excitement and neighborly generosity in rural Kansas.
While the men labored in the fields, the farm wives
worked in the kitchen. Cooking for lunch started in the
early morning, and as soon as the men were fed, dishes
would be washed and dinner preparation would begin.
Elaborate meals, fit for Sunday dinner, were produced in
those hot, bustling kitchens.

The meals were transported to the field, where folding chairs and long tables, spread with tablecloths and

dishes, would be set up on the wheat stubble. A harvest meal often consisted of fried chicken or chicken-fried steak, mashed potatoes and gravy, fresh corn-on-the-cob, garden-ripe tomatoes, green beans, cabbage salads, baked beans, homemade bread, ice tea, and lemonade. Dessert might include freshly baked pies or cakes and ice-cold watermelon. These large meals kept the men going, since the long days began early and often continued into the evening. It was a time of socializing for farm families, sharing the hard work as well as the meal.

Today, harvesting is somewhat easier, as the combines move effortlessly through miles of wheat fields. Neighbors still come together to help out, and nowadays many of the women work alongside the men. The elaborate harvest meals remain a tradition in Kansas, as the cooking duties are passed on from mother to daughter, ensuring that the favorite "harvest recipes" survive.

✳ Steam-Fried Chicken

Flora Smith, Ottawa

Flora Smith sends us this recipe for steam-frying chicken. She tells us that a tight-fitting lid on the skillet creates the steam, while the oil cooks and browns—hence, the "fast fry" effect. Flora says, "The number of servings depends on your 'chicken-eaters.' But be prepared, as it is irresistible."

1 whole frying chicken
1½ cups all-purpose flour
½ teaspoon paprika
1 teaspoon seasoning salt
½ teaspoon pepper
vegetable oil for frying

Cut the chicken into serving pieces. Rinse and drain on paper towels.

In a wide bowl, combine the flour, paprika, seasoning salt, and pepper. Dredge the chicken pieces in the flour mixture.

Fill a large, deep skillet one-third full with vegetable oil. Heat the oil on high and add several of the chicken pieces (do not crowd) to the skillet. Immediately cover the skillet with a tight-fitting lid and fry the chicken pieces for 5 to 8 minutes. Turn the pieces over, replace lid, and fry for 5 to 8 minutes more, or until golden brown and tender.

Remove the cooked pieces from the skillet and drain on a brown paper sack while frying the remaining pieces.

Serves 4.

❋ Crispy Oven-Fried Chicken

Joan Rockers, Garnett

Oven-fried chicken is a favorite of Joan Rockers's family for Sunday dinner. She adds that if you raise your own chickens, it isn't necessary to drizzle the chicken pieces with butter before baking, since home-fed chickens tend to have more fat than store-bought ones.

Joan likes to prepare a tossed green salad and baked potatoes alongside this dish for a quick and easy meal.

1 whole frying chicken
1¼ cups saltine crackers
¼ cup Parmesan cheese, grated
1 small bay leaf, crushed
1 tablespoon parsley
½ teaspoon oregano
½ teaspoon basil
¼ teaspoon paprika
½ teaspoon celery salt
½ teaspoon onion salt
¼ teaspoon salt
¼ teaspoon pepper
½ cup milk
¼ cup butter, melted

Cut the chicken into serving pieces, rinse, and pat dry with paper towels. Set aside.

Crush the saltine crackers and put them in a large bowl. Add the grated Parmesan cheese and the spices. Mix well to combine.

Pour the milk into a shallow bowl. Dip the chicken pieces into the milk and roll in the cracker crumb mixture to coat. Place the chicken pieces, skin-side up, in a lightly greased, large shallow baking dish. Drizzle the melted butter over the chicken pieces.

Bake the chicken uncovered at 375 degrees for about 1 hour, or until golden brown and the juices run clear when the chicken is pierced with a knife.

Serves 4.

✳ Roast Chicken with Pearl Onions

Roast chicken, once a popular method of preparing chicken, should not be forgotten by today's cooks. Simple yet elegant, it can be stuffed with dressing, fruits, or vegetables and basted with butter or drippings for crispy and flavorful skin.

In this recipe, the roast chicken is stuffed with pearl onions, which are served atop the chicken with the pan juices.

1 whole chicken
1 10-ounce carton pearl onions
1 tablespoon butter
⅓ cup water
¼ teaspoon parsley
⅛ teaspoon rosemary
⅛ teaspoon thyme
⅛ teaspoon salt
¼ teaspoon pepper
2 teaspoons butter, softened
¼ cup chicken broth
2 tablespoons dry white wine

Rinse the chicken and pat dry. Chill the pearl onions and peel with a sharp knife. (As an alternative, boil the onions for 3 minutes and rinse in cold water. Cut off the ends of each onion, and the skins will slide off easily.)

Melt 1 tablespoon of butter in a frying pan over low heat. Add the peeled onions and ⅓ cup of water. Cover and simmer for 10 to 15 minutes, or until the water evaporates. Uncover and brown the onions, shaking the pan frequently to brown evenly.

Remove the onions from heat and gently stir in the parsley, rosemary, thyme, salt, and pepper. Stuff the onion mixture into the cavity of the chicken. Close the chicken with toothpicks, or truss. Tie the legs together with string and hook the wing tips back behind the body joint, akimbo-style. Rub the outside of the chicken with the softened butter.

Place the chicken on a rack, breast-side up, in a baking dish or a shallow roasting pan. Roast at 400 degrees for about 1 hour, or until the juices run clear when the chicken is pierced with knife. After 30 minutes of baking, baste the chicken twice with the pan drippings.

Skim the grease from the pan juices and pour the juices into a small saucepan. Remove the onions from the cavity and place in the pan. Add the chicken broth and white wine and simmer over low heat for about 3 minutes. Cut the chicken into serving pieces. Garnish with the onions and top with the simmering juices.

Serves 4.

✳ Oven-Baked Chicken Tarragon

After the original French settlement of Silkville was abandoned in the 1880s, many of the colonists joined other French immigrants who had come from both Canada and France and had settled around Atchison, Leavenworth, Wathena, and Concordia.

Priding themselves on their culinary skills, the French had their own special methods of baking chicken. This simple, country-style French recipe makes use of clarified butter. Clarified butter does not brown or burn while the chicken is sautéing and therefore does not detract from the delicate flavor of the roasted chicken.

3 tablespoons butter, melted
(to make 2 tablespoons clarified butter)
1 whole chicken
salt and pepper, to taste
¼ cup white wine
½ cup whipping cream
1 teaspoon tarragon

Make the clarified butter by pouring melted butter into a narrow glass container—or simply microwave the butter until melted in a juice glass. After it stands for 1 to 2 minutes, remove the floating foam with a spoon, use the clear liquid, and discard the whey at the bottom.

Cut up a whole chicken into 8 pieces so that the backbone and rib cage are removed. Rinse and dry the chicken and season with salt and pepper.

In a skillet, sauté the chicken pieces over medium-high heat in the clarified butter until browned. Remove the pieces to a casserole that is large enough to hold the chicken in one layer.

Pour off all but 2 tablespoons of the drippings. Add the wine and let reduce over medium-high heat for about 1 minute. Add the cream and tarragon, stirring, for 1 to 2 minutes, or until the cream boils and begins to thicken.

Pour the sauce over the chicken and bake uncovered at 375 degrees for 25 to 30 minutes, or until tender. Test the thighs for doneness.

Remove the chicken pieces to a serving dish. Stir the sauce and pour over the chicken to serve.

Serves 4.

✳ Barbecued Chicken with Hot and Sweet Barbecue Sauce

Barbecued chicken is a summertime favorite in the Heartland. It is most often grilled for outdoor parties and picnics, complete with the backyard chef's own barbecue sauce.

This version stuffs the chicken with lemon, onion, celery tops, and garlic to make it moist and extra flavorful. It is then grilled (or oven-roasted, if you prefer) and basted with home-made Hot and Sweet Barbecue Sauce. The barbecue sauce im-proves with age, so make it the day before.

HOT AND SWEET BARBECUE SAUCE

1 15-ounce can tomato sauce
2 tablespoons molasses
2 tablespoons brown sugar
6 garlic cloves, whole
1½ teaspoons ground cumin
1 teaspoon celery salt
¼ teaspoon salt
1 teaspoon pepper
¼ teaspoon cayenne pepper
2 tablespoons red wine vinegar

1 whole chicken
½ teaspoon salt
¼ teaspoon pepper
1 small lemon
1 small onion, whole
1 or 2 celery tops
2 garlic cloves, whole

Hot and Sweet Barbecue Sauce: Combine all the ingredients for the barbecue sauce, except the red wine vinegar, in a saucepan. Add more cayenne pepper for extra hot sauce. Simmer over low heat, partially covered, for 15 minutes, stirring occasionally. Stir in the red wine vinegar and continue simmering for an additional 15 minutes. Remove the sauce from heat and cool to room temperature. Pour the sauce into a covered container and refrigerate until ready to use.

When ready to cook, pour ⅓ cup of the sauce into a small bowl for basting the chicken. Remove the giblets from the chicken. Rinse and pat dry. Sprinkle the salt and pepper in the cavity. With a fork, puncture the lemon on all sides and place it inside the chicken, along with the onion, celery tops, and garlic cloves. Truss the chicken and hook the wing tips back behind the body joint, akimbo-style.

Grill the chicken in a covered grill over indirect heat

by dividing the bed of coals and banking them on each side of a drip pan. Place the chicken, breast-side up, on the grill directly over the drip pan. Cover and cook for 30 minutes, then baste with the Hot and Sweet Barbecue Sauce. Continue cooking for an additional 20 to 30 minutes, basting occasionally. When the chicken is done, the juices should run clear when pierced with a knife.

Remove the lemon, onion, celery tops, and garlic. Cut the chicken into quarters and serve with the remaining barbecue sauce.

Serves 4.

Variation: To oven-roast, preheat the oven to 450 degrees. Place the chicken on a rack, breast-side up, in a large baking dish or shallow roasting pan. Place in the oven, uncovered, and immediately reduce heat to 350 degrees. Roast for 30 minutes, then baste with the barbecue sauce. Continue cooking for an additional 20 to 30 minutes, basting occasionally, until done.

✳ Butter-Basted Grilled Chicken

Rhonda Kessler, Sawyer

In this recipe, chicken pieces are placed in a buttery marinade for several hours before grilling over hot coals. A rice pilaf, green beans, and fresh sliced tomatoes would complete the meal.

1 whole chicken

MARINADE
2 cups water
1 cup apple-cider vinegar
1 teaspoon Worcestershire sauce
1 cup butter
2 tablespoons sugar
2 tablespoons salt
½ teaspoon coarsely ground pepper
2 garlic cloves, minced

Cut the chicken into serving pieces. Rinse, pat dry with paper towels, and place in a large bowl.

Marinade: In a large saucepan, combine all the ingredients for the marinade and bring to a boil. Remove from heat and cool to room temperature.

Pour the marinade over the chicken pieces. Cover and refrigerate for at least 3 hours, or overnight.

Remove the chicken from the marinade and place directly over medium-hot coals on a covered grill. Turn the chicken occasionally and baste often with the marinade. Cook until tender and nicely browned, 45 minutes to 1 hour.

Serves 4.

✳ Chicken Breasts with Leeks and Sweet Red Pepper

In earlier times, chicken—pan-fried or roasted—was often saved for special occasions. Nowadays, skinned and boned chicken breasts make a frequent appearance on Midwestern tables. A versatile cut, they lend themselves to broiling, baking, pan-frying, and grilling. Skinned and boned chicken breasts, or

4 *chicken breast halves*
2 *leeks*
1 *medium sweet red pepper*
¼ *cup butter*
salt, to taste

Skin and bone each chicken breast. Place each breast between 2 sheets of waxed paper and gently pound to ¼-inch thickness. Wrap chicken breasts in plastic wrap and refrigerate until ready to use.

Peel away the outer leaves of the leeks. Cut off the green tops ½ inch above the white section. Cut in half crosswise. Cut each piece lengthwise into long slender strips. Place the leeks in a bowl and rinse well to remove

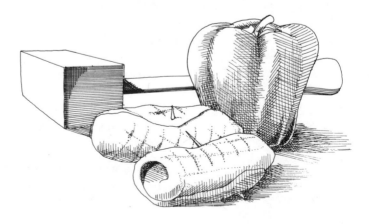

chicken fillets as they are sometimes called, cook quickly with little fuss and are excellent food for the dieter. They can be prepared in endless ways, as the following recipes show.

These rolled chicken breasts have a delicious filling of leeks and red pepper.

sand and dirt. Drain well. Slice the red pepper into thin strips, removing seeds and pith.

Melt the butter over low heat in a large frying pan. Add the leeks and red pepper and cover. Cook slowly over low heat until tender, about 15 minutes, stirring occasionally. Remove pan from heat and cool to room temperature.

Place some of the leek-and-red-pepper mixture, about 2 to 4 tablespoons per breast, on one end of each chicken breast. Salt each breast lightly and roll up, tucking in the sides. Secure with toothpicks.

Grill the chicken rolls directly over medium-hot coals, turning several times, for 10 to 15 minutes, until golden brown.

Serves 4.

✳ Smoked Chicken Salad with Curry Dressing

Prepare this delicious and attractive smoked chicken salad in the fall, when freshly picked apples and pecans are available.

4 chicken breast halves
2 tablespoons butter, melted
1 cup apple wood chips

CURRY DRESSING
½ cup mayonnaise
1 tablespoon sugar
½ teaspoon curry powder
4 teaspoons apple-cider vinegar
2 teaspoons whipping cream

1 pound fresh spinach
2 medium tart red apples
¼ cup pecans, coarsely chopped

Skin and bone the chicken breasts. Brush each chicken fillet with melted butter.

Place the apple wood chips on a piece of aluminum foil. Seal tightly to make a foil packet. Pierce the foil in several places to allow the smoke to escape. Place the foil packet directly on hot coals and replace the grid.

Grill the chicken fillets directly over the coals. Cover

and cook for 3 to 5 minutes each side, turning once and basting again with the melted butter. Remove the fillets from the grill and keep warm.

Curry Dressing: Place the mayonnaise in a small bowl. Add the sugar and curry powder and mix well with a wire whip. Add the vinegar and mix again. Add the cream and mix until smooth and creamy. Cover and chill until ready to use.

Wash the spinach, remove the stems, and drain well. Arrange the leaves on 4 dinner plates. Slice each chicken fillet into ⅜-inch slices and place each sliced breast on a bed of spinach, in the center of the plate. Core and slice the apples into ¼-inch wedges and arrange them to one side of the sliced chicken fillets. Drizzle about 2 tablespoons of the Curry Dressing over each chicken fillet. To garnish, sprinkle some chopped pecans on top of the sauce.

Serves 4.

✳ Country-Fried Chicken Breasts

The cook's secret of soaking meat in soda water adds a puffy lightness to the coating when this chicken fillet is fried.

4 chicken breast halves
1 teaspoon soda
1 cup water
½ cup all-purpose flour
½ teaspoon salt
1 teaspoon freshly ground pepper
½ teaspoon thyme
½ teaspoon celery salt
¼ cup vegetable oil

Skin and bone the chicken breasts and place them in a bowl. Combine the soda and water and pour over the chicken breasts. Let stand for 10 minutes.

In a shallow bowl, combine the flour, salt, pepper, thyme, and celery salt. Remove the chicken from the soda water and coat with the flour mixture.

Heat the oil in a large frying pan over medium-high

heat. Add the chicken breasts and fry for 3 to 5 minutes each side, or until golden brown.

Serves 4.

✳ Lemon Pepper Chicken with Artichoke Hearts

This contemporary recipe pairs sautéed chicken breasts with artichoke hearts, topped with a light lemon butter sauce.

4 chicken breast halves
2 teaspoons black peppercorns, coarsely crushed
salt, to taste
4 tablespoons butter, divided
1 13-ounce can artichoke hearts, drained and sliced
1 tablespoon lemon juice
1 tablespoon fresh parsley, chopped
3 tablespoons cold butter

Skin and bone the chicken breasts. Place each breast between 2 sheets of waxed paper and pound lightly with a kitchen mallet to ¼-inch thickness. Rub ½ teaspoon of pepper into both sides of each chicken breast. Sprinkle with salt.

Heat 2 tablespoons of the butter in a large frying pan over medium heat. Add the chicken breasts and cook, turning once, about 3 to 5 minutes each side. Remove the chicken from the pan and keep warm.

Add the remaining 2 tablespoons of the butter to the pan drippings. Add the sliced artichoke hearts and stir-fry over medium heat for 2 to 3 minutes. Remove them from the pan drippings and keep warm.

Add the lemon juice and fresh parsley to the drippings and stir over medium-high heat for about 15 seconds. Remove the pan from heat and immediately stir in the cold butter.

Arrange the chicken and artichokes on four plates. Pour the lemon butter sauce over and serve immediately.

Serves 4.

✳ Crème Fraîche Chicken

*Crème fraîche is
a staple in French
cookery and was
probably made by the
French who settled
in Kansas. All one
needed was a good
milk cow and the
ability to make
buttermilk.*

*Crème fraîche must
be made in advance, so
plan ahead. It may be
used in place of cream
or sour cream in soups
and sauces and as
a topping for fruits
or desserts. In this
recipe, it is used as a
marinade for chicken
breasts.*

CRÈME FRAÎCHE
1 cup whipping cream
1 tablespoon buttermilk or sour cream

3 garlic cloves, minced
¼ teaspoon celery salt
4 chicken breast halves
1¼ cups fresh bread crumbs
½ teaspoon tarragon
2 tablespoons Parmesan cheese, grated
3 tablespoons butter, melted

Crème Fraîche: In a small saucepan, heat the whipping cream to 90 to 100 degrees. Be careful not to overheat. Remove the pan from heat and stir in the buttermilk or sour cream. Pour the mixture into a container and cover. Let the mixture stand at room temperature (68 to 72 degrees) until it begins to thicken. This should take 12 to 16 hours.

When the Crème Fraîche begins to thicken, stir, then refrigerate for 24 hours before using. You may store it in the refrigerator for about 2 weeks.

Makes 1 cup.

Put ½ cup of Crème Fraîche in a shallow bowl. Stir in the garlic and celery salt. Skin and bone the chicken breasts and place them in the mixture, turning to coat. Cover and refrigerate for at least 8 hours, or overnight.

Mix the fresh bread crumbs, tarragon, and cheese in a shallow bowl. Remove the chicken breasts from the Crème Fraîche mixture and coat with the bread crumb mixture. Place the chicken in a lightly greased 9-inch baking dish and drizzle with the melted butter. Bake uncovered at 350 degrees for 25 to 30 minutes.

Place the chicken under the broiler for 1 to 2 minutes, until the tops are lightly browned.

Serves 4.

❋ Chicken and Morels in Brandy Cream

Morel mushrooms flourish in the state of Kansas in the spring-time. This highly prized fungus, with its delicate and nutty flavor, has earned an honored place in the world's finest kitchens.

The search for morels is a rite of spring in Kansas. Mushroom hunters comb the woods and creek beds early in the season to find the elu-sive morel. Its exact whereabouts continue to be a mystery even to the expert and a closely guarded secret by any-one who has discovered a patch.

This recipe pairs morels with chicken

2 tablespoons butter
8 ounces morel mushrooms,* sliced in half, or fresh button mushrooms, sliced
4 chicken breast halves
salt and pepper, to taste
2 tablespoons butter
¼ cup brandy
½ cup whipping cream

Melt 2 tablespoons of butter in a large frying pan over medium heat. Add the morels and cook until soft, 2 to 3 minutes. Remove them from the pan with a slotted spoon and keep warm.

Bone the chicken breasts, leaving the skins intact. Sprinkle lightly with salt and pepper. Add 2 tablespoons of butter to the frying pan and cook the chicken breasts over medium heat until golden, about 3 to 5 minutes on each side.

Remove the pan from heat. Pour the brandy over the chicken and immediately set aflame, shaking the pan until the flame dies. Remove the chicken from the pan juices and keep warm.

Return the pan to heat. Add the whipping cream and

*Never eat wild mushrooms you cannot positively identify.

*breasts, served in a
brandy cream sauce.*

boil rapidly over medium-high heat, stirring frequently, until the sauce turns a golden color and shiny bubbles form. Stir in the morels and heat throughout. Pour the sauce over the chicken and serve immediately.

Serves 4.

✳ Chicken Fillets with Tarragon Cream

*Chicken breast fil-
lets, sautéed in butter
and topped with a
tarragon-flavored
cream sauce, are quite
impressive but quick
to prepare. Serve them
with tender-crisp vege-
tables and a tossed
green salad.*

*4 chicken breast halves
salt, to taste
2 tablespoons butter
¼ cup dry white wine
½ teaspoon tarragon
½ cup whipping cream*

Skin and bone the chicken breasts and sprinkle with salt. Melt the butter in a large frying pan over medium heat. Add the chicken fillets and cook for 3 to 5 minutes each side. Remove the fillets from the pan and keep warm.

Add the wine and tarragon to the pan drippings and raise heat to medium-high. Boil until the liquid is reduced by about half. Add the cream and bring to a boil, stirring frequently, until it becomes thick and bubbly, 2 to 3 minutes. Pour the sauce over the chicken fillets and serve immediately.

Serves 4.

✳ Hunter's Chicken
(Pollo alla Cacciatora)

*Hunter's Chicken,
known to Italians as
Pollo alla Cacciatora,
is a favorite way to
prepare chicken in the
Italian communities*

*1 12-ounce can V8 juice
1 teaspoon beef bouillon
½ cup water
1 bay leaf
4 chicken breast halves
2 tablespoons butter*

of southeast Kansas. This simple version makes a quick rendition of hunter's-style chicken.

1 tablespoon olive oil
¼ *cup onion, finely chopped*
1 teaspoon tarragon
½ *cup dry vermouth*
freshly cooked pasta or rice

Put the V8 juice, bouillon, water, and bay leaf in a small saucepan and boil over medium heat until reduced by half, about 20 to 30 minutes.

In the meantime, skin and bone the chicken breasts. In a skillet over medium heat, melt the butter and olive oil. Add the onion and chicken breasts. Sauté quickly until the chicken is thoroughly cooked and moist but lightly browned, about 3 to 5 minutes on each side.

Remove the chicken and keep warm. Add the tarragon and vermouth to the pan. Stir until all the caramelized juices are liquid and then add the V8 mixture. Reduce heat to medium-low and boil the sauce gently for a few minutes, to reduce it slightly and combine the flavors.

Place the chicken breasts on the cooked pasta or rice. Pour the sauce over the chicken and serve.

Serves 4.

✳ Swiss Cheese Chicken Supreme

In this recipe, chicken breasts are baked in a vinegar and oil marinade and topped with fresh bread crumbs, Swiss cheese, and herbs.

4 *chicken breast halves*

MARINADE
3 tablespoons olive oil
1 tablespoon red wine vinegar
1 garlic clove, minced
2 green onions, chopped
⅛ *teaspoon salt*
⅛ *teaspoon pepper*

2 teaspoons Dijon mustard
2 cups fresh bread crumbs
½ *cup Swiss cheese, shredded*
½ *teaspoon marjoram*

½ teaspoon thyme
¼ cup butter, melted

Skin and bone the chicken breasts and place them in an 8- or 9-inch baking dish.

Marinade: Combine all the ingredients for the marinade in a small bowl. Mix well and pour over the chicken breasts. Let stand for 10 minutes, turning once.

Leaving the chicken in the marinade, spread ½ teaspoon of the Dijon mustard on the top of each chicken breast.

In a medium-sized bowl combine the bread crumbs, Swiss cheese, marjoram, and thyme. Cover the chicken breasts and marinade with the bread crumb mixture. Drizzle with melted butter.

Bake at 350 degrees for about 40 minutes, or until the chicken is tender and the topping is golden.

Serves 4.

✳ Blue Cheese Chicken Rolls

Chicken breast fillets, topped with a filling of blue cheese, cream cheese, and Parmesan cheese, are rolled up, dipped in cracker crumbs for a crispy coating, and baked until golden-brown. Serve with a green salad and a favorite vegetable.

4 chicken breast halves
1 ounce blue cheese, crumbled
3 ounces cream cheese
2 tablespoons Parmesan cheese, grated
1 tablespoon fresh parsley, finely chopped
¼ cup all-purpose flour
1 egg, beaten
1 cup club crackers, finely crushed
2 tablespoons butter, melted

Skin and bone the chicken breasts. Place each breast between 2 sheets of waxed paper and lightly pound to ¼-inch thickness. Set aside, or cover and refrigerate until ready to use.

In a small bowl, combine the cream cheese, blue cheese, and Parmesan cheese. Add the parsley and mix well. Spread about 1 tablespoon of the cheese mixture on each chicken breast. Starting at one end, roll up each breast, folding in the sides to seal tightly. Lightly coat each chicken roll with flour. Dip each roll in the beaten egg and roll in the crushed crackers.

Place the chicken rolls in a shallow baking dish. Drizzle with the melted butter. Bake at 400 degrees for 30 minutes, until lightly browned.

Serves 4.

✳ Lemon Pepper Chicken Fillets

Outdoor grilling can't get much easier than this! Just sprinkle chicken breast fillets with lemon pepper and grill with apple wood chips over medium-hot coals. This simple main course cooks in minutes and is a delight for dieters.

4 chicken breast halves
1 teaspoon lemon pepper
2 tablespoons butter, melted
1 cup apple wood chips (optional)

Skin and bone the chicken breasts. Rinse the chicken fillets and pat dry with paper towels. Rub ¼ teaspoon of lemon pepper into each fillet, about ⅛ teaspoon each side. Brush each one lightly with melted butter.

If desired, place the apple wood chips on a piece of aluminum foil. Seal tightly to make a foil packet. Pierce the foil in several places to allow the smoke to escape. Place the foil packet directly on the coals and replace the grid.

Cover and grill the chicken fillets directly over medium-hot coals for 3 to 5 minutes each side, turning once and basting again with the melted butter.

Serves 4.

Variation: Place the chicken fillets on a broiling rack. Set the rack inside a pan or on a baking sheet. Place the pan 4 to 6 inches under the broiler and cook as directed above.

✳ Chicken Bombay

In 1987, Frank represented Kansas in the National Chicken

MARINADE
¼ cup lemon juice
1 teaspoon salt

Cooking Contest, held in Jackson, Mississippi, and sponsored by the National Broiler Council.

His entry called for chicken breasts to be marinated, browned, then baked in yogurt with an exotic combination of spices.

6 chicken breast halves
½ cup all-purpose flour
2 tablespoons butter
2 tablespoons olive oil
1 onion, chopped
1 8-ounce carton plain yogurt
1 4-ounce can green chilies, drained and chopped
2 garlic cloves, minced
½ teaspoon cinnamon
½ teaspoon ginger
¼ teaspoon ground cloves
¼ teaspoon turmeric
¼ cup raisins
1 teaspoon orange peel, freshly grated
¼ cup sliced almonds
2 cups cooked white rice
fresh parsley sprigs
lemon slices

Marinade: In a small bowl, mix the lemon juice and the salt. Bone the chicken breasts, leaving the skins intact, and place them in a large shallow bowl. Pour the lemon mixture over the chicken and marinate at room temperature for 10 minutes, turning once.

Place the flour in a separate bowl. Drain the chicken breasts and dredge in the flour to coat on all sides, shaking off excess. Heat the butter and olive oil in a large frying pan over medium heat until the butter melts. Increase heat to medium-high and add the chicken. Brown quickly on both sides. Remove the chicken from the drippings and place in a 13 x 9–inch baking dish, skin side up, about 1 inch apart.

Add the chopped onion to the drippings and cook, stirring, for about 3 minutes. Remove the pan from heat and stir in the yogurt, green chilies, garlic, cinnamon, ginger, cloves, turmeric, raisins, and orange peel. Pour the yogurt mixture over the chicken breasts. Sprinkle with the almonds.

Bake, uncovered, at 375 degrees for 20 minutes. Cover and bake an additional 20 minutes, or until a fork can be inserted in the chicken with ease. Serve on a bed of white rice and garnish with parsley sprigs and lemon slices.

Serves 6.

✳ Chicken Pie

Chicken Pie is a classic in Midwestern cooking—a nourishing, everyday meal-in-one with simple flavors. In earlier times, a suet crust was used. This version calls for a basic pie crust and retains the traditional vegetables, but a sauce made of chicken broth and white wine makes it special enough for company.

2 chicken breast halves
1½ cups chicken broth
½ cup white wine
1 large carrot, sliced in half
1 stick celery, sliced in half
½ small onion
⅛ teaspoon thyme
¼ teaspoon salt
½ cup frozen peas
¼ cup butter
¼ cup all-purpose flour
2 cups reserved chicken broth
¼ cup cream (optional, for a richer sauce)
1 unbaked 9-inch double-crust pie shell

Place the chicken breasts in a large pot. Add the chicken broth, white wine, carrot, celery, onion, thyme, and salt. Bring to a boil, then reduce heat to low. Cover and simmer for about 20 to 30 minutes, or until the chicken is tender.

Remove the chicken from the pan to cool. Remove the

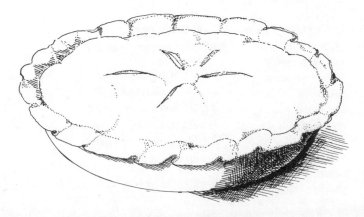

skin and bones and cut the meat into bite-size pieces.
Set aside. Strain the broth into a large measuring cup,
reserving the vegetables. There should be about 2 cups
of broth, but if not, add additional chicken broth or water
to make 2 full cups. Set aside. Dice the cooked carrot.
Finely chop 2 tablespoons each of the cooked celery
and onion and place the vegetables in a bowl. Place the
frozen peas in a strainer. Rinse with cold water just to
remove the frost. Drain well and add them to the bowl
of vegetables.

Melt the butter over low heat in a medium-sized saucepan. Add the flour and stir for about 1 minute. Add the
reserved chicken broth all at once and stir with a wire
whip until the mixture becomes thick and bubbly. Stir in
the whipping cream if desired, and heat just until bubbly.
Remove the pan from heat and stir in the chicken pieces
and vegetables. Cool slightly.

Pour the filling into an unbaked pie shell. Position the
top crust over the filling, cutting slits for the steam to
escape. Crimp and seal the edges.

Bake at 400 degrees for 45 to 55 minutes, or until the
crust is golden brown. Let the pie cool for 10 minutes
before cutting.

Serves 4 to 6.

✳ Chicken Rolls

Katherine Hahn Smith, Coffeyville

*During the late 1920s,
when nonlaying hens
sold for 6 cents a
pound, Katherine
Smith remembers
her mother making
these uniquely flavored
chicken rolls topped
with a chicken stock
sauce. Naturally, the
children enjoyed the*

1 whole chicken
salt and pepper, to taste

DOUGH
2 cups all-purpose flour
2 teaspoons baking powder
3/4 teaspoon salt
2 tablespoons shortening
3/4 cup cold milk

1/4 cup peanut butter

*unusual addition of
peanut butter.*

*2 cups chicken stock
¼ cup all-purpose flour*

Rinse the chicken, place it in a Dutch oven or large pot, and cover with water. Bring the chicken to a boil, reduce heat to low, and simmer until the meat is cooked and there is a nice stock, about 45 minutes. Remove the meat, discarding the skin and bones. Chop the chicken into small pieces and season with salt and pepper. Strain 2 cups of the stock and set aside to cool.

Dough: In a large mixing bowl, sift the flour, baking powder, and salt together. Cut in the shortening and stir in just enough cold milk to form the dough into a ball. On a lightly floured surface, work the dough gently and roll out to about ¼-inch thickness.

Spread the peanut butter on the dough and add the chopped chicken in an even layer. Roll up the dough in the style of a jelly roll and slice off rounds about 1 inch thick. Place the rolls on a greased baking sheet and bake at 375 degrees for about 12 minutes.

Meanwhile, put the cooled stock in a saucepan and whisk in ¼ cup of flour with a wire whip. Bring to a boil, reduce heat to low, and simmer for a few minutes to thicken and cook the flour. To serve, pour the sauce over the chicken rolls.

Serves 6.

✳ Homemade Chicken and Noodles

*Chicken and noodles
is a fine example of
comfort food in the
Heartland. It reminds
us of bygone days and
the dishes of our child-
hood. It was a dish
often prepared by our*

*2 chicken breast halves
4 chicken thighs
1 14-ounce can chicken broth
3 cups water
1 celery stalk with leaves
1 onion, sliced in half
2 medium carrots, peeled
1 sprig fresh parsley*

grandmothers and our great-grandmothers, since most of the ingredients were available on the farm, and because cooks of the past were well skilled in the art of noodle-making. With a little time and effort, you too can create some memories.

½ teaspoon salt
¼ teaspoon pepper

HOMEMADE NOODLES
1 cup all-purpose flour, sifted
1 egg, beaten
2 tablespoons milk
½ teaspoon salt

½ cup cold water
¼ cup all-purpose flour
salt and pepper, to taste

Place the chicken pieces in a large pot or Dutch oven. Add the remaining ingredients and bring the mixture to a boil over high heat. Reduce heat to low and simmer gently for 45 minutes, or until the chicken is tender.

Remove the chicken pieces from the pan and cool. Remove the meat, discarding the skin and bones. Cover and refrigerate the chicken pieces until ready to use.

Strain the broth into a clean pot and skim off the excess fat. Discard the parsley and all vegetables except the carrots. Chop the carrots into bite-size pieces and set aside.

Homemade Noodles: Sift the flour and set aside. In a large bowl, combine the egg, milk, and salt. Add as much of the flour as needed to make a stiff dough, stirring with a fork until it can be handled. Turn the dough onto a lightly floured surface and knead for 8 to 10 minutes, until smooth and elastic. Wrap the dough in plastic wrap and let rest for 20 minutes.

Divide the dough in half and roll out one portion to ¹⁄₁₆-inch thickness on a generously floured surface. Roll the dough up loosely and cut into slices about ½ inch wide. Unroll and separate the noodles. Repeat the procedure with the other portion of dough.

Return the chicken pieces and carrot to the chicken broth and bring to a boil over high heat. Add the noodles and continue boiling for about 5 minutes, or until the noodles are tender. Combine the water and flour in a small covered container. Shake to mix. Slowly stir in as much

of the mixture as needed to thicken the broth slightly.
Season with salt and pepper to taste. Boil for 1 minute
more and serve.

Serves 4 to 6.

✳ Deluxe Chicken and Rice Casserole

This recipe turns old-fashioned chicken and rice into something special by combining it with carrots, onion, and artichoke hearts. The addition of saffron adds a golden color to the casserole and gives off a mouth-watering aroma as it simmers.

1 whole chicken
1 cup all-purpose flour
1 teaspoon salt
¼ cup olive oil
3 carrots, peeled and sliced into 2-inch pieces
1 large onion, sliced into 8 wedges
1 celery stick with leaves, sliced in half
2¼ cups chicken broth
1 cup uncooked white rice
¼ teaspoon basil
⅛ teaspoon oregano
⅛ teaspoon saffron
1 13-ounce can artichoke hearts, drained and sliced in half

Cut the chicken into 8 serving pieces, rinse, and drain on
paper towels. Combine the flour and salt in a paper bag.
Place 2 or 3 chicken pieces at a time in the bag and shake
to coat.

Heat the olive oil in a large skillet over medium-high
heat. Add the chicken pieces and brown, turning once,
about 5 to 8 minutes on each side. Remove the chicken
pieces to a platter.

Place the carrots, onion, and celery in a large pot or
Dutch oven. Add the chicken broth, rice, basil, oregano,
and saffron, stirring to combine.

Arrange the chicken pieces on top of the vegetables
and rice. Bring the mixture to a boil over medium-high
heat. Reduce heat to low, cover, and simmer for 20 minutes. Add the sliced artichoke hearts, cover, and simmer
for 20 minutes more.

Serves 4.

✳ Chicken and Macaroni Casserole

Mrs. Robert G. Steele, Fort Scott

The only additions you'll need to this wholesome meal are garlic bread and a hearty appetite.

1 whole chicken
1 16-ounce package macaroni
1 10-ounce can cream of chicken soup, diluted with ½ can water
1 17-ounce can peas, drained
1 cup cheddar cheese, shredded

Boil the chicken in a large pot of water for 45 minutes, or until tender. Skin and bone the chicken, discarding all but the meat. Cut the meat into bite-size pieces. Cook the macaroni in a large pot of boiling water until tender. Drain and set aside.

In a large bowl, combine the cream of chicken soup, chicken, macaroni, peas, and cheese. Stir the mixture gently and pour into a 9-inch baking dish. Bake uncovered at 350 degrees for 40 minutes.

Serves 6.

✳ Eileen Ellenbecker's Roast Capon

Michael Ellenbecker, Lawrence

Michael Ellenbecker grew up on a farm near Marysville, where his family raised capons. He recalls that Thanksgiving dinner was always capon instead of turkey, and in his opinion, capon is the superior bird.

Michael sends the following recipe for

1 8-pound capon
salt and pepper, to taste
3 cups water

GRAVY
pan juices
6 tablespoons cornstarch
3 cups cold water
salt and pepper, to taste

Rinse the capon and pat dry with paper towels. Sprinkle the cavity with salt and pepper. Fasten the neck skin to

his mother's Roast Capon, in which she recommends using cornstarch instead of flour for thickening the gravy. Serve it with mashed potatoes, broccoli, and cranberry sauce.

the back with a skewer. Tie the legs securely to the tail. Hook the wing tips back behind the body joint, akimbo-style.

Place the capon on a rack in a roasting pan. Roast, uncovered, in an oven preheated to 400 degrees for 30 to 45 minutes, or until the bird is lightly browned. Remove from the oven and drain the fat. Add the water to the pan and cover tightly. Roast the bird for 2½ to 3 hours at 350 degrees. The capon is done if the juices run clear when the thigh is pierced with a knife and the drumstick meat feels very soft when pressed between fingers. Remove the capon from the pan and let stand for 15 minutes before carving.

Gravy: Place the pan juices in a saucepan and heat to simmering over medium heat. Combine the cornstarch and water, mixing well. Gradually pour the cornstarch and water mixture into the juices, stirring constantly, until the desired thickness is achieved. Season with salt and pepper to taste. Simmer the gravy gently for 5 minutes.

Serves 8 to 10.

✳ Creamed Capon on Corn Bread

Eileen Ellenbecker, Marysville

Eileen Ellenbecker has found a creative way to use leftover capon.

3 cups cooked capon
½ cup onion, chopped
½ cup celery, chopped
1 cup fresh button mushrooms, sliced
2 garlic cloves, minced
4 cups chicken broth or water
3 tablespoons cornstarch
1 cup water
¼ cup cream (optional)
salt and pepper, to taste
freshly baked corn bread, cut into 4 to 6 servings

Cut the leftover capon into bite-sized pieces and place in a 4-quart soup kettle. Add the onion, celery, mushrooms, and garlic. Add the chicken broth or water (or half chicken broth, half water). Bring to a boil, reduce heat to low, and simmer uncovered for 20 to 30 minutes, until the vegetables are tender.

Mix the cornstarch and water together in a small bowl. Add gradually to the simmering mixture, stirring constantly, until the desired thickness is achieved. Simmer for 3 to 5 minutes. If desired, add the cream and reheat to simmering. Season with salt and pepper to taste.

To serve, ladle the capon mixture over warm corn bread.

Serves 4 to 6.

✳ Grilled Capon

Steve Albright, McLouth

Steve Albright suggests a capon roasted on the grill as an alternative to the traditional oven-roasted turkey for the holidays. "Be sure to use high-quality, freshly cracked pepper when making this recipe," says Steve. "I'll guarantee, you'll love the results!"

3 heads unpeeled garlic, baked
1 7-to-9-pound capon
½ teaspoon salt
1 teaspoon pepper
1 whole lemon
juice of 1 lemon
¼ cup butter, softened
1 to 2 tablespoons pepper, coarsely ground

BASTE
1¼ cups butter
2 cups orange juice

SAUCE
pan juices
¼ cup dry white wine

To bake the garlic, wrap the garlic heads tightly in aluminum foil. Bake them at 375 degrees for 45 to 60 minutes, or until softened.

Rinse the capon thoroughly inside and out. Pat dry with paper towels. Sprinkle the salt and pepper in the cavity. Place 1 whole lemon, pricked several times with a fork, and the baked heads of garlic inside the cavity. Fasten the neck skin to the back with a skewer. Tie the legs securely to the tail. Hook the wing tips back behind the body joint, akimbo-style.

Squeeze the juice of 1 lemon over the bird to freshen. Rub the outside with the softened butter and sprinkle with coarsely ground pepper.

Baste: Melt the butter in a small pan over low heat and stir in the orange juice.

Grill the capon, breast-side up, over indirect heat in a covered grill with a large drip pan directly below the bird. (For indirect heat, divide the bed of hot coals, banking them on each side of the drip pan.)

Grill the capon for approximately 2 to 2 ½ hours, basting every 30 minutes. If necessary, after 1 hour, add more hot coals to the fire to maintain a constant temperature. During the last hour of cooking, baste with some of the accumulated pan drippings, if desired.

The capon is done if the juices run clear when the thigh is pierced with a knife and the drumstick meat feels very soft when pressed between fingers. Remove the lemon from the cavity and discard. Serve the garlic cloves as a spread for bread.

Sauce: Remove the drip pan from the grill. Skim the excess fat from the pan juices and pour the juices into a saucepan. Add the wine and boil over high heat until the mixture is reduced by half. Serve over the capon.

Serves 8 to 10.

✳ Traditional Roast Turkey

Roast turkey is America's favorite for Thanksgiving and other holiday meals. It traditionally graces the table with gravy and dressing and a variety

1 15-pound turkey (wild or domestic)
salt
6 to 8 cups prepared stuffing

GRAVY
pan juices
¼ cup all-purpose flour

of colorful vegetables. Roast turkey is versatile and economical and usually provides delicious leftovers for sandwiches, soups, salads, and casseroles.

Some people believe the wild turkey is superior in flavor to the domestic variety. Two types of wild turkey can be found in Kansas. The Eastern Turkey is found in the timber areas in the eastern part of the state, while the Rio Grande Turkey, a plains species, is found in central and western Kansas. The season is open statewide during spring and fall.

1 cup water
salt and pepper, to taste

Rinse the turkey and pat dry. Sprinkle the cavity lightly with salt. Pull back the neck skin and sprinkle with salt. Stuff the turkey with a stuffing of your choice. (Do not pack because the stuffing will expand.) Fasten the neck skin to the back with a skewer. Tie the legs securely to the tail. Bend the wing tips back behind the body joint, akimbo-style.

Place the turkey on a rack in a large roasting pan. Tent with foil and roast at 325 degrees for approximately 4 to 5 hours, or until a meat thermometer inserted in the thigh reads 185 degrees. For golden brown skin, remove the foil and baste the turkey with the pan juices during the last 30 minutes of cooking. Remove the turkey from the pan. Remove the dressing from the cavity and keep warm. Cover the turkey and let stand for 15 minutes before carving.

Gravy: Skim the excess fat from the pan juices and pour the juices into a saucepan. Heat to simmering over medium heat. Combine the flour and water in a small covered container. Shake vigorously to blend. Gradually pour the mixture into the simmering juices, stirring con-

stantly, until the desired thickness is achieved. Season with salt and pepper to taste.

Serves 12 or more.

✳ Turkey with Apple-Tarragon Baste

Here is a simple and no-fuss way to grill the economical turkey— a tasty alternative for the Thanksgiving feast as well as for outdoor parties. Grilled turkey cooks reasonably fast, creating crisp, beautiful brown skin, and retaining its succulent flavor.

1 8-to-10-pound turkey

APPLE-TARRAGON BASTE
¼ cup butter
5 tablespoons apple cider or apple juice
3 tablespoons applejack or brandy
1 tablespoon brown sugar
½ teaspoon tarragon

Rinse the turkey and pat dry with paper towels. Fasten the neck skin to the back with a skewer. Tie the legs securely to the tail. Hook the wings back behind the body joint, akimbo-style.

Apple-Tarragon Baste: Melt the butter in a small saucepan. Add the remaining ingredients and simmer over low heat for 5 minutes, stirring occasionally. Cool slightly and pour baste into a plastic spray bottle or bowl.

In a covered grill, bank hot coals on each side of a large metal drip pan or around heavy-duty aluminum foil. Lightly grease the grill. Place the turkey in the center of the grill, breast-side up, directly over the drip pan or foil. Cover the grill.

After the turkey has cooked for about 1 hour, spray or brush the turkey with the Apple-Tarragon Baste about every 20 minutes until done. If necessary, after 1 hour add more hot coals to the fire to maintain a constant temperature. Grill for 2 to 2½ hours, or until a meat thermometer inserted in the thigh registers 185 degrees. If the turkey begins to turn too brown, cover with a tent of aluminum foil.

Serves 8 to 10.

❊ Turkey Apple Sausage

*This recipe makes
a very lean and de-
licious sausage for
breakfast. Serve in the
morning to overnight
guests with waffles or
pancakes.*

1 pound ground turkey
3 tablespoons applesauce
1 teaspoon thyme
½ teaspoon ginger
¼ teaspoon nutmeg
½ teaspoon coarsely ground pepper
1 teaspoon salt
2 to 3 tablespoons butter

Combine all ingredients in a large bowl. Shape the sausage into a roll about 2½ inches in diameter. Cover with plastic wrap. Refrigerate and let the flavors blend for 6 hours, or overnight.

Cut the sausage into ½-inch rounds. Pat to about ¼-inch thickness. Heat the butter in a skillet over medium heat and fry the patties until golden brown.

Makes about 16 small patties.

❊ Baked Prairie Chicken with Corn Bread Dressing

*The prairie chicken
is a type of prairie
grouse that has found
in Kansas a suitable
habitat. The Greater
Prairie Chicken re-
sides in the Flint Hills
of east-central Kansas,
while the Lesser Prai-
rie Chicken keeps
to the high plains of
southwest Kansas.
    Prairie chickens
were once threatened
with dangerous decline
in numbers, due to a
change in their habitat*

2 prairie chickens
salt

CORN BREAD DRESSING
¼ cup butter
1 cup onion, finely chopped
¼ cup pecans, coarsely chopped
2 cups corn bread stuffing
1 teaspoon summer savory
¼ cup raisins
¼ to ½ cup chicken broth
salt and pepper, to taste

6 fresh bacon strips (unsmoked)

GRAVY
pan juices

from soil erosion and the Dust Bowl of the 1930s, as well as to the lack of regulations on hunting. However, prairie chickens now flourish in Kansas and can be hunted during the designated season —from November to January.

This recipe for prairie chicken is an updated version of an 1874 recipe from The Kansas Home Cookbook, *which contained contributions from the Ladies of Leavenworth (Leavenworth, 1874).*

1 tablespoon all-purpose flour
½ to ¾ cup half and half
salt and pepper, to taste

Rinse the prairie chickens in cold water, drain, and pat dry. Lightly salt the cavity of each bird.

Corn Bread Dressing: Heat the butter over low heat in a large pan or Dutch oven. Add the chopped onion and cook slowly, stirring often, until tender. Add the chopped pecans and stir for 2 minutes more. Remove the pan from heat and add the corn bread stuffing, summer savory, and raisins, mixing well. Stir in the chicken broth a little at a time until the dressing is moist but not sticky. Add salt and pepper to taste.

Stuff each chicken with half of the dressing. Hook the wing tips back behind the body joint, akimbo-style, truss, and tie the legs together. Wrap each chicken with 3 strips of fresh bacon, securing with toothpicks.

Place the chickens, breast-side up, on a rack in a shallow baking dish. Place them in an oven preheated to 450 degrees. Immediately reduce the temperature to 350 degrees and bake for 1 to 1½ hours, or until the juices run clear when the thigh is pierced with a knife. Baste twice with the accumulated drippings during baking.

When the chickens are done, remove the bacon and toothpicks and discard. Cut the strings and remove the dressing from the cavity of each chicken and keep warm.

Gravy: Skim the excess fat from the pan juices and pour the juices into a saucepan or skillet. Heat the juices over medium heat. Add the flour and stir for about 1 minute. Add the half and half slowly, stirring until the desired consistency is reached. Continue stirring until bubbly. Add salt and pepper to taste.

Slice the prairie chickens in halves or quarters. Serve with Corn Bread Dressing and Gravy.

Serves 4.

Variation: If prairie chickens are unavailable, 4 Cornish game hens may be substituted. Prepare as directed above, using only 2 bacon strips to wrap each hen.

✳ Fried Pheasant

Lanora L. Webb, Liberal

The pheasant-hunting season in Kansas begins in November and runs through January. Pheasants are highly prized by Kansas hunters, as well as by the thousands of out-of-state hunters who come here each year. Pheasants are mostly found in the south-central and western part of the state, around grain fields, marshes, and abandoned farm sites.

Lanora Webb prepares this recipe for her son and his hunting party. She writes, "They'll furnish the rest of the supper if Mom will fry the pheasant."

1 pheasant
1 quart of cold water
2 teaspoons salt
1 cup buttermilk
2 cups all-purpose flour
vegetable oil for frying
salt and pepper, to taste

Skin the pheasant and rinse well. Fill a large bowl with the cold water and stir in the salt. Place the pheasant in the salt water. Cover and refrigerate overnight.

Drain the pheasant and slice the breast into ¼-inch slices. Pour the buttermilk into a shallow bowl and place the flour in a separate bowl. Dip the pheasant slices in the buttermilk and dredge in the flour.

Pour the oil, about ½ inch deep, in a large skillet. Heat the oil over medium-high heat until hot enough to sizzle. Add some of the pheasant slices (do not crowd) and pan-fry, covered, until golden brown, about 2 to 3 minutes on each side. Drain on paper towels and add salt and pepper to taste.

Serves 4.

Option: To cook the legs and thighs, sprinkle them with meat tenderizer and set aside for several minutes. Follow the directions above, frying until tender and golden brown.

✳ Hunter's Pheasant with Red Wine Sauce

Jay Pruiett, Lawrence

Jay Pruiett recalls, "When I began hunting pheasants nearly

1 young pheasant
2 or 3 small onions, peeled
1 large carrot, cut into chunks

25 years ago, I soon discovered that those who would eat wild pheasant face two significant obstacles. The first involves actually shooting a pheasant, as opposed to hunting them; the second is finding a recipe which does not somehow involve cream of mushroom soup. As to the first, I can only suggest that very little choke, a load of good 7-½s, and taking only very close shots might be helpful. The following recipe should make dining upon wild pheasant something to be anticipated, rather than the price one must pay for having shot the damned bird in the first place."

Jay suggests selecting a young pheasant, the fatter the better, and preferably one that has not been "shot up with a load of 6s, or worse, 4s." A young pheasant may be identified by leg spurs which are easily bent and rounded rather than pointed.

3 to 4 whole garlic cloves, peeled
12 juniper berries*
6 strips bacon or salt pork

RED WINE SAUCE
¼ cup dry red wine
1 medium onion, finely chopped
1 small bay leaf
¼ teaspoon thyme
5 whole black peppercorns
1 tablespoon butter
½ teaspoon all-purpose flour
reserved juices
salt and pepper, to taste

Stuff the pheasant with the onions, carrot, and garlic cloves. Cut small slits under the skin, particularly in the breast area, and insert the juniper berries. Wrap the strips of bacon or salt pork around the bird, securing them with toothpicks.

Place the bird on a rack in a preheated shallow baking pan. Roast, uncovered, at 450 degrees for 15 minutes on each side and for 15 minutes more, breast-side up. The pheasant is done when the legs rotate easily in their sockets and when the juices run clear when the meat is pierced with a knife.

Allow the bird to cool slightly and slice the meat from the carcass. Reserve the pan juices for the wine sauce.

Red Wine Sauce: Pour the wine into a saucepan. Add the onion, bay leaf, thyme, and peppercorns. Simmer over low heat until the liquid reduces by half. Combine the butter and flour and stir into the wine mixture. Strain the sauce through a fine sieve. Stir in reserved juices and add salt and pepper to taste. Serve the sauce over the sliced pheasant.

Serves 4.

*Juniper berries are from the juniper, an evergreen shrub. They are often used in game recipes and can be purchased at gourmet and health food stores.

✳ Smothered Quail

Marna Lovgren, Oswego

Quail are native to Kansas, and the state has two species. The Bobwhite is found throughout the state but most abundantly in the eastern part, and the Scaled Quail (also known as blue quail) lives in the arid, sandy, grassland regions of extreme southwest Kansas. Quail are usually found in areas where food, shelter, and nesting-cover occur in close proximity, preferably near a mixture of grassland, cropland, and woodland areas.

This highly sought-after game bird is considered a delicacy by those who hunt. The season in Kansas, which is considered one of the best quail-hunting states in the nation, begins in early fall.

8 quail breasts
½ cup butter
1 small onion, thinly sliced
½ cup apple-cider vinegar or dry white wine
2 teaspoons fresh parsley, finely chopped
1 tablespoon sugar
½ teaspoon salt
⅛ teaspoon pepper

Rinse the quail breasts and pat dry with paper towels. Melt the butter in a large frying pan over medium-high heat. Add the quail breasts and brown quickly, about 2 to 3 minutes on each side. (Reduce the heat to medium if the butter begins to burn.) Remove the breasts from the pan and set aside. Add the thinly sliced onion to the pan drippings and reduce heat to low. Cook slowly, turning often, until tender, 5 to 10 minutes.

Return the quail breasts to the pan. Add the vinegar or white wine, parsley, sugar, salt, and pepper. Stir gently and bring the mixture to a boil. Cover tightly, reduce heat to low, and simmer for 10 to 20 minutes, or until the breasts are tender.

To serve, place the quail breasts on a platter and top with the onion and pan juices.

Serves 4.

✳ Braised Wild Duck

Aletha Hensleigh, Winchester

Kansas has always been a nomadic cross-way and no less so for ducks and geese. The sky has literally been blackened with flocks of these birds during their winter migration.

This recipe braises wild duck in red wine and herbs, creating deliciously moist meat.

4 wild ducks, giblets and necks included
1½ cups water
1 teaspoon ground cloves
1 teaspoon salt
1 teaspoon pepper
8 shallots, peeled
4 tablespoons butter
4 tablespoons butter, softened
½ cup dry red wine
⅓ cup vinegar
2 teaspoons lemon peel, grated
½ teaspoon honey or brown sugar
1 bay leaf
1 teaspoon chervil
2 teaspoons parsley
½ teaspoon tarragon or rosemary
½ teaspoon cornstarch
1 tablespoon water
½ cup croutons

Place the duck giblets and necks in a large pan. Add the water and simmer over low heat until tender. Remove from heat and cool.

Combine the ground cloves, salt, and pepper and rub the inside of each duck with some of the mixture. Place a set of giblets, 2 peeled shallots, and 1 tablespoon of butter in the cavity of each bird. Truss the birds. Cover the breast of each bird with 1 tablespoon softened butter. Place the birds snugly in a casserole.

In a small bowl, combine the wine, vinegar, grated lemon peel, and honey or brown sugar. Pour the mixture over the birds. Using a small piece of cheesecloth, make a bouquet of the bay leaf, chervil, parsley, and tarragon or rosemary. Tie the cheesecloth securely with string and place it in the casserole.

Roast the casserole uncovered at 500 degrees for 15 minutes. Lower heat to 300 degrees, cover, and braise for an additional 25 minutes, or until the birds are tender. Baste the birds occasionally with the pan juices.

Remove the ducks from the casserole, cut the strings, and discard the stuffing. Skim the fat from the pan juices and place the juices in a saucepan. Simmer the juices over low heat. Combine the cornstarch and water and pour the mixture into the juices, stirring until the sauce begins to thicken. Boil the sauce gently for 1 minute. Pour the sauce over the ducks and garnish with croutons.
Serves 4 to 6.

✳ Grilled Breast of Dove with Grapes

Jay Pruiett, Lawrence

There are estimates that the average hunter will connect with a dove once in about every four shots, according to Jay Pruiett. "I have a little trouble with this estimate," says Jay, "particularly when I recall the day I shot over four boxes of number 8s without hitting a single dove. The point of all this is that I have never had to trouble myself overmuch about how to cook the miserable few doves I manage to bag each September. What I have found is one excellent recipe for eight doves, which will serve quite nicely as an appetizer for an elegant

8 dove breasts, skinned

MARINADE
2 cups dry red wine
½ cup olive oil
2 garlic cloves, minced
4 green onions, chopped

2 cups commercial grapevines, for smoking
2 bacon strips
whole wheat bread, sliced ¾-inch thick and toasted
1 bunch seedless white grapes

Place the skinned dove breasts in a large shallow dish.

Marinade: Combine the ingredients for the marinade, mixing well. Pour over the dove breasts. Cover and refrigerate overnight, turning at least once.

About 1 hour prior to serving, start a bed of coals that just covers the bottom of the grill, spacing the coals about 1 inch apart. Put the grape vines in a container, cover them with water, and set aside.

Remove the dove breasts from the marinade and drain briefly. Slice the bacon strips in half. Wrap each dove with a half strip and secure with toothpicks.

game feast for four, or as a romantic light dinner for two, served along with wild rice and some fresh fruit."

When the coals are ready, drain the grapevines and toss them on the hot coals. Replace the grid and immediately place the dove breasts, bone side down, on the grid. Cover and grill for 12 minutes. Turn the breasts over and grill for an additional 6 minutes. Remove the breasts and discard the bacon and toothpicks.

Serve the dove breasts on toasted whole wheat bread and garnish with white grapes.

Makes 4 appetizers or 2 main courses.

✳ Perfect Deer Steaks

Barney Pontious, Parsons

Deer are plentiful in Kansas and two types of Whitetail and the Rocky Mountain Mule Deer reside here. This recipe marinates deer steaks overnight and pan-fries them, as you would beef steaks.

4 deer steaks, or 8 deer loin chops
1 egg, beaten
1 12-ounce can evaporated milk
1½ cups all-purpose flour
1 teaspoon salt
½ teaspoon pepper
¼ cup vegetable oil or shortening

Rinse the deer steaks in salted water, drain, and trim off any excess fat. Place them in a large baking dish. In a small bowl, combine the beaten egg and the evaporated milk. Pour over the steaks, cover, and refrigerate overnight.

Combine the flour, salt, and pepper in a shallow bowl. Remove the steaks from the milk mixture and dredge in the seasoned flour.

Heat the oil or shortening over medium heat. Add the steaks and fry for 3 to 5 minutes each side, or until desired doneness is achieved.

Serves 4.

Please Pass the Prairie Dog

David Hann of Lawrence contributed this story from his great-grandfather's memoir, "Incidents in My Life." The event occurred after his great-grandparents, John and Ella Fuller, settled near Millbrook in Graham County in 1882. (Millbrook was destroyed by a tornado in 1887 and never rebuilt.)

John Fuller wrote, "One of my neighbors was helping me dig a well. We went out one day and shot four prairie dogs. I dressed them, kept two for myself and gave the other two to my neighbor. When I took them home I told my wife they were rabbits. She said they didn't look like the rabbits in Illinois and I told her they were just fatter. She cooked the prairie dogs for dinner the next day. My neighbor was still helping with the well and was with us for that meal. We each took a piece of the meat and my bite kept getting bigger and bigger until I couldn't swallow it. I was sitting close to a window which was open and that bite went out the window. As the meal neared an end, I forgot myself and told my neighbor to pass me the prairie dog. My wife reared back and said, 'I knew those weren't rabbits!' She would never cook anything in that kettle again."

Ella evened the score one April Fool's Day by mixing cotton into John's biscuits.

✳ Barbecued Rabbit

Susie Bermudez, Lawrence

The abundant cotton-tail rabbit makes for good hunting throughout the state, and its meat may be substituted in many chicken recipes.

In this recipe, the

1 rabbit
1½ cups all-purpose flour
1 teaspoon salt
¼ cup vegetable oil
1 8-ounce can tomato sauce
⅓ cup brown sugar
1 teaspoon chili powder
1 to 3 teaspoons liquid smoke, to taste

rabbit is floured, browned, then baked with a barbecue sauce. Serve it with fried potatoes and corn-on-the-cob.

Cut the rabbit into serving pieces, rinse, and drain. In a shallow bowl, combine the flour and salt. Dredge the rabbit pieces in the flour mixture, shaking off excess.

Heat the vegetable oil in a large skillet over medium-high heat. Add the rabbit pieces and brown quickly, turning once. Place the pieces in a large baking dish.

In a small bowl, combine the tomato sauce, brown sugar, chili powder, and liquid smoke to taste. Pour over the rabbit and bake uncovered at 350 degrees for about 1 hour, or until tender.

Serves 4.

✳ Bar-B-Q Beaver

Barney Pontious, Parsons

Barney Pontious traps beaver around creek beds and rivers in Kansas during the winter hunting season. He says the meat tastes very much like beef and is delicious served with barbecue sauce on buns.

1 beaver, 30 to 60 pounds, dressed
2 bay leaves
salt and pepper, to taste
barbecue sauce, to taste
hamburger buns

Remove all fat from the beaver and discard. Cut the meat into several large chunks and place in a large pot or Dutch oven. Add the bay leaves and cover with water. Bring to a boil over high heat. Reduce heat to low and simmer for 2 to 3 hours, or until the meat is tender.

Remove the meat from the pot and cool. Remove the bones and cut the meat into bite-size pieces.

Place the meat in a large pan and add salt, pepper, and barbecue sauce to taste. Reheat over low heat for 5 minutes.

Serve the beaver on hamburger buns.

Serves a large crowd.

✳ FISH

I n earlier days, fish was an available source of food to both the Indians and the pioneers who lived near the Kansas rivers and streams. Kansas fish—such as catfish, crappie, and several species of bass—are still abundant in lakes and rivers across the state and are much sought after by avid fishermen during the summer months. For less active fish-lovers who prefer not to cast a hook into the water, farm-raised catfish is now a growing consumer industry in Kansas.

Unlikely as it seems for a land-locked state, seafood specialties have long been available to Kansans. Once the railroads were built, seafood, along with other first-rate continental cuisine, was transported across the state on rails. "Meals by Fred Harvey" became a prime drawing card for the Santa Fe Railroad passenger traffic. The seventy-five cent dinner menu on westbound trains in 1888 featured such delicacies as Blue Points on Shell, Filets of Whitefish, and Lobster Salad au Mayonnaise.

Salted cod, fresh or canned salmon, and smoked and fresh oysters also graced the late nineteenth-century Midwestern tables—specialties that were apt to be considered holiday food. Their availability was a blessing to Easterners and homesick immigrants who longed for a taste of the sea.

Today, all varieties of fresh seafood and fish are shipped to specialty shops and supermarkets on a regular basis, and Kansans enjoy these delights of the sea as part of

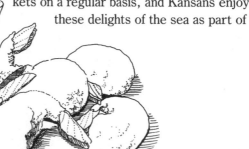

their regular diet. A number of recipes in this chapter feature Kansas's native catfish, including the prize-winning recipe for Catfish Grilled in Corn Husks. There are ideas for two other Kansas fish as well, in the recipes for Broiled Bass with Tarragon Butter and Crispy Baked Crappie Fillets. Imported shellfish are rendered with Heartland overtones, as in the recipe for shrimp fried in a whole wheat or cornmeal beer-batter.

✳ Grilled Lemon Catfish

Catfish, native to Kansas, can be caught in lakes, rivers, and ponds throughout the state. The pioneers undoubtedly took up fishing as another food source and as a way to vary their diets. Catfish would have been a reliable and plentiful catch. Today, farm-raised catfish, sweet and finely textured, is a growing Kansas industry.

The following recipes for catfish provide a number of mouth-watering ways to prepare this Kansas fish.

4 catfish fillets, about 2 pounds

LEMON MARINADE
¼ cup olive oil
2 tablespoons lemon juice
¼ teaspoon dill
⅛ teaspoon salt
¼ teaspoon pepper, coarsely ground

Wash the catfish fillets and pat dry with paper towels. Place them in a large, shallow dish.

Lemon Marinade: In a small bowl, combine all the ingredients for the marinade, mixing well. Pour the marinade over the catfish fillets. Cover and refrigerate for about 30 minutes, turning once.

Remove the catfish fillets from the marinade and place on the grill, directly over medium-hot coals. Cook, uncovered, for 5 to 8 minutes on each side. Baste lightly with the remaining marinade before turning over. Cook until the fish flakes easily with a fork.

Serves 4.

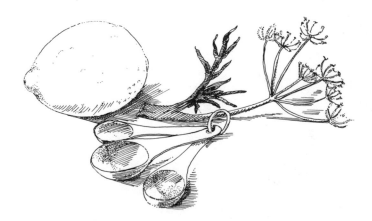

✳ Neosho River Catfish

Nadine Herridge, Oswego

Chetopa, Kansas, is known for the very large catfish caught in the area and has been dubbed the "Catfish Capital." Nadine Herridge's husband likes to fish there, just ten miles south of their home in Oswego. Nadine deep-fries the catfish, whole or fillets, in her special batter and serves them piping hot.

4 pan-size catfish fillets, or 4 whole catfish, dressed
½ cup pancake mix
1 egg
1 cup pancake mix
1 12-ounce can 7-Up
vegetable oil or shortening, for deep-fat frying

Place ½ cup pancake mix in a shallow bowl. Dip the catfish fillets or whole catfish in the pancake mix and place on a baking sheet to dry for 20 minutes.

In a mixing bowl, beat the egg slightly. Add 1 cup of pancake mix and the 7-Up, stirring to combine.

In a large pan or Dutch oven, heat the oil or shortening to about 350 degrees. Dip the fish into the batter and carefully lower into the hot oil. Deep fry until the fish is golden brown and flakes easily with a fork. Drain and serve immediately.

Serves 4.

✳ Catfish Grilled in Corn Husks

John Bowden, Lawrence

Independence Days, a Fourth of July celebration, is held annually in Lawrence. In July 1988, the First Annual River City Catfish Cook-Off became part of the festivities. John Bowden took first prize with this unique recipe that grills the catfish in fresh corn husks. The fresh corn makes a perfect accompaniment. A wide

4 pan-size catfish
salt and pepper, to taste
4 fresh corn husks
1 pound tomatillos, husks removed
8 large whole garlic cloves, unpeeled
2 sweet red peppers
2 yellow banana peppers
2 green chili peppers

Skin and behead the catfish. Wash them and pat dry. Sprinkle each fish with salt and pepper to taste. Cover and refrigerate until ready to use.

To prepare the corn husks, peel off the outer husks from the corn and discard. Carefully peel off the inner

variety of peppers and
southwestern vege-
tables like the tomatillo
is available in most
Kansas supermarkets.

husks, keeping them in one piece, and remove the silks. Rinse well. In a large pot of boiling water, blanch the husks for 30 seconds. Remove them from boiling water and immediately plunge them into a pan of ice water. Leave the husks in the water, or seal them in a plastic bag with some water. Refrigerate until ready to use.

Roast the tomatillos and peppers on a grill over hot coals, turning frequently, until the skins begin to wrinkle and blacken. Enclose them in a paper bag for 15 minutes or more to steam them for easier peeling. Wrap the garlic in foil and roast on hot coals until soft, about 10 minutes.

Remove the skins from the tomatillos and puree them in a blender or a food processor. Pour the pureed tomatillos into a wide bowl. Peel the peppers, removing the pith and the seeds. Rinse the peppers with cold water and slice them into 1-inch strips. Peel the whole garlic cloves and set aside.

Place the fish in the bowl of pureed tomatillos and coat well with the mixture. Put 2 cloves of garlic and a few pepper strips inside each fish. Place each fish on a corn husk and arrange a few more strips of the peppers on top. Wrap the husks around each fish and secure with thin strips of extra husks or string.

Grill them directly over hot coals for about 40 minutes, 20 minutes each side. The fish is done if it flakes easily with a fork.

Serves 4.

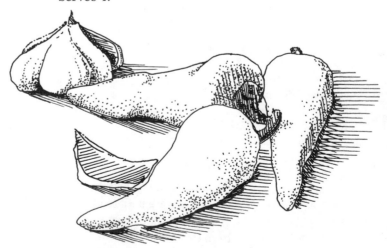

✳ Catfish with Orange and Lemon Slices

Bob Schaffer, Lawrence

This recipe won second place at the River City Catfish Cook-Off and its completely different flavoring shows the versatility of this fish. The catfish is stuffed with colorful orange and lemon slices and topped with a spicy seasoning.

4 whole catfish, skin and heads removed
salt and pepper, to taste
8 thin slices of lemon
8 thin slices of orange
Cavendar's Greek seasoning, to taste

Sprinkle salt and pepper inside each catfish. Arrange the orange and lemon slices inside the fish. Place the fish on the grill over medium-hot coals and sprinkle generously with the Greek seasoning.

Grill over hot coals for a total of 40 minutes, 20 minutes each side, adding more seasoning after turning.
Serves 4.

✳ Catfish Kabobs

Bill Simon, Eudora

Bill Simon, an outdoor cooking enthusiast, has a hobby of entering cooking contests. His recipe for marinated catfish, skewered with fresh vegetables, makes a colorful and tasty kabob.

2 pounds catfish fillets

MARINADE
¼ cup olive oil
¼ cup lemon juice
¼ cup fresh pineapple juice
2 tablespoons soy sauce
1 teaspoon fresh parsley, chopped
1 teaspoon salt
1 teaspoon pepper

8 large mushroom caps
2 lemons, sliced into ¼-inch rounds
2 large green peppers, seeded and cut into 1-inch pieces
3 small onions, sliced in half
8 cherry tomatoes, whole

Rinse the catfish fillets and drain well. Cut the fish in 1- to 2-inch squares and set aside while preparing the marinade.

Marinade: Combine all the ingredients for the marinade in a large bowl, mixing well.

Place the catfish squares in the marinade. Cover and let marinate at room temperature for 1 hour, turning occasionally. Drain the fish, reserving the marinade.

Place the mushroom caps in a large bowl. Boil water and pour over the mushrooms. Let stand for 1 minute. Drain well.

On 6 skewers, alternate the fish with the mushroom caps, lemon slices, green pepper, onion halves, and cherry tomatoes.

Grill the kabobs over medium coals for 8 to 10 minutes, turning and basting frequently with the marinade.

Serves 6.

✳ Catfish with Horseradish Sauce

Patty Boyer, Lawrence

*This unique recipe
seals in the moistness
of the fish by creating
a delicate blanket of
meringue that avoids
the heaviness of most
batters.*

*4 catfish fillets
2 teaspoons lemon pepper
2 egg whites
2 tablespoons sour cream
2 green onions, chopped
2 garlic cloves, minced
¼ teaspoon basil*

HORSERADISH SAUCE
*2 tablespoons butter
2 tablespoons all-purpose flour
1 cup milk
3 to 4 tablespoons prepared horseradish, to taste
½ teaspoon paprika*

Sprinkle each catfish fillet with ½ teaspoon of lemon pepper. Place the fillets on a lightly greased baking sheet.

In a mixing bowl, beat the egg whites until stiff peaks form. Fold in the sour cream, green onion, garlic, and basil. Spoon some of the mixture on top, completely covering each fillet.

Bake the fillets uncovered at 375 degrees for 20 to 25 minutes, until the topping is browned and the fillets flake easily with a knife.

Horseradish Sauce: In a saucepan, melt the butter over low heat. Stir in the flour until smooth and bubbly. Stir in the milk and horseradish and stir constantly over medium heat until thick and bubbly. Stir in the paprika and serve over the catfish fillets.

Serves 4.

Meals by Fred Harvey

Fred Harvey, one of America's most prominent restaurateurs, was an Englishman who eventually settled in Leavenworth, Kansas. When he first arrived in this

country in 1850 at the age of fifteen, he worked in restaurants in New York and New Orleans and then became
one of the first mail clerks on the railroad. Before he had
opened his first Harvey House, he had already achieved
success as a general agent for the Northern Missouri
Railroad, as an advertising salesman for the *Leavenworth
Times*, as a cattle rancher, and as an investor in the Ellsworth Hotel (a few years before that boom town boasted
the largest cattle yards in the state in 1872).

In his frequent travels as an agent for the railroad,
Harvey—an enterprising man and a lover of fine dining—
must have been disgusted by the crude meals and hurried
pace at the railroad's watering stops. It was through his
vision that fine dining came to the Wild West.

In 1876, Harvey made contractual agreements with the
Atchison, Topeka, and Santa Fe Railroad to establish restaurants along the route that would allow passengers to
dine in high style. The first restaurant opened that year
in Topeka. Harvey Houses were a far cry from the dismal
outposts of the competition. The standards for service
and food preparation were very strict. In 1881 at Raton,
New Mexico, one of Harvey's surprise visits resulted in
the firing of the entire all-male staff. The new manager
replaced the waiters with attractive young girls, and a
new dimension to western dining—feminine charm—was
added to the restaurants. During the day, the waitresses
wore black poplin dresses with white caps and aprons,
changing to all-white attire in the evening. With the combination of fine food and pleasant service, "Meals by Fred
Harvey" became a primary drawing card for passengers
traveling throughout the West.

"As a student at the University of Kansas in the 1920s,
my sisters and I signed on to work as waitresses in the
Harvey House at Ashland, Arizona," says Mrs. Alice P.
Morgan of Lawrence. "The Japanese janitor would watch
for the train. Once we knew it was coming, we had about
20 minutes to prepare the tables for the passengers. The
diners could choose from the menu for about $2.25 a
plate or order a la carte from the lunch counter."

Harvey Houses served not only rail passengers, for
the local residents often considered them the finest res-

taurant in town. Fresh and sometimes exotic items, like lobster and wild game, were found on Harvey menus. Since Harvey's contracts with the railroads included free shipment of supplies, he enjoyed an enormous advantage over his competition. One of the first restaurant chains, Harvey Houses continued as reliable dining places for automobile travelers well into the 1950s.

✳ Crappie Meunière

Crappie is a native Kansas fish that thrives in many lakes across the state and is plentiful during the summer months. With a live minnow and some patience, even the novice can land this culinary treat—and a simple recipe will turn this deliciously mild fish into an elegant meal.

1 to 1½ pounds crappie fillets or other lean white fish fillets
1 cup all-purpose flour
1 teaspoon salt
¼ cup butter
2 tablespoons lemon juice
¼ cup butter
2 tablespoons fresh parsley, chopped

Rinse the crappie fillets and drain. Combine the flour and salt in a shallow bowl. Roll the fillets in the flour mixture and shake off excess.

Melt ¼ cup of butter in a large frying pan over medium heat. Add about half the fillets to the pan. Cook the fillets for 3 to 5 minutes on each side, or until they flake easily with a fork. Remove them from the pan and keep warm. Add the remaining fillets and more butter if necessary and cook as directed.

Add the lemon juice to the pan drippings and cook, stirring for 1 minute. Add ¼ cup of butter, reduce heat

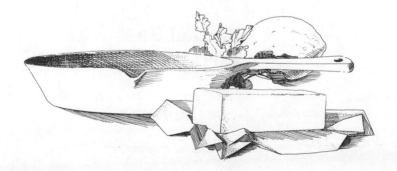

to medium-low, and slowly brown the butter. Pour the butter sauce over the crappie fillets and sprinkle with fresh chopped parsley.

Serves 4.

✳ Crispy Baked Crappie Fillets

Grace B. Anderson, Lawrence

"What could be better than Kansas crappie!" exclaims Grace Anderson. Grace says her husband fishes for crappie at Clinton Lake, just outside of Lawrence. They like to share his catch with their family and friends, and this recipe is Grace's favorite way to prepare the fillets.

¼ cup butter or margarine, melted
¼ teaspoon paprika
¼ teaspoon lemon pepper
½ cup saltine or club-style crackers
½ cup potato chips
1 pound crappie fillets or other lean white fish fillets

Melt the butter and pour into a shallow bowl. Add the paprika and lemon pepper. Crush the crackers and the potato chips. Mix them together in a small bowl and pour the crumbs onto a plate or waxed paper. Dip the fish fillets in the butter mixture and coat with the crumbs. Place the fillets in a single layer in a shallow baking pan.

Bake at 350 degrees for 8 minutes for small fillets, 10 minutes for large ones. Turn the oven to broil and cook the fish for 5 to 7 minutes, or until nicely browned.

Serves 4.

Option: Drizzle the remaining butter mixture over the fillets just before broiling.

✳ Broiled Bass with Tarragon Butter

Bass is native to Kansas and a popular game fish throughout the state. The lean

1½ pounds white bass fillets or other lean white fish fillets
salt and pepper, to taste
½ cup dried bread crumbs, finely crushed
lemon slices, ⅛-inch thick

white fish has a firm texture and is a good choice for oven broiling. Prepare a green salad and a vegetable to accompany this light summer entree.

¼ cup butter, softened
¼ teaspoon tarragon

Place a large piece of aluminum foil on a cookie sheet. Turn up the edges slightly to catch the juices. Salt and pepper the fillets and place them on the cookie sheet.

Sprinkle each fillet with about 1 tablespoon of the bread crumbs. Place 1 lemon slice in the center of each fillet.

In a small bowl, combine the butter and tarragon. Dot each fillet with 1 to 2 teaspoons of the tarragon butter.

Preheat the oven broiler. Place the fish 4 to 6 inches from the heat. Broil for 5 to 10 minutes, or until the fish is golden brown and flakes easily with a fork. If the fillets begin to brown too quickly, lower the rack several inches and continue broiling.

Serves 4.

✳ Beer-Batter Shrimp with Spicy Shrimp Sauce

Because we are quite a distance from the beach, fried shrimp has always been a special treat to Midwesterners. This recipe gives a choice of two beer batters, featuring two of Kansas's finest products—wheat and corn—and a spicy shrimp sauce for dipping.

2 pounds large shrimp (10 count per pound)

SPICY SHRIMP SAUCE
1 cup catsup
2 tablespoons horseradish
1 teaspoon lemon juice
dash of Worcestershire sauce
dash of hot pepper sauce

WHOLE WHEAT BEER-BATTER
¼ cup whole wheat flour
¾ cup unbleached white flour
1½ teaspoons baking powder
½ teaspoon salt
¼ teaspoon onion powder
¼ teaspoon garlic powder
¼ teaspoon paprika
1 egg, beaten
¾ cup flat beer

CORNMEAL BEER-BATTER
¾ cup cornmeal
¾ cup unbleached white flour
2 teaspoons baking powder
1 teaspoon salt
½ teaspoon onion powder
½ teaspoon garlic powder
¼ teaspoon paprika
1 egg, beaten
¾ cup flat beer

vegetable oil or shortening for deep-fat frying

Shell and devein the shrimp. For an attractive appearance, leave the tails intact and cut part way through the center of each shrimp to butterfly. Rinse well and drain. Cover and refrigerate until ready to use.

Spicy Shrimp Sauce: In a small bowl, combine all the ingredients for the sauce. Cover and refrigerate until ready to use.

Beer-Batter (of your choice): In a large bowl, combine all

the dry ingredients, mixing well. Add the beaten egg and the beer and beat with a wire whip just until smooth.

Heat the oil in a medium-sized, heavy-bottomed pan over high heat, until hot enough to sizzle.

Dip the shrimp in the batter and gently lower into the hot oil. Fry 2 or 3 at a time. Turn each shrimp once and cook until the coating is golden brown, 1 to 2 minutes. Remove the shrimp with a slotted spoon and drain on paper towels. Repeat the process with the remaining shrimp. Serve immediately with the Spicy Shrimp Sauce.

Serves 4.

✳ Shrimp Quantrill

Landon Hollander, Lawrence

Landon Hollander calls this recipe Shrimp Quantrill because the taste will raid your tastebuds —not, we hope, as violently as its notorious Confederate namesake!

1 pound medium-large shrimp

MARINADE
¼ cup olive oil
½ cup dry white wine
2 tablespoons bottled clam juice
3 tablespoons Dijon mustard
1 tablespoon Worcestershire sauce
hot pepper sauce, to taste
2 garlic cloves, minced
2 tablespoons red pepper flakes, crushed
1 teaspoon rosemary

Shell and devein the shrimp. Butterfly them by slicing part way through the center.

Marinade: In a bowl or dish, combine the ingredients for the marinade, mixing well.

Add the shrimp to the marinade, cover, and refrigerate for 1 to 2 hours.

When the coals are hot, remove the shrimp from the marinade and place on double skewers to facilitate turning them on the grill. Cook directly over the hot coals for about 2 minutes each side.

Serves 4.

Variation: Place the skewered shrimp on a cookie sheet under the oven broiler. Turn frequently, using a hot pad to grip the skewers. Cook for 2 minutes each side.

✳ # Skewered Scallops with Garlic and Red Pepper

Scallops are often available to Kansans now that supermarkets supply fresh seafoods. Grilling sea scallops with fresh vegetables from the garden will bring the ocean a little closer to your own backyard.

1 pound sea scallops

GARLIC AND RED PEPPER MARINADE
¼ cup olive oil
4 teaspoons red wine vinegar
4 garlic cloves, minced
¼ teaspoon red pepper flakes
⅛ teaspoon salt
¼ teaspoon pepper

1 green pepper, seeded and chopped into 1-inch pieces
1 sweet yellow or orange pepper, seeded and chopped into 1-inch pieces
8 cherry tomatoes
8 whole mushrooms

Rinse the scallops and drain on paper towels. Place them in a large shallow bowl.

Garlic and Red Pepper Marinade: Combine all the ingredients for the marinade and mix well.

Pour the marinade over the scallops and toss to coat. Cover and refrigerate for 15 minutes.

Remove the scallops from the marinade and place on 4 metal skewers, alternating them with the chopped peppers, cherry tomatoes, and whole mushrooms.

Grill, uncovered, over hot coals, or place the skewers on a cookie sheet under the oven broiler. Turn frequently, using a hot pad to grip the skewers. Cook for 5 to 8 minutes. When done, remove scallops and vegetables from the skewers immediately. Serve with lemon wedges.

Serves 4.

✳ Seafood with Red Pepper Noodles

Lindi Ensminger Waldman, Prairie Village

RED PEPPER NOODLES
1 large red bell pepper
1 egg yolk
1 cup all-purpose flour

12 ounces lobster meat
7 ounces small shrimp
1 tablespoon vegetable oil
2 tablespoons shallots, chopped
1¼ cups fish stock or clam juice
¾ cup dry white wine
1 teaspoon lemon juice
2 tablespoons dry sherry
3 cups heavy cream, divided
¼ cup green onion tops, cut on the bias

Red Pepper Noodles: Roast the red bell pepper over an open flame or under the oven broiler until the outer skin is slightly charred on all sides. Immediately place the roasted pepper in a brown paper bag and seal shut for approximately 1 hour. This allows the skin to loosen for easier peeling. Remove the skin and the seeds and discard. Dry the pepper with paper towels and puree until smooth in a blender. Measure 2½ ounces of puree, about ¼ cup.

Add the egg yolk to the pepper puree and combine thoroughly. Add the flour slowly to the mixture. It should resemble cornmeal, but when gathered, it should stick together. If the dough balls up, add additional flour. Knead until smooth and elastic, about 10 minutes.

Roll out the dough in a pasta machine, starting on 1 and repeating the procedure until ending with 5. Cut the dough into fettuccine or any wide flat pasta shape. (If cutting by hand, roll out the pasta on a lightly floured surface to ¹⁄₁₆-inch thickness and cut into fettuccine or desired shape.) After cutting, dredge the pasta in flour to prevent sticking. Place the finished pasta on a cookie sheet to dry for approximately 4 hours.

Just before serving time, prepare the cream sauce, in which the pasta is cooked.

Blanch the lobster meat in boiling water. Shell and devein the shrimp and boil for 2 to 3 minutes, until tender. Set aside.

Heat the oil in a large frying or sauté pan. Sauté the shallots for 1 minute over medium heat. Add the fish stock or clam juice and the white wine. Simmer until the liquid reduces to ¾ cup.

Add the lemon juice, sherry, and 2½ cups of the heavy cream. Bring the mixture to a boil over high heat for about 2 minutes. Add the dried red pepper pasta. Cook, occasionally stirring the pasta, until the cream stock is reduced and thickened, about 3 minutes. Add the lobster meat, shrimp, green onion tops, and the remaining ½ cup of heavy cream. Stir to combine and heat throughout. Serve immediately.

Serves 4.

Variations: Substitute other seafoods, such as small pieces of orange roughy or langostinos, for the lobster meat. Use chicken broth instead of the fish stock or clam juice.

✳ Fried Frog Legs

The lakes, ponds, and rivers of Kansas afforded the Plains Indians one of their delicacies—frog legs. They skinned the legs and broiled them over an open fire or dipped them in a batter of wild-fowl eggs and cornmeal for pan-frying. In this version,

2 pounds frog legs
1 cup yellow cornmeal
½ teaspoon marjoram
½ teaspoon thyme
1 teaspoon salt
¼ teaspoon pepper
½ cup vegetable oil

Rinse the frog legs and set aside. Combine the cornmeal, marjoram, thyme, salt, and pepper in a large bowl.

Heat the oil in a large frying pan over medium-high

the frog legs are rolled in a cornmeal mixture and pan-fried.

heat. When the oil is hot enough to sizzle, roll the frog legs in the cornmeal mixture and place them in the frying pan. Reduce heat to medium-low and fry for about 15 to 20 minutes, turning the legs occasionally to brown evenly on all sides.

Serves 4.

✳ PASTAS, GRAINS, AND CASSEROLES

Many of the foods we eat combine sauces, meats, or vegetables with starch foods like yeast doughs, pastas, or grains. All cultures have variations on these supporting cast-members. Indeed, the kind of starch food used often may identify a meal's cultural origin.

Of all the Europeans, Italians have best refined pasta (literally, "paste"), creating many shapes and uses. Though pasta is well established in the Italian populations of southeastern Kansas, other "pastes," in the form of dumplings and egg noodles, have been popularized in Kansas through German and Czech influence. Today, the widespread use of pastas in Kansan diets may have more to do with the contemporary desire for lighter and more versatile meals served hot or cold over noodles than with ethnicity.

Grains are also enjoying a resurgence in popularity. A recognition of the health benefits of fiber has prompted new interest in foods with bran, which is the outer portion, or ground husk, of wheat and other grains. The whole grain, used in cracked wheat or bulgur, is common in recipes of the Lebanese families who came to Kansas in the 1890s and settled in Wichita. Rice is a grain often served hot as a side dish, as in Risotto.

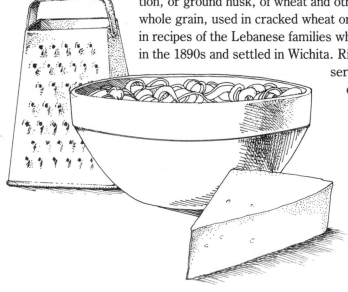

However, like pasta, rice is being tried more often in cold dishes tossed with vegetables and dressings. Rice, pasta, and cornmeal continue to be the common starch support for casseroles baked with vegetables or meats and served on the side or as an entire meal.

Recipes for yeast dough dishes include Bohne Berogge (pronounced BONE-nah brog-ee), a bun which uses a sweetened bean mixture for filling. This meal is popular among the Swiss and German communities of central Kansas and can be eaten hot or cold. By far the most common meal using yeast dough is pizza. This dish is so pervasive today that it needs no definition. Pizza has been completely absorbed into American culture; once a finger food in college-town restaurants, it is now a fixture in the landscape of American eateries.

Included in this section are a wide array of dishes, such as the frugal Italian Cabbage Casserole, the natural Lamb's Quarters Lasagne, and the gourmet Risotto with Artichoke Hearts.

✳ Homemade Pasta

Making your own pasta is not as difficult as it sounds, and the difference in taste and texture makes it well worth the effort. A hand-crank pasta machine can help with the final kneading and is most desirable when cutting the dough into uniform noodles.

1½ cups all-purpose flour, unsifted
2 large eggs

Pour the flour onto a smooth countertop. Make a well in the center and add the eggs. With a fork, gently beat the eggs, incorporating some of the flour as you stir, until there is a pastelike mass. With your hands, continue to incorporate as much of the flour as possible, creating a stiff ball of dough.

Knead the dough, adding more flour at first to keep it from being sticky, until it is very firm but elastic. To knead it properly takes a full 10 minutes. Wrap the dough in plastic and let rest 15 minutes before cutting.

If using a machine to cut the dough, divide it into quarters and progressively extrude it to the proper thickness. If cutting the pasta by hand, divide it in half and roll it out as thin as possible. Dust it with flour, roll it up, and cut it into ¼-inch wide strips.

Cook the pasta fresh (it should take only about 3 minutes) in a generous amount of rapidly boiling water or let it dry completely for storage.

Makes 4 main courses of fettuccine.

The Little Balkans

The Balkan Peninsula of southeastern Europe was a politically volatile area in the late nineteenth and early twentieth centuries, its peoples characterized as belligerently independent. The extreme southeastern corner of Kansas, with its diverse mix of immigrant groups, became known for its political ups and downs as well as mysterious disappearances, murders, and labor strikes. The parallel nature of events in these two regions led former Governor Walter Stubbs during the 1920–21 coal strike to state, "I feel as if I'm Governor of the Balkans."

The appellation stuck. What was once a wisecrack has now become a term of endearment. The people of the

Little Balkans are proud of their heritage and are still strong advocates of freedom of expression. Immigrants from Italy, Austria, Germany, Yugoslavia, England, Wales, Scotland, France, and Belgium began moving into the area in 1874, with Italians and Austrians being the largest groups. These immigrants came to do the arduous and dangerous work in the coal and zinc mines and in other industries that eventually developed in the area. Their motives for migration varied from political oppression and high taxes to poverty and unemployment in their native countries.

As its diversity might suggest, there is no such thing as a simple meal in the Little Balkans. A dinner here might consist of a mixture of dishes from a variety of countries. Nor is this merely peasant cooking; according to *The Little Balkans Cookbook* (Pittsburg: Pittsburg Area Festival Association Corporation, 1986), "some of the miner's wives had worked as cooks in palatial mansions in Europe before coming to Kansas to live in tiny company houses." The best of their recipes and cooking tips have been exchanged "over the fence," which occasionally blurs the lines of ethnic culinary demarcation. Traditionally, more than one kind of meat is prepared for a meal—and a variety of vegetables as well. Freshly made sausages might be served with chicken and dumplings, pasta, homemade wine and cheese, and pickled peppers.

Most homes around Pittsburg, Frontenac, and Parsons nurture a vegetable garden during the warm months. Fresh herbs are a must; many of their recipes call for rosemary, thyme, dill, and fennel. Garlic and other aromatics are commonly grown to supplement the daily fare in a part of the state where exotic dining is commonplace.

✳ Pasta with Italian Tomato Sauce

Today more emphasis is placed on the

3 tablespoons olive oil
1 cup onion, chopped

pasta as an equally important ingredient in the dish, not just a starch support for the sauce. Attitudes about sauces have changed as well. Rather than a sauce with a multitude of ingredients, there is more interest in the classic thick tomato sauces seasoned with herbs and lightly sweetened with sugar. With these richer sauces, less sauce is served with the pasta.

3 garlic cloves, minced
1 14-ounce can Italian tomatoes, undrained and chopped
1 8-ounce can tomato sauce
2 teaspoons basil
¼ teaspoon oregano
2 teaspoons sugar
¼ teaspoon salt
⅛ teaspoon pepper
10 to 12 ounces angel hair pasta, or thin spaghetti, freshly
   cooked
¼ cup Parmesan cheese, grated

Heat the oil in a large frying pan over low heat. Add the onion and garlic and cook slowly until tender. Add the tomatoes, tomato sauce, basil, oregano, sugar, salt, and pepper.

Simmer over low heat, stirring occasionally for about 20 minutes. Serve the sauce over freshly cooked pasta and sprinkle with grated Parmesan cheese.

Serves 4.

❊ Buttered Noodles with Toasted Bread Crumbs

Czechs were among those Europeans who brought along their love of egg noodles to their Kansas settlements. This modest garnish, inspired by a Czech recipe, makes simple noodles into an attention-getting side dish that complements any main course. Though both the seasoned bread crumbs and the noodles may

1½ cups fresh bread crumbs
2 tablespoons garlic salt
8 ounces freshly made noodles (or good-quality dried pasta)
¼ cup Parmesan cheese, freshly grated
2 tablespoons butter, room temperature

To make fresh bread crumbs, take 2 to 3 slices of dense white bread and process them with the steel knife in a food processor. Preheat the broiler and place the crumbs on a cookie sheet. Toast the crumbs for about 20 seconds until lightly browned, watching very carefully. Remove from the broiler, quickly stir, and return the crumbs to the broiler. Toast again for about 10 to 20 seconds, stir, and once again return to the broiler for 10 seconds for

be successfully store-
bought, the essence
of the dish lies in its
homemade charm.

the final browning. Toss the crumbs with the garlic salt and set aside.

Make the noodles fresh or prepare them according to the package directions. In a warm bowl, toss the noodles, butter, Parmesan, and half the toasted garlic crumbs until well mixed. Garnish each plate or a serving dish with the remaining crumbs or pass at the table.

Serves 4 to 6.

✳ Drukla Noodles

Esther Reilly, Dorrance

*Esther Reilly says that
Drukla Noodles are
just one example of the
many delicious recipes
brought from Russia
by the Volga Germans
who settled in Kansas.*
  *Drukla means
"dry." The noodles
are cooked, simmered
in a small amount of
cream to coat them,
and tossed with cooked
onion and browned
bread crumbs. Serve
them as a side dish
with fried chicken or
pork chops.*

6 cups water
2 teaspoons salt
8 ounces wide egg noodles
½ cup half and half
salt and pepper, to taste
¼ cup butter
½ cup onion, diced
1 cup fresh bread crumbs, about 2 slices

In a large pan or Dutch oven, bring the water to a rapid boil. Add the salt and the egg noodles. Boil for 3 to 5 minutes, or until the noodles are tender.

Drain the noodles and return them to the pan. Add the half and half and salt and pepper to taste. Simmer on low heat, stirring often.

Melt the butter in a frying pan over medium heat. Add the onion and sauté until lightly browned. Stir in the bread crumbs and brown.

Toss the onion and bread crumb mixture with the noodles. Serve immediately.

Serves 4.

The Industrious Germans

The German influence on Kansas culture far surpasses that of any other ethnic group in Kansas history. Though enough Germans lived in Atchison in the 1860s to support a German-language newspaper, soon after the Civil War as many as forty thousand more came from eastern states to settle in Kansas. Many of them were third-generation Pennsylvania Dutch, who included Lutherans, Amish, Dunkards, and River Brethren. These groups spread throughout the state, bringing with them their love of the soil, industriousness, religious devotion, and famous culinary skills.

A hundred years earlier, in 1762, Catherine the Great had invited the ancestors of these Germans to establish colonies in Russia. Communities sprang up in the Volga region in the southern part of the country. The empress hoped that the German immigrants—hard-working, dependable, law-abiding, and skilled in advanced farming techniques—would serve as models for her struggling peasants. In 1874, Alexander II did not renew Catherine's pledge to the Germans to exempt them from military service. Since bearing arms was unacceptable to their religious beliefs, they were forced to emigrate. C. B. Schmidt, in Europe to promote settlement for the Santa Fe Railroad, helped to convince nearly fifteen thousand of these Germans from the Volga region and the southern part of Russia to come to Kansas. His similar efforts in Germany added twenty thousand more Catholics, Lutherans, and Baptists to the German population of the state. As their settlements succeeded, so did Kansas. Each religious group settled in different areas of the state and, due to their industrious nature and love of the land, each soon found prosperity.

Perhaps most significant for the future of Kansas, the German Mennonites brought with them the seeds of the Turkey Red wheat, which was eventually to become the most important crop in Kansas. With the profits from the year's harvest, the Mennonites increased their land holdings to establish the large farms typical of wheat-growing country.

Cultural differences among the Germans, though much diminished, are still apparent today in their foods. The Mennonites are excellent cooks and still prepare their traditional dishes, such as their favorite bread, Zwieback. Another specialty is Bohne Berogge, a yeast roll filled with sweetened mashed pinto beans and served with a sweetened cream sauce. The Mennonites are probably best known in the region for their delicious sausage, produced in many small towns of central Kansas, such as Peabody, Hillsboro, and Hesston. The taste of the sausage differs from town to town, as each sausage-maker has his or her own secret recipe. These traditional recipes—and much more—can be sampled at the Menno-nite Central Committee Relief Sale, an annual fund-raiser held in Hutchinson.

The Volga Germans still prepare such specialties as Bierocks, their version of a Russian dish called *pirozhki*. This baked pastry, filled with ground beef and cabbage, is well known to central Kansas residents. Käse Maul-taschen, or Cheese-Filled Noodle Pockets, is another Volga German dish, usually served as a meatless meal or as a side dish. The annual Oktoberfest, held in Hays, draws thousands of people throughout Kansas to cele-brate the Volga German heritage of Ellis County. The festivities include German singers and dancers, tradi-tional German foods, and, of course, a variety of beers.

✳ Cheese-Filled Noodle Pockets

(Käse Maultaschen)

Mrs. Frank (Anna) Schippers, Victoria

Anna Schippers sends us this traditional Volga German recipe for noodle pockets. These ingredients would be easy to come by on the farmstead and would create a

CHEESE FILLING
12 ounces dry-curd cottage cheese
½ cup sugar
1 egg, beaten
½ teaspoon cinnamon, or ¼ teaspoon allspice

DOUGH
2 cups all-purpose flour

filling, meatless meal for the hard-working family. This recipe is a familiar one to Kansans of German descent around Ellis County.

Käse Maultaschen makes a complete vegetarian meal or a side dish with beef or pork.

½ teaspoon salt
2 eggs, lightly beaten
4 tablespoons milk

TOPPING
¼ cup butter
½ cup whipping cream, or sour cream

GARNISH
2 tablespoons melted butter
1 cup fresh bread crumbs

Cheese filling: In a mixing bowl, combine all the ingredients for the filling and set aside.

Dough: Combine the flour and salt in a medium-sized bowl. Add the beaten egg and mix with a fork. Add the milk a tablespoon at a time, until the dough is smooth and moist but not sticky. Let the mixture stand for 10 minutes.

Turn the dough onto a lightly floured surface and roll out to ⅛-inch thickness. Cut into 6-inch squares and place a heaping tablespoon of the cheese filling in the center of each square. To form the noodle pockets, bring the four corners of each square to a point and pinch to seal the edges.

Drop the noodle pockets into a large pot of boiling water. (Add ½ teaspoon of salt to the water, if desired.) Boil the noodle pockets until they rise to the top, then continue boiling for 2 minutes more. The total cooking time should be approximately 20 minutes. Remove the cooked noodle pockets with a slotted spoon and place in an oven-proof serving bowl. Cover and keep warm in the oven while preparing the topping.

Topping: Melt the butter over low heat in a heavy skillet. Stir in the cream or sour cream and heat until the mixture is hot and bubbly. Pour the topping over the noodle pockets.

Garnish: Melt the butter in a small skillet over medium heat. Add the bread crumbs and fry, turning often, until golden brown. Sprinkle the buttered bread crumbs over the noodles and serve immediately.

Serves 4.

✳ Lamb's Quarters Lasagne

Kelly Kindscher, Lawrence

The use of wild foods, both in cooking and for medicinal purposes, evokes a rich American vista of pioneer life. Today, gathering wild greens adds a special dimension to cooking and becomes sport for the naturalist, but it's important to make certain that the right species is picked. For best and safest results, learn from someone who knows both the plant and when it should be harvested.

Kelly Kindscher, author of Edible Wild Plants of the Prairie: An Ethnobotanical Guide *(Lawrence: University Press of Kansas, 1987), tells us, "Lamb's quarters are an ancient food. Stockpiles of their seeds have been found in ruins near St. Louis that are 5,000 years old." Lamb's quarters are a common weed, so weeding your garden in the spring or early summer might produce enough for dinner.*

"Lamb's quarters are a wonderful addition to a more traditional dish, such as my recipe for Lamb's Quarters Lasagne," adds Kelly. "I can serve it and receive no complaints, from even the most domesticated Americans."

8 lasagne noodles
1 cup ricotta cheese, or cottage cheese
1 egg, beaten
salt and pepper, to taste
1 15-ounce can tomato sauce
2 garlic cloves, minced (optional)
1 tablespoon fresh basil, chopped (optional)
1 cup lamb's quarters, washed and chopped
⅓ cup Parmesan cheese, grated
½ pound mozzarella cheese, shredded

Cook the lasagne noodles according to the package directions. Rinse and drain well.

Combine the ricotta or cottage cheese with the egg in a small bowl. Add salt and pepper to taste.

Pour the tomato sauce into a small saucepan. Add the garlic and basil, if desired, and heat to simmering. Pour a small amount of the tomato sauce into the bottom of a 9-inch baking dish. Place 4 of the lasagne noodles on top of the sauce. Spread half of the cheese and egg mixture on the lasagne. Add half of the lamb's quarters, pour some of the sauce over, and sprinkle with some of the mozzarella and Parmesan cheese. Add a second layer, ending with the cheese on top.

Bake uncovered at 350 degrees, for 30 to 40 minutes, or until hot and bubbly. Let stand for 5 minutes before cutting.

Serves 4.

✳ Spinach Lasagna

Mary Terrill Pattie, Topeka

This casserole makes a great meatless meal, and with no sauce to prepare, it can be assembled quickly.

1 8-ounce package lasagna
2 10-ounce packages frozen spinach
1 24-ounce carton cottage cheese
2 eggs, beaten
2 tablespoons fresh parsley, chopped, or 1 tablespoon dried parsley
½ teaspoon garlic powder
¼ teaspoon salt
¼ teaspoon pepper
1 8-ounce package Monterey jack cheese, shredded
1 cup Parmesan cheese, freshly grated

Cook the lasagna noodles and the frozen spinach according to package directions. Drain well, press the water out of the spinach, and set aside. While the noodles and spinach are cooking, combine the cottage cheese, eggs, parsley, garlic powder, salt, and pepper in a blender or food processor and blend until smooth.

Using a lightly greased 13 x 9–inch baking dish, cover the bottom with a layer of lasagna noodles, then a third each of the cottage cheese mixture, the Monterey jack cheese, the cooked spinach, and the Parmesan cheese.

Repeat the layers two more times, ending with the Parmesan cheese.

Bake at 350 degrees uncovered for 40 to 45 minutes, or until lightly browned and bubbly. Let the casserole stand about 10 minutes before cutting and serving.

Serves 6 to 8.

✳ Macaroni and Cheese

In earlier times, macaroni was often combined with eggs, cream, chicken or ham and steamed in a mold. These days, macaroni and cheese is usually served as a quick vegetarian entree or a side dish.

Jayni's grand-mother, Beulah Amos, always took special care in preparing this dish for her children and grandchildren. "Three generations later," says Jayni, "we can still count on our favorite comfort food at family gatherings."

1 10-ounce bag shell macaroni
1 cup cheddar cheese, shredded
1 cup milk
2 tablespoons all-purpose flour
½ teaspoon salt
salt, to taste
1 teaspoon pepper, coarsely ground (optional)

Cook the macaroni in a large pot of boiling water until tender. Pour the macaroni into a colander to drain. Return it to the pan and add the shredded cheese, mixing well.

Pour the milk into a plastic container, or a jar with a lid. Add the flour and salt. Cover and shake well to combine. Place the pan of macaroni and cheese over medium-low heat and slowly add the flour mixture, stirring well. Cook and stir until thick and bubbly, 3 to 5 minutes. Add salt to taste and pepper, if desired. Serve immediately.

Serves 4 to 6.

✳ Cottage Cheese Casserole

Von Schroeder, Overland Park

This casserole of macaroni and two cheeses needs only the complement of a crisp green salad and garlic

2 tablespoons butter or margarine
½ cup onion, finely chopped
½ cup celery, finely chopped
½ cup fresh mushrooms, thinly sliced
2 garlic cloves, minced

bread for a healthful and satisfying meatless meal.

1 6-ounce can tomato paste
4½ cups water
1 teaspoon sugar
¼ teaspoon marjoram
1½ teaspoons salt
4 cups elbow macaroni
2 cups cottage cheese
⅓ cup Parmesan cheese, grated
¼ cup fresh parsley, chopped

In a large skillet or Dutch oven, melt the butter or margarine over medium-low heat. Add the onion, celery, mushrooms, and garlic and cook until tender, stirring frequently.

Stir in the tomato paste, water, sugar, marjoram, salt, and macaroni. Simmer slowly over low heat until the macaroni is tender, 10 to 20 minutes. Stir the mixture frequently to prevent sticking.

Place half of the macaroni mixture in a greased 9-inch baking dish. Top with half of the cottage cheese, Parmesan cheese, and parsley. Repeat the layers with the remaining ingredients.

Bake uncovered at 350 degrees for 40 minutes. Let the casserole stand for 10 minutes before cutting.

Serves 4 to 6.

✳ Potato Dumplings

Anna Marie Krusic, Frontenac

"This dumpling recipe was handed down to me from my mother," writes Anna Marie Krusic. "Potato Dumplings were served as part of our Sunday meal with pork roast or chicken with gravy."

2 to 3 slices of white bread
¼ cup butter
5 large potatoes, peeled and grated
cold water
½ cup mashed potatoes
2 teaspoons salt
¼ teaspoon white pepper
4 cups all-purpose flour

Melt the butter over medium heat in a large frying pan. Cut the bread slices into ½-inch cubes. Add the bread cubes to the pan and brown, turning occasionally. Remove the cubes from the pan and set aside.

Place the grated potatoes in a large bowl. Cover with cold water and let stand for 20 to 30 minutes, until the starch settles to the bottom of the bowl. Pour off the water, keeping the starch with the potatoes. Add the mashed potatoes, salt, and pepper. Gradually mix in the flour, adding as much as necessary to form a soft dough.

To make the dumplings, take one bread cube and wrap a small portion of the dough around it to form a ball about 2 inches in diameter. Repeat this procedure until the potato mixture is used up.

Drop the dumplings into a large pot of boiling salted water and cook for about 20 to 25 minutes, or until the dumplings are completely cooked. Drain and serve at once.

Makes 18 to 20.

✴ Baked Cornmeal Dumplings

Nearly every culture has its own version of dumplings. The pioneers made them often, because they were an inexpensive and filling staple that could be made or seasoned with whatever was on hand.

This modern version is made with cornmeal, bits of cooked cabbage and onion, and Parmesan cheese. Serve with soup and salad, or as a side dish to beef and pork entrees.

3 tablespoons butter
1 cup cabbage, finely chopped
½ cup onion, chopped
½ teaspoon sugar
½ cup cold water
¾ cup yellow cornmeal
1 cup chicken broth
1 cup water
¼ cup Parmesan cheese, grated
2 tablespoons butter, melted

Melt the butter in a medium-sized skillet over low heat. Add the chopped cabbage and onion and cook, turning occasionally, until tender. Stir in the sugar and remove from heat.

Pour ½ cup of cold water into a mixing bowl. Slowly

pour in the cornmeal, stirring until the mixture is smooth and has no lumps.

Bring the chicken broth and water to a boil in a large pan or Dutch oven. Slowly pour in the cornmeal mixture, stirring constantly. Reduce heat to low and continue stirring for 5 to 8 minutes, until the mixture is thick. Remove from heat and stir in the cabbage mixture and the Parmesan cheese.

Pour the cornmeal mixture into a bowl and cool just until it can be handled, about 10 to 15 minutes. Form the mixture into balls about 1½ inches in diameter and place them on a lightly greased cookie sheet. Brush the dumplings with melted butter and bake for 25 to 30 minutes, until lightly browned.

Makes 16 to 18.

✳ Cornmeal Mush

Cornmeal mush was often prepared by the Indian tribes who inhabited Kansas. Nineteenth-century settlers also relied heavily upon corn, because it was versatile, practical, and nutritious. Freshly cooked ears of corn were a seasonal favorite, while breads, pud-

dings, pancakes, and cornmeal mush were filling variations on a theme. White flour was sometimes difficult to come by in those days and corn ground into meal was a common substitute.

In the past, cornmeal mush was most often sliced, fried, and served with sor-

ghum, honey, or gravy. Today, this historic food is sometimes updated with the addition of grated cheese or topped with a meat or vegetable sauce and served as a main course. It can also complement a highly seasoned chili or stew.

3 cups water
1 cup cornmeal
1 teaspoon salt
1 cup cold water
½ cup sharp cheddar cheese, grated (optional)

Boil 3 cups of water in a large pan or Dutch oven. Combine the cornmeal, salt, and cold water in a bowl, stirring to combine. Slowly pour the cornmeal mixture into the boiling water, stirring constantly. Bring the mixture to a full boil. Reduce heat to medium-low and stir constantly with a large spoon for 10 to 15 minutes, or until the mixture is thick. If desired, add the grated cheese during the last 2 minutes of cooking.

Turn the mush into a lightly greased loaf pan. Cool for 1 hour. Turn onto a plate, cover, and chill until ready to use.

Slice the cornmeal mush into ½-inch slices and fry in butter over medium heat until lightly browned. Serve with butter and sorghum.

Serves 6.

✳ Fried Oatmeal

Frugal cooks of the past never wasted anything, including leftover hot cereals. For example, cooked oatmeal could be sweetened and made into a loaf for frying later. This version dresses fried oatmeal up a bit with cinnamon and raisins. Add coconut, wheat germ, dried fruits, or nuts for a healthful change of pace.

Serve fried oatmeal as the main dish for breakfast or as a side with bacon and eggs. For a sweet treat, it may be topped with sorghum or honey.

3 cups water
1 teaspoon salt
4 cups oatmeal
½ cup brown sugar
½ teaspoon cinnamon
½ teaspoon vanilla extract
½ cup raisins (optional)
butter, for frying

Bring the water and salt to a boil over high heat in a large saucepan. Stir in the oatmeal and immediately reduce heat to low. Simmer uncovered for 3 minutes, stirring frequently to prevent sticking. Cover the pan and remove it from heat. Let the oatmeal stand for 5 minutes.

Stir in the brown sugar, cinnamon, vanilla, and raisins, if desired, while the oatmeal is still warm. Pour the mixture into a buttered loaf pan. Cool to room temperature. Cover and chill overnight.

Carefully remove the oatmeal loaf from the pan and cut into slices about ⅜ inch thick. Melt butter in a skillet and fry the oatmeal slices over medium heat until crispy and golden brown.

Serves 6 to 8.

✳ Pepperoni Pizza with Pineapple and Green Pepper

Sometimes Kansans forget that pizza wasn't invented here. Perhaps it's because those who grew up in Kansas in the 1960s were introduced to pizza by Tony's of Salina and Pizza Hut of Wichita, now two of the nation's largest pizza producers.

This pizza recipe is reminiscent of a popular variation served at the former Campus Hideaway restaurant of Lawrence (established in 1957). Several generations of University of Kansas students enjoyed some of the best pizza in Kansas there for over twenty-five years.

PIZZA CRUST
2 packages dry yeast
pinch of sugar
½ cup warm water
3½ cups all-purpose flour
1 teaspoon salt
¼ cup olive oil
¾ to 1 cup warm water

SAUCE
1 12-ounce can tomato paste
½ cup tomato sauce
4 garlic cloves, minced
1 tablespoon basil
¼ teaspoon oregano
1 teaspoon sugar

TOPPING
4 ounces pepperoni
1 green pepper, seeded
1 8-ounce can unsweetened pineapple chunks
¾ pound whole milk mozzarella cheese*
3 tablespoons pesto* (optional)

4 teaspoons yellow cornmeal

Pizza Crust: Dissolve the yeast and sugar in ½ cup of warm water. Measure the flour and salt into a large bowl. Add the yeast mixture and olive oil, mixing well. Add the warm water slowly, stirring until the dough can be handled. Turn the dough onto a lightly floured surface and knead it for 10 minutes, or until the dough is smooth and elastic. Place the dough in a lightly greased bowl, turning once to grease the top. Cover and let rise in a warm

*Whole milk mozzarella cheese is available in Italian and specialty food shops. Pesto may be homemade or purchased in specialty food shops.

place until doubled in size, 1 to 1½ hours. Meanwhile, make the sauce.

Sauce: In a medium-sized pan, combine all the ingredients for the sauce. Simmer over low heat for 5 to 10 minutes, stirring frequently. Remove from heat and set aside while preparing the topping.

Topping: Slice the pepperoni into thin slices. Chop the green pepper. Drain the pineapple chunks and slice in half. Shred the mozzarella cheese into a large bowl. If desired, add the pesto to the cheese and stir to combine. Refrigerate the cheese until ready to use.

When the dough has risen, punch down and knead lightly on a floured surface. Divide the dough in half and roll out one half to fit a 12-inch pizza pan. Sprinkle 2 teaspoons of cornmeal on a lightly greased pizza pan and place the dough on the pan, turning up the edges to create a slight ridge. Spread half of the tomato sauce on the pizza. Arrange half of the pepperoni slices and the green pepper on top. Place a few pineapple chunks on the pizza and top with half of the cheese.

Cook the pizza on the lowest oven rack in a preheated oven of 500 degrees for about 10 minutes. The crust should be lightly browned and the toppings golden and bubbly. Repeat the procedure with the remaining half of

the dough. Cut the pizzas with a pizza cutter or a sharp knife and serve immediately.

Makes 2 12-inch pizzas.

To freeze: Prepare pizzas as directed, except omit the cheese. Reduce the cooking time to 7 minutes. Remove from the pan and cool on a wire rack. Add the cheese. Wrap securely with plastic wrap and cover with aluminum foil. Freeze up to 2 months.

To reheat: Place the pizza on a pizza pan and bake at 350 degrees for 10 to 12 minutes.

✳ Barbecued Cheese and Pepper Pizza

John Bowden, Lawrence

Kansans' love of barbecuing goes beyond ribs and steaks. John Bowden offers this recipe for grilling pizza, using a commercially made ceramic pizza stone on a covered grill to work like a wood-fired oven.

PIZZA CRUST
1 package dry active yeast
pinch of sugar
¼ cup warm water
¼ cup rye flour or whole wheat flour
2 tablespoons extra-virgin olive oil
½ teaspoon salt
½ cup warm water
1¾ cups unbleached white flour

TOPPINGS
1 sweet red or orange pepper
2 green chilies
2 yellow banana peppers
1½ cups Monterey jack cheese
¼ cup Parmesan cheese

all-purpose flour or cornmeal
1 tablespoon extra-virgin olive oil

Pizza Crust: In a large bowl, dissolve the yeast and sugar in ¼ cup of warm water. Stir the rye or whole wheat flour into the yeast mixture. Cover and let stand in a warm

place until the mixture begins to bubble and rise, 15 to
20 minutes.

Stir in the olive oil, salt, and ½ cup warm water. Add
the flour, ½ cup at a time, stirring until the dough can be
handled. Add additional flour if the dough is too sticky to
handle. Turn the dough onto a lightly floured surface and
knead for about 10 minutes, or until smooth and elastic.
Place the dough in a lightly greased bowl, turning once to
grease the top. Cover and let rise in a warm place until
doubled in size, about 1 hour. Meanwhile, prepare the
toppings.

Toppings: Place the peppers on a grill over hot coals, or
under the oven broiler, turning frequently until the skins
begin to wrinkle and blacken. Remove and enclose in
a paper bag for 15 minutes or more to steam them for
easier peeling. Peel the peppers, removing the pith and
seeds. Rinse them with cold water and slice into 1-inch
strips.

Shred the Monterey jack cheese and grate the Parmesan cheese. Combine the cheeses in a bowl, cover, and
refrigerate until ready to use.

Wait until the coals have reached their hottest point
and begin to cool down to medium-hot before cooking the
pizza. Place a pizza stone on the grid directly over the
coals and allow it to preheat for 10 minutes.

When the dough has risen, punch down and knead
lightly on a floured surface. Roll out the dough to desired
thickness and place on a pizza paddle that has been generously floured or sprinkled with cornmeal. Sprinkle the
olive oil over the pizza dough. Arrange the pepper slices
on the dough—work quickly or the pizza will stick to the
paddle. Top with the cheeses and quickly slip the pizza
onto the pizza brick.

Cover the grill and cook for 12 to 15 minutes, or until
the crust is golden and the cheeses have melted.

Makes 1 large pizza.

Variation: Top with any combination of the following
ingredients: sliced pepperoni, cooked sausages, sun-
dried tomatoes, anchovies, jalapeño peppers, sliced raw

or cooked onion, canned tomatoes (chopped and well drained), mozzarella or Romano cheese.

✳ Bohne Berogge

Lorraine J. Kaufman, Moundridge

"A pioneer wife looked for foods that could be served hot for the first meal, but were equally delicious served cold at the next," writes Lorraine Kaufman. In pioneer days, these recipes were considered "convenience foods" —dishes that resisted spoilage, used the on-hand farm products, and could eliminate an otherwise unnecessary trip to town.

"From the sturdy Swiss German immigrant farmers," continues Lorraine, "comes this recipe for Bohne Berogge (pronounced BONE-nah brog-ee)—beans in bread. These rolls, served with a rich sauce, were a meal in themselves. They were also a convenient snack for a hungry boy to slip in his pocket as he passed through the kitchen on his way to the fields or to play."

FILLING
2 cups dry pinto beans
1⅓ cups sugar
1⅓ teaspoons salt

SWEET DOUGH
2 packages dry yeast
½ cup warm water
½ cup shortening
½ cup sugar
2 teaspoons salt
⅔ cup milk
⅓ cup water
2 eggs, beaten
4½ to 5 cups all-purpose flour, sifted

SAUCE
1 cup whipping cream
1 cup milk, divided
½ cup sugar
1½ tablespoons cornstarch

Filling: Wash the pinto beans and simmer in a generous amount of water until tender, about 2 hours. Drain the water and mash the beans until smooth and uniform in texture. Add the sugar and salt and mix well. Allow the beans to cool completely before using them for the filling.

Sweet Dough: Dissolve the yeast in the warm water and set aside.

Melt the shortening in a heavy pan. Add the sugar, salt, milk, and ⅓ cup of water and heat just until lukewarm. Stir in the beaten eggs and the yeast. Transfer to a large bowl.

Mix the flour into the liquid a little at a time until a soft dough forms. Turn the dough onto a floured surface and knead until smooth and elastic, about 10 minutes. Put the dough into a greased bowl and cover. Let rise until doubled in bulk, about 1 hour. Punch down the dough and let rise again.

Shape the dough into buns about the size of a walnut and arrange them on a greased baking sheet so that they do not touch. Cover and let rise until doubled in size.

Off the baking sheet, flatten the buns into a circle and place a large spoonful of bean filling in the center. Pull the dough up around the filling and pinch the edges together along the top. Return the buns to the baking sheet, allowing enough room so that they will not touch after rising. Let rise until doubled in size. Bake for 15 minutes at 375 degrees.

Sauce: In a heavy saucepan, bring the cream, ½ cup of milk, and the sugar to a simmer. Mix the cornstarch with the remaining ½ cup of milk and add to the hot mixture, stirring constantly until the sauce is slightly thickened.

To serve, pour the hot sauce over the warm Bohne Berogge.

Makes about 3 dozen.

✳ Cracked Wheat with Green Peas

Cracked wheat makes a delicious alternative to potatoes or rice. To complement your main course, substitute any vegetable of your choosing.

2½ cups water
2 teaspoons chicken or beef bouillon
1 cup cracked wheat
1 cup frozen peas

Bring the water and the bouillon to a boil in a medium-sized saucepan over high heat. Slowly stir in the cracked wheat. Bring the mixture to a boil, cover, and reduce heat to low. Cook for 5 minutes, then quickly stir in the peas. Cover and continue cooking for 2 to 5 minutes more, until the liquid is absorbed. Remove from heat and let stand, covered, for 10 minutes before serving.

Serves 6.

✳ Bulgur Wheat Dish

Beulah Farha, Wichita

Many Lebanese families migrated to Kansas in the 1890s and settled in Wichita, giving it the largest Lebanese population in the state. The Lebanese have retained numerous traditional dishes, such as this delicious one shared by Beulah Farha, which she serves as a side dish for chicken.

⅓ cup salad or vegetable oil
1 cup rosemarina or small pieces of vermicelli
1 cup coarse bulgur wheat, rinsed
1 onion, finely chopped
¼ teaspoon nutmeg
2 tablespoons dried parsley
½ to 1¼ teaspoons salt, to taste
¼ teaspoon pepper
2¾ cups boiling chicken broth or water

Heat the oil in a large saucepan over medium heat. Stir in the rosemarina or vermicelli and sauté until it is golden brown. Remove the pan from heat and add the bulgur wheat, onion, nutmeg, parsley, salt to taste, and pepper. Mix well and add the chicken broth or water, or a combination of both. Return to heat, cover, and simmer over low heat for 20 minutes. Let stand until ready to serve.
　　Serves 6.

✳ Tomato and Brown Rice Casserole

Patricia Habiger, Spearville

The use of rice was extended throughout the United States by European immigrants who preferred it to the potato. Southerners, too, brought rice into Kansas as their choice for a starch side dish. Though the heavy German influence seems to put the potato on our plates more often than

¼ cup olive oil
2 onions, chopped
1 green pepper, seeded and chopped
3 to 4 stalks celery, chopped
4 cups fresh tomatoes, peeled and chopped, or 2 16-ounce
　　cans whole tomatoes, undrained and chopped
1 cup brown rice
1 tablespoon lemon juice
1 tablespoon basil
1 teaspoon salt
cayenne pepper, to taste
1 cup cheddar cheese, shredded

rice, recipes such as this one are common fare in Kansas.

The secret to making this dish outstanding is using fresh, home-grown tomatoes. Serve as a vegetarian meal or as a side dish to almost any entree.

Heat the oil over medium heat in a large pan or a Dutch oven. Add the onion and fry, stirring frequently, until golden brown. Add the green pepper and celery and fry for 3 minutes more. Add the fresh chopped tomatoes and cover. Reduce heat to low and simmer until the tomatoes liquify, about 5 minutes. (If using canned tomatoes, add them to the pan and proceed to the next step.)

Add the brown rice, lemon juice, basil, salt, and cayenne pepper, to taste. Bring the mixture to a boil. Reduce heat to low, cover, and simmer for 45 to 55 minutes, or until the rice is tender and the liquid is absorbed.

Add the shredded cheese and stir to melt. (Or pour the rice mixture into a 9-inch baking dish and sprinkle the cheese on top. Place the baking dish under the broiler for a few seconds, until the cheese is melted and golden.)

Serves 6.

✳ Risotto with Artichoke Hearts

Risotto is a creamy dish made with Arborio rice, a variety of plump rice from Italy. Many versions of this dish, brought to Kansas by Italian

2 tablespoons butter
¼ cup green onion, chopped
1 cup Arborio rice, rinsed and drained
1 bay leaf
1 14-ounce can chicken broth
½ cup dry white wine
1½ cups water

immigrants, are still popular in the Italian communities of Kansas.

Serve this savory rice dish with grilled chicken or pork. Though long-grain white rice works well, authentic results require the Arborio variety. You can find this rice (also known as Italian rice) in specialty food stores or Italian markets.

1 14-ounce can artichoke hearts, drained and sliced
¼ cup Parmesan cheese, grated

Melt the butter in a large heavy-bottomed saucepan. Add the chopped green onion and cook over low heat until tender. Add the rice and the bay leaf and cook for 3 minutes, stirring occasionally.

Combine the chicken broth, white wine, and water in a medium-sized pan and heat to simmering. Add ½ cup of the simmering liquid to the rice. Cook slowly, uncovered, over low heat, allowing the rice mixture to simmer gently, without boiling. Continue cooking, stirring occasionally to prevent sticking, until all of the liquid is absorbed, about 3 to 5 minutes. Add another ½ cup of the simmering liquid and repeat the process. Continue adding the liquid ½ cup at a time. Stir more frequently, as the rice will tend to stick to the pan as it cooks. Add the artichokes and the grated cheese when you add the last ½ cup of liquid, and cook until most of the liquid is absorbed and the rice mixture is creamy. Remove from heat. For best results, serve immediately. The entire process will take 30 to 40 minutes.

Serves 6.

✳ Savory Cabbage and Brown Rice Casserole

This hearty casserole makes a perfect accompaniment to chicken or wild fowl.

2½ cups water
1 cup brown rice
¼ cup butter
3 cups cabbage, thinly sliced
¼ cup raisins
2 tablespoons sliced almonds
½ cup milk
1 tablespoon soy sauce
1 egg, beaten

Bring the water to a boil in a large pan over high heat. Add the rice and bring to a boil again. Reduce heat to low, stir, and cover. Cook for 50 to 60 minutes, or until all of the water is absorbed. Turn the rice into a large bowl and set aside.

Melt the butter in a large frying pan over medium-low heat. Add the sliced cabbage, raisins, and almonds. Cook, stirring occasionally, until the cabbage is tender, about 5 minutes. Remove from heat. Stir the cabbage mixture into the rice.

In a small bowl combine the milk, soy sauce, and egg. Pour over the rice and cabbage, mixing well.

Turn the mixture into a lightly greased 2-quart casserole. Cover and bake at 350 degrees for 30 minutes.

Serves 6.

✳ Wild Rice Club Supper

This recipe won Jayni the grand prize in the 1987 Uncle Ben's Long Grain & Wild Rice 25th Anniversary Recipe Contest (Fast and Easy category). Her easy-to-prepare creation combines ingredients reminiscent of a club sandwich.

1 5.2-ounce package Uncle Ben's Long Grain & Wild Rice
  Chicken Stock Sauce With Vegetables
1½ cups cooked chicken or turkey, coarsely chopped
1 tomato, chopped
1½ cups romaine lettuce, sliced
3 slices bacon, cooked and crumbled

Cook the contents of the rice and seasoning packets according to the package directions, using a medium-sized pan.

Stir in the cooked chicken or turkey and tomato and heat throughout. Remove from heat and stir in the lettuce. Garnish with the crumbled bacon.

Serves 4.

✳ Corn and Oyster Casserole

Virginia Nordyke, Ottawa

Once the railroads came to Kansas, perishable foods could

1 16-ounce can golden cream-style corn
1 cup milk
1 egg, well beaten

*be shipped overland
to homesick settlers
yearning for a taste
of the sea. Oysters
became somewhat
common and ap-
peared often during
the holiday season
as casseroles and
stuffings for roast fowl.*

*The combination of
cream-style corn and
oysters, baked with a
butter-crumb topping,
makes a good vegetable
side dish for roast tur-
key or ham. Virginia
Nordyke considers it
a "must" for special
holiday meals.*

2 8-ounce cans oysters, drained and chopped
1 cup cracker crumbs
¾ teaspoon salt
¼ teaspoon pepper

TOPPING
1 tablespoon butter, melted
½ cup cracker crumbs

In a large bowl, combine the cream-style corn and milk.
Stir in the beaten egg. Add the chopped oysters, cracker
crumbs, salt, and pepper, mixing well. Pour the mixture
into a large greased baking dish.

Topping: In a small bowl, combine the melted butter and
½ cup of cracker crumbs. Sprinkle on top of the casserole.

Bake uncovered at 350 degrees for 20 to 25 minutes.
Serves 8.

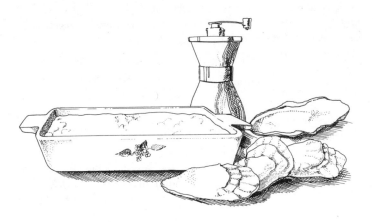

✳ Farmer's Corn Casserole

Kay Marshall, Tribune

*Vegetable casseroles
serve double duty by
supplying the vegetable
as well as the starch.*

1 egg
½ cup butter or margarine, softened
¾ cup sour cream
1 17-ounce can whole kernel corn, drained

This tasty dish with its cheery yellow color complements almost any meal. It's a great choice for a potluck occasion.

1 17-ounce can cream-style corn
¼ teaspoon salt
½ cup milk
1 8-ounce box corn muffin mix
1 cup cheddar cheese, shredded

In a large mixing bowl, beat the egg. Add the butter or margarine and sour cream, mixing well. Stir in the drained corn, cream-style corn, salt, and milk. Add the corn muffin mix, mixing well. Pour the mixture into a lightly greased 9-inch baking dish and top with the cheese.

Bake, uncovered, at 350 degrees for 40 to 45 minutes. Serves 6 to 8.

✳ # Italian Cabbage Casserole

Olga Saia, Frontenac

Olga Saia's mother brought this recipe from Italy. Times were difficult in those days and wasting food was unthinkable. Her recipe makes use of stale bread and a favorite garden vegetable, the cabbage.

Born of frugal times, this casserole may be embellished in many ways. Cooked and diced chicken pieces may be added, or other kinds of cheeses may be used. For extra seasoning, add a generous pinch of dried oregano to the tomato sauce.

1 medium-sized head of cabbage, cut into 1-inch strips
12 medium-sized slices stale Italian bread, sliced ½-inch thick
1 15-ounce can tomato sauce
1 cup Parmesan cheese, finely grated
1 cup reserved cabbage water

Cook the cabbage strips, uncovered, in a pot of boiling water for about 10 minutes, or until tender. Drain the cabbage, reserving 1 cup of the water.

In a buttered 9-inch baking dish, place a layer of bread slices. Top with a layer of cabbage and spread half of the tomato sauce on the cabbage. Sprinkle the sauce with half of the Parmesan cheese. Make a second layer, ending with the cheese on top. Pour the reserved cabbage water into the baking dish.

Bake the casserole uncovered at 350 degrees for about 45 to 50 minutes, or until bubbly and nicely browned. Serves 4.

✳ Tofu-Spinach Enchiladas

Kate Shreves, Overbrook

Soybeans are a major crop in Kansas, which produced over 66.5 million bushels in 1987. Soybean protein is a complete protein; its amino acid pattern conforms closely to that of milk. It is extremely low in saturated fats and contains no cholesterol. In the United States, soybeans are produced mainly for the oil (with the protein by-product used to feed livestock), but in China and Japan, tofu (or soybean curd) is a major source of protein in the diet, much as bread and dairy products are here.

Tofu has been embraced by many cooks as an adaptable substitute for meat, with little change in recipes or cooking techniques. Bland in taste, tofu takes on the flavor of the dish it is in. At one time, tofu could be purchased only in specialty shops, but now it is produced in Kansas and can be found in most supermarkets.

2 tablespoons safflower oil
½ pound tofu, cut into small cubes
1 large onion, chopped
3 garlic cloves, minced
1 teaspoon summer savory
1 pound fresh spinach, stemmed and chopped
1 teaspoon oregano
½ teaspoon salt
¼ teaspoon pepper
1 tablespoon dry white wine
½ cup Parmesan cheese, grated
2 8-ounce cans tomato sauce
1 10-ounce can enchilada sauce
1 tablespoon chili powder (optional)
12 corn tortillas
2 cups Monterey jack cheese, shredded
1 6-ounce can pitted black olives, drained and chopped

Heat the safflower oil in a large skillet over medium heat. Add the tofu, onion, garlic, and summer savory and sauté for 3 minutes, or until the onion is tender-crisp.

Add the chopped spinach, oregano, salt, pepper, and wine. Cover and cook over low heat until the spinach is wilted, about 3 to 5 minutes. Remove from heat and stir in the Parmesan cheese.

In a medium saucepan, combine the tomato sauce, enchilada sauce, and chili powder, if desired. Bring the mixture to a boil over high heat. Reduce heat to low and simmer for 10 minutes.

With a pair of tongs, dip a tortilla in the sauce for a few seconds, until flexible. Drain briefly and lay on a plate. Spoon some of the tofu and spinach filling on top. Roll up and place in a greased 13 x 9–inch baking dish. Repeat the procedure with the remaining tortillas.

Cover the enchiladas with the remaining sauce. Cover the baking dish with foil and bake at 350 degrees for 30 minutes. Uncover and top with the Monterey jack cheese and black olives. Return to the oven and bake uncovered for 5 minutes, or until the cheese is melted and bubbly.

Serves 4.

✳ Tomato-Cheese Rarebit

This dish is a varia-tion of Welsh rabbit (or rarebit), the cheese and ale sauce served over toast, crackers, or sliced tomatoes. If tomatoes are added to the sauce, it is some-times called "blushing bunny." It makes a quick comfort meal of wholesome ingredi-ents, especially when using homemade bread and canned tomatoes put by in the summer.

2 tablespoons butter
2 tablespoons onion, finely chopped
4 cups canned tomatoes, drained and chopped
1 egg
2 cups cheddar cheese, shredded
½ teaspoon Worcestershire sauce
pinch of cayenne, or 1 teaspoon dry mustard
¼ teaspoon salt
4 slices of toasted homemade bread

In a saucepan, melt the butter over medium heat and cook the onion until soft and transparent. Add the toma-toes and simmer for 5 to 10 minutes. Remove the pan from heat.

In a mixing bowl, beat the egg well. Stir in a spoonful of the hot tomato mixture, then add the cheese. Stir in a little more of the tomatoes. Pour the cheese mixture into the saucepan. Return the pan to low heat and cook until the cheese is melted. Remove from heat and add the Worcestershire, cayenne or dry mustard, and salt. Immediately pour over the toasted bread and serve.

Serves 4.

✳ VEGETABLES

After acquiring their homestead, Kansas pioneers first built a home and then plowed and seeded their land with income crops. Next came the all-important task of planting a vegetable garden. The entire family took part in the difficult job of turning over the rigid prairie soil for garden space. They first planted corn, beans, squash, and pumpkins, as had the Indians, spending much of their time hauling water and praying for rain. Sometimes the scorching heat of prairie summers ruined the plants, or the grasshoppers ate the vegetables, but in better times, the rains came and the garden blossomed into a cornucopia of vegetables, enough to get a pioneer family through the winter.

These days, both farm and town families enjoy the pleasure of a backyard garden that supports a variety of luscious vegetables. The pleasure of watching the vegetables grow is matched only by the pleasure of sharing them. In July and August, as gardens begin to yield their treasures, the talk among friends and neighbors often starts with, "Got any ripe tomatoes yet?" "How's the corn looking?" or "Do you need any green beans?"

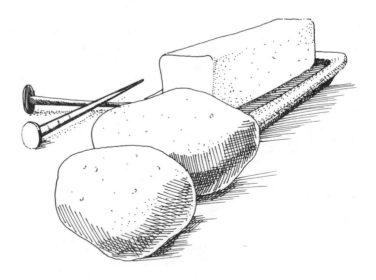

Usually these conversations end with an exchange of some of those garden delights.

The versatility of vegetables is presented in this chapter. Recipes for two classics, Baked Potatoes and Real Mashed Potatoes, give the cook detailed instructions for the very best results. Recipes for steamed, grilled, and boiled vegetables include contemporary dishes such as Steamed Squash with Tomato-Basil Butter, Grilled Sweet Potato Sticks, and Corn with Anise Butter. Vegetables in cream sauces—Spinach with Horseradish Cream and Sour Cream Beets—are also featured. An assortment of recipes for root vegetables, greens (both wild and domestic), and vegetable casseroles suggest vegetable dishes to fit almost any meal.

✳ Baked Potatoes

The potato is a simple and noble vegetable. Baked, it has remained a staple in hearty Midwestern cooking and is truly loved by all. However, today's busy or careless cooks often end up with an insipid baked potato, because they overcook it, undercook it, or bombard it with microwaves until its firm flesh shrivels into pasty submission.

M. F. K. Fisher comments on the baked potato in her book The Art of Eating *(New York: Random House, 1976): "If, baked and pinched open and bulging with mealy snowiness, they offset the fat spiced flavor of a pile of sausages— then and then alone should they be served.*

Then they are dig-nified. Then they are worthy of a high place, not debased to the deadly rank of daily acceptance. Then they are a gastronomic pleasure, not merely 'tubers used for food.'"

This simple recipe for baking potatoes gives clear and easy instructions for making the very best baked potatoes.

4 large russet potatoes
8 potato baking nails, common 16d aluminum nails, well
     washed, or metal skewers*
olive oil
salt
butter
pepper, coarsely ground
sour cream (optional)

Wash the potatoes and pat dry with paper towels. Cut out a shallow spot the size of a nickel in each potato. Insert two nails in each potato, one in each end, or run a skewer through each potato. Rub potatoes with olive oil and sprinkle with salt.

Place the potatoes in a preheated oven of 400 degrees, directly on the rack and centered in the middle of the oven. Bake for 45 minutes to 1 hour, or until the potatoes can be pierced easily with a sharp knife. (The insertion of the nails or skewer speeds up the baking time.)

Remove the nails with an oven mitt and serve the pota-

*Aluminum baking nails are available at specialty kitchen stores.

toes immediately with butter and a few grindings of high quality black pepper. Top with a dollop of sour cream if desired.

Serves 4.

✳ Yogurt Stuffed Potatoes

This recipe offers the perfect solution for what to do with leftover baked potatoes. Simply scoop out the insides of the potatoes from the skins, mix in a few simple ingredients, and return the mixture to the shells for a new version of the old favorite, twice-baked potatoes. Serve with beef steak or fish in place of a baked potato.

4 large baking potatoes
¾ cup plain yogurt
½ teaspoon salt
¼ teaspoon pepper
⅓ to ⅔ cup milk, scalded
2 green onions, chopped
½ cup sharp cheddar cheese, shredded
3 tablespoons butter, melted

Wash potatoes and pierce them several times with a fork. Bake them at 400 degrees for about 1 to 1½ hours, or until soft.

Remove potatoes from the oven and cool for 10 minutes. Slice the potatoes open lengthwise and scoop out the insides, being careful not to tear the skins. Set the skins aside. Place potato in a mixing bowl and mash with a hand-masher or electric mixer. Add the yogurt, salt, and pepper. Add the milk, as needed, until the potato mixture is smooth and light. Stir in the green onion and cheese. Spoon the potato mixture into the shells. Top each potato half with about 1 teaspoon of melted butter.

Place the potato halves in a large baking dish. Bake uncovered at 400 degrees for 30 minutes, or until tops are golden.

Serves 4 to 8.

✳ Real Mashed Potatoes

Never think of mashed potatoes as merely a perfunctory side dish. There is a pleasant texture to their starchy blandness that stands alone or provides a palette upon which to present other delicious tastes—such as gravy or simply butter. Mashed potatoes were another version of that basic staple in the pioneer's diet, a hearty starch for hungry farm hands and field workers, comfort food for the sick and frail, and by today's standards, just good country cooking.

The most common way to serve mashed potatoes is to ladle a rich gravy into the well made with the back of a spoon. These days, many people skip the gravy, because, if made correctly, mashed potatoes are a treat by themselves. This version gives detailed instructions to achieve perfection.

6 medium red potatoes
1 teaspoon salt
3 tablespoons butter
1 teaspoon salt
⅓ cup hot milk

Peel the potatoes, quarter, and place in a large pot of cold water. Bring the water to a boil and add 1 teaspoon of salt. Boil gently until the potatoes are tender when pierced with a table knife. Drain off the water and mash the potatoes by hand with a potato masher. Add the butter and salt and mash again. Slowly add the hot milk, mixing with an electric mixer, until smooth and thoroughly blended.
      Serves 8.

✳ Old-Fashioned Potato Cakes

What do you do with those leftover mashed potatoes? The answer is, make potato cakes! Serve this traditional favorite for breakfast, lunch, or dinner.

3 cups cooked mashed potatoes, chilled
¾ cup all-purpose flour
¼ cup butter

Shape the mashed potatoes into cakes about 3 inches in diameter and ½ inch thick. Dust with flour, shaking off excess.

Heat the butter in a large frying pan over medium heat. Fry the potato cakes until lightly browned, about 3 to 5 minutes each side, turning carefully. Add more butter to the pan if necessary.

Serves 4 to 6.

Variation: Mix finely chopped green onion, grated cheese, herbs, or minced garlic into the potatoes before frying. Serve with a dollop of sour cream.

✳ Garlic Potatoes Supreme

Here's a deliciously different way to serve mashed potatoes on a warm summer day.

2 to 3 large red potatoes, peeled and quartered (about 1½ pounds)
6 tablespoons extra-virgin olive oil
4 garlic cloves, minced
½ teaspoon salt
⅛ teaspoon pepper
1 to 3 tablespoons tarragon vinegar or white wine vinegar, to taste
1 tablespoon fresh parsley, finely chopped
¼ cup red onion, chopped

Place the peeled and quartered potatoes in a pan of cold water and bring to a boil. Boil gently until the potatoes are tender. Drain off the water and coarsely mash the potatoes with a handmasher or a fork. Do not use an electric mixer, because they should not be completely smooth.

Add the olive oil, garlic, salt, and pepper. Mix well. Add the vinegar to taste. Stir in the chopped parsley and red onion. Serve warm or at room temperature.

Serves 4.

✳ Fried Potatoes with Garlic and Onion

Almost everyone grew up on some kind of fried potatoes. In earlier times, potatoes were fried in large amounts of lard or bacon fat. This version adds onion and fresh garlic and fries the potatoes in a small amount of olive oil—fulfilling both our quest for less fat in our diet and our expectations of the dish.

3 medium potatoes (about 3 cups, peeled and diced)
1 large onion
¼ cup olive oil
3 garlic cloves, minced
salt and pepper, to taste

Peel and dice the potatoes into ½-inch cubes. Finely chop the onion.

Heat the olive oil over medium-high heat in a large, nonstick skillet. When hot enough to sizzle, add the potatoes and onion and reduce heat to medium. Fry, turning the mixture frequently, until the potatoes and onion are tender and golden, about 20 minutes. During the last 5 minutes of cooking, reduce heat to medium-low and add the minced garlic. Sprinkle with salt and pepper to taste.

Remove the potatoes from the pan and drain briefly on paper towels, if desired.

Serves 4 to 6.

✳ Pommes Frites

Pommes Frites, or fried potatoes, are a standard in French country cooking and were most certainly included in the meals of French settlers here in Kansas. What makes these simple fried potatoes outstanding is the care with which they are cooked. Watching the pan temperature and turning the potatoes carefully as each surface becomes golden brown will result in a crispy texture and a colorful complement to many main courses.

4 medium red potatoes
2 tablespoons butter
2 tablespoons olive oil
2 tablespoons fresh parsley, minced

Peel and quarter the potatoes. Place them in a pan, cover with water, and boil until they can be pierced with a table knife. Drain the potatoes in a strainer, or pat them completely dry before frying.

In a skillet, heat the butter and olive oil together over medium-high heat and add the boiled potatoes. Brown the potatoes on all sides by turning them individually. Adjust the heat as necessary to cook them evenly, until golden brown. Sprinkle the minced parsley over the potatoes just before serving.

Serves 4 to 6.

✳ German Potato Pancakes
(Kartoffelpuffer)

Potato pancakes remain a favorite in the German communities of Kansas. Made with shredded potatoes and onion, they are fried to a crispy golden brown on the outside but remain soft and creamy on the inside.

2 medium potatoes
1 medium onion
1 egg
2 tablespoons all-purpose flour
½ teaspoon salt
2 teaspoons fresh parsley, finely chopped
dash of nutmeg
bacon fat, vegetable oil, or shortening, for frying

Peel and shred (or grate) the potatoes and onion and place them in a large bowl. In a small bowl, beat the egg. Gradually add the flour, salt, parsley, and nutmeg, beating with a wire whip. Pour the mixture over the shredded potatoes and onion, stirring to combine.

Over medium heat, add bacon fat, vegetable oil, or shortening to a depth of ¼ inch in a large frying pan. When hot enough to sizzle, pour in some of the potato mixture. With a spatula, shape the mixture into a pancake about 4 inches in diameter. Repeat with the remaining potato mixture, making 4 to 6 pancakes. Do not crowd.

Fry the potato pancakes for 3 to 5 minutes each side, or until golden brown. Drain briefly on paper towels and serve warm.

Serves 4 to 6.

✳ Scalloped Potatoes

Charlene Mason Simpson, Garland

"About fifty years ago, when I was ten years old, I was expected to prepare the noon meal while my mother helped my dad with the farm work," recalls Charlene Simpson.

3 to 4 medium potatoes
½ cup onion
2 tablespoons butter
salt and pepper, to taste
2 tablespoons all-purpose flour
1¾ cups milk
1 cup cheddar cheese, shredded

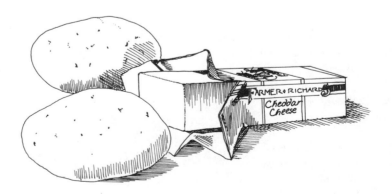

*"We always had pota-
toes in some form, as
they were a staple in
our diet. We fixed a lot
of scalloped potatoes
for the threshing crew
during harvest time
because it was an easy
dish to prepare."*

Peel and thinly slice the potatoes and finely chop the onion. Arrange half the potato slices in a 9-inch baking dish. Sprinkle with half the onion. Dot with 1 tablespoon of the butter and add salt and pepper. Sprinkle with 1 tablespoon of the flour. Place the remaining potato slices in the dish and layer as before. Pour the milk over all and bake covered at 350 degrees for 45 minutes.

Sprinkle the cheddar cheese over the potatoes, uncover, and continue baking for 30 to 45 minutes, or until the potatoes are tender and the sauce thickens.

Serves 6.

✳ New Potatoes with Dill and Butter

*Most backyard gar-
deners delight in
digging a few potatoes
in early summer, for
there is nothing so
special as the fresh,
earthy taste of new
potatoes. This very
simple method for
preparing them is
probably the best way
to enjoy their naturally
delicious flavor.*

1 pound new potatoes
2 tablespoons butter
2 teaspoons fresh dill, chopped, or ½ teaspoon dry dill
salt and pepper, to taste

Wash the potatoes. Carefully peel off a thin strip of the skin to create a ring around the center of each potato. Drop the potatoes into a large pot of boiling water and cook them just until tender, 15 to 20 minutes. Remove and drain well.

Melt the butter in a large frying pan over medium-low heat. Add the potatoes and shake the pan until they are well coated with butter. Cook the potatoes, shaking the pan occasionally, to brown them evenly. Sprinkle with dill and add salt and pepper to taste. Shake to mix and serve.

Serves 4.

Nicodemus: Promised Land of the Prairie

In 1877, the site of Nicodemus—believed to be named for the first slave to buy his freedom in America—was promoted to blacks in Kentucky by two land speculators, one white (W. R. Hill) and one black (W. H. Smith). Hill's sales pitch told tales of abundant game, wild horses, adequate water and timber, and fertile land. Appealing to blacks' sense of economic disadvantage in the white-dominated South, Hill and Smith's circular claimed that Nicodemus would become the "Largest Colored Settlement in America." Meanwhile, in Topeka, Reverend Simon Roundtree and four other blacks from Kentucky and Tennessee formed the Nicodemus Town Company. They arrived in Nicodemus in July 1877 and were joined over the next three years by freed slaves from Kentucky, Tennessee, and Mississippi.

Unfortunately, Nicodemus was not the promised land of the prairie touted by the promoters. Building materials were scarce and animals, farm implements, and provisions were in short supply. The colony was forced to seek aid from the governor and nearby communities to survive. Over time, however, the community grew and prospered to seven hundred residents, becoming one of the largest communities in northwest Kansas. The black settlers were proud of their town and their proven ability to survive as a community independent of white society.

Like hundreds of other small Midwestern towns, the railroad never came to Nicodemus and the population began to decline in 1910. In 1988 the residents numbered fewer than one hundred. But Nicodemus is not forgotten by those who moved away. Every summer, the Annual Homecoming is held during the last weekend of July and families who once lived there or whose ancestors settled Nicodemus come home to celebrate. The festivities include a special program and parade, ending with a church service and dinner on Sunday.

Celebrations of this kind as well as "camp meetings" held by black settlements were usually for religious and political purposes. They also gave families a chance to socialize. Cracklin' corn bread, meats roasted over a fire pit, greens, and sweet potatoes were some of the foods that probably graced the tables of these past celebrations.

✳ Aunt Jane's Sweet Potatoes

Mary Mize, Topeka

"I remember visiting my Great-Aunt Jane as a young girl, and she would serve these sweet potatoes," says Mary Mize. "It seems that the recipe dated back to before the Civil War." Mary likes to serve this special dish to family and friends on the holidays.

4 sweet potatoes
½ cup butter or margarine
¾ cup all-purpose flour
¼ cup sugar
salt and pepper, to taste
pinch of cinnamon (optional)

Peel and quarter the sweet potatoes. Melt the butter or margarine in a small pan over low heat. In a shallow bowl, combine the flour and sugar. Add salt and pepper to taste, and cinnamon if desired. Dip the sweet potatoes in the butter or margarine, turning to coat well. Roll them in the flour and sugar mixture and set aside.

Pour the remaining melted butter or margarine into a 13 x 9–inch baking dish to coat. Place the sweet potatoes in the baking dish. Bake uncovered at 350 degrees for 30 to 40 minutes, or until tender. Gently turn the potatoes over after 15 to 20 minutes of baking.

Serves 6 to 8.

✳ Candied Sweet Potatoes

Marj Thompson, Hutchinson

Candied Sweet Potatoes are a universal holiday selection of children as well as adults. Serve them with roasted turkey, ham, or capon.

4 sweet potatoes, unpeeled
½ cup brown sugar
salt, to taste
¼ cup butter or margarine

SAUCE
½ cup brown sugar
1 tablespoon cornstarch
½ teaspoon cinnamon
¼ teaspoon allspice
1 cup apple or pineapple juice
2 tablespoons butter or margarine
¼ cup pecans, coarsely chopped (optional)

Drop the unpeeled sweet potatoes into a large pot of boiling water and cook just until tender, about 25 minutes. Drain and cool. Peel and cut the potatoes into thick slices. Place them in a 13 x 9–inch baking dish. Sprinkle the potato slices with brown sugar and add salt to taste. Dot with butter or margarine and bake uncovered at 325 degrees for 30 minutes. Meanwhile, make the sauce.

Sauce: In a saucepan, blend the brown sugar, cornstarch, cinnamon, and allspice together. Stir in the apple or pineapple juice and add the butter or margarine. Bring the sauce to a boil over medium-high heat and stir for 2 minutes.

When ready to serve, pour the sauce over the sweet potatoes and sprinkle with chopped pecans, if desired.

Serves 6 to 8.

✳ Grilled Sweet Potato Sticks

For a colorful alternative, substitute sweet potatoes as the starch side dish for an outdoor meal.

4 large sweet potatoes
melted butter or sesame oil
salt and pepper, to taste

Boil the well-washed sweet potatoes in their jackets in a covered pot of salted water. When tender, drain off the water and dry them by shaking the pan over the heat. When cool enough to handle, pull off the skins. Cut them into thick lengthwise strips.

Brush the strips with butter or sesame oil. Grill directly over hot coals, carefully turning often until golden brown, or broil on a broiler pan in the oven. Sprinkle with salt and pepper to taste.

Serves 6 to 8.

Corn Is King

By 1860, more than ten thousand farms were operating in the state and the most important crop was corn. George Hildt wrote of planting his corn in 1857: "Mon-

day I planted my acre of corn in the sod. . . . I planted
mine with an axe . . . by chopping in the sod at a suitable
distance apart and putting in three or four grains of corn
and stamping it under with your foot or axe. It requires
no further attention the first year as weeds do not bother
you."

Corn's central position in the life of Kansans was
shown in 1899, when the Atchison Corn Carnival drew an
estimated twenty-five thousand people. One of the most
successful celebrations held in the state of Kansas, the
entertainment included a corn show, brass bands, the-
ater, a carnival, fireworks, and a baseball game between
the Kansas City Blues and the Atchison Corn Carnival
Colts.

After the 1905 carnival, Henry Field, writer for the
Shenandoah (Iowa) *World*, wrote in *The Atchison Corn
Carnival, 1905*, "The Atchison Corn Carnival was one of
the great events of my life. It is a passion; an outburst;
a glorification of King Corn, and the Spirit of the West.
It is peculiar to Atchison, and an amazing thing is it is
all free."

Though botanically the word "corn" simply means
grain, to Americans it signifies maize. Two types are
commonly grown: field corn, which is used for fodder,
and sweet corn, native to this country and a vital crop
for centuries. In fact, the United States is one of the few

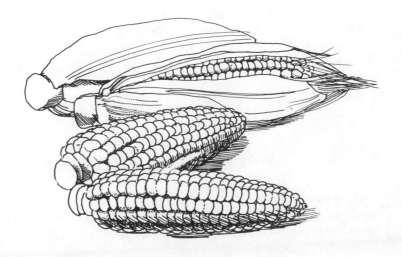

countries where sweet corn, cooked as a vegetable, plays an important dietary role.

Kansas is part of the Corn Belt and an important producer of corn and corn products. Popcorn, another kind of corn that has small kernels, is also grown in the state, as is a recently introduced variety of blue corn.

✳ Barbecued Sweet Corn

A real campfire treat is to bake corn in mud casings. Good old Kansas mud, the reddish clay variety, seems to work best. Pack the mud around each unhusked ear and bury it in the hot coals of a campfire. In about an hour, the clay should be baked and the kernels should show some light browning. The following recipe describes an easier way to barbecue corn on the backyard grill.

6 ears of fresh sweet corn in the husks
ice water
salt (optional)

Pull back the husks, remove the silk, and replace the husk. Tie the husks with string or fine wire at the center and at the tip of the cob, making sure the kernels are covered. Place the ears of corn in a pan of ice water, salted if desired, and soak for 15 to 30 minutes.

Drain the ears and place them directly over hot coals for 10 to 20 minutes, turning frequently, until the kernels are tender. Just before serving, remove the husks. If tied with wire, snip the hot wires with wire cutters, wearing gloves or using hot pads.

Serves 6.

✳ Corn with Anise Butter

It is surprising that corn remains a uniquely American

ANISE BUTTER
½ teaspoon aniseed
1 teaspoon boiling water

food. It was taken back
to Europe centuries
ago by explorers, but it
is rarely served there
as a vegetable. Im-
migrants to Kansas,
however, depended
on corn as a staple
in their diets, as a
vegetable as well as a
grain. This recipe uses
anise to spice up an
old standard.

2 tablespoons butter, slightly softened
⅛ teaspoon anise flavoring
1 tablespoon fresh parsley, chopped

4 fresh ears of sweet corn, or 1 17-ounce can corn

Anise Butter: Place the aniseed in a small cup. Pour
1 teaspoon of boiling water over it and soften for 30 minutes. With a fork, stir in the butter, anise flavoring, and
chopped parsley.

Boil the ears of corn in a large pot until tender, or simmer the canned corn, undrained, in a saucepan over low
heat.

To serve, spread the Anise Butter on the ears of corn,
or drain the canned corn and stir in the Anise Butter.

Serves 4.

✳ Swiss Corn Casserole

Sharon K. Wienck, Barnes

This great potluck dish
was a contest winner
for Sharon Wienck,
who studies home eco-
nomics education at
Kansas State Uni-
versity. Her recipe
won first place in the
vegetable category at
the 1987 Washing-

1 16-ounce can cream-style corn
¼ cup all-purpose flour
3 ounces cream cheese, diced
½ teaspoon onion salt
1 16-ounce can whole kernel corn, drained
1 6-ounce can sliced mushrooms, drained
¾ cup Swiss cheese, shredded
1½ cups fresh bread crumbs
2 tablespoons butter, melted

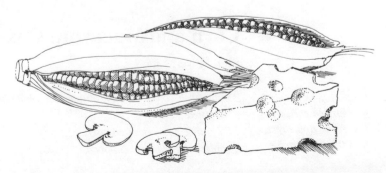

ton County Tasting Luncheon.

Combine the cream-style corn and flour in a large saucepan. Add the diced cream cheese and the onion salt. Cook over medium heat, stirring constantly, until the cream cheese melts. Add the whole kernel corn, mushrooms, and the shredded cheese.

In a small bowl, combine the bread crumbs and melted butter and set aside.

Pour the corn mixture into a lightly greased 1½-quart casserole dish. Cover and bake at 350 degrees for 30 minutes. Top with the buttered bread crumbs and bake uncovered for an additional 20 to 25 minutes, or until top is lightly browned.

Serves 8.

✳ Creamy Corn

Eileen Cox, Lakin

For large family dinners, this easy corn dish is terrific because you can "fix and forget" it while preparing other items that need more attention.

4 cups fresh corn, or 2 10-ounce packages frozen corn
2 tablespoons sugar
1 8-ounce package cream cheese
½ cup butter or margarine
6 tablespoons water

Combine all ingredients in a slow cooker and cover. Cook on low for 4 hours, stirring occasionally. Or cover and cook slowly in a heavy saucepan over very low heat for 1 hour, stirring occasionally.

Serves 8.

✳ Corn and Macaroni Casserole

Ruth Meyer, Linn

Ruth Meyer uses her homegrown corn in this recipe and says that this "easy and

2 cups fresh corn, or 1 17-ounce can whole kernel corn, drained
1 17-ounce can creamed corn
2 tablespoons onion, chopped

*fast" dish is popular
with her family and
at potluck dinners.*

2 tablespoons green pepper, chopped
1 cup processed cheese, cubed
1 cup macaroni, uncooked
½ cup butter or margarine, melted
salt, to taste

In a large bowl, combine all of the ingredients. Pour the mixture into a large casserole. Cover and bake at 350 degrees for 30 minutes. Uncover and bake for an additional 30 minutes.

Serves 6.

People of the South Wind

The state of Kansas took its name from the Kansa Indians, or "people of the south wind." By the 1830s, Kansas was not only inhabited by the Kansa, Cheyenne, and Osage tribes but also had become the home of the Kickapoos, Potawatomis, Cherokees, Delawares, and other tribes that were relocated by the United States government.

Of the tribes located in Kansas, only those tribes that relied strictly on bison for meat were considered Plains Indians. The men gathered periodically for organized hunts, and the women tended the crops, which consisted primarily of the "holy threesome"—corn, beans, and squash. Because corn, the mythological food of the gods, by itself did not provide adequate nutrition, the Indians augmented their meals with beans and squash. Dried corn was ground into meal, baked as bread, used as batter to fry meats, and cooked as porridge. When traveling, Indians carried a high-protein food called pemmican, which was made of powdered buffalo jerky bound with berries and a small amount of lard. The Indians dried fruits and vegetables as well and stored the surplus in cool, underground pits where the food was preserved and protected from predators. Early settlers in Kansas learned many of these Indian practices.

The Kickapoo, Potawatomi, Iowa, Sac, and Fox tribes

still maintain reservations in Kansas today, although their populations have dwindled since a century ago. Tribal meetings and gatherings are occasionally held on the reservations, with traditional foods being an important part of the festivities.

✳ Autumn Squash

Squash was an important vegetable to the Kansa, Osage, and Pawnee Indians who inhabited Kansas. These tribes lived in villages of large earth lodges and cultivated corn and beans, as well as squash. The early settlers learned from the Indians, and these vegetables became some of the first ones they planted.

This recipe, featuring two kinds of squash, combines the beautiful fall colors of yellow and orange —making it as pretty as a maple tree in a Kansas autumn.

2 acorn squash
½ cup water
2 tablespoons butter
2 yellow squash, thinly sliced
1 onion, sliced in rings
6 tablespoons sour cream
¼ teaspoon salt
¼ teaspoon pepper

TOPPING
¼ cup Parmesan cheese, grated
1 cup fresh bread crumbs, finely chopped
½ teaspoon herb blend (equal parts parsley, thyme, oregano or tarragon)
2 tablespoons butter, melted

Cut the acorn squash in half lengthwise and remove the seeds. Place the halves in a large baking dish cut-side down. Add the water and bake uncovered at 350 degrees for about 25 minutes, or until fork-tender.

Meanwhile, in a large skillet, melt the butter over medium heat and cook the sliced yellow squash and onion together until both vegetables are soft and translucent. Remove from heat and add the sour cream, salt, and pepper, stirring until well mixed.

Fill each half of the acorn squash with the yellow squash filling and return to the oven for about 5 minutes to reheat.

Topping: In a small bowl, combine the Parmesan cheese, bread crumbs, and herb blend. Sprinkle the topping over the filling, drizzle the melted butter on top, and place under the broiler to brown.

Serves 4.

✳ Savory Squash Cobbler

Though this cobbler looks very much like a peach cobbler, it is actually cooked butternut squash in a savory sauce of chicken broth, cinnamon, and sour cream covered with a bread crumb and almond topping.

1 butternut squash, about 2½ to 3 pounds
½ cup water
salt, to taste
3 bacon strips
1 medium onion, finely chopped
2 tablespoons butter
2 tablespoons all-purpose flour
½ teaspoon cinnamon
1¼ cups chicken broth
¼ cup sour cream

TOPPING
1 cup fresh bread crumbs
2 tablespoons almonds, finely chopped
2 tablespoons butter, melted

Cut the butternut squash in half lengthwise and remove the seeds. Place the halves in a large baking dish cut-side down. Add the water and bake uncovered at 350 degrees for about 30 to 40 minutes, or until fork-tender. Remove from the pan and cool. Cut the squash lengthwise into several large slices. Slice the pulp from the rind and cut into 1-inch cubes. Measure 4 cups of squash. Sprinkle with salt to taste and set aside.

Fry the bacon in a large skillet over medium-low heat. Drain and crumble. Set aside. Add the onion to the drippings and cook until tender. Add the butter to skillet. Stir the flour and cinnamon together in a small cup and sprinkle it over the skillet mixture, stirring for 1 minute. Slowly add the chicken broth, stirring until it begins to thicken and boil. Remove the pan from heat and stir in the sour cream. Combine the sauce with the squash and crumbled bacon and pour into a 2-quart baking dish.

Topping: Combine the bread crumbs and almonds in a small bowl. Stir in 2 tablespoons of melted butter and sprinkle the topping over the squash.

Bake uncovered at 350 degrees for 25 to 30 minutes, or until hot and bubbly. Let stand for 10 minutes before serving.

Serves 6.

✳ Sweet and Nutty Butternut Squash

Baked squash is an ideal fall dish to serve with roast turkey or wild fowl. In this recipe, it is lightly sprinkled with butter, brown sugar, spices, and ground nuts.

1 large butternut squash
½ cup water
2 tablespoons brown sugar
⅛ teaspoon cinnamon
⅛ teaspoon ginger
⅛ teaspoon salt
2 tablespoons butter
1 tablespoon pecans or English walnuts, ground

Cut the squash in half lengthwise and remove the seeds. Place the halves in a large baking dish, cut-side down.

Add the water and bake uncovered at 350 degrees for 30 to 40 minutes, or until fork-tender. Remove the squash from the pan and cool. Slice the squash into lengthwise strips about ½ inch wide. Cut the strips into 3-inch lengths. Slice the pulp from the rind and arrange the squash strips in a 9-inch baking dish.

In a small bowl, combine the brown sugar, cinnamon, ginger, and salt. Sprinkle the mixture over the squash and dot evenly with butter. Top with ground pecans or walnuts.

Bake uncovered at 350 degrees for 15 minutes. Serves 4.

✳ Steamed Squash with Tomato-Basil Butter

Fresh yellow crookneck squash is a Kansas garden favorite and is readily available in the summertime. This tasty recipe contrasts the bright yellow squash with a dollop of rose-colored Tomato-Basil Butter.

TOMATO-BASIL BUTTER
¼ cup butter, slightly softened
4 teaspoons tomato paste
½ teaspoon dried basil

STEAMED SQUASH
1 pound yellow crookneck squash,
*   sliced into ⅛-inch rounds*
salt, to taste

Tomato-Basil Butter: In a mixing bowl, cream the butter until it is light and fluffy. Add the tomato paste and the basil, mixing well. Cover and refrigerate for 30 minutes. Set the butter out to soften slightly for about 10 minutes before using.

Steamed Squash: Pour water into a vegetable steamer and bring it to a boil over medium-high heat. Slice the squash and place in the steamer. Steam for 5 to 8 minutes, or until the squash is tender.

Remove the squash from the steamer and sprinkle with salt to taste. Place a serving of squash on each plate and top with a dollop of the Tomato-Basil Butter.

Serves 4.

✳ Fried Yellow Squash

The combination of flour and cornmeal makes a delicious coating for fried squash.

2 small yellow squash
1 egg
½ cup all-purpose flour
½ cup yellow cornmeal
½ teaspoon salt
¼ cup vegetable oil

Wash the squash and pat dry. Slice into ⅛-inch slices. In a small bowl, beat the egg well. In a shallow bowl, combine the flour, cornmeal, and salt.

Heat the oil in a large frying pan over medium heat. Dip the sliced squash in the beaten egg and coat with the flour and cornmeal mixture. Place in the frying pan and cook for about 3 minutes each side, or until golden. Drain on paper towels and serve immediately.

Serves 4.

✳ Onions with Herbs and Butter

In the spring, early settlers pulled wild onions to flavor foods and enhance stews. Once a garden was established on the homestead, they cultivated several varieties of onions, as they were easy to grow.

This recipe, which treats the onion as a vegetable, is a grilled favorite in the summer when the onions are mild and sweet. If you grow your own herbs, use fresh ones, but double the amounts.

4 medium yellow onions
¼ teaspoon marjoram
¼ teaspoon thyme
¼ teaspoon basil
¼ teaspoon tarragon
salt and pepper, to taste
½ cup butter

Skin the onions. From the top, make a crisscross cut three-quarters of the way through each one. Place each onion on a large square of aluminum foil. Combine the marjoram, thyme, basil, and tarragon in a small bowl. Sprinkle ¼ teaspoon of the herb mixture over each onion. Sprinkle with salt and pepper to taste. Top each one with 2 tablespoons of butter. Wrap the foil securely around each onion to seal in the juices.

Place the onions over medium-hot coals on a covered grill and bake for 45 to 60 minutes, or until easily pierced with a knife and the juices begin to caramelize.

Serves 4.

Variation: Bake the onions in the oven at 400 degrees for 1 hour, or until tender.

✳ Grilled Carrots and Leeks

The classic combination of carrots and leeks can accompany all grilled foods.

1 large leek
4 to 5 carrots
1 tablespoon olive oil
¼ teaspoon marjoram
¼ teaspoon thyme
¼ teaspoon tarragon
⅛ teaspoon salt
⅛ teaspoon pepper
2 tablespoons butter

Peel away the outer leaves of the leek. Cut off the green tops 1 inch above the white section. Slice the leek into

¼-inch rounds. Place the slices in a bowl and rinse well to remove sand and dirt. Drain well. Peel the carrots and cut in half crosswise. Slice each half lengthwise into narrow strips.

Place the leek slices and carrot strips in a bowl. Add the olive oil, marjoram, thyme, tarragon, salt, and pepper, stirring to coat the vegetables.

Turn the vegetables onto a large sheet of aluminum foil. Dot with the butter. Seal the foil tightly and grill over indirect heat on a covered grill for about 45 to 60 minutes, or until the vegetables are tender.

Serves 4.

✳ Scalloped Carrots

Mrs. Wallace E. McClenny, Valley Falls

This baked carrot casserole is a good choice when a vegetable dish is needed for a picnic or potluck dinner.

4 cups carrots
3 tablespoons butter or margarine
1 medium onion, finely chopped
1 10-ounce can cream of celery soup
½ cup cheddar cheese, shredded
½ teaspoon salt
¼ teaspoon pepper

TOPPING
1½ cups dry bread crumbs, or seasoned stuffing mix
3 tablespoons butter, melted

Peel and slice the carrots into ⅛-inch rounds. Measure 4 cups of carrots and boil them just until tender-crisp. Drain well and place in a greased 9-inch baking dish.

Melt the butter or margarine over low heat in a medium-sized frying pan. Add the onion and cook until tender. Remove the pan from heat and add the soup, cheese, salt, and pepper, mixing well. Pour the mixture over the carrots.

Topping: In a small bowl, combine the dry bread crumbs or stuffing mix and 3 tablespoons of melted butter. Sprinkle on top of the casserole.

Bake uncovered at 350 degrees for 30 to 40 minutes, or until the topping is golden and the mixture is bubbly. Serves 6 to 8.

✳ Mint Glazed Carrots

Clarinda Burchill, El Dorado

This recipe and the next—for Sour Cream Beets—were two favorite vegetable dishes at the Birch-Hill Dining Room, once located in an old stone hotel in Augusta. Clarinda Burchill and her husband owned and operated the dining room from 1937 to 1941. "In those days we had very little modern equipment and few modern appliances," writes Clarinda. "Also, no mixes and packaged foods. Everything was made from scratch. Perhaps those were the good old days."

1½ pounds carrots
½ teaspoon salt
¼ cup butter or margarine
½ cup sugar
2 tablespoons mint leaves, finely chopped

Peel and cut the carrots into sticks or slices. Place them with the salt in a pot of boiling water. Cook the carrots until they are tender-crisp. Drain and set aside.

In a large frying pan or a Dutch oven, melt the butter or margarine over low heat. Add the sugar and cook, stirring until the sugar is dissolved. Add the carrots, turning gently until glazed, about 3 to 5 minutes. Remove from heat and gently stir in the chopped mint leaves.

Serves 6 to 8.

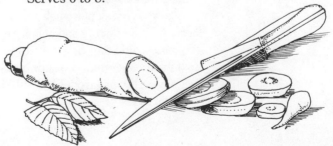

✳ Sour Cream Beets

Clarinda Burchill, El Dorado

The English were the first to bring beets to the United States. This colorful tuber, when combined with sour cream, makes a delicate complement to any pork dish.

3 bacon strips, diced
1 teaspoon all-purpose flour
1 teaspoon sugar
½ teaspoon salt
1 cup sour cream
2 tablespoons lemon juice
1 16-ounce can beets, drained and shredded

In a large frying pan or a Dutch oven, fry the diced bacon over medium-low heat until crisp. Add the flour and stir to combine. Stir in the sugar, salt, sour cream, and lemon juice. Cook for 2 minutes, stirring constantly. Add the shredded beets, mixing well, and heat throughout.
    Serves 4.

✳ Snow Peas, Carrots, and Onions

This colorful vegetable medley goes well with grilled red meats.

¾ cup carrots
¼ cup butter
½ cup canned pearl onions, rinsed and drained
⅓ pound fresh snow peas
salt, to taste
fresh or dried dill, to taste

Peel and slice the carrots into ⅛-inch rounds. Cook in boiling water until tender. Drain well.
    In a large frying pan, melt the butter over medium heat. Add the carrots and onions to the pan and sauté for 2 minutes. Add the snow peas to the pan and sauté for 2 to 3 minutes, or until the snow peas are tender-crisp.
    Remove the pan from heat, salt lightly, and sprinkle with dill to taste.
    Serves 4.

✳ Peas with Fresh Mint

Fresh peas and mint make this dish a springtime favorite. Frozen peas (or snow peas) may also be used in place of fresh ones.

⅓ cup water
⅛ teaspoon salt
1 pound fresh or frozen peas
1 teaspoon lemon juice
pinch of sugar
¼ cup butter
1 tablespoon fresh mint leaves, finely chopped

Pour the water into a medium-sized pan. Add the salt and bring to a boil. Add the peas, lemon juice, and a pinch of sugar. Reduce heat to low, cover, and simmer for about 10 minutes, or until tender-crisp.

Drain the water from the pan and add the butter and fresh mint. Stir gently and serve.

Serves 6 to 8.

✳ Spring Peas with Lettuce

Freshly shelled peas and lettuce from a Kansas spring garden make up this favorite vegetable dish. Serve it with roast chicken or wild fowl.

8 lettuce leaves, rinsed
2 cups freshly shelled peas, or 1 10-ounce package frozen peas
1 teaspoon water
2 green onions, chopped
¼ teaspoon fresh dill, or ⅛ teaspoon dried dill

½ teaspoon sugar
¼ teaspoon salt
⅛ teaspoon pepper
2 tablespoons butter

Line the bottom of a large skillet with the lettuce leaves. Cover with the peas and sprinkle with 1 teaspoon of water. Add the chopped green onion and sprinkle the top evenly with the dill, sugar, salt, and pepper. Dot evenly with the butter. Cover the skillet tightly and simmer over low heat for 10 to 15 minutes, or until the peas are tender.
    Serves 4.

✳ Layered Vegetable Casserole

Beverly J. Corcoran, Pittsburg

The cook has time to prepare nearly any entree while this vegetable casserole bakes lazily in the oven. For a meal-in-one, try putting a meat loaf of lean ground beef on top of the layered vegetables. Once the meat loaf is ready, the vegetables will be waiting underneath.

2 large potatoes, thinly sliced
1 medium zucchini, thinly sliced
1 large sweet onion, thinly sliced
1½ cups broccoli flowerets
2 to 3 medium tomatoes, peeled and sliced
1 carrot, peeled and shredded
salt and pepper, to taste
1 tablespoon butter
¼ cup water

Butter a large casserole or Dutch oven and layer the sliced vegetables in the pan in the order of the ingredients list. Sprinkle the vegetables with salt and pepper and dot the top with butter. Add the water, cover, and bake at 325 degrees for 1½ hours. The casserole can also be simmered slowly over very low heat on top of the stove for 2 to 3 hours, or until all the vegetables are tender.
    Serves 6 to 8.

✳ Collard Greens and Turnips

Leanna Galloway, Lawrence

Leanna Galloway moved to Lawrence from Mississippi twenty-seven years ago. She is eighty-six years old and still loves to garden. She even raised cotton in her yard once, which led to her picture appearing in the local paper.

Leanna grows a variety of vegetables, including several kinds of greens. She learned about wild greens after coming to Kansas. In the summer, her grandchildren still take her to the country to pick the wild varieties, which she often puts up for later use. "I'd rather eat wild greens. They taste better than the domestic ones," says Leanna.

Greens have a historic place in Kansas cooking. Pioneers gathered such wild greens as dandelion, pig weed, and lamb's quarters on their homesteads. They usually boiled the greens with salt pork or ham hocks. Sometimes potatoes or turnips, when available, were added to create a hardy dish.

Leanna suggests serving corn bread with these greens.

½ pound salt pork
4 cups water
1 bunch collard greens
2 to 3 medium turnips

Place the salt pork in a large pan or Dutch oven. Add the water and bring to a boil over high heat. Reduce heat to low, cover, and simmer for 1 hour. (For a less salty flavor, cover the salt pork with water and boil for several minutes. Drain well and boil again as directed.)

Wash the collard greens several times in cold water. Remove tough stems and tear large leaves into several pieces. Place the greens in the pan with the salt pork and remaining water. Cover and simmer over low heat for 30 minutes.

Peel and quarter the turnips and add to the pan. Simmer uncovered for 30 minutes more, or until the turnips are tender.

Serves 4.

✳ Spinach with Horseradish and Cream

In this recipe, fresh spinach, combined with cream and horseradish, makes a richly flavored side dish.

1 pound fresh spinach, or 1 10-ounce package frozen
    chopped spinach
½ cup whipping cream
2 teaspoons prepared horseradish
⅛ teaspoon salt
⅛ teaspoon pepper
1 tablespoon butter, softened

Wash the fresh spinach and chop. Place the spinach in a large pan without water, except for the drops that cling to the leaves. Cover and cook over low heat until leaves are tender, 3 to 5 minutes. (If using frozen spinach, cook according to package directions.) Drain the spinach in a large colander and press out the water.

Return the spinach to the pan and add the cream, horseradish, salt, and pepper. Bring the mixture to a boil over medium-high heat and cook until the cream thickens slightly. Remove from heat and stir in the butter.

Serves 4.

✳ Apples and Swedes Sauté

There are three kinds of turnips: the French navet, the common white turnip, and the yellow turnip. The yellow turnip is also known as the rutabaga or simply "the swede," indicating its place of origin. Swedes are considered to have the strongest flavor of the three and are preferred by those who appreciate the assertive flavor of turnips. Many Kansans of northern European descent have found swedes to be a pleasant complement to pork chops and ham.

1 pound rutabagas, diced
2 tablespoons butter
2 tablespoons brown sugar
¼ cup cider or applejack (optional)
2 tart apples, coarsely chopped
salt, to taste

In a large pot, boil the diced rutabagas just until tender, about 15 minutes. Melt the butter in a skillet and add the brown sugar. If desired, stir in the cider or applejack. Drain the rutabagas and add them with the apples to the skillet. Cook over medium-high heat, stirring occasionally until the rutabagas are glazed and lightly browned, about 8 to 10 minutes.

Serves 4 to 6.

✳ Souffléed Turnips

In The WPA Guide to 1930s Kansas *(Lawrence: University Press of Kansas, 1984),* one writer's tale gives the turnip a special role in the settlement of an area just east of Abilene: "This region was settled in the 1870s and 1880s by Germans from Wisconsin who lived in ox-drawn wagons until they built their homes. In later years the settlers declared that they came to Kansas because they had heard that here they might pull and eat turnips in the fields on Christmas. During the hardships that followed their moving, the pioneers often wondered why they had left comfortable homes for the occasional privilege of pulling turnips in December."

Perhaps this light and airy side dish of turnips would have provided some consolation!

3 medium turnips, about 1½ pounds
½ teaspoon salt
1 tablespoon butter, softened
1 egg yolk, beaten
¼ cup milk
½ teaspoon salt
¼ teaspoon pepper
¼ cup cheddar cheese, shredded
1 egg white

Peel and quarter the turnips. Place them in a large pan, cover with water, and add ½ teaspoon of salt. Boil until the turnips are tender, about 25 minutes. Drain well and mash thoroughly.

Add the butter, egg, milk, salt, and pepper to the mashed turnips, mixing well. Stir in the shredded cheese.

In a separate bowl, beat the egg white until stiff and gently fold into turnip mixture.

Pour the mixture into a buttered 1½-quart casserole. Bake uncovered at 375 degrees for about 25 minutes, or until lightly browned and an inserted knife comes out clean.

Serves 6.

✳ Zucchini with Pecans

Lisa Albright, McLouth

Lisa Albright, an organic gardener, says, "We Kansans come from diverse ethnic backgrounds. No matter how different our preferences are for culinary delights, we all have one thing in common: the precious soil that converts one tiny seed into a shining bouquet of deep green zucchini (that is, if harvested before baseball-bat size!). Conserving the soil and passing on this rich heritage to the coming generations is the original recipe for good eats!"

3 cups zucchini
1 to 2 teaspoons olive oil
2 garlic cloves, minced
¼ teaspoon pepper, freshly ground
salt, to taste
3 tablespoons pecans, chopped

Cut the zucchini into julienne strips. Coat a large skillet with the olive oil and place over medium-high heat. Add the zucchini and garlic and sauté just until tender-crisp. Add the remaining ingredients and toss gently.
   Serves 4.

✳ Broccoli with Lemon Cream

To retain the broccoli's bright green color, boil uncovered. The Lemon Cream adds contrast and elegance to this popular vegetable.

1 head broccoli

LEMON CREAM
1 cup whipping cream
1 egg yolk
½ teaspoon grated lemon rind
1 teaspoon lemon juice

Rinse the broccoli in cold water. Remove the leaves and trim off the tough part of the stalks. Cut the broccoli lengthwise into 4 to 6 servings. Place in a large pot of boiling water and cook uncovered for 5 to 10 minutes, or until tender-crisp.

Lemon Cream: Pour the whipping cream into a small saucepan. Boil over high heat for about 5 minutes, or until the sauce reduces to about ¾ cup. Remove from heat. Place the egg yolk in a small bowl and beat well. Stir 2 tablespoons of the hot cream into the egg yolk, then slowly add the egg mixture to the cream, stirring to combine. Return the mixture to low heat and continue stirring for 1 minute, or until slightly thickened. Do not boil. Remove the pan from heat and add the lemon rind and lemon juice.

Pour over the broccoli and serve immediately.
Serves 4 to 6.

✳ Escalloped Cabbage

Mrs. Wallace E. McClenny, Valley Falls

Cabbage is a versatile vegetable and has many uses, both cooked and raw. This baked cabbage casserole goes well with roast pork or chicken. For the best flavor, choose a firm, fresh head of cabbage free

1 small head of cabbage, cored and chopped into 1-inch pieces
3 tablespoons butter or margarine
½ teaspoon salt
¼ teaspoon pepper
1 cup cheddar cheese, shredded
3 cups cracker crumbs
1 egg, beaten
1 cup whipping cream, or half and half

*of yellow leaves and
decayed spots.*

Place the chopped cabbage in a large pan with the butter
or margarine, salt, and pepper. Add just enough water
to cover. Bring to a boil, reduce heat to low, and simmer
until the cabbage is tender, 5 to 10 minutes. Drain the
cabbage well.

Butter a 9-inch baking dish and add half of the cabbage.
Sprinkle half of the shredded cheese on top. Top with
half of the cracker crumbs. Repeat the layers, using the
remaining cabbage, cheese, and cracker crumbs.

In a small bowl, combine the beaten egg and the cream
or half and half. Pour the mixture over the cabbage,
cover, and bake at 350 degrees for 20 minutes. Remove
the cover and continue baking for 10 minutes more. Let
the casserole stand for 10 minutes before cutting.

Serves 6 to 8.

✳ Fried Okra Patty

Selan U. Hall, Jr., Lawrence

*In this recipe, sliced
okra, coated with
cornmeal and fried
with chopped onion
and jalapeño peppers,
is formed into a large
patty and topped with
cheese.*

*1 pound okra
1 cup yellow cornmeal
½ teaspoon salt
¼ teaspoon pepper
bacon drippings or vegetable shortening for frying
1 large onion, finely chopped
4 to 8 jalapeño peppers, seeded and chopped (to taste)
1 cup sharp cheddar cheese, shredded*

Cut the caps off the okra and slice in half lengthwise. In
a paper sack, combine the cornmeal, salt, and pepper.
Drop the sliced okra into the bag and shake to coat.

In a large frying pan, melt the bacon drippings or
shortening to a depth of ½ inch over medium heat. When
hot, add the okra and fry until well browned on the bottom, 10 minutes or longer. Turn over gently and add the
chopped onion and peppers to the pan. Fry for 10 minutes more, or until the vegetables are tender and well
browned. (The vegetables will stick together and form
a patty; do not try to separate.)

Sprinkle the shredded cheese over the vegetables. Reduce heat to low, cover, and continue cooking for 1 minute, or until the cheese melts.

With a large spatula, remove the patty from the pan and drain on paper towels. Cut into wedges and serve.

Serves 4 to 6.

✳ Green Beans with New Potatoes

In early summer, when the green beans and new potatoes are ready to harvest, this classic garden combination is a rite of the season for many cooks.

This recipe is a new twist on an old favor-ite. The smoked ham hock and onion give it that old-time flavor, while the use of sum-mer savory and fresh garlic adds a con-temporary flair. The cooking time has been shortened to make the vegetables tender but not mushy.

Green Beans with New Potatoes is a traditional vegetable side dish, but it is hearty enough for a one-course meal.

1 pound green beans, broken in half
1 onion, chopped
1 smoked ham hock
1 garlic clove, whole
½ teaspoon summer savory
1 teaspoon salt
¼ teaspoon pepper
1 pound new potatoes

Place all the ingredients, except the new potatoes, in a large pot or Dutch oven. Cover with cold water and bring to a boil over high heat. Reduce heat to low and partially cover the pan. Simmer for 45 minutes, stirring once or twice.

Add the new potatoes and continue cooking until the potatoes are tender, about 30 minutes more.

Take the ham hock out of the pot. Remove the bones and trim off the fat. Cut the meat into small pieces and return to the pot. Simmer for a few more minutes before serving.

Serves 4 to 6.

✳ Sweet and Sour "Schnibbled" Beans

(Schnibbelbohnen)

Janice Raven Hornbostel, Junction City

As a young woman, Sophie Bomhoff Lohmeyer traveled alone from Germany to Kansas. She settled here and raised a family, and they remember many of the fine recipes she brought with her from the old country. Though most were never written down, her family, three generations later, has recorded some of them so that they might be shared.

3 to 4 bacon strips, cut into 1-inch pieces
1 small onion, finely chopped
1 tablespoon all-purpose flour
½ cup sugar
½ cup apple-cider vinegar
½ cup water
2 15-ounce cans French-style green beans, drained
2 15-ounce cans great northern beans, drained
salt and pepper, to taste

In a large skillet, brown the bacon and onion over medium heat. Adjust heat as necessary to avoid burning the onion. Pour off all but 1 tablespoon of the drippings and stir in the flour. Continue cooking for 1 to 2 minutes.

Combine the sugar, vinegar, and water in a mixing bowl. Pour it slowly into the skillet, stirring constantly. Add the beans and simmer for 20 minutes, stirring occasionally. If possible, make a day ahead to enhance the flavor. Reheat before serving.

Serves 6 to 8.

✳ Lima Beans Brittany Style

(Flageolets à la Bretonne)

Simone Johnson, Topeka

Flageolets, small beans found in France, "are a cross between navy beans and lima beans," says Simone Johnson. "They are not available here, but I have found lima beans

2 10-ounce packages frozen baby lima beans
6 bacon strips, diced, or ¼ pound salt pork, diced
1½ cups onion, chopped
1 tablespoon garlic, minced
2 teaspoons fresh thyme, chopped, or 1 teaspoon dry thyme
1 cup tomatoes, peeled, seeded, and coarsely chopped
1 tablespoon fresh parsley, chopped

to be a good substitute in this recipe."

Fresh tomatoes, onion, garlic, and herbs from a summer garden lend themselves well to this recipe. This dish is traditionally served with roast leg of lamb.

Place the lima beans in a large pan and cook according to the package directions. Drain well.

In a large frying pan, cook the diced bacon or salt pork over medium-low heat until golden brown. Remove the bacon or salt pork and set aside, reserving 2 to 3 tablespoons of the fat in the pan. Add the onion and garlic and cook until tender, turning occasionally. Add the thyme and tomatoes and simmer slowly until the mixture thickens slightly. Stir in the cooked lima beans and continue cooking over low heat for 10 minutes more. Return the bacon or salt pork to the mixture, if desired. Sprinkle with fresh parsley and serve.

Serves 6 to 8.

✳ Swedish Brown Beans

(Bruna Bönor)

Mrs. Julia Peterson Hampton, Oskaloosa

Mrs. Julia Hampton grew up in Assaria, where her Swedish grandparents had settled in the 1860s. Her recipe for Swedish Brown Beans has been handed down through at least four generations. The slow cooking of these beans results in a rich and creamy texture.

1 pound dried Swedish brown beans*
1 cup butter
¾ cup brown sugar
2 teaspoons salt
2 tablespoons vinegar

Rinse the beans and soak in a large bowl overnight. Drain and transfer to a large pot or Dutch oven. Add water to cover and simmer over low heat for 1 hour. (The beans will have an unusual odor when they first begin to cook.) Add the butter, brown sugar, and salt. Continue cooking for another hour and add the vinegar. Replenish with water occasionally, as the liquid begins to evaporate. Cook for 2 to 4 hours more, until the mixture thickens and the beans are tender. When it begins to thicken, stir gently about every 20 minutes to prevent scorching.

Serves 6.

*Swedish brown beans can be found in specialty or Swedish food stores.

✳ German Baked Beans

Mary L. Kelling, Hays

"What is a picnic nowadays without baked beans?" says Mary Kelling. She sends us the recipe for baked beans that her mother brought from Germany to Kansas many years ago. This version is made with dried beans and cooked in a slow oven.

1 quart dried pea beans or Great Northern beans
½ to 1 pound diced salt pork, bacon, or ham
1 onion, chopped
½ cup catsup or barbecue sauce
¼ cup molasses
⅓ cup sugar
⅓ cup brown sugar
prepared mustard, chili powder, salt, and pepper, to taste

Wash the beans and place them in a large bowl. Cover with cold water and soak overnight.

Drain the beans and place them in a large pan or stock pot. Add water to cover and simmer over low heat for 1 hour. Drain, reserving the cooking liquid, and place the beans in a large earthenware pot or casserole dish. Add the remaining ingredients and ½ cup of the cooking liquid. Mix well and bake covered in a slow oven of 250 degrees for 6 to 8 hours, or until the beans are tender. Uncover during the last hour of baking. If the beans

become dry during cooking, add some of the reserved cooking liquid.

Serves 10 or more.

✳ Skillet Baked Beans

This quick-and-easy version of barbecued baked beans can be made in the skillet in minutes. Serve with hamburgers or hot dogs for a quick meal.

4 bacon strips, diced
½ cup onion, chopped
½ cup green pepper, seeded and chopped
1 16-ounce can pork and beans
1 15-ounce can red beans, drained
½ cup barbecue sauce
2 to 4 tablespoons brown sugar, to taste
⅛ teaspoon cayenne pepper

Brown the diced bacon in a large skillet or Dutch oven over medium-low heat. Remove the bacon and reserve. Add the chopped onion and green pepper to the drippings. Cook, stirring occasionally, until the vegetables are tender.

Add the beans, barbecue sauce, brown sugar (to taste), cayenne pepper, and the reserved bacon. Simmer slowly over low heat for 15 minutes, stirring occasionally. Adjust seasonings with additional barbecue sauce, brown sugar, or cayenne pepper.

Serves 6 to 8.

✳ Mom's Caraway Sauerkraut

Agnes Sabatka Reeh, Atwood

Agnes Sabatka Reeh has shared this recipe with many others, exactly as it was handed down to her through her family of Czech descent.

"As a child," Agnes writes, "I remember my parents making a crock jar full of sauerkraut in the fall of the year and storing it in a cool cellar to keep it from spoiling. Since there were not many fresh vegetables in the grocery stores and [few] refrigerators in those days, this recipe was a nice accompaniment with meat. Our family especially likes it with pork dishes and dumplings."

4 slices bacon
¾ cup onion, diced
4 tablespoons all-purpose flour
1 14-ounce can sauerkraut
1¾ cups water
3 teaspoons caraway seed

In a large skillet, fry the bacon until crisp. Remove the bacon and cut it into small pieces. Add the diced onion to the skillet and sauté over medium heat until soft and transparent. Stir the flour into the onions and cook for 2 minutes.

Rinse the sauerkraut and drain well. In a saucepan, bring the sauerkraut, water, and caraway seed to a boil. Add the onion and flour mixture and the bacon pieces and stir until thickened.

Serves 4.

✳ SALADS

The word "salad" can mean many things: green leaf salads, vegetable salads, molds, or medleys with meat, grains, or fruit. Depending on the culture or the period of history, salad on the menu meant an appendage to the main course that might be served first or last. A pungent dressing with herbs often accompanied the leaves of lettuce, which, from Roman times, were believed to "arouse the appetite," "aid digestion," or "encourage sleep."

Salads of meat and cooked vegetables were popular during the settlement period of Kansas. In the 1870s, the most common ingredients were chicken, cabbage, potatoes, and eggs; green salads, as we know them today, did not become popular until the 1900s. Near the turn of the century, the discovery of vitamins and their source —fresh vegetables—prompted cooks to include a variety of raw greens more often in their menus. These fresh ingredients were already commonly used in Midwestern recipes due to the ready access of garden produce.

In 1905, a Pennsylvania housewife won a national contest with a jellied salad. James Beard, in *James Beard's American Cookery* (Boston: Little, Brown and Company, 1972), remarks that from this event, popularity of congealed salads grew "alarmingly" and was "without question, an American innovation." These

salads, ever popular at church dinners and potlucks, are a refreshing combination of sweet and sour that complements the steadfast heartiness of a typical Kansas main course.

Today, many kinds of salads are served as lunch entrees, first courses, side dishes at dinner, or even as the complete evening meal. Ingredients have also become more cosmopolitan, with such extravagances as black beans, hearts of palm, and colorful varieties of peppers.

In this section, there are suggestions for "garden-variety" salads composed of fresh-picked greens. Other offerings combine meat and vegetables, such as Frontier Chicken Salad, a re-creation of a popular salad in the 1800s, and Herring Salad, a traditional feature of the Swedish smorgasbord. Kaw Valley Potato Salad, Black Bean Salad, and Patio Corn Salad are all examples of recipes for picnics and potlucks. Discover some salads for contemporary tastes with Heartland roots, such as Cracked Wheat Salad and Nasturtium-Spinach Salad.

✳ Lettuce Salad with Garlic Vinaigrette

"For a good salad, four persons are required, a spendthrift for oil; a miser for vinegar; a man of judgment for salt; and a madman for stirring the dressing," commented Eliza Leslie in 1857 (quoted in Food On *The Frontier by Marjorie Kreidberg [St. Paul: Minnesota Historical Society Press, 1975]).*

The salads of Miss Leslie's day were likely to be blanched vegetables tossed in a dressing of vinegar or mayonnaise. Raw vegetable salads gained in popularity in the late nineteenth century as rural cooks experimented with fresh garden greens. Today, lettuce salads are part of an everyday meal.

1 to 2 heads bibb or butter lettuce
2 medium carrots
2 green onions
2 medium tomatoes

GARLIC VINAIGRETTE
1 cup olive oil
⅓ cup red wine vinegar
3 garlic cloves, minced
⅛ teaspoon salt
¼ teaspoon pepper, coarsely ground

Wash the lettuce, drain and chill. Finely shred the carrots, chop the green onion, and peel and wedge the tomatoes. Cover and chill all the ingredients until ready to use.

Garlic Vinaigrette: Combine all the ingredients for the vinaigrette in a small bowl, mixing well.

To serve, arrange the lettuce leaves, whole or torn, on salad plates. Place a spoonful of the shredded carrot in the center of each salad and sprinkle the chopped green onion on top. Garnish with tomato wedges. Stir the dressing and spoon some over each salad.

Serves 4 to 6.

✳ Stuffed Lettuce Salad

Olga Saia, Frontenac

In this unique recipe, a head of lettuce is stuffed with a blue cheese filling, making a beautiful and delicious presentation when the head is cut into wedges to serve.

1 large compact head of lettuce
2 3-ounce packages cream cheese, softened
½ cup blue cheese, crumbled
¼ cup mayonnaise
2 tablespoons green pepper, finely chopped
1 tablespoon sweet red pepper, finely chopped
2 tablespoons onion, finely chopped
2 tablespoons fresh parsley or chives, finely chopped
1 teaspoon Worcestershire sauce
3 to 4 drops of red pepper sauce (optional)

Core the head of lettuce and hollow out the center, leaving a shell about 1 inch thick. Wash the lettuce thoroughly and drain.

In a bowl, beat the cream cheese, blue cheese, and mayonnaise together until smooth. Add the chopped green and red pepper, onion, parsley or chives, and Worcestershire sauce, mixing well. Add a few drops of red pepper sauce, if desired.

Pack this mixture into the head of lettuce. Wrap the lettuce with damp paper towels and then with foil to hold its shape. Chill for 2 hours or overnight.

To serve, cut the head into wedges and place on a leaf of lettuce for garnish.

Serves 6 to 8.

✳ Wilted Lettuce

Wilted greens is one of the oldest types of green salads. Early settlers probably made this salad with freshly-picked wild greens.

This updated version is made with fresh

4 cups fresh leaf lettuce, torn

DRESSING
2 tablespoons apple-cider vinegar
2 tablespoons water
1 tablespoon sugar
⅛ teaspoon salt
⅛ teaspoon pepper

leaf lettuce, and it con-
tinues to be a favorite
of those with backyard
gardens.

3 slices bacon, cut into ½-inch pieces
3 green onions, chopped
1 hard-boiled egg, chopped (optional)

Rinse and tear the lettuce leaves and place them in a large bowl.

Dressing: In a small bowl, combine all the ingredients for the dressing. Set aside.

Brown the bacon pieces in a frying pan over medium heat. When nearly done, add the chopped green onion and stir-fry for 1 to 2 minutes. Pour the dressing into the frying pan and simmer for 1 minute.

Pour the hot dressing over the lettuce and toss to coat. You may garnish with chopped egg, if desired. Serve immediately.

Serves 4.

✳ Summer Salad with Citrus Dressing

During the summer
months in Kansas, all
of the vegetables in this
salad can be picked in
vegetable gardens or
purchased at farmer's
markets. This salad
blends well with grilled
chicken or pork for
a cool summertime
meal.

1 pound fresh spinach
1 small cucumber
1 small red onion
1 green pepper
1 sweet red pepper
1 yellow or orange pepper

CITRUS DRESSING
½ cup olive oil
2 tablespoons lemon juice
2 tablespoons orange juice
½ teaspoon orange peel, grated
1 teaspoon fresh basil, finely chopped, or ½ teaspoon dried
   basil
¼ teaspoon sugar
⅛ teaspoon salt
pinch of ground saffron (optional)

2 tablespoons pecans, coarsely chopped

Wash and stem the spinach. Drain and chill for at least 30 minutes before using. Peel and thinly slice the cucumber and red onion. Place in separate bowls, cover, and chill.

To prepare the peppers, slice them in half and remove the seeds and pith. Put them on a baking sheet and place them about 6 inches under the oven broiler until the skins wrinkle and blacken. Place the peppers in a paper bag and seal tightly for at least 15 minutes. Remove them from the bag, peel, and rinse under cold water. Drain and slice them into ¼-inch strips. Place the pepper strips in a small bowl and set aside.

Citrus Dressing: In a small bowl, combine all the ingredients for the dressing, mixing well.

Arrange the spinach leaves, whole or torn, on individual salad plates. Place the cucumber slices around the edges of the plate and the onion rings on top.

Stir 2 tablespoons of the dressing into the sliced peppers. Pour some of the dressing over each salad. Top each with some of the pepper slices. Garnish with chopped pecans.

Serves 4 to 6.

✳ Nasturtium-Spinach Salad

Nasturtium leaves and blossoms are both edible and delicious. They have an earthy flavor, somewhat resembling the taste of a mild radish. A wild variety once grew on the plains and were harvested by the Indian tribes.

In this ornamental salad, the nasturtium leaves are combined with fresh spinach

1 pound fresh spinach
1 cup small, young nasturtium leaves
2 green onions, chopped

HONEY SALAD DRESSING
½ cup safflower oil
3 tablespoons lemon juice
1 tablespoon honey
⅛ teaspoon salt
⅛ teaspoon fresh ground pepper

nasturtium flower blossoms, rinsed

Rinse the spinach leaves and nasturtium leaves several times in cold water and drain well. Place the spinach

and garnished with its colorful blossoms. To avoid the danger of insecticides, grow your own nasturtiums.

leaves, torn or whole, in a large salad bowl. Add the nasturtium leaves and chopped green onion.

Honey Salad Dressing: Combine all the ingredients for the salad dressing in a small bowl, mixing well.

Stir the dressing and pour over the greens. Toss lightly. Place the salad on salad plates and garnish with the blossoms.

Serves 4 to 6.

✳ Baby Grandma's Hot Polk Salad

Selan U. Hall, Jr., Lawrence

Selan Hall learned to identify and cook wild greens from his grandmother, whom he fondly nicknamed "Baby Grandma" because of her height —just over five feet. "A 'mess of greens' serves four or more," says Selan. "All of these wild greens in the recipe can be found in Kansas and some can be found right in town."

Never eat wild greens you cannot identify. Some wild greens, such as polk, can make you ill if eaten raw, so be sure to cook them thoroughly before eating. For the less adventurous cook, domestic varieties, such as spinach, mustard, collard, or turnip greens, may be purchased at the supermarket and make good substitutes.

1 mess of polk, or 1 pound of domestic greens
wild greens such as dandelion greens, lamb's quarters,
*   young thistle (optional)*
3 bacon strips
1 small onion, finely chopped
2 tablespoons balsamic vinegar
1 teaspoon pepper
toasted sesame seed, or coarsely chopped cashew nuts

Rinse your choice of greens (wild or domestic) several times in cold water. Drain briefly and place in a large pot. Add ¼ cup of water and cover tightly. Simmer over low heat for 6 to 8 minutes, or until tender. Drain the greens and keep warm.

Fry the bacon strips in a medium-sized skillet over medium heat until crispy. Remove from the pan, drain, and crumble. Add the chopped onion to the pan drippings and fry, turning often until tender. Stir in the balsamic vinegar and pepper.

Add the onion mixture and crumbled bacon to the greens, tossing gently to coat. Add more vinegar and pepper if desired. Top the greens with toasted sesame seed or chopped cashew nuts.

Serves 4.

✳ Tomato and Basil Salad

The sound of fireworks heralds more than Independence Day—it means the first tomatoes are ripe! Tomatoes and basil flourish in Kansas, and a popular theory of gardeners even recommends planting them together to improve the taste of the tomatoes. This recipe puts that great garden combination on your plate.

4 or 5 large tomatoes
½ cup fresh basil leaves, finely chopped
3 green onions, chopped

VINAIGRETTE
½ cup olive oil
2 tablespoons red wine vinegar
2 garlic cloves, minced
⅛ teaspoon salt
¼ teaspoon pepper

Peel and core the tomatoes and cut them into wedges. Place them in a large bowl. Add the chopped basil leaves and green onion.

Vinaigrette: In a small bowl, combine the ingredients for the vinaigrette, mixing well.

Pour the vinaigrette over the tomato mixture. Stir gently to combine. Cover and chill for 2 hours before serving.

Serves 4 to 6.

✳ Harvest Tomato Salad

Sally Hubbard, Lyons

Sally Hubbard sends us this old family recipe for a refreshing tomato salad. "I helped my mother make this salad back in the 1920s for the harvest threshing crews," she told us. "We made a dishpan-full everyday and it was always gone by the time the meal was over."

3 cups fresh tomatoes
2 medium cucumbers
1 mild onion
¼ cup cider vinegar
¼ cup sugar

Peel and chop the tomatoes, cucumbers, and onion and place them in a large bowl. Combine the cider vinegar and the sugar in a small bowl. Stir to dissolve the sugar and pour over the vegetables. Stir gently, cover, and refrigerate until ready to serve.

Add salt only when serving because the salad will become too watery if added sooner.

Serves 6 to 8.

※ # Marinated Herbed Tomato Salad

Marlene Neufeld, Buhler

Backyard gardeners can show off their productive gardens when making this refreshing vegetable salad. The dressing calls for fresh herbs, but dried ones may be used if fresh herbs are unavailable; simply cut the amounts in half.

For a colorful presentation, serve in a glass bowl or on lettuce leaves on individual salad plates.

6 medium tomatoes, peeled and cut into wedges
3 sweet peppers (green, red, and yellow), sliced or diced
1 red onion, thinly sliced into rings
1 cup pitted black olives

HERB DRESSING
⅔ cup vegetable oil
¼ cup apple-cider vinegar
¼ cup green onion, chopped
¼ cup fresh parsley, snipped
1 teaspoon fresh basil, finely chopped
1 teaspoon fresh marjoram, finely chopped
1 teaspoon sugar
1 teaspoon salt
¼ teaspoon pepper

Combine the cut-up tomatoes, peppers, and onion in a large bowl. Add the olives and set aside.

Herb Dressing: In a screw-top jar or lidded container, combine the ingredients for the dressing. Shake or mix well.

Pour the dressing over the vegetables and stir gently. Cover and refrigerate for 3 hours before serving. Stir again before serving.

Serves 6 to 8.

※ # Marinated Garden Salad

Theodora Dixon, Caney

Use any combination of the vegetables listed to create a salad that suits your taste.

tomatoes, peeled and cut into wedges
green, red, or yellow peppers, seeded and chopped
sweet red or white onion, chopped
green onions, chopped

This flexible recipe allows you to make just enough for your family, or enough for a party.

cucumbers, sliced
broccoli tops
cauliflowerets
fresh peas
carrots, sliced (cooked or uncooked)
fresh button mushrooms
corn, cooked and drained
pitted black olives

DRESSING
¾ cup vegetable oil
¼ cup vinegar
1 teaspoon sugar
½ teaspoon salt
pepper, to taste
garlic salt, to taste
½ teaspoon basil or marjoram
fresh chopped parsley, to taste

Wash and cut 4 or 5 vegetables of your choosing into bite-size pieces. Place them in a large bowl.

Dressing: Combine all the ingredients for the dressing in a small bowl, mixing well.

Pour the dressing over the vegetables. Stir to coat. Cover and refrigerate at least 3 hours, stirring occasionally, before serving.

Makes 1 cup.

✳ Hearts of Palm Salad with Jalapeño Relish

Midwestern tastes have been greatly influenced by the Mexicans who began immigrating to Kansas in the late 1860s, bringing with them recipes for delicious relishes and sauces featuring

JALAPEÑO RELISH
6 tablespoons olive oil
2 tablespoons red wine vinegar
2 garlic cloves, minced
⅛ teaspoon salt
⅛ teaspoon pepper
1 to 2 jalapeño peppers, seeded and finely chopped
2 large tomatoes, peeled and chopped

jalapeño peppers.

Jalapeños, now a regular feature in Kansas gardens, ripen in late summer and add spicy flavor to summer salads. This festive salad makes an elegant first course for a summer barbecue. If fresh tomatoes are unavailable, use high-quality canned ones.

1 head Boston or butter lettuce, washed and drained
1 14-ounce can hearts of palm, drained and sliced

Jalapeño Relish: In a medium-sized bowl, combine the olive oil, vinegar, garlic, salt, and pepper. Add the chopped jalapeños to taste. Gently stir in the chopped tomatoes. Let the dressing stand 1 hour or more before serving to allow the flavors to blend.

Arrange the lettuce leaves on salad plates. Slice the hearts of palm into long, thin strips. Arrange them on the lettuce leaves. Top each salad with 1 to 2 tablespoons of the jalapeño relish.

Serves 4 to 6.

✳ Black Bean Salad

In the recipes of yesteryear, bean salads—a standard in Kansas cooking—often featured several kinds of beans or a combination of beans and hard-boiled eggs.

This colorful and

2 15-ounce cans black beans
1 17-ounce can corn (no salt)
2 medium tomatoes, peeled and chopped
3 green onions, chopped

DRESSING
6 tablespoons olive oil
2 tablespoons red wine vinegar
½ teaspoon ground cumin

contemporary recipe calls for black beans, corn, and tomatoes marinated in a cumin and garlic dressing.

3 garlic cloves, minced
⅛ teaspoon pepper

Rinse the black beans and the corn in a large colander and drain well. Place them in a large bowl and add the chopped tomatoes and green onion.

Dressing: In a small bowl, combine all the ingredients for the dressing, mixing well.

Pour the dressing over the black bean salad. Stir gently to combine. Cover and refrigerate, stirring occasionally, for 8 hours or overnight.

Serves 10 to 12.

✳ Kidney Bean Salad

Rhonda Kessler, Sawyer

This recipe exemplifies the kind of bean salads prepared by previous generations of cooks. The combination of red beans, diced hard-boiled eggs, and sweet pickles makes a colorful salad medley.

2 16-ounce cans red kidney beans, drained
6 hard-boiled eggs, diced
1 teaspoon onion, finely chopped
¼ cup sweet pickles, chopped
¼ teaspoon celery seed
1 tablespoon apple-cider vinegar, or to taste
salt and pepper, to taste
pinch of sugar

Combine all the ingredients in a mixing bowl. Adjust seasoning to taste. Refrigerate overnight. Stir before serving.

Serves 6 to 8.

✳ Patio Corn Salad

Theodora Dixon, Caney

Colorful corn headlines this salad—perfect for potluck din-

2 17-ounce cans corn, drained
1 medium cucumber, diced
¼ cup onion, diced

ners or served with
barbecued ribs.

¼ cup sour cream
2 tablespoons mayonnaise
1 tablespoon vinegar
¼ teaspoon dry mustard
¼ teaspoon celery seed
½ teaspoon salt
2 small tomatoes, chopped

Place the drained corn in a large serving bowl. Add the cucumber and onion, mixing well.

In a small bowl, combine the sour cream, mayonnaise, vinegar, dry mustard, celery seed, and salt. Mix well and gently stir into the vegetables. Scatter the tomato pieces on top of the salad. Cover and chill for at least 2 hours before serving.

Serves 6 to 8.

✳ Grandmother's Pea Salad

Mrs. Cleo Carson, Erie

This old-fashioned,
country-style salad
is still a favorite that
shows up often at
picnics and church
suppers. It pairs nicely
with cold fried chicken
and other potluck
dishes.

1 16-ounce can peas, or 2 cups fresh or frozen peas
¼ cup onion, grated
¼ cup sweet or dill pickles, diced
¼ cup celery, diced
2 hard-boiled eggs, chopped
¼ cup longhorn cheddar cheese, shredded
½ cup sour cream

Drain the peas and place them in a large bowl. (If using fresh or frozen peas, cook for a few minutes in a small amount of water, just until tender-crisp. Rinse in cold water to cool and drain well before using.)

Add the onion, pickles, celery, eggs, and cheese. Fold in the sour cream. Chill at least 2 hours before serving.

Serves 4 to 6.

✳ Kaw Valley Potato Salad

Irene S. Vogel, Lawrence

Potatoes have been grown commercially in the Kaw Valley since the 1930s. As a young girl, Irene Vogel used to carry water on her pony Rex to the field hands harvesting potatoes on her family's farm in Grant Township, located on the banks of the Kaw River.

Her recipe for classic, Midwestern-style potato salad makes a perfect accompaniment to picnics, barbecues, and potluck dinners.

2 pounds small new potatoes
4 hard-cooked eggs, diced
8 small green onions, chopped
½ cup celery, chopped (optional)
¼ cup sweet pickles, chopped (optional)
1 cup mayonnaise
2 to 3 tablespoons mustard, to taste
sugar, to taste (optional)
½ teaspoon salt
¼ teaspoon pepper
dash of paprika

Boil the potatoes in a large pot until tender but not mushy. Drain and peel. Chill for an hour or so, then dice into bite-size pieces. Place the potatoes, eggs, and green onion in a large mixing bowl. If desired, add the celery and pickle.

In a small bowl, combine the mayonnaise, mustard to taste, sugar if desired, salt, and pepper. Stir the mixture into the potato salad. Cover and chill 2 hours. Sprinkle with paprika before serving.

Serves 8 to 10.

✳ Croatian Potato Salad

George Samskey, Jr., Kansas City

The simplest recipes are often the most impressive. The potatoes in this Croatian salad absorb the flavor of the dressing and complement sausages, hamburgers, and most picnic foods.

5 pounds red potatoes, washed
½ cup white vinegar
¾ cup corn oil
1 to 2 tablespoons salt, to taste
2 teaspoons pepper
⅓ cup onion, finely chopped

In a large pot, cover the potatoes with water, add ¼ cup of vinegar, and bring to a boil. Cook until tender.

Cool the potatoes by running cold water over them. Drain and remove the skins while they are still warm. Cut the potatoes into ½-inch cubes. Place them in a large mixing bowl.

In a small bowl, combine the corn oil, ¼ cup of vinegar, salt to taste, pepper, and the chopped onion. Mix well and pour over the potatoes, stirring gently to coat. Cover and refrigerate for about 1 hour, or until thoroughly chilled. Stir well before serving.

Serves 10 to 12.

✳ Dilled New Potato Salad

The dill vinaigrette and the special vegetable additions add a new twist to this potato salad.

1 pound new potatoes
1 cucumber, thinly sliced
1 large tomato, peeled, seeded, and chopped

DILL VINAIGRETTE
½ cup olive oil
2½ tablespoons wine vinegar
1 garlic clove, minced
½ teaspoon dill
⅛ teaspoon salt
⅛ teaspoon pepper

Boil the potatoes just until tender. Rinse with cold water, drain, and remove the skins. Dice the potatoes and place them in a large bowl. Add the sliced cucumber and chopped tomato.

Dill Vinaigrette: In a small bowl, combine the ingredients for the vinaigrette, mixing well.

Pour the vinaigrette over the vegetables and stir gently to coat. Cover and refrigerate for 1 hour or more, stirring occasionally.

Serves 6.

✳ Sweet and Sour Cabbage Slaw

Rose Mary Dietz, Hoisington

Modern cole slaws derive from older ethnic recipes that required a quick blanching of the cabbage before it was tossed with a dressing. The following recipe, handed down to Rose Mary Dietz, is a fine example of a traditional slaw of German heritage.

1 medium-sized head of cabbage, shredded
½ cup sugar
¼ cup vinegar
½ teaspoon salt
1 onion, finely chopped
5 bacon strips
pepper to taste

In a saucepan, cover the shredded cabbage with water and bring to a boil. Cook for a few minutes until softened. Drain, pressing out the excess water.

In a large mixing bowl, combine the sugar, vinegar, salt, and onion until well blended. Add the cooked cabbage and toss until well mixed.

Cut the bacon into small pieces and fry in a skillet until brown and crisp. Drain the bacon and toss with the slaw. Add the pepper and adjust seasonings with sugar and

vinegar. Cover and chill the slaw for 2 hours or overnight to allow its flavors to steep and mellow.

Serves 6 to 8.

✳ Tart Potato Slaw

Mrs. Robert G. Steele, Fort Scott

The unusual addition of potatoes and bacon add extra flavor and texture to this slaw.

3 to 4 medium potatoes, peeled
3 cups cabbage, thinly sliced
1 teaspoon salt
¼ teaspoon celery seed
¼ teaspoon onion salt

DRESSING
½ cup salad oil
¼ cup vinegar
2 garlic cloves, minced
1 teaspoon pepper, coarsely ground
1 teaspoon sugar
2 tablespoons water

Boil the potatoes until tender. Cool and dice them.

Measure 4 cups of the diced potatoes and combine them with the sliced cabbage, salt, celery seed, and onion salt in a large mixing bowl.

Dressing: Combine all the ingredients for the dressing in a small bowl, mixing well.

Pour the dressing over the vegetables. Cover and refrigerate for 1 hour or more to blend flavors.

Serves 6 to 8.

Sauerkraut Salad

Marjorie Fox, Coffeyville

Introduced early to this country, cabbage became quite popular as an easily grown vegetable. A source of vitamin C, cabbage was typically paired with vinegar, which brought a desirable amount of acidity to a meal. Sauerkraut, a dish most certainly prepared by those Kansas settlers who immigrated from eastern European countries, was a means of preserving cabbage by pickling. It was served hot with roasted meats, as well as cold with sausages.

In this recipe, the addition of sauerkraut enhances a fresh vegetable salad. "My mother-in-law gave me this recipe, which she had gotten from her mother, so it's really quite old, but like many things, it's stood the test of time," writes Marjorie Fox. "It's sweet, crunchy, and so easy to make. Almost any fresh vegetable can be used in this salad."

¼ cup apple-cider vinegar
1 cup sugar
1 cup green pepper, chopped (or use half red pepper for color)
1 cup celery, chopped
1 red or white onion, chopped
1 cup cauliflower, broken into small flowerets
1 14-ounce can sauerkraut

Boil the cider vinegar and the sugar together in a small pan, stirring until the sugar is completely dissolved, about 1 minute. Set aside to cool.

Place the chopped vegetables in a large bowl. Drain the sauerkraut in a strainer and rinse under cold water. Press out the excess moisture. Add the sauerkraut to the bowl of vegetables. Pour the vinegar and sugar mixture over the vegetables. Mix well.

Cover and chill for at least 4 hours, or overnight for best results.

Serves 6.

❋ Polish-Style Cucumbers in Sour Cream

(Ogorki ze Smietana)

Stephanie Swieton Mroz, Mission

Stephanie Swieton Mroz tells us that her mother brought this delicious cucumber recipe to Kansas from her homeland of Poland. Her family has many special memories of a cucumber patch they once owned a few miles west of Bonner Springs where the Kansas Turnpike now runs. Her father would sometimes make his entire meal of a large serving of this dish, accompanied only by rye bread or mashed potatoes with sautéed onion.

The dish is an excellent accompaniment to any kind of meat and is best when prepared a day or two in advance.

3 medium cucumbers
3 tablespoons salt
2½ tablespoons vinegar
⅔ cup sour cream
¼ teaspoon pepper

Peel and slice the cucumbers into a large bowl. Add the salt and mix well. Cover and refrigerate at least 2 hours, or overnight.

Put the cucumbers in a colander and rinse well. Press out the excess moisture by placing an empty bowl, a little smaller than the colander, on top of the cucumbers. Press down firmly for about 1 minute while the water seeps out. Or take the cucumbers out of the bowl by handfuls and squeeze as tightly as possible with both hands.

Place the cucumbers in a large bowl. Combine the vinegar, sour cream, and pepper in a small bowl and pour over the cucumbers. Mix gently until well combined. Cover and refrigerate for 1 to 2 hours to enhance the flavor.

Serves 6.

Variation: Add 1 tablespoon of finely chopped mild onion or green onion, 1 teaspoon fresh dill weed, or 1 tablespoon finely chopped green pepper to the bowl of cucumbers before adding the vinegar and sour cream.

❋ Asparagus Spears Vinaigrette

When buying asparagus, choose spears that are straight, with a good green color. They

2 pounds fresh asparagus

VINAIGRETTE
½ cup olive oil

*should puncture easily
and have well-formed,
tightly closed tips.
Thick or thin stalks
are equally tender and
tasty.*

*A simple salad of
fresh asparagus spears
served on a bed of
lettuce is the perfect
finishing touch to an
elegant meal.*

2½ tablespoons wine vinegar
2 green onions, chopped
¼ teaspoon dry mustard
1 garlic clove, minced
⅛ teaspoon salt
¼ teaspoon pepper

lettuce leaves

Trim the ends of the asparagus spears. Wash well to remove the sand. Boil in a large pot for about 5 minutes, until tender-crisp. Drain the spears and immediately place them in a bowl of ice water for several minutes. Drain well and chill for at least 30 minutes.

Vinaigrette: In a small bowl, combine all the ingredients for the vinaigrette, mixing well.

To serve, place 1 or 2 large lettuce leaves on each salad plate. Arrange the asparagus spears on the lettuce leaves and top with the vinaigrette.

Serves 6.

❋ Perfection Salad

Kathryn Long, Edna

*Perfection Salad was
a prize winner in a
contest sponsored
by Charles Knox of
Knox Gelatin, Inc.,
in 1905. This recipe
has survived the years
and still shows up
at church dinners
and potlucks in the
Heartland.*

*Kathryn Long
sends us another
version of this old-
time recipe from her*

½ cup cold water
2 envelopes unflavored gelatin
2 cups boiling water
½ cup vinegar
½ cup sugar
1 teaspoon salt
1 cup cabbage, finely chopped
2 cups celery, finely chopped
¼ cup sweet red pepper, seeded and chopped
lettuce leaves
mayonnaise

Pour the cold water into a large bowl. Add the gelatin and dissolve for 5 minutes. Add the boiling water, vinegar,

mother's collection. It appeared in Favorite Recipes, published by the Trinity Methodist Church of Hutchinson more than fifty years ago.

sugar, and salt, stirring well. When the mixture is cool, add the chopped cabbage, celery, and red pepper.

Turn the mixture into a 2-quart mold or a 13 x 9–inch baking dish. Cover and chill until firm.

Place lettuce leaves on a large platter. Unmold the salad, or slice servings and place on the lettuce leaves. Top with mayonnaise to serve.

Serves 12.

✳ Asparagus Mold

Patricia Habiger, Spearville

Molded salads were much in vogue at the turn of the century for luncheons and buffet parties. This updated one is flavored with asparagus soup and filled with crunchy vegetables and pecans.

1 10-ounce can cream of asparagus soup
1 3-ounce package lemon gelatin
1 8-ounce package cream cheese, softened
½ cup cold water
½ cup mayonnaise
¾ cup celery, finely chopped
½ cup green pepper, finely chopped
1 tablespoon onion, grated
½ cup pecans, coarsely chopped
lettuce leaves

Pour the soup into a large saucepan and bring to a boil over medium-high heat. Remove from heat and add the gelatin, stirring until dissolved. Add the cream cheese and stir until melted, or blend with an electric mixer. Stir in the water and mayonnaise. Fold in the celery, green pepper, onion, and pecans.

Turn the mixture into a mold or 8-inch pan. Cover and chill until firm. To serve, unmold or slice, and place on a bed of lettuce leaves.

Serves 6 to 8.

✳ Lemon Chicken Aspic

*Aspics, always popu-
lar in Europe, found
another home in the
United States. An
aspic is a spiced or
seasoned jelly tradi-
tionally made from
reduced meat stocks
that are rich in the
gelatin needed to mold
the chosen foods.*

*This modern
chicken aspic, served
on a bed of lettuce
leaves, is the perfect
light entree for hot
Kansas summers.*

4 chicken breast halves
2 3-ounce packages lemon gelatin
1 cup boiling water
1 cup mayonnaise
2 cups sour cream
1 cup celery, finely chopped
1 tablespoon onion, minced
1½ tablespoons garlic powder
lettuce leaves

In a large pan or Dutch oven, cover the chicken breasts
in water and simmer until tender, about 30 minutes.
Remove from the pan and drain. When cool enough to
handle, remove the meat from the bones and cut into
bite-size pieces. Place the chicken pieces in a covered
bowl and refrigerate until ready to use.

Place the gelatin in a large mixing bowl. Pour in the
boiling water and stir until dissolved. Cool and add the
mayonnaise, sour cream, celery, onion, garlic powder,
and the chicken pieces, stirring until well blended.

Pour the mixture into a mold or a large loaf pan and
refrigerate until firm. To serve, unmold the aspic onto a
bed of lettuce leaves.

Serves 6 to 8.

✳ Frontier Chicken Salad

*Many salads of the
1800s were "com-
posed" of meats and
cooked vegetables. If
a salad included a
raw vegetable, it was
usually cabbage.*

*This chicken salad
is reminiscent of a
nineteenth-century cre-*

4 chicken breast halves
¼ teaspoon celery salt
2½ cups cabbage, chopped
¼ cup sweet red pepper, seeded and chopped
½ cup mayonnaise
1 tablespoon lemon juice
2 teaspoons sugar
½ teaspoon curry powder
½ teaspoon dry mustard
¼ teaspoon celery seed

ation—but with a few
modern-day touches.

lettuce leaves
2 hard-boiled eggs, chilled and sliced
1 tablespoon capers, drained

Cook the chicken breasts in a pan of boiling water until tender, about 30 minutes. Drain and cool completely. Remove the skin and bones. Chop the chicken into bite-size pieces.

Place the chicken pieces in a large bowl. Add the celery salt and toss to coat. Stir in the chopped cabbage and red pepper.

In a small bowl, combine the mayonnaise, lemon juice, sugar, curry powder, dry mustard, and celery seed. Gently fold this mixture into the chicken mixture. Cover and chill at least 1 hour before serving.

To serve, arrange lettuce leaves on salad plates. Put some of the chicken salad on the lettuce leaves. Garnish with egg slices. Top each salad with a few capers.

Serves 4 to 6.

Little Sweden

Swedes first came to Kansas soon after the territory was opened for homesteading in the 1850s. By 1859, other families had migrated from Sweden as well as from eastern and northern states, spreading into settlements near Olsburg and Walsburg and in the Blue River Valley, which is now the Tuttle Creek Reservoir. Large tracts of land were also purchased by Swedish land companies in the Smoky Hill Valley for colonies. In 1863, the town of Lindsborg, now nicknamed "Little Sweden," was founded. Other Scandinavians settled in the state, but except for the Danish town of Denmark in Lincoln County, their populations were too small to retain their national identity. According to the 1890 census, Swedes outnumbered other Scandinavians ten to one in Kansas.

Two-thirds of Lindsborg's population has Swedish ancestry, and the town boasts three major Swedish festivals each year. On the third Saturday in June, the

Midsummer's Day Festival is held to welcome the return of summer. The town is crowded with traditionally
costumed dancers, and the air is filled with the aro-
mas of fresh-baked Swedish rye bread and *jast krans,* a
ring-shaped pastry. The *dala* horse, a brightly painted,
wooden horse, is the town's symbol of its Swedish heritage and decorates the entrances of homes. Local stores
feature Swedish arts and crafts, and the groceries stock
the potato sausage, lingonberry preserves, and pickled
herring that are essential to the authentic dishes of their
ancestry.

The festival day is crowned with a traditional smorgasbord. Translated, smorgasbord means "butter-goose-
bread" and is virtually a buffet of appetizers. The presentation is beautiful: long tables filled with an array of
colors, scents, and flavors, each overflowing with individually decorated portions of herring salad, dilled potatoes, Swedish meatballs, brown beans, and the famous
rennet-thickened custard, ost kaka, just to name a few.

In October of odd-numbered years, Svensk Hyllnings-
fest repeats this grand custom in order to pay tribute
to the Swedish-American pioneers. It too features the
arts, crafts, folk dancing, and smorgasbord that befit
a traditional Swedish festival.

In Lindsborg as well as Sweden, the celebration of
Christmas begins on the second Saturday of December
with the St. Lucia Festival. According to eighteenth-
century tradition, the eldest daughter brings special buns
and cookies to each family member to re-enact the leg-
end of St. Lucia, who brought food and drink to the hungry during a period of famine. The whole town celebrates
the festival, with live Christmas music, folk dancing, and
the "crowning" of St. Lucia, the symbol of light and hope
to the world.

✳ Herring Salad

(Sill Sallad)

Mrs. Julia Peterson Hampton, Oskaloosa

Herring salad is a very special part of Swedish gatherings and holiday celebrations. Swedes say that one must acquire a taste for pickled herring to appreciate this special dish, which is a traditional favorite among the Swedish communities of Kansas.

Julia Hampton sends us her recipe with her grandmother's decorative variation for Christmastime.

1 8-ounce jar pickled herring, drained
1 quart pickled beets, drained
1 quart boiled potatoes, drained
1 pound cooked lean beef
½ small onion, chopped
¼ to ½ cup cream

Chop or grind each ingredient to a medium-coarse texture. Combine the ingredients except the cream in a large bowl, mixing well. Cover and refrigerate for at least 24 hours.

Add the cream, approximately 1 teaspoon per cup of salad, to the chilled salad.

Serves 10 or more.

Variation: Place the salad in a decorative bowl and smooth the surface. Mark the center of the salad with a star-shaped cookie cutter. Remove the cutter and fill in the pattern with the chopped yolk of 2 hard-boiled eggs. Fill the points of the star with chopped egg white. Fill the remaining surface with chopped pickled beets. (The last step should be done immediately before serving so that the beets do not discolor the egg whites.)

✳ Curried Tuna Salad

Mrs. Cleo Carson, Erie

In James Beard's American Cookery (Boston: Little, Brown and Company, 1972), Beard writes, "Since tuna fish in oil first became a staple item on

1 6-ounce can of white tuna, in water
¼ cup mayonnaise
¼ teaspoon curry powder
1 8-ounce can unsweetened pineapple rings, drained
½ cup celery, thinly sliced
⅓ cup pecans, chopped
2 hard-boiled eggs, diced

grocery shelves, it has been one of the great American standards for salads."

Serve this simple, tasty version for lunch or as a light dinner.

⅓ cup shredded carrot
lettuce leaves

Drain the tuna and set aside. In a mixing bowl, stir the mayonnaise and curry powder together until well blended. Dice the pineapple rings into small chunks and add them to the bowl. Stir in the tuna and the remaining ingredients. Mix gently until all the ingredients are well coated with the mayonnaise. Chill thoroughly. To serve, place the curried tuna on lettuce leaves.

Serves 4.

Variation: Toast 8 slices of bread and spread with curried tuna, making 4 sandwiches. Cut each sandwich into quarters.

✳ # Cracked Wheat Salad with Lemon Vinaigrette

Kansas wheat comes in many forms and today's cooks are rediscovering its natural state. This healthy salad, made with cracked wheat and fresh vegetables, is a refreshing summertime salad as well as a terrific picnic dish.

2 cups water
1 cup cracked wheat

LEMON VINAIGRETTE
¼ cup olive oil
2 tablespoons lemon juice
2 garlic cloves, minced
¼ teaspoon salt
¼ teaspoon pepper

1 cup cucumber, peeled, seeded, and diced
1 large tomato, peeled and diced
2 green onions, chopped

In a medium-sized saucepan, bring the water to a boil over high heat. Slowly stir in the cracked wheat. Bring the mixture to a boil and cover. Reduce heat to low and cook for 7 minutes, or until the water is absorbed. Remove from heat and cool at room temperature for 1 hour with the lid on. Refrigerate, covered, until well chilled.

Lemon Vinaigrette: In a small bowl, combine all the ingredients for the vinaigrette and set aside.

Put the cracked wheat in a serving bowl. Pour the lemon vinaigrette over and stir to coat. Add the cucumber, tomato, and green onion and toss gently. Cover and chill for 1 hour before serving.

Serves 6.

✳ Brown Rice Salad

When health foods gained in popularity in the 1970s, cold rice salads such as this were one result. This filling salad, topped with sunflower seeds, can serve as a meatless meal-in-one.

2½ cups water
1 cup brown rice
½ teaspoon salt
¼ cup mayonnaise
¼ cup plain yogurt
1 2-ounce jar stuffed Spanish olives, drained
1 4-ounce jar marinated mushrooms, drained and sliced
*   in half*
¼ cup sunflower kernels

Bring the water to a boil in a large pan over high heat. Add the rice and salt and return to boiling. Reduce heat to low and stir. Cover and cook for 50 to 60 minutes, or until all the water is absorbed. Cool the rice to room temperature.

Place the rice in a large bowl. Add the mayonnaise and yogurt and mix well. Stir in the olives, mushrooms, and sunflower kernels.

Cover and chill at least 2 hours before serving.
Serves 6 to 8.

✳ Rice and Spice Salad

This chilled rice salad combines white rice with fruits and sliced

2 cups water
1 cup white rice
1 tablespoon wild rice (optional)

*almonds. Serve it with
chicken or fish.*

*¼ teaspoon salt
¼ cup mayonnaise
¼ cup plain yogurt
½ teaspoon ground allspice
1 8-ounce can unsweetened pineapple chunks, drained
¼ cup raisins
2 tablespoons sliced almonds*

Bring the water to a boil over high heat in a medium-sized saucepan. Add the white rice, wild rice if desired, and salt. Bring to a boil, stir, and cover. Reduce heat to low and cook for 14 minutes, or until all the water is absorbed. Let the rice cool in the covered pan for 15 minutes. Place the cooked rice in a large bowl and continue cooling to room temperature.

In a small bowl, combine the mayonnaise, yogurt, and allspice. Stir the mixture into the rice. Add the drained pineapple chunks, raisins, and almonds, mixing well. Cover and chill for at least 2 hours before serving.

Serves 6.

✳ Pineapple Beets

Agnes Gladden, Dodge City

*This delicious sweet-
and-sour combination
of pineapple and beets*

*¼ cup brown sugar
2 tablespoons cornstarch
¼ teaspoon ginger*

½ teaspoon salt
1 16-ounce can sweetened pineapple chunks, juice reserved
⅓ cup vinegar
½ cup water
2 16-ounce cans cut beets, drained
lettuce leaves (optional)

makes a decorative salad served on lettuce leaves or a tasty side dish to grilled or roasted meats.

In a saucepan, combine the brown sugar, cornstarch, ginger, and salt. Drain the juice from the pineapple and stir it into the brown sugar mixture along with the vinegar and water.

Cook the mixture over medium heat, stirring constantly, until the sauce is thick and bubbly. Stir in the drained pineapple chunks and beets. Serve warm or cold. Arrange chilled Pineapple Beets on a bed of lettuce leaves, if desired.

Serves 8.

✳ Banana-Peanut Salad

Mrs. Bettye Bartlett, Fowler

Bettye Bartlett sends us a recipe that has stood the test of time. Her mother-in-law served it some fifty years ago to the harvest crews. Bettye continued to serve it to the crews when she took over the job of cooking, and now her daughter-in-law carries on the tradition.

This cool banana salad with a sweetened dressing and salty peanuts is sure to satisfy your own "crew" on a hot summer day.

1 cup brown sugar
2 tablespoons all-purpose flour
½ cup milk
½ teaspoon vanilla extract
5 to 6 medium bananas, sliced
⅓ cup salted peanuts, coarsely ground

In a small saucepan, combine the brown sugar and flour. Slowly stir in the milk. Cook over medium heat, stirring,

until the sauce thickens and begins to bubble. Remove
from the heat, stir in the vanilla, and cool. Serve the
sauce at room temperature, or place in a covered container and chill until ready to use.

Slice the bananas into a large bowl. Pour the sauce
over the bananas and sprinkle the ground peanuts on top.

Serves 4 to 6.

✳ BREADS AND BREADSTUFFS

According to Marjorie Kreidberg, author of *Food on the Frontier* (St. Paul: Minnesota Historical Society Press, 1975), "The absence of bread in rural or urban kitchens was as hard on morale as it was on health. Bread was not only a basic food, but the quality and goodness of the loaves that each housewife produced was considered the ultimate yardstick of her domestic accomplishments."

Bread remains an essential part of the meal for families in Kansas. In researching and creating bread recipes, we found that nearly every culture present in the state has its own special breads, each with its own special history. Native Americans still make fry bread, and the familiar yellow corn bread that accompanies navy beans, stews, and fried chicken is a direct descendant of the pioneer's johnnycake. The Swedes of Lindsborg consider bread so important that, in true Swedish tradition, their famous Swedish Rye Bread is served as a first course

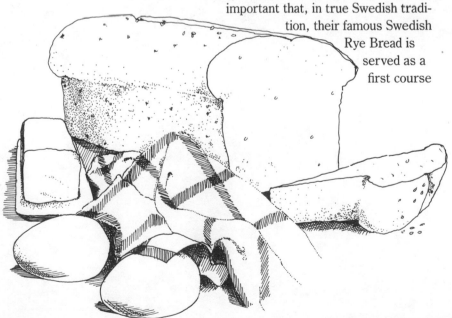

—a humble symbol of the nourishment they are about
to receive. The Czechoslovakians around Wilson pride
themselves on their traditional Christmas bread, Houska,
while the German Mennonites of central Kansas still
bake their beloved Zwieback on Saturday afternoons for
the Sunday meal.

With today's busier lifestyles, what was once daily
bread baking has become a weekend hobby of both men
and women—but the emphasis is again on health. Breads
are often made with nutritious whole wheat flour and
whole grains, sometimes sweetened with honey, and
loaded with fruits and nuts.

The baking of bread is a unique domestic event. The
beginning baker will find the experience relaxing and,
in a way, comforting. Even a less-than-perfect loaf fresh
from the oven will always produce an astonishing singular
flavor. What a pleasant experience it is to fill a home with
the aroma of freshly baked bread, to eat it hot from the
oven, and to share the goodness with family and friends!

✳ Honey Whole Wheat Bread

Esther Fenton Mauk, Bonner Springs

"Every ingredient for bread was available on the homestead," recalls Esther Mauk. The winter wheat, harvested before the Fourth of July, was ground into all-purpose flour. Chickens provided the eggs —at the same time,

"they kept the grass mowed, the snakes away, and the bugs down." Fall butchering supplied the lard for cooking, and bees gave the honey. Even the yeast was made at home.

"I love the flavor of fresh ground wheat so

much that I purchased a hand-cranked grain mill," adds Esther. She still produces most of her ingredients on the farm just like her folks did in the early days, but now she buys her yeast from the store.

2 cakes yeast, or 2 packages dry yeast
3 cups warm water
½ cup honey
2 tablespoons vegetable oil, or lard
1 egg, beaten
1 teaspoon salt
5 cups whole wheat flour
5 to 6 cups all-purpose flour

In a large mixing bowl, dissolve the yeast in the water. Add the honey, vegetable oil or lard, and the beaten egg. Add the flour and salt, stirring until the dough is firm but still moist.

Turn the dough onto a floured surface and knead until smooth and elastic, about 10 minutes. Cover and let rise in a warm place until doubled in size, about 1 hour. Punch down and let rise again for 1 hour. Punch down, divide the dough into thirds, and place in 3 greased loaf pans.

Allow the loaves to rise for 1 hour. Bake at 350 degrees for about 40 minutes.

Makes 3 loaves.

❇ Sunflower State Whole Wheat Bread

Nothing identifies Kansas more than wheat and sunflowers. This hearty whole wheat bread is filled with delicious sunflower kernels. For a real treat, serve it fresh from the oven with butter.

2 packages dry yeast
1 tablespoon brown sugar
2 cups warm water
⅓ cup vegetable oil
2 teaspoons salt
¾ cup powdered milk
5 tablespoons brown sugar
½ cup unsalted sunflower kernels
5 to 6 cups whole wheat flour

In a large bowl, dissolve the yeast and brown sugar in the warm water. Add the oil, salt, powdered milk, brown sugar, and sunflower kernels and stir to combine. Gradually stir in as much of the flour as needed, until the dough is moderately stiff.

Turn the dough onto a lightly floured surface and knead for 8 to 10 minutes, until smooth and elastic, adding more flour if necessary. Form the dough into a ball and place in a greased bowl, turning once to grease the top. Cover and let rise in a warm place until doubled in size, 1 to 1½ hours.

Punch down and divide dough in half. Shape the halves into loaves and place in greased loaf pans. Cover and let rise in a warm place until doubled, 45 to 60 minutes.

Bake at 400 degrees for 15 minutes. Reduce heat to 350 degrees and bake for 30 minutes more. Remove the loaves from pans and cool on wire racks.

Makes 2 loaves.

❇ Kansas-Style Honey Wheat French Bread

In 1869, the Frenchman Ernest Valeton de Boissiere set up

2 packages dry yeast
pinch of sugar
2 cups warm water

a socialist colony in
Franklin County to
raise silkworms for a
silk industry. These
French settlers were
credited with some of
the finest cooking in
Kansas at that time.
They made rich sauces
for wild game, gour-
met casseroles and
stews, and, of course,
baked some of the best
bread in the county.

The following recipe
for French bread is
made with whole wheat
flour and is lightly
sweetened with honey.

¼ cup honey
1½ teaspoons salt
3 cups stone ground whole wheat flour
2 to 3 cups unbleached white flour
cornmeal
1 egg white
1 tablespoon water

In a large bowl, dissolve the yeast and the sugar in the warm water. Stir in the honey and salt. Gradually add the whole wheat flour, stirring until smooth. Stir in as much of the white flour as needed, until the dough is moderately stiff.

Turn the dough onto a lightly floured surface. Knead for 8 to 10 minutes, until the dough is smooth and elastic, adding more flour if necessary.

Shape the dough into a ball and place in a lightly greased bowl. Cover and let rise in a warm place for 1 to 1½ hours, until doubled in size. Punch down and turn onto a lightly floured surface. Divide the dough in half. Cover and let rest for 10 minutes.

Roll each half into a 15 x 12–inch rectangle. Roll up tightly from the long side. Moisten and seal well, tapering the ends. Grease French bread pans or a large baking sheet and sprinkle generously with cornmeal. Place each loaf in a pan, or on the baking sheet, seam side down. Cover and let rise in a warm place until doubled in size, 45 to 60 minutes.

In a small bowl, combine the egg white and water and brush the loaves lightly with the mixture. Make 5 diagonal cuts about ½ inch deep across the tops of the loaves.

Bake at 375 degrees for 40 to 45 minutes. Brush the bread with the egg white and water mixture after 20 minutes of baking. Cool on a wire rack.

Makes 2 loaves.

Requisite for Good Bread

"The first requisite for *good bread* is good flour," instructs the 1874 *Kansas Home Cook-Book* by the Ladies of Leavenworth, "and three other things must also be exactly right: the quality of the yeast, the fermentation of the dough, and the heat of the oven. No exact rules can be given to determine these points, but they may be easily learned by a little careful observation.

Bread rises much quicker in the daytime when the kitchen is warm, than at night when the fire is out; therefore, five or six hours in the day are equal to twelve at night.

Many housekeepers mix their bread at night, mould and put it into baking-pans the first thing in the morning, thus economizing time."

✳ Best White Bread

Nothing smells so good while baking, or tastes so delicious when done, as basic white bread enriched with butter and eggs. Simply serve warm with butter or toasted. This firm white bread also makes excellent French toast.

1 cup milk
6 tablespoons butter
2 tablespoons sugar
1 teaspoon salt
1 package dry yeast
pinch of sugar
¼ cup warm water
1 egg, slightly beaten
4 to 5 cups all-purpose flour

Pour the milk into a saucepan and heat over medium heat until hot but not boiling. Remove the pan from heat and pour the milk into a large bowl. Add the butter, sugar, and salt. Stir and let the mixture cool to lukewarm.

Dissolve the yeast and sugar in the warm water. Add the yeast mixture and the egg to the milk mixture, and beat with a large spoon. Add the flour, 1 cup at a time, beating well until the dough is firm enough to handle.

Turn the dough out onto a lightly floured surface. Knead for about 10 minutes, until the dough is smooth and elastic. Shape the dough into a ball and place in a lightly greased bowl, turning once to grease the top. Cover and let rise in a warm place for about 1 hour, until doubled in size.

Punch down and divide in half. Shape into 2 loaves and place in greased loaf pans. Cover and let rise in a warm place for 30 to 40 minutes, until doubled.

Bake at 375 degrees for about 40 minutes, or until golden brown.

Makes 2 loaves.

✳ Fruit Yeast Sourdough Starter

Carol Kennedy Zacharias, Topeka

"The sourdough starter made from the yeast of fruits has an entirely different flavor than ones made from yogurt or commercial yeast," says Carol Zacharias. "It takes some patience and sometimes a couple of tries to get started, but it is well worth the effort." Carol prefers to use locally grown fruit for her starter and Kansas flour in

1 to 2 pounds fresh ripe grapes, strawberries, or
    blueberries
2½ cups room temperature distilled or
    deionized water, divided
2¾ cups hard wheat flour, divided
1 teaspoon sugar

Let the fruit stand at room temperature for 24 hours. Place in a bowl and soak in 2 cups of the distilled or deionized water for 25 minutes. Strain the water into a crock, or a heavy light-proof nonmetallic container with a lid. The fruit may then be used for another purpose.

Add 1½ cups of the flour to the water and mix well. Stir in the sugar. Cover and let stand in a warm place (80 to 85 degrees), stirring 2 times a day. In the winter, a

her breads.

Sourdough starters can be finicky and may not perform well—one reason they were cherished and passed on to friends and family. Don't be discouraged if your first effort isn't a success—try again!

Following the recipe for the starter are two of Carol's favorite sourdough bread recipes.

good place is on the floor by the furnace. After bubbles appear (24 to 48 hours), stir in ¾ cup of the flour.

In 2 to 3 days, when the mixture is bubbly, stir and refrigerate for 24 hours. This will discourage any bacteria, if present.

Remove from the refrigerator, stir, and add ½ cup of the flour and ½ cup of the water. Let the mixture stand for 2 to 4 days until it develops its characteristic odor. Refrigerate again for 24 hours.

Remove the starter from the refrigerator, warm to room temperature, and use as directed in sourdough bread recipes.

When using the starter, replace the amount you use with three-fourths the amount of water and twice the amount of flour as liquid. (Example: Your recipe calls for 2 cups of starter. After removing the starter, add 1½ cups of water and 3 cups of flour.) Mix well and let the starter stand at room temperature for 18 to 20 hours before refrigerating.

✳ Sourdough French Bread

Carol Kennedy Zacharias, Topeka

Pioneers used sourdough starter because it was a dependable and replenishable source of leavening that did not spoil easily. Starters with good flavor were passed on to friends and families. Some of these batches have been kept active for generations.

Not only does sourdough make delicious bread, it can be used in pancakes, biscuits, muffins, breads, and cookies.

1 cup sourdough starter
2 cups warm water
4 cups all-purpose flour
2½ teaspoons sugar
1½ teaspoons salt
4 cups all-purpose flour
cornmeal
1 egg white, slightly beaten
1 teaspoon water

Combine the starter, water, and 4 cups of flour in a large bowl. Mix well, cover, and let stand in a warm place for at least 8 to 10 hours, or preferably overnight.

When ready to use, the mixture should be full of bubbles and spongy-looking. Stir in the sugar, salt, and enough of the flour to make a stiff dough.

Turn the dough onto a lightly floured surface and knead for 10 minutes, or until smooth and elastic. Place the dough into a greased bowl, turning once to grease the top. Cover and let rise in a warm place until doubled in bulk, about 1 to 2 hours.

Punch the dough down and divide in half. Roll each half into an oblong cylinder-shaped loaf. Grease French bread pans, or a large baking sheet, and sprinkle with cornmeal. Place the loaves in the pans or on the baking sheet. Cover and let rise until almost doubled, about 1 hour.

Preheat the oven to 400 degrees. Place a shallow pan of boiling water in the oven on the bottom rack. With a very sharp knife, make several slashes diagonally across the top of each loaf. In a small bowl, combine the egg white and water and brush the tops of the loaves.

Bake the loaves at 400 degrees for 10 minutes. Brush with the egg white mixture and remove the pan of water. Bake 15 to 20 minutes more, or until the loaves are lightly browned and make a hollow sound when tapped.

Makes 2 loaves.

✳ Sourdough Potato Bread

Carol Kennedy Zacharias, Topeka

This bread freezes well and keeps for a week when stored in a cool place.

1 cup sourdough starter
2 cups warm water
4 cups all-purpose flour
1 cup hot water
2 tablespoons butter or margarine, softened
1 cup instant potato flakes
⅔ cup milk
2 tablespoons sugar
2 teaspoons salt
4 cups all-purpose flour

Combine the starter, water, and 4 cups of flour in a large bowl. Mix well, cover, and let stand in a warm place for at least 8 to 10 hours, or preferably overnight.

When ready to use, the mixture should be full of bubbles and spongy-looking. Pour the hot water into a medium-sized bowl. Add the butter or margarine to the hot water to melt. Stir in the potato flakes and mix until well blended. Stir in the milk, sugar, and salt. When the mixture cools to lukewarm, add it to the sourdough mixture. Add enough flour to make a stiff dough.

Turn the dough onto a lightly floured surface and knead for 10 minutes, or until smooth and elastic. Place the dough in a greased bowl, turning once to grease the top. Cover and let rise in a warm place until doubled in bulk, 1 to 2 hours.

Punch the dough down and divide into 3 pieces. Form each piece into a ball and place in round 8- or 9-inch cake or bread pans. Cover the loaves and let rise until almost doubled, 1 to 2 hours.

Combine the egg and milk and brush the tops of the loaves. Slash the tops of the loaves ½ inch deep with a sharp knife in a crisscross pattern.

Bake at 375 degrees for 30 to 35 minutes, or until the loaves are lightly browned and make a hollow sound when tapped.

Remove the loaves from the pans and cool on wire racks.

Makes 3 loaves.

Breadbasket of the World

The history of growing wheat in Kansas parallels the transformation of the Central Plains. A soft-grained wheat was the first wheat brought from Europe and was grown east of Missouri. Planted in the spring, it adapted better to mild summers. When settlers tried to grow spring wheat in central and western Kansas, however, it rarely had time to mature before the arrival of the hot, drying winds of summer. With blistering summers being one of the few reliable aspects of Kansas weather, the crop often perished, leaving the pioneers with little grain for winter storage.

It was not until the German Mennonites brought the seeds of the hardy Turkey Red wheat from Russia in 1874 that a stable way of life on the plains began to develop. The Turkey Red wheat, or Hard Red Winter wheat as it is now known, thrived in Kansas, producing enormous yields. Planted in the fall and harvested in early summer, Kansas wheat is now recognized around the world for its superb quality. Kansas ranks first in the United States in total wheat production and in flour milled. Since the introduction of those small seeds, Kansas, a major exporter of wheat, has truly earned the title of "Breadbasket of the World."

✳ Whole Wheat Soybean Bread

Mrs. Otto (Emogene) Harp, Marienthal

Many Kansas cooks grind their own wheat, claiming the virtue of freshly ground flour. For years, Emogene Harp has ground wheat, corn, and even milo for her baking endeavors. When her husband began raising soybeans, they too became grist for her mill. Her experiment with soy flour was not only successful but prolifically award-winning. This bread, when submitted to the Kansas State Fair, won a blue ribbon in its class, Sweepstakes, Dillon's Best of Show, and a Special Award from the Wheat Commission! Emogene travels

4 eggs, beaten
3 packages dry yeast
3 cups warm water
½ cup honey
1 cup soy oil
4 teaspoons salt
6 cups all-purpose flour, divided
2 cups soybean flour, sifted before measuring
4 cups whole wheat flour
¼ cup soy margarine, melted (optional)

In a large bowl, mix the eggs, yeast, water, honey, soy oil, salt, and 1 cup of the all-purpose flour. Stir until well blended. Add the remaining flours, 1 cup of each at a time, mixing well after each addition. Incorporate only enough additional all-purpose flour so that the dough becomes stiff and does not stick to the bowl or hands. Knead the dough on a surface sprayed with a vegetable spray (you may spray your hands also) until smooth and elastic, about 8 to 10 minutes.

Place in a lightly oiled bowl, cover, and let rise in a warm place until doubled, about 1 hour.

Punch down the dough and divide it into 4 parts. Let

throughout Kansas as a spokesperson for the Kansas Soybean Association.

stand a few minutes and shape into 4 loaves. Place the loaves into lightly oiled loaf pans and let rise until almost doubled, 45 to 60 minutes.

Bake at 375 degrees for 45 minutes or until golden brown. Remove the loaves from the pans and brush the tops with melted soy margarine, if desired. Cool on wire racks.

Makes 4 loaves.

✳ Oatmeal Bread

Marilyn Eck, Bartlett

The combination of rolled oats and sorghum favored by those of German and Scottish heritage gives this old-fashioned bread a natural sweetness.

1 cup rolled oats
1 tablespoon salt
2 tablespoons shortening
2 cups boiling water
1 package dry yeast
⅔ cup warm water
⅔ cup sorghum
5½ cups all-purpose flour

Place the rolled oats, salt, and shortening in a large bowl. Stir in the boiling water and set aside. Let cool to lukewarm.

Dissolve the yeast in the warm water. Add the yeast mixture and the sorghum to the rolled oats mixture and mix well. Stir in the flour 1 cup at a time, until the dough is firm enough to handle. Add additional flour if necessary. Turn the dough onto a lightly floured surface and knead until smooth and elastic, about 8 minutes. The dough will be slightly sticky because of the oatmeal.

Place the dough in a lightly greased bowl and cover. Let rise in a warm place until doubled, about 1 hour. Punch down and knead lightly. Divide the dough in half and shape into loaves. Place the loaves in 2 greased loaf pans. Cover and let rise again until almost doubled, 30 to 45 minutes. Bake at 350 degrees for 45 minutes.

Makes 2 loaves.

✳ Sage Bread

David A. Gaddy Cox, Kansas City

Indians gathered the leaves of wild sage to burn as incense and reportedly ate the seeds raw or ground into meal (Kelly Kindscher, Edible Wild Plants of the Prairie *[Lawrence: University Press of Kansas, 1987]). In this recipe, the potent flavor of sage is incorporated into a tasty bread.*

1 package dry yeast
¼ cup lukewarm water
2½ cups all-purpose flour
¼ teaspoon baking powder
2 teaspoons dried sage
1 tablespoon sugar
1 teaspoon salt
½ cup piñon nuts, shelled
1 egg
1 cup dry cottage cheese
1 tablespoon lard or shortening, melted
1 tablespoon butter or shortening, melted

In a small cup, dissolve the yeast in the water. In a bowl, combine the flour, baking powder, sage, sugar, salt, and piñon nuts. In a separate large bowl, beat the egg with the cottage cheese until smooth. Add the melted lard or shortening and the yeast.

Add the dry ingredients to the cottage cheese mixture in small amounts, beating well after each addition, until a firm dough forms.

Cover the dough with a cloth and let rise in a warm place for about 1 hour, or until doubled. Punch down and knead the dough for about 1 minute. Shape into a smooth ball and place in a greased loaf pan or baking dish. Cover and let rise in a warm place for 40 minutes, or until doubled.

Bake in an oven preheated to 350 degrees for 50 minutes. Remove from oven and brush the top with melted butter or shortening.

Makes 1 loaf.

✳ Pumpkin Yeast Bread

Patty Boyer, Lawrence

Pick-your-own pumpkin patches seem to flourish in the fall in eastern Kansas. A family drive through the country in late October is an autumn ritual for those seeking just the right jack-o'-lantern for Halloween or a good pie pumpkin for pies and breads. Fresh pumpkin puree should be first choice for this recipe, but a good-quality canned variety will do.

1 package dry yeast
¼ cup warm water
1 cup pumpkin puree, fresh or canned
2 eggs, beaten
¼ cup butter, softened
1 tablespoon chili powder
2 tablespoons sugar
1 teaspoon salt
½ cup raisins
¼ cup toasted pumpkin seeds or sunflower seeds
4½ to 5 cups unbleached white flour

To make pumpkin puree: Cut a pie pumpkin in half and remove the seeds and fibers. Quarter each half and place in a large baking dish. Bake at 350 degrees for about 1 hour, or until the pulp is tender. Scrape the pulp from the skin and puree in a blender or food processor. Measure 1 cup of puree and reserve the remainder for another use.

Dissolve the yeast in the warm water. Pour the pumpkin puree into a large bowl. Add the dissolved yeast, eggs, butter, chili powder, sugar, salt, raisins, and pumpkin or sunflower seeds, mixing well. Gradually stir in the flour until the dough is firm enough to handle.

Turn the dough onto a lightly floured surface and knead

for about 10 minutes, or until smooth and elastic. Form the dough into a ball and place in a lightly greased bowl. Cover and let rise in a warm place until doubled in size, about 1 hour. Punch down and divide the dough in half. Shape into 2 loaves and place in greased loaf pans. Cover and let rise in a warm place until doubled, about 45 minutes.

Bake at 375 degrees for 35 to 40 minutes. Remove the loaves from the pans and cool on a wire rack.

Makes 2 loaves.

✳ # Swedish Rye Bread

Mrs. Lambert Dahlsten, Lindsborg

Traditionally, Swedes do not serve bread to complement the main course. It is considered such an important food in the Swedish diet that it is presented on a large plate as a first course before the entree. Butter, the accompaniment, is shaped into balls or long curls.

This recipe for Swedish Rye Bread has been a favorite in Mrs. Dahlsten's family for four generations. It was brought to the United States by her grandmother, who emigrated from Sweden in the 1800s.

Mrs. Dahlsten says her bread recipe makes plenty for family and

2 potatoes
2 cups reserved potato water
2 yeast cakes, or 2 packages dry yeast
1 quart buttermilk
4 cups rye flour
1 cup all-purpose flour
4 teaspoons salt
1 cup sugar
1 cup molasses
½ cup shortening
1 tablespoon caraway seeds
½ cup orange peel, grated
10 to 12 cups all-purpose flour
1 egg white
1 tablespoon cold water

In a large pan of water, boil the potatoes until soft. Drain, reserving 2 cups of the potato water. To make the starter, mash the potatoes in a large bowl and add the reserved potato water. In a saucepan, warm the buttermilk just until lukewarm and add it to the potato mixture along with the yeast, rye flour, 1 cup of all-purpose flour, and salt. Stir well. Cover and let rise for about 1 hour, until doubled in size.

for much-appreciated gifts during the holiday season.

While the starter is rising, combine the sugar, molasses, shortening, caraway seeds, and orange peel in a large pan. Bring the mixture to a boil over medium heat, stirring often, just until the sugar dissolves. Remove it from heat and cool to lukewarm.

Stir the sugar and molasses mixture into the sponge until completely combined. Work in 10 to 12 cups of all-purpose flour, until the dough is no longer sticky and can be easily handled.

Turn the dough onto a lightly floured surface and knead until it is smooth and elastic, about 10 minutes.

Form the dough into 4 large or 6 medium-sized loaves. Place on lightly greased baking sheets or in greased loaf pans. Cover and let rise in a warm place until doubled, about 1 hour or more.

When the loaves are ready to bake, combine the egg white and water and gently brush the tops of the loaves. Bake the loaves at 375 degrees for 1 hour. Brush the loaves again after 20 minutes.

Makes 4 to 6 loaves.

✳ Houska *Vánočka*

(Czechoslovakian Christmas Bread)

Mrs. Sylvia G. Vopat, Wilson

name Houska perhaps Moravian origin

During the Christmas season in Wilson, the "Czech Capital of Kansas," you are likely to find Houska at local celebrations and family gatherings.

Houska is a Czechoslovakian bread traditionally served at the holidays and often given as a gift. This elaborate version has a truly festive appear-

1 package dry yeast
1¼ cups warm water
¼ cup sugar
¼ cup brown sugar
1 teaspoon salt
⅓ cup powdered milk
¼ cup instant potatoes
¼ teaspoon orange peel, grated
¼ teaspoon lemon peel, grated
4 cups all-purpose flour, divided
1 egg, beaten
¼ cup shortening, melted
1 teaspoon cinnamon

ance and represents the heritage of at least three generations of the Vopat family. Sylvia Vopat has modernized it a bit by substituting instant potatoes for fresh and adding the spices. Other fruits can also be used to decorate the bread, such as pineapple, dried apricots, and papayas.

¼ teaspoon nutmeg
¼ teaspoon allspice
¼ teaspoon ginger
pinch of mace
1 cup white raisins
1 cup currants
1 cup walnuts or pecans, chopped
1 tablespoon honey
1 teaspoon vanilla extract
½ teaspoon almond extract

GLAZE
1 egg yolk
1 teaspoon sugar
2 tablespoons milk
sesame, poppy, anise seeds, for decoration
2 tablespoons sliced almonds

ICING
1 cup powdered sugar
2 to 3 tablespoons milk

red and green maraschino cherries

In a large mixing bowl, dissolve the yeast in the warm water. Stir in the sugar, brown sugar, and salt. Add the powdered milk, instant potatoes, orange peel, lemon peel, 2 cups of the flour, and the egg. Beat the mixture well with a wooden spoon. Continue beating while incorporating the melted shortening.

In a separate bowl, sift together the remaining 2 cups of flour, cinnamon, nutmeg, allspice, ginger, and mace. Gradually add the dry mixture to the dough, mixing well. Add the raisins, currants, nuts, honey, vanilla, and almond extract to the dough, mixing well. Turn the dough onto a floured surface and gently knead until smooth and elastic, about 10 minutes. Place the dough in a lightly greased bowl and cover. Let rise in a warm place until doubled in size, about 1 hour.

Punch down, knead lightly, and divide the dough into 5 portions. Roll each portion into long strands. Braid 3 of the strands and place on a greased cookie sheet. Gently dent the center of the braid and twist the remaining 2 strands together. Lay the twisted strands on top of the braid, tucking under each end. Lightly grease the bread with vegetable oil, cover with plastic, and let rise in a warm place for 1 hour or until doubled in size.

Cover the bread with a foil tent and bake at 400 degrees for 20 minutes. Slip a second cookie sheet under the bread and bake for another 20 minutes, removing the foil if a darker loaf is desired.

Glaze: Combine the egg yolk, sugar, and milk in a small bowl. Brush over the bread. Sprinkle with seeds to decorate. Add the almonds to the remaining glaze and brush them evenly over the bread. Return the bread, uncovered, to the oven to brown, about 5 minutes.

Icing: Place the powdered sugar in a small bowl. Add the milk a tablespoon at a time, until it is the consistency of honey. When the bread is cool, dribble the icing on top and decorate with red and green maraschino cherries.

Makes 1 loaf.

✳ Polish Nut Bread

Julia Egnatic, Kansas City

Nut-flavored yeast breads are popular at holiday time on Strawberry Hill, an ethnic community in Kansas City, Kansas. The Croatians call it povotica *(pronounced* poh-va-TEET-za)*, and it is also referred to as Polish nut bread. There are many versions, all delicious.*

One Christmas, Jayni was lucky

2 packages dry yeast or yeast cakes
½ cup warm water
1 cup milk, scalded
¼ cup sugar
¼ cup butter
1 teaspoon salt
4 to 5 cups all-purpose flour
2 eggs, beaten

NUT FILLING
½ cup milk, scalded
½ cup butter
2 pounds English walnuts, ground
1 cup sugar
¼ cup brown sugar

enough to be the recipient of one of Julia Egnatic's loaves of nut bread with its delicious English walnut filling. She says, "Be sure to use real butter in the nut filling. There is no substitute!"

1 teaspoon cinnamon
¼ cup honey
½ teaspoon vanilla
2 eggs, beaten

1 egg, beaten

Dissolve the yeast in the warm water. To scald the milk, pour it into a saucepan and cook over medium heat until hot but not boiling. Remove from heat. Pour the milk into a large bowl. Add the sugar, butter, and salt. Cool to lukewarm. Add 3 cups of the flour, and beat well. Stir in the yeast mixture and the eggs. Add enough of the remaining flour to make a soft dough.

Turn the dough onto a lightly floured surface and knead for 10 minutes, or until the dough is smooth and elastic.

Place the dough in a lightly greased bowl, turning to grease the top. Cover and let rise in a warm place until doubled in size, about 1 hour. Punch down and let rise again until doubled. While the dough is rising, make the filling.

Nut Filling: In a small pan, scald the milk. Pour it into a large bowl. Add the butter and stir until it begins to melt. Stir in the English walnuts, sugar, brown sugar, cinnamon, honey, and vanilla. Add the eggs and mix well. Set aside.

When the dough has doubled again, punch it down and divide it in half. Roll out each half of the dough on a lightly floured surface until almost paper thin. Spread half of the filling on each and roll up in the style of a jelly roll. Fold the rolls in half, laying the legs of the U-shaped rolls side by side into two 9 x 5 x 3–inch loaf pans.

Let rise until doubled. Brush each loaf with the beaten egg. Bake at 350 degrees for 45 to 50 minutes, or until golden.

Makes 2 loaves.

✳ No-Knead Whole Wheat Rolls

Anna Ruth Beck, Halstead

Howard and Anna Ruth Beck grow, harvest, and mill their wheat on the farm in Halstead that has been in Howard's family since 1880. Anna Ruth uses stone-ground whole wheat flour for a large part of her baking. This is her favorite recipe for whole wheat rolls.

1 cup milk, scalded
½ cup butter or margarine
¼ cup sugar or honey
1 teaspoon salt
1 package dry yeast
¼ cup lukewarm water
1¾ cups stone-ground whole wheat flour
1 egg, beaten
1¾ cups unbleached white flour

Pour the milk into a saucepan and heat over medium heat until hot but not boiling. Remove from heat. Place the butter or margarine, sugar or honey, and salt in a large bowl. Pour the hot milk over it, stir, and cool to lukewarm.

Dissolve the yeast in the warm water. Add the whole wheat flour to the milk mixture. Beat with an electric mixer for 7 minutes. Add the dissolved yeast and the egg. Beat until the mixture is smooth. Stir in the unbleached white flour. The dough should be somewhat soft. Add more flour if necessary. Cover and let rise in a warm place until doubled in size, about 1 hour. Punch down and let rise again.

Punch down and shape into rolls. Place them on a greased baking sheet and bake at 375 degrees for 12 to 15 minutes.

Makes about 2 dozen.

✳ Cornmeal Rolls

Merle Bird, Rossville

This roll recipe derives from Anadama Bread, which differs in its use of molasses instead of sugar.

2 cups milk
⅔ cup yellow cornmeal
½ cup butter or margarine
2 packages dry yeast
⅓ cup warm water

½ cup sugar
1 teaspoon salt
3 eggs, beaten
6 cups all-purpose flour

Pour the milk into a saucepan. Slowly stir in the cornmeal, mixing well. Cook over medium heat, stirring constantly, until all of the milk is absorbed into the cornmeal
and the mixture thickens, 5 to 8 minutes. Remove from
heat and add the butter. Cool to lukewarm.

Dissolve the yeast in the warm water. When the cornmeal mixture has cooled, add the sugar, salt, eggs, and
dissolved yeast, mixing well. Gradually stir in the flour
to make a soft dough. Cover and let the dough stand for
5 minutes.

Turn the dough onto a lightly floured surface and knead
for about 3 to 5 minutes. Form the dough into a ball and
place in a greased bowl. Turn to grease the top. Cover
and let rise in a warm place for about 1 hour, or until
doubled in size. Punch down and roll out on a lightly
floured surface to ½- to ¾-inch thickness. Cut the dough
into circles with a 2½-inch biscuit cutter. Place them on a
lightly greased baking sheet. Cover and let rise in a warm
place until doubled, 30 to 45 minutes.

Bake the rolls at 375 degrees for about 10 minutes, or
until golden.

Makes 3 dozen.

✳ Zwieback

Georgina Johnson, Hillsboro

2 cups milk
½ cup butter or margarine
¼ cup sugar
2 teaspoons salt
2 tablespoons dry yeast
¼ cup warm water
5 cups all-purpose flour

ZWEE-bok). This
traditional bread is a
community favorite
and is usually served
with Sunday dinner.

Pour the milk into a medium-sized pan. Add the butter or margarine, sugar, and salt. Warm over low heat, just long enough to melt the butter. Pour the milk mixture into a large mixing bowl and cool.

Dissolve the yeast in the warm water. When the milk mixture has cooled, add the yeast mixture. Stir in the flour, about 2 cups at a time, until it can be kneaded. Add more flour if necessary. It should be slightly softer than bread dough.

Turn the dough onto a lightly floured surface and knead until it is smooth and elastic, 5 to 10 minutes. Place the dough in a lightly greased bowl, cover, and let rise in a warm place until doubled in size, about 1 hour. Punch down and let rise again.

Punch down and shape the dough into buns by pinching off 2-inch balls. Place them on a greased cookie sheet. Pinch off 1½-inch balls and press them down gently on top of the larger balls of dough. Leave a few inches of space between the buns and allow them to rise until doubled in size.

Bake at 425 degrees for 12 minutes, or until golden brown.

Makes 2 to 3 dozen.

✳ Orange Bow-Knots

Eunice M. Pittman, Bloom

"I grew up in a Swedish family that came to Kansas around the turn of the century," writes Eunice Pittman. "The best parts remembered were not the labor we did, but the holidays and other special family gatherings, when we got together to see all the new additions to the family. It seems like the biggest share of the time we mostly ate and did our catching up over a cup of coffee!

Many times, after we got cars, we gathered at Grandpa's on Sunday afternoons for an early evening supper, as we all had to get back home in time to do the chores. Usually everyone brought some kind of food along, to put together with Grandma's big pot of coffee. Somewhere along the way one of my aunts began making Orange Bow-Knots to go along with the coffee. Now, when we have our family

1 cup milk
½ cup butter or butter flavored shortening
½ cup sugar
1 teaspoon salt
2 packages dry yeast
2 teaspoons sugar
½ cup warm water
2 eggs, beaten
½ cup frozen orange juice concentrate (undiluted)
5 to 6 cups all-purpose flour, sifted

ORANGE ICING
1 cup powdered sugar, sifted
2 tablespoons frozen orange juice concentrate (undiluted)
1 tablespoon butter, softened

In a small saucepan, scald the milk. Pour the milk into a large bowl. Add the butter or shortening, sugar, and salt. Cool to lukewarm.

In a measuring cup, dissolve the yeast and sugar in the warm water. Add to the cooled milk mixture. Add the eggs and orange juice concentrate, beating well. Gradually stir in enough flour to make a soft dough. Cover and let stand in a warm place for 10 minutes.

Turn the dough onto a lightly floured surface and knead for 5 to 10 minutes, until smooth and pliable. Form the dough into a ball and place in a greased bowl, turning to grease the top. Cover and let rise in a warm place until doubled, 1 to 2 hours. Punch down and let the dough rest for 15 minutes.

Roll the dough out on a lightly floured surface into a 10 x 16–inch rectangle, about ½ inch thick. Cut into strips 10 inches long and ¾ inch wide. Make each strip round by lightly rolling it with your palms and tie in a simple loose knot, allowing room for the dough to expand.

Arrange the bow-knots on baking sheets, tucking the

*reunions, I've some-
how inherited the job
of making those rolls."*

ends under. Cover and let rise in a warm place until
doubled, about 45 to 60 minutes.

Bake at 400 degrees for 12 minutes, or until delicately
browned. Remove the bow-knots from the baking sheets
and cool on a wire rack.

Orange Icing: In a mixing bowl, combine the powdered
sugar, orange juice, and butter. Mix until smooth and
brush on the bow-knots with a pastry brush.
Makes about 3 dozen.

✳ Poppy Seed Rolls
(Mak Kuchen)

Lorraine J. Kaufman, Moundridge

*The Swiss German
Mennonites brought
poppy seed and their
recipe for Mak Kuchen
when they immigrated
to Kansas from Russia
around 1874.*

*Some of their de-
scendants in central
Kansas still plant
poppy seed in the early
spring, preferring
the homegrown seed
over the store-bought
ones. In ten to twelve
weeks, the plants are
a mass of white or
pinkish blossoms. Har-
vest occurs when the
seed pods are com-
pletely dry and can
be snapped from the
plant. The pods are
then slit open and the*

1 package dry yeast
½ cup warm water
1½ cups warm water
½ cup shortening, melted
½ cup sugar
2 teaspoons salt
4½ to 5 cups all-purpose flour

POPPY SEED FILLING
3 cups poppy seed
3 cups sugar
1 cup plus 2 tablespoons half and half

melted butter

Stir the yeast into the ½ cup of warm water and set
aside. In a large bowl, combine the shortening, warm
water, sugar, and salt. Mix well. Sift in 1 cup of the flour
and add the dissolved yeast. Stir in the remaining flour
to make a soft dough. Turn the dough onto a floured surface and knead about 10 minutes until smooth. Place the
dough in a greased bowl. Cover and let rise in a warm
place until doubled in size, about 45 minutes. Punch down

tiny seeds shaken out. Sorting is usually done by hand, so that any seeds less than perfect can be discarded. The purple-blue seeds are cleaned by winnowing or washing. Afterwards, to thoroughly dry, they are either hung outside in a cloth bag in the sunshine for several days or put in a warm oven.

the dough. Let rise again until doubled in size, about 1½ hours. Meanwhile, prepare the filling.

Poppy Seed Filling: Grind the poppy seed in an electric mill, blender, or food processor, using the finest blade. If using a blender, grind ¾ cup of seed at a time for about 12 seconds at the highest speed or until the seed is finely ground.

Place the ground poppy seed in a saucepan. Add the sugar and mix well. Add the half and half a little at a time, taking care that the mixture doesn't become thin. Place over low heat, stirring constantly, until the sugar is completely dissolved. Remove from heat and cool.

When the dough has doubled, divide it into 3 equal portions. Cover and let rise again on a floured surface for 30 minutes.

Roll out each portion to 14 x 15 inches and about ⅛ inch thick. Spread each portion with one-third of the poppy seed mixture. If the mixture is too thick, add a small amount of half and half until spreading consistency is reached. Roll up in the style of a jelly roll, pinching the dough together at the ends.

Place the rolls, seam-side down, in a greased 10 x 15 x 1–inch jelly roll pan. Bake at 375 degrees for 30 minutes. Remove from oven and lightly brush the tops of the rolls with melted butter.

Cool the rolls in the pan. To serve, slice into ½-inch servings.

Makes about 24 slices per roll. Serves 18.

✳ One-Rise Cinnamon Rolls

Ms. Terry L. Ryan, Tecumseh

There is nothing more welcome in the morning than fresh-baked cinnamon rolls. Terry Ryan, a fourth-

3 to 3½ cups all-purpose flour
1 package dry yeast
1 cup very warm water (120 to 130 degrees)
1 egg
¼ cup sugar

generation Kansan
"and proud of it,"
writes that she per-
fected this recipe over
ten years. That's a lot
of good mornings.

1 teaspoon salt
2 tablespoons butter or margarine, softened

FILLING
2 tablespoons butter or margarine, melted
¼ cup sugar
1 teaspoon cinnamon
½ cup chopped pecans or walnuts

TOPPING
2 tablespoons butter or margarine, melted
2 tablespoons sugar
½ teaspoon cinnamon

GLAZE
2 cups powdered sugar
2 tablespoons butter or margarine, softened
4 to 5 tablespoons orange juice

In a large bowl, blend 1½ cups of the flour with the yeast, warm water, egg, sugar, salt, and butter. Beat well for 3 minutes. Gradually stir in enough of the remaining flour until the dough gathers into a ball. Turn the dough onto a floured surface and knead for 1 minute. Roll the dough into a 15 x 8–inch rectangle about ⅛ inch thick.

Filling: Brush the melted butter over the prepared dough. Combine the sugar and cinnamon and sprinkle over the dough. Top with the chopped nuts. Starting at the long side, roll the dough up tightly, and moisten and seal the seam. Cut into ¾-inch slices and place the rolls in a lightly greased 13 x 9–inch baking pan.

Topping: Brush the rolls with the melted butter. Combine the sugar and cinnamon and sprinkle on top. At this point, you may cover the rolls and refrigerate up to 24 hours, or cover and let them rise in a warm place until light and doubled in size, about 40 to 45 minutes.

When leavened, bake the rolls at 400 degrees for 18 to 20 minutes until golden brown, watching the baking time carefully.

Glaze: In a small bowl, combine the powdered sugar, butter, and orange juice to a pouring consistency. Drizzle over the hot rolls and serve immediately.

Makes 15 to 20.

✳ Indian Fry Bread

David A. Gaddy Cox, Kansas City

Fry bread is a staple within the Indian communities of Kansas. The quickly fried, soft bread is a cross between a tortilla and pita bread and is used with many dishes. For an alternative to the popular Indian Tacos, make rounds of dough and fill with cooked, chopped meat. Fold, seal, and fry in deep fat. Fry bread also makes a tasty dessert when brushed with melted butter and sprinkled with powdered sugar.

2 cups all-purpose flour
3 teaspoons baking powder
½ teaspoon salt
1 cup milk or water
2 tablespoons shortening
vegetable oil or shortening for deep-fat frying

In a large bowl, mix the flour, baking powder, and salt together. Heat the milk or water in a saucepan until warm. Remove pan from heat and add the shortening, stirring until melted.

Mixing with a fork, add as much of the milk mixture as necessary to the dry ingredients to form a soft dough. Do not overwork the dough. Place the dough on a floured surface and pat or roll out to a thickness of ⅛ to ¼ inch. Cut the dough into 5 x 5–inch diamond-shaped pieces and make a short slit through the dough in the center. Or cut into rounds, about 5 inches in diameter.

To cook, fry the bread in deep oil or shortening, turning once, until golden brown.

Makes 6.

✳ Black Walnut Bread

Edna McGhee, Madison

The native black walnuts found along most any Kansas stream make a moist and tasty

3 cups all-purpose flour, sifted
3 teaspoons baking powder
½ teaspoon salt
1 egg, slightly beaten

*loaf of bread. Edna
McGhee notes that
black walnuts produce
enough oil so that no
shortening is needed
in this recipe.*

1 cup milk
1 cup black walnuts, ground

Combine the dry ingredients in a large mixing bowl. Add
the egg and milk and blend until smooth. Stir in the black
walnuts.

Pour the batter into a greased loaf pan and let stand for
20 minutes.

Bake at 325 degrees for 20 minutes. Raise the temperature to 375 degrees and bake for an additional 40
to 45 minutes, or until an inserted toothpick comes out
clean.

Makes 1 loaf.

✳ Sour Cream Corn Bread

*The Indian tribes of
Kansas made a simple
version of corn bread
by mixing cornmeal
with boiling water
and baking it. The
pioneer version, a
well-established recipe
in the eastern states,
was called johnnycake
(a name derived from*

1 cup yellow cornmeal
1 cup all-purpose flour
¼ cup sugar
4 teaspoons baking powder
½ teaspoon salt
1 egg, slightly beaten
1 cup milk
¼ cup vegetable shortening
½ cup sour cream
1 7-ounce can of corn, drained

"journey cake," as the bread often accompanied the traveler) and was a filler in their diets when meat was scarce. This modern version is enriched with sour cream and whole corn kernels.

In a large bowl, combine the cornmeal, flour, sugar, baking powder, and salt. Add the egg, milk, and shortening. Beat with a wire whip or an electric mixer, just until smooth. Do not overbeat. Fold in the sour cream and corn. Pour the mixture into a greased 9-inch baking dish. Bake at 400 degrees for 20 to 25 minutes, until an inserted toothpick comes out clean.

Serves 6.

✳ Cracklin' Corn Bread

Deanna Lovejoy, Lawrence

"Cracklins" are the browned pieces of fried salt pork used in many recipes of southern origin. This corn bread

½ pound salt pork
1¼ cups cornmeal
¾ cup all-purpose flour
2 teaspoons baking powder
¼ cup sugar

½ teaspoon salt
1 cup milk
1 egg, beaten
¼ cup rendered fat, or vegetable oil

Place the salt pork in a pan and cover with water. Bring to a boil over high heat and boil for 5 minutes. Drain the salt pork, remove, and discard the rind. Dice the salt pork into small pieces and place in a skillet. Fry over low heat, turning occasionally for 15 to 30 minutes, until crispy and well browned. Drain the cracklings on paper towels and measure ½ cup. Reserve the rendered fat for the next step or for another use.

In a large bowl, combine the dry ingredients. In a separate bowl, combine the milk, egg, and rendered fat or oil. Pour the milk mixture into the dry ingredients, stirring to combine. Stir in the cracklings. Pour the batter into a greased 9-inch baking dish or greased muffin tins. Bake at 400 degrees for 20 to 25 minutes, or until an inserted toothpick comes out clean.

Serves 6.

Variation: Use crispy-fried bacon pieces in place of the cracklings.

❋ Grandmother's Corn Bread

Maxine Todd, Sedan

*Maxine Todd's grand-
mother taught her
to make corn bread
when she was a child.
She says, "Over the
years I have also cre-
ated a Mexican-style
variation to please my
family's 'south of the
border' taste." Her
variation is included.*

2 cups stoneground yellow cornmeal
1 cup all-purpose flour, sifted
1½ teaspoons baking powder
2 tablespoons sugar
1 teaspoon salt
2 eggs, slightly beaten
1½ cups milk
2 tablespoons melted shortening or lard

Preheat the oven to 350 degrees. Combine all of the dry ingredients in a large bowl. Add the eggs, milk, and melted shortening or lard. Beat well with a wire whip or a large spoon.

Heat a greased 9-inch baking dish or iron skillet in the oven for about 5 minutes. Pour the batter into the preheated baking dish. Bake for 20 minutes or until an inserted toothpick comes out clean.

Serves 6.

Variation: For Mexican-style corn bread, follow the recipe above, but use vegetable oil in place of shortening and do not sift the flour. To the batter, add ½ cup chopped onion, ½ cup chopped green chilies, 1 tablespoon chopped and seeded jalapeño, 1 cup drained canned corn, and 2 tablespoons chopped pimentos.

Bake in a preheated 13 x 9–inch pan at 350 degrees for 30 minutes.

Serves 8.

❋ Better Biscuits

You can fill them with raisins and sprinkle the tops with cinnamon, but there is only one right way to make

2 cups all-purpose flour, sifted
3 teaspoons baking powder
½ teaspoon salt
¼ cup shortening
¾ cup cold milk

biscuits, according
to Frank's grand-
father, Charles Dwight
Carey, Sr., and that
was his way. "First,
get a fifty pound sack
of flour," he would say,
"and throw away that
mixing bowl because
the only way to make
biscuits is to mix them
up right in the sack."

No one, to Frank's
knowledge, ever pre-
sented his grandfather
with a fifty-pound
sack of flour to test
that claim, but one
must agree that careful
attention to technique
does result in a finer
biscuit.

In a large mixing bowl, add the dry ingredients and sift again to mix thoroughly. Cut in the shortening with a pastry blender until well combined, but do not overwork the mixture. Even the warmth of your hands can cause the shortening to melt and make the dough sticky and heavy.

Add the milk all at once. This is the most important step, because overmixing the dough will create a pasty mixture. Using a large wooden spoon, try to blend the dough by circling the bowl and cutting the moist part into the drier mixture. Keep these strokes to a minimum, about 10 total.

Place the dough onto a cool, floured countertop. Finish mixing the dough with a light kneading action—very few strokes, just until it will stay together to form the biscuits. Add more flour, as necessary, to keep it from sticking.

Pat the dough into a circle about ½-inch thick and cut the biscuits with a 2-inch cookie cutter. Re-form the remainder of dough to cut more biscuits. Biscuits rise best when they are cut cleanly.

Place the biscuits on an ungreased cookie sheet and bake at 450 degrees for 12 to 15 minutes.

Makes 10 to 12.

* ## Elegant Biscuits

Elizabeth M. Skinner, Wichita

Biscuits were not just breakfast food to home-steaders in Kansas; they appeared on the table for lunch and dinner as well. Today, Midwesterners still appreciate biscuits anytime, but now vege- *table shortening has taken the place of lard, bacon fat, or chicken fat, which were once common ingredients.*

As Elizabeth Skinner tells us, "Making biscuits is an art—not to be *lost!" She claims she has found the "very best" biscuit recipe available. The biscuits are soft and flaky on the inside, crusty on the outside, and they reheat beautifully in the microwave.*

3 cups all-purpose flour
¾ teaspoon cream of tartar

½ teaspoon salt
4½ teaspoons baking powder
2½ tablespoons sugar
¾ cup shortening
1 cup milk
1 egg, beaten

In a large bowl, sift together the dry ingredients. Cut the shortening into the flour mixture with a pastry blender until the mixture resembles coarse meal. Add the milk and egg and mix just until the dough is moist.

Place the dough on a floured board and knead very gently, just until all ingredients are moist. Roll out the dough to ½-inch thickness and cut with a 2½-inch biscuit cutter.

Place the biscuits on an ungreased baking sheet and bake at 450 degrees for 12 to 15 minutes.

Makes 12.

✳ Whole Wheat Buttermilk Biscuits

Joan Larson Bader, Berryton

These whole wheat "refrigerator biscuits" can be made up to five days ahead and baked freshly as needed. Joan Bader suggests using the biscuits as a topper for chicken or meat pies. "And of course," says Joan, "there is always the favorite 'biscuits and gravy.'"

1 package dry yeast
½ cup warm water
5 cups whole wheat flour
2 teaspoons salt
1 teaspoon baking soda
3 tablespoons baking powder
3 tablespoons sugar
¾ cups shortening
2 cups buttermilk

Dissolve the yeast in the warm water. Combine the dry ingredients in a large bowl. Cut the shortening into the dry ingredients with a pastry blender or a fork until the mixture is crumbly.

In a bowl, combine the buttermilk with the dissolved

yeast and pour the mixture into the dry ingredients, stirring just to moisten.

Cover the bowl and refrigerate until ready to use. The dough will keep up to 5 days.

To make the biscuits, roll the dough out on a lightly floured surface to ½-inch thickness. Cut with a biscuit cutter and place on an ungreased baking sheet. (They do not need to rise.) Bake at 400 degrees for about 12 minutes.

Makes 30.

❋ Whole Wheat Sesame Drop Biscuits

Kate Shreves, Overbrook

These easy drop biscuits, made with healthful ingredients, will open your day with a nutritious good morning. For a special treat, top the hot biscuits with butter and sorghum.

½ cup whole wheat flour
½ cup all-purpose flour
2 teaspoons baking powder
¼ teaspoon salt
¼ cup wheat germ
¼ cup sesame seed
2 tablespoons butter
½ cup milk

Combine the dry ingredients in a large bowl. Cut the butter into the dry ingredients with a pastry blender or a fork. Add the milk slowly, stirring just until combined.

Drop about 2 tablespoons of the mixture, 2 inches apart, onto a greased cookie sheet. Bake at 450 degrees for 12 to 15 minutes.

Makes 9 to 10.

✳ Amaranth Muffins

Nila Denton, Stockton

Amaranth, now grown in Kansas, is an ancient grain, first cultivated by the Aztec Indians nearly five thousand years ago. They considered it the grain of the gods. Today, amaranth is being rediscovered for its nutritional benefits.

In this recipe, amaranth flour is combined with un-bleached white flour and coarsely cracked wheat to make delicious, healthy muffins.

1 cup coarsely cracked wheat*
1 cup milk
1 egg
¼ cup vegetable oil
½ cup amaranth flour
¾ cup unbleached white flour
1 tablespoon baking powder
¼ teaspoon salt
¼ cup sugar

In a small bowl, combine the cracked wheat and milk. Cover, and depending on desired degree of crunchiness, let stand for 5 minutes or overnight.

Beat the egg and oil into the cracked wheat mixture. Sift the dry ingredients into a large bowl. Stir the cracked wheat mixture into the dry ingredients just until moistened. Spoon the batter into greased muffin tins, filling two-thirds full.

Bake at 375 degrees for 20 to 25 minutes, until lightly browned on top.

Makes 12.

* You can crack your own wheat: Put about a ¼ cup of whole wheat kernels into a food processor, and process for about 15 seconds with the steel knife attachment.

✳ Sunrise Muffins

Patricia Habiger, Spearville

Patricia Habiger says these hearty whole wheat muffins complement any meal, especially breakfast.

1⅔ cups whole wheat flour
¾ cup brown sugar
1 teaspoon baking soda
½ teaspoon baking powder
1 teaspoon cinnamon

½ teaspoon nutmeg
½ teaspoon salt
⅓ cup vegetable oil
1 egg, slightly beaten
1 cup unsalted sunflower kernels
¾ cup raisins
1 cup carrot, finely grated
¼ cup water

In a large bowl, combine the flour, brown sugar, baking soda, baking powder, cinnamon, nutmeg, and salt. Add the oil and egg and stir just to moisten. Add the sunflower kernels, raisins, grated carrot, and water, mixing to form a smooth batter. Do not overmix.

Pour the batter into greased muffin tins about three-fourths full and bake at 375 degrees for 20 to 25 minutes, or until an inserted toothpick comes out clean. Let the muffins cool for 5 minutes before removing from the tins. Makes 12.

✻ Blueberry Muffins

Judith Bird, Dodge City

Judith Bird was kind enough to submit the booklet of muffin recipes that she wrote for friends and family. Included here are

2 cups all-purpose flour, sifted
2 teaspoons baking powder
½ cup sugar
½ teaspoon ground cinnamon (optional)
1 egg, unbeaten
1 cup sour cream

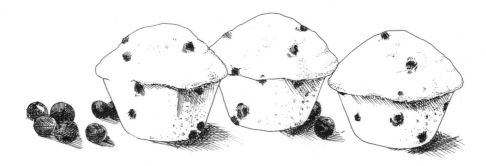

four of her well-tested and uniquely flavored recipes.

1 cup fresh blueberries, destemmed and rinsed
sugar for topping

In a large bowl, combine the flour, baking powder, sugar, and cinnamon. Mix well.

Make a well in the center of the dry ingredients and add the egg and the sour cream. Beat with a fork until well combined. Gently fold in the blueberries.

Spoon the batter into lightly greased muffin tins, filling to three-fourths full. Sprinkle the top of each muffin with sugar. Bake at 425 degrees for about 20 minutes. Serve hot.

Makes 12.

✳ Beer Rye Muffins

Judith Bird, Dodge City

Great with soup on Friday nights.

1 cup all-purpose flour, sifted
¾ cup rye flour
2 tablespoons brown sugar
2 teaspoons baking powder
2 teaspoons caraway seed
½ teaspoon salt
1 egg
1 cup flat beer
¼ cup vegetable oil
1 cup cheese, shredded (optional)

In a large mixing bowl, combine the flours, brown sugar, baking powder, caraway seed, and salt. Mix well and set aside.

In another bowl, beat the egg, beer, oil, and cheese, if desired, together. Add the egg mixture to the dry ingredients all at once, stirring just until moistened. The batter should appear coarsely mixed. Spoon into greased muffin tins, filling each about three-fourths full.

Bake at 400 degrees for 20 to 25 minutes, until lightly browned. Immediately remove from the pan to a wire rack. Serve warm.

Makes 12.

✳ Strawberry-Rhubarb Muffins

Judith Bird, Dodge City

What better way to welcome Spring!

2½ cups all-purpose flour, sifted
1 teaspoon baking soda
1 egg
1½ cups brown sugar, lightly packed
1¼ cups buttermilk
¼ cup corn oil
1 teaspoon vanilla extract
1 cup rhubarb, finely chopped
½ cup strawberries, coarsely chopped
½ teaspoon cinnamon
2 tablespoons sugar

In a mixing bowl, combine flour with the baking soda. Mix well.

In another large bowl, beat the egg and stir in the brown sugar, buttermilk, oil, and vanilla. Mix well. Stir in the rhubarb. Fold in the flour mixture until the dry ingredients are moistened. Gently fold in the strawberries.

Fill lightly greased muffin tins three-fourths full. Combine the cinnamon and sugar and sprinkle on top of each muffin. Bake at 375 degrees for 20 to 25 minutes. Serve warm.

Makes 12.

✳ Oatmeal Spice Muffins

Judith Bird, Dodge City

The aroma of these muffins will spur any lazy morning appetite.

½ cup all-purpose flour, sifted
½ cup whole wheat flour
¾ cup rolled oats
1 teaspoon baking powder
¾ teaspoon baking soda
1¼ teaspoons cinnamon
½ teaspoon nutmeg
1 4-ounce jar strained carrots

¾ cup brown sugar
½ cup vegetable oil
1 egg
½ teaspoon vanilla extract
⅓ cup nuts, chopped (optional)

In a large mixing bowl, combine the flours, oats, baking powder, baking soda, cinnamon, and nutmeg. Mix well.

In another bowl, mix together the strained carrots, brown sugar, oil, egg, vanilla, and nuts if desired. Add to the dry ingredients, stirring just until moistened. Spoon the batter into greased muffin tins, filling two-thirds full.

Bake at 400 degrees for 15 to 20 minutes. Serve warm.

Makes 12.

✳ Stack o' Wheats

Pancakes, also known as flapjacks or griddle-cakes, were a mainstay for previous generations. They were easy to prepare, and the ingredients were always available on the homestead. Cora Skinner Ream, writing for the Kansas City Star *about her childhood in the 1870s in* Kansas, *said, "Pancakes should decorate the coat of arms of the pioneers, for surely pancakes were the salvation of the early settlers—pancakes, sorghum and gravy"* (quoted in Mary Margaret McBride, Harvest of American Cooking *[New York: G. P. Putnam, 1957]).*

Pancakes were made from every kind of flour. They were enriched with milk and leavened with eggs or baking powder, depending on what was at hand. Prepared either as breakfast or a side dish, the following recipes reveal pancakes at their best—past and present.

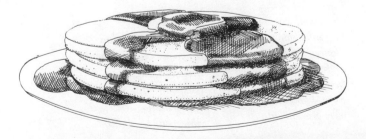

¾ cup cake flour, or all-purpose flour
¾ cup whole wheat flour
1½ tablespoons baking soda
½ teaspoon salt
3 tablespoons sugar
3 egg yolks
3 tablespoons molasses
1 cup buttermilk
½ cup water
3 egg whites
maple syrup or sorghum
½ cup pecans, chopped (optional)

Sift the cake flour or all-purpose flour into a large bowl. Add the whole wheat flour, baking soda, salt, and sugar and sift again.

To the dry ingredients, add the egg yolks, molasses, buttermilk, and water, mixing just to moisten.

Beat the egg whites with an electric mixer until stiff peaks form. Gently fold the beaten egg whites into the batter. If the batter appears too thick, stir in 2 to 4 tablespoons of water.

Pour a large spoonful of batter (enough to make pancakes 3 to 4 inches in diameter) on a hot, lightly greased griddle, or in a similarly prepared large frying pan. Turn the pancakes when bubbles begin to form and break and the edges are set. Brown lightly and serve hot. Top with maple syrup or sorghum and chopped pecans, if desired.

Makes 14 to 16 small pancakes.

✳ Cornmeal Griddlecakes

Cornmeal was an important staple in the pioneer kitchen, and with it, pioneers made tasty griddlecakes. Served for breakfast, they also substituted

1 cup cornmeal
¼ cup all-purpose flour
2 teaspoons baking powder
2 teaspoons sugar
¼ teaspoon salt
1 egg, beaten
2 tablespoons salad oil

*as bread or as a fill-
ing side dish at other
meals.*

1 cup milk
butter
maple syrup

In a large bowl, combine the dry ingredients, mixing well. Add the egg, oil, and milk, stirring until the batter is smooth.

Pour 2 to 3 tablespoons of the batter (enough to make the griddlecakes 3 to 4 inches in diameter) on a hot, lightly greased griddle or in a similarly prepared large frying pan. Turn when bubbles form and break and the edges are set. Brown lightly and serve hot with butter and maple syrup.

Makes 12 to 14 small pancakes.

"Pancake Hub of the Universe"

Each year on Shrove Tuesday, the Kansas town of Liberal swells to almost twice its normal population, with spectators coming from all over the nation to witness an international event—Pancake Day.

The event has its roots in religious custom of over 500 years ago, when accumulated cooking fats, forbidden during Lent, were used up by baking pancakes on Shrove Tuesday. English tradition has it that a woman in Olney, engrossed in her pancakes, forgot the time until she heard the church bells calling everyone to the shriving service. She ran to the church, skillet in hand, to become the first pancake racer. Neighbors joined in the next year, and it became a contest to see who could reach the church steps first, thereby collecting a kiss and the blessing "The Peace of the Lord Be Always With You."

In 1950, R. J. Leete, then president of the Liberal Jaycees, saw a picture in a magazine of the race in Olney, with housewives running to the church, skillets in hand and flipping pancakes as they ran, to vie for a kiss from the bellringer. Leete cabled Vicar Ronald Collins, who headed up the English race, challenging housewives of Olney to compete against women of Liberal. The vicar readily accepted, and every year since that time, the challenge is repeated in the spirit of international good-will and friendship.

The race begins and with a flip, they're off. In parallel competitions, the housewives of Olney, England, and Liberal, Kansas, each outfitted in the required "housewifely" garb of scarves and dresses, run a 415-yard S-shaped course, skillet in hand, through the streets of their respective communities. The race is for the best time and is completed with a final flip of the pancake before the finish line.

Pancake Day in Liberal has grown into a two-day celebration with many groups and organizations in charge of different events—including the race itself, pancake breakfast, talent show, shriving service, and parade followed by the Eating, Flipping, and Cooking Contest. Liberal, currently suffering a losing streak, has earned its title of "Pancake Hub of the Universe."

※ # Oatmeal Raisin Pancakes

Mrs. Thomas Hood, Liberal

These tasty pancakes promise to be a favorite of young folks.

¾ cup all-purpose flour
½ cup quick or instant oatmeal
¼ cup packed brown sugar
¼ cup raisins
2 teaspoons baking powder
½ teaspoon salt
1 cup milk
1 egg, beaten
1 tablespoon oil

Combine all dry ingredients in a large bowl. Beat the milk, eggs, and oil together and add to the dry ingredients. Stir just until the dry ingredients are moistened.

Pour a spoonful of the batter (enough to make pancakes 3 inches in diameter) on a hot, lightly greased griddle or in a similarly prepared large frying pan. Turn when bubbles form and break and the edges are set. Brown lightly and serve with butter and maple syrup.

Makes about 18 3-inch pancakes.

✳ Yogurt Pancakes

Mrs. Thomas Hood, Liberal

This recipe uses yogurt instead of buttermilk for a tart richness.

1 tablespoon sugar
1 teaspoon baking powder
1 teaspoon soda
½ teaspoon salt
1½ cups all-purpose flour
4 eggs, beaten
1 cup yogurt (flavored or plain)

Mix the sugar, baking powder, soda, salt, and flour together in a large bowl. Add the eggs and the yogurt and mix until smooth.

Pour a spoonful of the batter (enough to make pancakes 4 inches in diameter) on a hot, lightly greased griddle or similarly prepared large frying pan. Turn when bubbles form and break and the edges are set. Brown lightly and top pancakes with flavored syrup or fruit.

Makes 12 4-inch pancakes.

✳ German Apple Pancakes

Mrs. Thomas Hood, Liberal

These rich pancakes are sprinkled with cinnamon sugar, filled with cooked apples or applesauce, and rolled up to eat.

6 eggs, lightly beaten
1½ cups all-purpose flour, sifted
¼ teaspoon salt
1 tablespoon sugar
2 cups milk
2 to 3 tablespoons butter
2 tablespoons sugar
1 teaspoon ground cinnamon

1 lemon, quartered
2 cups cooked apples or applesauce

In an electric blender, combine the eggs, flour, salt, sugar, and milk. Blend until the batter is thin, smooth, and lump-free, about 3 to 5 minutes.

Melt the butter a tablespoon at a time as needed in a large frying pan over high heat. Using a ¼-cup measure, pour the batter into the pan and tilt the pan back and forth quickly to form a large, thin pancake. Once the top appears dry, turn the pancake to cook the other side.

At the table, serve the combined sugar and cinnamon, the lemon, apples or applesauce, and the pancakes. Let everyone assemble their own pancake, as follows. Sprinkle the sugar mixture over each pancake. Add a squeeze of the lemon. Spread some of the cooked apples or applesauce over each pancake and roll up.

Makes 14 to 16 large pancakes.

✳ Pancake Omelet

(Schmarren)

Eleanor Schippers, Victoria

The Volga Germans settled the German community of Herzog in 1876. They were very religious people; so, as Eleanor Schippers reports, Fridays and other days of abstinence required meatless meals. It was on days such as these that eggs would be put to use in turning out dishes that would be satisfying and nutritious. A familiar yet tasty meatless recipe was for a pancake omelet that was prepared in a cast-iron skillet and then cut or slashed into pieces, giving it its German name, Schmarren.

2 large eggs, or 3 small eggs
⅓ cup milk
½ cup all-purpose flour
¼ teaspoon salt
3 tablespoons butter

In a mixing bowl, beat the eggs and the milk together. Add the flour and salt and mix well until smooth.

Melt the butter over medium-high heat in a heavy skillet, preferably cast iron. Pour the egg and milk mixture into the skillet. When the batter is lightly browned on one side, cut in half and turn over. Tear the pancake into rough pieces with two knives. Continue cooking and turning the pieces over until they are golden brown on both sides.

Serves 1 to 2. For more servings, repeat the recipe as directed.

Variation: For a sweetened version, add 1 tablespoon of sugar and ¼ teaspoon of baking powder to the batter. Drizzle the pancake omelet with maple syrup.

✳ RELISHES AND PRESERVES

Preserving foods in the old days was a necessity. When winter suspended growth until spring, there simply were no foods available to the settlers other than those they had been able to "put by." Besides the annual task of butchering and storing meats, settlers gathered wild foods in the spring and summer as well as harvested those grown in their gardens and orchards. These fruits and vegetables had to be safely preserved by either canning or drying.

Drying foods in the sun is an ancient method of reducing the water content of fruits and vegetables so that spoiling organisms cannot grow. Canning, a relatively new procedure, was developed in the early 1800s. By employing heat and an airtight seal to prevent spoilage, a whole new variety of foods—namely, vegetables and fruits—were able to be preserved in a condition close to their original color, texture, and taste.

Canning, not thoroughly understood at first, was sometimes unreliable. Heat and an airtight seal alone are not enough to preserve food. To safely put foods by, the addition of salt, sugar, and/or vinegar might be required, depending on

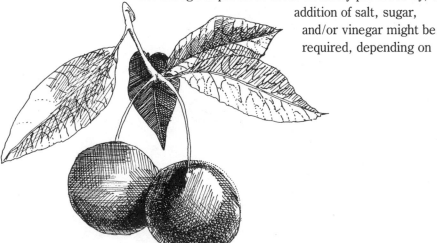

the item, to discourage bacterial growth. This knowledge evolved through experimentation. From the beginning, because canning required heating the food to be preserved, recipes developed combining vegetables or fruits with herbs and spices. By World War II, home canning had undergone nearly a century of refinement and was routine in most kitchens.

In the early days, home canning was a convenience that had not yet been taken over by commercial canneries. Not only were simple ingredients put by, but sauces, relishes, and preserves were made ready to use "right from the jar." Canning shows that a homemaker's skill extends from the garden, to the kitchen, and into the cellar. Months later, when the chill of winter grips the home, a jar, tightly packed with the color of springtime, is brought out like a vintage wine. Silence reigns until the "hiss of safety" can be heard, reassuring the anxious cook that the jar was well sealed. Then, the family enjoys spoonfuls of garden-fresh preserves that send the taste buds reeling back to summer.

There is practically no other way to taste these rural Kansas specialties than to make them yourself. (Inexperienced canners should consult a reliable reference on preserving foods.) Sand Hill Plum Butter, Wild Mulberry Jam, and Prickly Pear Jelly are flavors available occasionally in specialty stores but are free for the picking with permission from the landowner. Dutch Honey is a great change from maple syrup, and there is no substitute for a homemade treat such as Jalapeño Pepper Relish. This chapter also offers recipes for simple cheese making, for an experience right from the homestead of the past.

✳ Sand Hill Plum Butter

Doris Kaufman, Wichita

Doris Kaufman says that Sand Hill plums were known to the early settlers of Kansas as "berries of the plains" and that they grew abundantly in the sandy soil. The Swiss German settlers made lotvark, *or plum jam, from them. They mixed the pulp with sugar and cooked it in large kettles on wood-burning stoves until the right consistency was reached. The jam was then stored in stone crocks covered only with paper and cloth.*

Times have changed and the once-common bushes have disappeared from the plains as the land has been ploughed for farming. However, Sand Hill plum bushes still thrive along the roadsides and fence rows in central Kansas. They bloom in late March and early April and ripen in July and August. Many agree that nothing quite equals the flavor of the wild Sand Hill plum.

4 to 5 pounds wild Sand Hill plums (6 cups plum pulp)
2 cups applesauce
10 cups sugar (or to taste)

Cut the plums in half, or crush them with the bottom of a heavy glass jar, and place them in a large pan or Dutch oven. Cook the plums in their own juices, stirring frequently, over low heat until the pulp is soft, about 20 minutes. Push the cooked plums through a strainer to rid the fruit of the skins and pits. Measure 6 cups of plum pulp.

Place the plum pulp, applesauce, and sugar in a large heat-proof crockery pan or baking dish. Cook over low heat, stirring until the sugar is partially dissolved.

Place the pan or baking dish in the oven and cook uncovered at 350 degrees for 1 hour. Reduce heat to 300 degrees and cook for 1¼ hours more, stirring occasionally. The plum butter should be thick but still moist on top. Remove from the oven and quickly ladle the plum butter into sterilized canning jars, leaving ½-inch headspace. Wipe the jars, adjust the lids, and process in a boiling-water bath for 10 minutes. (Inexperienced canners should consult a reliable reference on preserving foods.)

Makes 3 to 4 pints.

❋ Apple Butter

Mrs. Edward Kauffman, Haven

Every April, the Mennonite community in Hutchinson sponsors a fund-raiser, the Mennonite Central Committee Relief Sale. If you attend, your nose will undoubtedly lead you to the booth where apple butter is being freshly made. The applesauce is combined with cider and slowly stirred in a huge copper kettle. The warm apple butter is then spooned into jars for eager buyers.

Mrs. Edward Kauffman was kind enough to share the recipe that has been in her family since the early 1900s. Spread it on homemade biscuits or toasted English muffins. Or just eat it by the spoonful!

1 bushel of Jonathan apples
4 gallons apple cider
10 pounds sugar

Wash and core the apples. Do not peel them. Cut the apples into quarters and place them in a large kettle with a small amount of water. Cook the apples over low heat, stirring occasionally until tender. Drain off the liquid and press the apples through a cone-shaped colander, discarding the waste. Measure 4 gallons of applesauce and set aside. (The juice that is drained can be canned and processed for 10 minutes in a boiling-water bath for apple juice.)

To make the apple butter, pour the apple cider into a large copper kettle. Bring the cider to a boil and cook until it is reduced by about half. Continue boiling and add the applesauce. Cook, stirring continually to prevent scorching, until the mixture is again reduced by half. Add the sugar and continue cooking and stirring for 20 to 30 minutes more. Remove the kettle from the heat and immediately spoon the apple butter into hot sterilized jars, leaving ½-inch headspace.

Cover the jars with metal lids and screw the bands on tightly. Process the jars in a boiling-water bath for 10 minutes. (Inexperienced canners should consult a reliable reference on preserving foods.)

Makes 4 gallons.

❋ Wild Mulberry Jam

Ruth Deckert, Pawnee Rock

Ruth Deckert developed this recipe because she likes to use the native fruits, in the tradition of the early settlers.

1 gallon wild black mulberries (4¾ cups berry pulp)
¼ cup lemon juice
1 package powdered fruit pectin
8½ cups sugar
2 packages black raspberry powdered drink mix

To make the berry pulp: Thoroughly wash the mulberries. Place the berries in a large kettle and add just enough water to cover. Bring to a boil over high heat, reduce heat to low, and simmer for 10 minutes.

Strain the juice through a jelly cloth and reserve. Put the berries through a food mill to remove the stems and many of the seeds. Measure 4¾ cups of berry pulp into a 6- to 8-quart kettle.

Add the lemon juice and 1 cup of reserved mulberry juice. Add the pectin and stir until dissolved. Bring the mixture to a full rolling boil over high heat, stirring to prevent scorching. Add the sugar and continue stirring the mixture. Boil for 4 minutes. Stir in the black raspberry powdered drink mix and boil for 2 more minutes.

Skim the jam and pour immediately into hot sterilized canning jars, leaving ½-inch headspace. Wipe the jars, adjust the lids, and process in a boiling-water bath for 10 minutes. (Inexperienced canners should consult a reliable reference on preserving foods.)

Makes 10 cups.

✳ Corn Cob Jelly

Lorraine J. Kaufman, Moundridge

Little is ever wasted on the farm, and that applies to both past and present. This jelly is a tasty way to extract some good flavor from field corn before you "give it away" to the hogs.

12 to 14 cobs of red field corn
1 package powdered fruit pectin
3 cups sugar

Choose freshly shelled corn cobs that have not been treated with chemicals. Remove the tips of the cobs. Wash them well to remove any chaff. In a large stock pot, cover the cobs with water and boil gently for 30 minutes.

Strain the juice through a cloth and measure 3 cups into a saucepan. Add the pectin, mix well, and bring to a hard boil. Stir in all the sugar at once. Bring to a full boil again, stirring constantly, and boil hard for 3 to 5 minutes or until it sheets all tines of a fork.

Remove the jelly from the heat. Skim off any foam and pour the jelly into hot sterilized jars or ornate molds, leaving ½-inch headspace. Seal at once with hot melted paraffin. (Inexperienced canners should consult a reliable reference on preserving foods.)

Makes 3 cups.

✳ Prickly Pear Jelly

Ruth Deckert, Pawnee Rock

Prickly pear cactus grows in Kansas, thriving in the dry soil of prairie, pastures, and along roadsides. The Indians who lived on the plains and prairies ate the fruit of the prickly pear both raw and dried.

This recipe uses the ripe red fruit of the cactus to make a delicious jelly. When harvesting the fruit, take along pruning shears, kitchen tongs, and gloves for protection from the cactus needles.

1 gallon ripe prickly pear fruit
¼ cup lemon juice
¾ cup water
1 package powdered fruit pectin
5 cups sugar

Wash the cactus fruit and place it in a large kettle. Add just enough water to cover. Bring the mixture to a boil. Reduce heat to low, and simmer for 5 minutes, or until the fruit begins to soften. Crush the fruit with a potato masher and continue simmering until tender. Strain the juice through 2 or 3 thicknesses of cloth (such as a sheet or piece of muslin), reserving 2½ cups.

In a 6- to 8-quart kettle, add the cactus juice, lemon juice, and water. Add the pectin, stirring until dissolved. Bring the mixture to a full rolling boil. Add the sugar and stir to dissolve. Bring the mixture again to a full rolling boil and boil for 2½ minutes.

Skim the jelly and pour it into hot sterilized jars, leaving ½-inch headspace. Seal at once with hot melted paraffin. (Inexperienced canners should consult a reliable reference on preserving foods.)

Makes 6 cups.

✳ Dandelion Jelly

Von Schroeder, Overland Park

Von Schroeder has never considered the dandelion a weed.

1 quart of dandelion blossoms, stemmed (picked early in the morning)
1 quart water

Indeed, gathering the bright yellow blossoms early in the morning and making them into a jelly that tastes like honey turns a gardening chore into a pleasant task.

Be sure to pick dandelions in areas not treated with harmful chemicals.

1 package powdered fruit pectin
1 teaspoon lemon or orange extract
4½ cups sugar

In a large saucepan, boil the dandelion blossoms in the water for 3 minutes. Strain off 3 cups of the liquid into a clean saucepan and mix in the pectin, extract, and sugar. Discard the blossoms. Return to heat and boil for 3 minutes.

Remove the jelly from the heat and skim. Pour the jelly into sterilized jars, leaving ½-inch headspace. Seal at once with hot melted paraffin. (Inexperienced canners should consult a reliable reference on preserving foods.)

Makes 4 cups.

✳ Applesauce

As the apple orchards of northeast and central Kansas begin to produce their fruit in early fall, it's hard to resist making this simple old-time favorite. Use freshly picked apples for the best results. Not only is applesauce a great dessert or snack, it's also a good side dish for pork, ham, or chicken.

2 pounds tart apples
¼ cup water
2 to 4 tablespoons sugar, to taste
¼ teaspoon cinnamon (optional)

Core the apples and cut them into quarters. Do not peel. Place them in a large pot or Dutch oven. Add the water and cover. Cook slowly over low heat for about 20 minutes, or until the apples are tender. Put the apples through a food mill. Return the applesauce to the pot and add the sugar to taste. Add cinnamon, if desired. Cook over low heat, stirring occasionally, for 5 to 10 minutes. Serve warm or chilled.

Serves 6.

For longer storage, the applesauce may be canned as follows: Pour the hot applesauce into hot sterilized canning jars, leaving ½-inch headspace. Wipe the jars, adjust lids, and process in a boiling-water bath for 10 minutes. (Inexperienced canners should consult a reliable reference on preserving foods.)

Makes 1 quart.

✳ Mincemeat

Marilyn Neill, Fredonia

"I could never find a recipe for mincemeat in a cookbook to suit me. So, through trial and error I finally put this recipe together," writes Marilyn Neill. She says that her recipe makes delicious pies and cookies and that the amount of vinegar or sugar may be adjusted according to your own tastes.

4 pounds beef chuck roast
1 pound suet
6 pounds apples, cored and chopped (unpeeled)
1½ pounds raisins
3 cups sugar
2 cups brown sugar
2 cups light corn syrup
1 12-ounce can frozen lemonade concentrate
1 12-ounce can frozen orange juice concentrate
3 tablespoons cinnamon
1 tablespoon ground cloves or allspice
1 tablespoon salt
¾ cup vinegar
3 cups water

Place the roast in a roasting pan. Add ½ cup of water. Cover and roast at 350 degrees for 2½ to 3 hours, or until tender.

Cool the roast and cut into large pieces, removing the bone and fat. Coarsely grind or chop the meat and the suet in a grinder or food processor.

Place the meat and suet in a very large pot or a Dutch oven. Add the remaining ingredients and simmer uncovered over low heat for about 2 hours, stirring occasionally.

Cool the mincemeat and place in quart containers. Store in refrigerator or freeze for longer storage.

Makes 7 quarts.

Dutch Honey

Mrs. Violet Parsons, Alden

"If you are ever at Aunt Violet's," Violet Parsons overheard her nephew say, "and you taste something better than anything you have ever tasted before —it's Dutch Honey."

Violet's mother learned to make this recipe when she belonged to the Kansas Farm Bureau back in the early 1920s. "It was very quick and easy, and at that time it was inexpensive because we had plenty of country cream," says Violet.

This homemade topping is excellent on biscuits, pancakes, and ice cream.

1 cup sugar
1 cup brown sugar
1 cup corn syrup, light or dark
1 cup whipping cream
1 teaspoon vanilla extract or maple syrup

Combine all the ingredients, except the vanilla, in a saucepan. Stir continually over high heat, bringing the mixture to a rolling boil. Continue stirring and boiling vigorously for 1 minute. Remove from heat and stir in the vanilla extract or maple syrup. Serve warm, or cover and refrigerate for later use.

Makes 2 cups.

Canning Club

Many years of experimentation led to improved canning methods. A canning club was started in the 1930s in Glenwood—Helen Fenton's part of the country that lies just south of Basehor, Kansas. Women from around the region met every month to learn how to can food.

"The first can recommended for tomatoes was tin with a recess around the edge of the lid," writes Mrs. Fenton. "When the can was filled with hot tomatoes, a hot 'gook' called sealing wax was poured around this lid. To open the can you tapped the wax with a kitchen knife so it would shatter. Sometimes, if not sealed well, the lid would blow off."

Other methods of preserving were tried. Cabbage was made into kraut and cucumbers were put into stone crocks or wooden barrels to make pickles. "Sweet corn, packed in salt, was preserved with somewhat of a loss in flavor," recalls Mrs. Fenton. "It would have to be cooked and drained two or three times before you could eat it."

✳ Pickled Asparagus

Karen Pendleton, Lawrence

Because of almost ideal conditions, many Kansans proudly cultivate small asparagus patches in their backyards. Pickling asparagus is a delicious way to avoid wasting a bumper crop. Karen Pendleton suggests using the top four to five inches of the asparagus spears for pickling and the bottoms for making asparagus soup.

4½ pounds fresh asparagus spears
3 garlic cloves, peeled
1 teaspoon pickling spice
3 cups water
2 cups vinegar (5% acidity)
1 tablespoon pickling salt

Snap off the tough ends of the asparagus and rinse well to remove any sand. Pack the spears tightly into 3 hot sterilized wide-mouth pint jars, leaving ¼-inch headspace. Place a clove of garlic in each jar.

Remove the cloves from the pickling spices and reserve for another use. Put the remaining spices in a medium saucepan. Add the water, vinegar, and pickling salt. Bring the mixture to a boil and pour over the asparagus, leaving ¼-inch headspace.

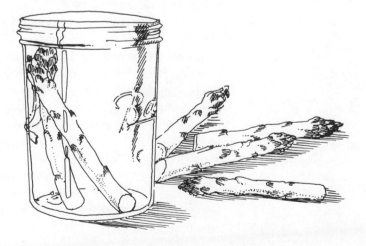

Wipe the jars, adjust the lids, and process in a boiling-water bath for 15 minutes. (Inexperienced canners should consult a reliable reference on preserving foods.)

Makes 3 pints.

✳ Crisp Icicle Pickles

Lillabelle Stahl, Burlingame

The preparation of homemade pickles requires time, patience, care, and good judgment. Crispy sweet pickles add interest to any meal and serve well as a snack straight out of the jar. Lillabelle Stahl says she has made this pickle recipe a number of times, always with great results.

2 gallons cucumbers
2 cups canning salt
2 tablespoons powdered alum
2 quarts vinegar
1 box pickling spices
16 cups sugar
2 tablespoons turmeric (optional)
green food coloring (optional)
fresh grape leaves (optional)

Rinse and slice the cucumbers into spears or rounds. Place in a 4-gallon crock. Add the canning salt to 1 gallon of water and bring to a boil. Pour over the cucumbers and cover. Let stand for one week. Once or twice during the week, skim off any white scum that forms on top.

On the seventh day, drain the liquid from the cucumbers and discard. Cover again with 1 gallon of boiling water. Let stand overnight.

On the eighth day, drain the liquid and discard. Dissolve the powdered alum in 1 gallon of boiling water and pour over the cucumbers. Let stand overnight.

On the ninth day, drain the liquid and discard. Place the pickling spices in a cheesecloth bag. In a large pot, add the vinegar, the bag of pickling spices, and sugar. Stir in the turmeric and green food coloring, if desired. Bring the mixture to a boil and pour over the cucumbers. Let stand overnight.

On each of the next three days, drain off the vinegar mixture, reserving it. Pour the mixture into a large pot, bring to a boil, and pour back over the cucumbers. Let stand.

On the thirteenth day, drain off the vinegar mixture and reserve. Pack the pickle spears or rounds into hot sterilized jars, leaving ½-inch headspace. For added crispness, add a grape leaf to each jar, if desired. Bring the vinegar mixture to a boil, remove the pickling spice bag, and pour over the pickles, leaving ½-inch headspace. Wipe the jars and adjust the lids.

Process the jars in a boiling-water bath for 10 minutes for pint jars and 15 minutes for quart jars. (Inexperienced canners should consult a reliable reference on preserving foods.)

Makes 8 quarts or 16 pints.

✳ Homestead Cucumber Relish

Mrs. Virginia Love Krey, Garden City

Homemade relishes are often produced wherever there are prolific gardens. This relish is great on hamburgers and hot dogs. Kids love it!

5 to 6 cucumbers, about 10 cups
4 green peppers, seeds and pith removed
4 sweet red peppers, seeds and pith removed
8 medium onions, peeled
4 cups crushed ice
¼ cup pickling salt

1 teaspoon turmeric
1 teaspoon mustard seed
1 teaspoon pepper
3 cinnamon sticks
1 teaspoon whole cloves
1 teaspoon allspice
2 cups vinegar
4 cups sugar

Grind or chop finely all the vegetables, or combine them in a food processor and process until minced. Put the vegetables in a large bowl, cover with the crushed ice, and stir in the pickling salt. Let stand uncovered for 30 minutes, then drain.

Add the spices, vinegar, and sugar to the vegetable mixture, mixing well. Pour the mixture into a large pot and boil for 5 minutes.

Pour the relish into sterilized jars, leaving ¼-inch headspace. Wipe the jars, adjust the lids, and process in a boiling-water bath for 10 minutes. (Inexperienced canners should consult a reliable reference on preserving foods.)

Makes 6 to 8 pints.

✳ Green Tomato Relish

Caroline Wittman, Topeka

Making homemade relish is an excellent way to use those last green tomatoes before the first frost.

4 cups onion
4 cups cabbage
4 cups green tomatoes
1 sweet red pepper
1 green pepper
½ teaspoon salt
4 cups vinegar
2 cups water
6 cups sugar
1 tablespoon celery seed
1 tablespoon mustard seed

Thoroughly wash and finely chop the onion, cabbage, green tomatoes, and peppers, or use a food processor. Place the chopped vegetables in a large bowl, sprinkle with salt, cover, and let stand in the refrigerator overnight. Rinse with cold water and drain well.

Bring the vinegar, water, sugar, celery seed, and mustard seed to a boil in a large pot or Dutch oven. Pour the chopped vegetables into the boiling liquid, reduce heat to low, and simmer for 3 minutes.

Put the relish into sterilized pint jars, leaving ¼-inch headspace. Wipe the jars, adjust the lids, and process in a boiling-water bath for 10 minutes. (Inexperienced canners should consult a reliable reference on preserving foods.)

Makes 8 pints.

Fiestas in Kansas

By the 1920s, Mexicans were the second largest ethnic group of immigrants to settle in Kansas. Many had come to work on the railroads between 1865 and 1870, seeking better jobs and incomes. When the railroads extended into Colorado, some stayed to work as farm laborers cultivating and harvesting sugar beets in western Kansas. Although the railroads continued to dominate the employment of Mexican labor until World War II, some Mexicans worked in salt mining, coal mining, oil, and meat-packing.

Communities with large Mexican populations may have the good fortune to enjoy a Mexican fiesta. This traditional celebration is often held at Catholic churches throughout the state to raise money for the church and parochial schools. The fiestas consist of lively music, games, traditional costumes, handicrafts, and, of course, genuine Mexican foods.

The style of Mexican cooking in the Midwest may differ from other areas of the United States because, as with all transplanted cultures, the availability of ingredients affects traditional recipes. At fiestas in Topeka, for example, potatoes and peas are common additions to many of the dishes.

Mexican-American families are close-knit, and often the whole group gathers to prepare the traditional foods of their homeland. Susie Bermudez of Lawrence recalls, "We would meet at my uncle's house and the women would cook all day. Depending on the occasion, they would invite other families and we'd have a feast."

Susie also remembers more typical Midwestern meals. "At home, Mom would make American recipes for Sunday dinner. We would have fried chicken, meat loaf, pot roast, mashed potatoes, and salads. This was a real treat, for as Mexican foods are to you, American foods were to us."

Mexican food has become increasingly popular in Kansas. It is not unusual for backyard gardeners to grow the many varieties of peppers, including the jalapeño, that are essential to Mexican cuisine. Fresh homegrown tomatoes, onions, and chili peppers are turned into spicy salsas and used in other Mexican specialties. Grocery stores now carry competing brands of ingredients for Mexican cookery, and Mexican restaurants are commonplace across the state—additional testimony to the role of Mexican food in Kansan diets.

✳ Jalapeño Pepper Relish

Susie Bermudez, Lawrence

Susie Bermudez's grandfather immigrated from Mexico to El Paso, Texas, in the 1890s to work on the railroads. Her parents met in Quinimo, Kansas, and moved to Ottawa after they married.

Susie says that her family used to cook everything from beans to ears of corn outdoors when she was a child. "They cooked in tubs of water or steamed foods in a hole dug in the ground and covered with corn husks. Chilies hung everywhere. Everything was canned or dried due to the lack of refrigeration.

I remember Dad had an orchard of apples, peaches, and grapes. He also planted corn, potatoes, and peppers." Susie recalls the happy times when the family would gather to cook and share meals. "Fires were built and pots would hang above them. The aroma of beans and tortillas would fill the air. The kids would run all over the place under the moonlight. I always felt a sense of security and love."

Susie's family recipe for pepper relish accompanied many of those meals her family shared together. Serve it with grilled meats or traditional Mexican dishes.

¾ *cup vinegar*
½ *cup olive oil*
½ *cup water*
2 *tablespoons sugar*
1 *teaspoon oregano*
1 *teaspoon salt*
¼ *teaspoon pepper*
¼ *to* ½ *pound jalapeño peppers, sliced in half and seeded*
1 *small celery stalk, thinly sliced*
2 *carrots, peeled and thinly sliced*
1 *medium head of cauliflower, cut into flowerets*
1 *white onion, chopped*
1 *2-ounce jar stuffed Spanish olives, drained*

In a large pan or a Dutch oven, combine the vinegar, olive oil, water, sugar, oregano, salt, and pepper. Add the sliced jalapeño peppers, celery, carrot, and cauliflower. Bring the mixture to a boil, reduce heat to low, and simmer uncovered for 4 minutes. Add the chopped onion and simmer for 1 minute more. Remove the pan from the heat and stir in the olives. Cool and serve.

Serves 8 or more.

✳ Hot Dog Relish

Relish is a must on the all-American hot dog. This colorful version has a German twist, combining sauerkraut with bread and butter pickles. It can be freshly made in minutes and is great on hamburgers, fish, and vegetable salads.

½ *cup sliced bread and butter pickles*
½ *cup sauerkraut, drained*
1 *small red onion, coarsely chopped*
1 *garlic clove, minced*
¼ *teaspoon pepper*
3 *drops Tabasco sauce, or to taste*

Put all the ingredients in a food processor. Using the steel knife blade, pulse a few times, just until the mixture is uniform in texture. (Or put all the ingredients on a cutting board and mince with a chef's knife.) Place the relish in a jar or covered container and chill for at least 24 hours for a blending of flavors.

Makes 1½ cups.

Carrot Crunch

Lorraine J. Kaufman, Moundridge

A spoonful of this colorful relish will brighten any summer plate. Its healthy appeal and zesty flavor are bound to spark everyone's appetite.

4 large carrots
1 large lemon
1 cup sugar
½ cup walnuts, coarsely chopped

Peel the carrots or wash them thoroughly. Finely grate the carrots or use a food processor. Place them in a large bowl. Finely grate the peel of the lemon and add it to the grated carrot. Squeeze the lemon and add the juice and sugar to the carrot mixture, stirring until the sugar granules are completely dissolved. Store the mixture, covered, in the refrigerator for three days. This allows the relish to ripen and gives it a marvelous flavor.

Just before serving, stir in the chopped walnuts.

Makes 1 pint.

Drying Fruits and Vegetables

"Years ago storing food for winter was a problem," writes Elton Fenton of Bonner Springs. "I was born in 1911 and even when I was a kid drying food was a good way to store it.

Most every farm had an orchard. In our orchard grew the Ben Davis apple, a good variety to dry. It was a big red apple with light-colored streaks, and very dry and mealy. We kids complained about the apples not having much flavor (a little like cardboard), but they sure dried well. All fruits and vegetables are much sweeter when dried.

Folks dried fruit in the sun mostly. They put it out on a flat roof on bedsheets and some thin cloth on top to keep the flies off. Days when the sun never shined, the apples were put in the oven of an old wood cookstove. The heat was hard to control so the oven door was left open most of the time.

Sweet corn was very good dried. It was dried mostly

in the oven. Because it was so sticky and sweet when cut off the cob, the flies were hard to keep off it. So the kitchen oven seemed to be best.

We have a better way to dry everything now. We built a drier four feet high and two feet square with six trays made of stainless steel mesh wire. A small gas stove sits under the trays with two fans to even out the heat.

Most everything dries in twenty-four hours. We dry apples, pears, grapes, cantaloupes, bananas, cabbage, turnips, carrots, celery, onions with the green tops, sweet corn, and tomatoes.

No sulfur or other preservatives are added."

If you visit the Lawrence Farmer's Market (open Saturday mornings from May through October), you can sample Mr. Fenton's dried fruits and vegetables.

✳ Farmer's Cheese

Nadine Herridge, Oswego

In years past, cheese making was common practice on the homestead. Nadine Herridge is proud of her heritage and recalls her life on the farm. "I grew up in Chetopa, ten miles south of Oswego, in a family of eight children. We always had plenty to eat because we raised or made most everything we needed on the farm. We raised our own hogs and chickens, canned homegrown goods, and made lye soap. During the depression, one of the things we made was our own cheese."

This recipe makes a mild cheese, but if a stronger flavor is desired, pimentos, caraway seed, diced hot peppers, or garlic powder may be added.

1 gallon thick clabbered milk*
3 tablespoons butter
½ teaspoon soda
½ cup thick sour cream
1 teaspoon salt
½ teaspoon yellow food coloring (optional)

* Clabbered milk can be made by allowing safe raw milk to stand. For best results, inexperienced cooks should consult a reliable reference.

Heat the clabbered milk in a large pot or Dutch oven to 110 degrees, stirring frequently. (This temperature is slightly higher than what is ordinarily used in making cottage cheese.) Hold at this temperature for 30 minutes and continue stirring. Remove from heat and drain off the whey. Pour the curds into a colander and press the liquid from the curds until they are very dry. Place the curds in a large bowl and add the butter and soda. Mix well and let stand for 2 hours.

Add the sour cream, salt, and food color, if desired. Turn the mixture into the top of a double boiler, stirring constantly over low heat until all the ingredients melt and blend into a smooth mass. Pour the cheese into a buttered mold or bowl. Cover and chill.

Makes 1 pound.

✳ German Cheese

(Käse)

Eleanor Schippers, Victoria

According to Eleanor Schippers, food which could be made of items produced on the farm were especially preferred in the old days. Milk, always in abundance, often appeared on the table as cottage cheese.

Eleanor writes, "In the summer and fall months a familiar sight was Mutter's [Mother's] cottage cheese bag hanging from a nail in the warm attic with a dish pan beneath it to catch the whey. The home-made cottage cheese was not only eaten as it was, but it was sometimes garnished with finely chopped winter onions. Often it appeared as a filling for noodle pockets or was used for making Käse."

1 16-ounce bag or carton dry cottage cheese*
1 teaspoon soda
1½ teaspoons salt
½ cup butter or margarine, softened

*A bag or carton of dry cottage cheese can be purchased at country stores, health food stores, or German specialty food shops.

1 large egg, beaten
3 small drops of yellow food coloring (optional)

Squeeze the bag of cottage cheese until completely dry,
or drain in a strainer. Place the cottage cheese in a mixing bowl and add the soda, salt, and butter or margarine.
Mix well. Let stand for 10 minutes.

Place the cheese mixture in a heavy skillet over low
heat. Stir the mixture over very low heat until completely
melted. When melted, add the egg and stir until well
blended. Stir in the yellow food coloring, if desired.

Pour the cheese into a well-buttered dish and chill at
least 24 hours. Slice to serve.

Makes 1 pound.

✳ DESSERTS

When asked what their really special recipes are, Kansas cooks overwhelmingly reply, "Desserts!"

The answer is not so surprising considering the legacy of recipe exchanges and the intense—if polite—rivalries at county fairs. Making (and baking) desserts has always been an opportunity to show a little creative flair, to be neighborly, or to say you are "sweet" on someone.

Sweetened foods had humble beginnings in Kansas, for refined sugar was expensive and often unavailable. Early settlers frequently used molasses or sorghum and the honey harvested from their bees as sweeteners. At first, pawpaws, wild plums, persimmons, and various berries were the only fruits available. Before the apple orchards flourished in Kansas, mock apple pies were made of sheep sorrel, crackers, and tartaric acid; though remarkably similar in taste, they were no substitute for the real thing. More common desserts were rice or suet pudding, bread pudding, and vinegar cobbler.

White flour was also considered rare and a delicacy. Though wheat was grown on most farms, it was costly to

have it milled, and as the cash crop, as much as possible
was sold in order to buy the sugar needed to preserve
vegetables and fruits for the winter. In addition to the
difficulties of adjusting to a strange new land, European
cooks who brought to Kansas their heritage of fine desserts were challenged by the limited availability of ingredients. However, desserts often meant more than a
sweet treat to these immigrants; even a simple cake or
fruit pie might remind them of their homeland or sym-
bolize the triumph of prosperity and civilization over
their rugged existence. Their skill at farming, as well as
homemaking, resulted in comfort and security—priceless
commodities on the plains. In Willa Cather's *My Antonia*,
the shy children of immigrant settlers show off their new
cellar:

> They said nothing, but, glancing at me, traced on
> the glasses with their finger-tips the outline of the
> cherries and strawberries and crabapples within,
> trying by a blissful expression of countenance to
> give me some idea of their deliciousness.
> "Show him the spiced plums, mother. Ameri-
> cans don't have those," said one of the older boys.
> "Mother uses them to make *kolaches*," he added.

The simple desserts of the early settlers endure today.
Re-created in this chapter, they may not seem fanciful in
terms of decoration or presentation, but they showcase
high-quality ingredients and a perfected technique (as in
the ripeness of the fruit and the flakiness of the crust).
Kansans still cook the vinegar cobbler and suet pudding
of the past—not just to commemorate their ancestors but
because they are great desserts. As for apple pies, there
are six recipes here, each representing distinct variations
on the traditional Heartland favorite. Other fruit desserts, using fresh apricots, persimmons, and peaches,
are included, along with many more beloved desserts
from church socials and harvest gatherings.

Classic Apple Pie

Becky Ott, Eudora

Floyd and Becky Ott have an apple orchard in Eudora. Becky likes to bake apple pies with Jonathan, McIntosh, or Yellow Delicious apples. "We now have many producing trees," says Becky, "but when we started our orchard, each apple was valuable to us and to be able to prepare a dessert with our own fruit was very special."

Included is the recipe for Flaky Pie Crust, given to her by a German lady over forty years ago, along with a pie plate and a rolling pin, as a wedding gift.

FLAKY PIE CRUST
2 cups all-purpose flour
1 teaspoon salt
1 cup shortening
1 tablespoon white vinegar
⅓ cup cold milk

FILLING
2 pounds tart apples
¾ cup sugar
2 tablespoons all-purpose flour
1 teaspoon cinnamon
¼ teaspoon nutmeg

2 tablespoons butter

Flaky Pie Crust: In a large bowl, add the flour and salt. Cut in the shortening with a pastry blender or a fork until the mixture resembles small peas. Stir in the vinegar. Stir in the milk a tablespoon at a time, just until the mixture is moistened. Cover and chill for 30 minutes.

Divide the dough in half and roll out to ⅛-inch thickness on a lightly floured surface. Line a 9-inch pie plate with half the dough and use the other half for the top crust.

Filling: Peel and slice the apples and place them in a large bowl. In a separate bowl, combine the sugar, flour, cinnamon, and nutmeg. Pour the mixture over the apples, stirring gently to combine.

Spoon the apple mixture into the unbaked pie shell. Dot with butter. Position the crust over the apples, cutting slits for the steam to escape. Trim and seal the edges.

Bake at 425 degrees for 15 minutes. Reduce heat to 375 degrees and bake for 30 to 40 minutes more, until the filling is bubbly and the crust is golden brown.
Serves 6 to 8.

Hint: If the apples are not tart, add 1 tablespoon of lemon juice to the filling before baking.

✳ Simple and Delicious Apple Pie

Elda Wenzel, Wichita

This apple pie is similar to a French apple tart, with the wholesome goodness of cream for thickening and richness.

5 cups tart apples (6 to 8 apples)
¾ to 1 cup sugar, to taste
1½ tablespoons all-purpose flour
½ teaspoon cinnamon
⅛ teaspoon nutmeg
1 unbaked 9-inch pie shell
1 cup whipping cream

Peel and slice the apples into a large bowl. In a separate bowl, combine the sugar, flour, cinnamon, and nutmeg. Pour the mixture evenly over the apples, mixing well. Spoon the apple mixture into an unbaked pie shell, without heaping. Pour the whipping cream evenly over the apples.

Bake the pie at 425 degrees for 15 minutes. Reduce heat to 350 degrees and bake for 30 to 40 minutes more. Cool to room temperature before serving.

Serves 6 to 8.

The Marvelous Apple

The apple was probably the first fruit cultivated by man. Crisp, juicy, sweet, and firm, its white interior holds the very promise of health. Throughout Western culture, the apple has assumed symbolic importance. Scandinavian folklore indicates it was the source of wisdom for the gods. In the Judeo-Christian tradition, the apple has symbolized temptation—the forbidden fruit on the tree of knowledge, of which Adam and Eve ate. It has represented both trust, as when William Tell set an apple atop his son's head, and deceit, as in the poisoning of Snow White with the scarlet fruit. And inspiration, it is said, came to Sir Isaac Newton in the form of a falling apple. It is no wonder that the New England colonists brought their homeland with them to the New World in the form of apple trees. They planted and cultivated the seedlings

DESSERTS

and, by the next century, were shipping apples back to England.

The apple tree first moved across the midsection of the United States in the 1840s on the back of a folk hero named Johnny Appleseed. John Chapman, his real name, was wise enough to establish nurseries for the seedlings rather than actually sow the seeds, for the seeds do not bear true to the tree.

His legendary efforts brought the trees as far as Indiana. As the pioneers moved into Kansas Territory, they too planted a number of varieties: the Wolf River giants; bright red French Fameuses with flesh so white they were also called Snow; the mottled but mouth-watering little brown Russets; and the Westfield Seek-No-Furthers. The most prolific varieties for Kansas, however, were the Jonathan, the McIntosh, Winesap, the Ben Davis, and the Rome Beauty. Many homesteads had small fruit orchards. Apples supplemented the diet with the vitamins found in fresh fruit. When stored in a cool place, apples kept very well, and they were easily processed and canned as applesauce or dried for longer periods—always a consideration in pioneer days. Because climatically apple trees require only a winter dormancy to produce fruit, they became established in most of the United States.

Kansans soon discovered, as New Englanders had, that apples made an excellent cash crop. It was the Rome Beauties and the Ben Davises that became the "mortgage raisers" in late nineteenth-century Kansas. To succeed in the market, apple trees had to be productive and their fruit had to be salable. Many varieties did not meet those requirements, and as the apple industry developed in the Northwest, those that were too delicate to ship also disappeared. It is sad to report that of the seven thousand varieties grown in the United States, only a dozen or so are grown commercially. Consumers have chosen the flawless, tough-skinned, and uniform red exterior of the Red Delicious apple over the more flavorful "antique" varieties, as they are now known.

Today it is still possible to taste the apples of our ancestors in the orchards and farmers' markets of Kansas.

Floyd Ott and Fred W. Leimkuhler are two of the growers
who maintain antique varieties of apples. The older
types of Jonathans and McIntoshes that they grow in
their northeastern Kansas orchards may not be picture-
perfect, but their flavor is astonishing.

With an abundance of fine apples, Kansas has an equal
supply of fine apple recipes. Apples lend themselves to
a variety of cooking methods. Sautéed with diced beets
and onions, for example, they are ideal with roast beef,
roast pork, and roast duck. Baked apples—their cavities
filled with raisins and brown sugar and served with or
without cream—make a delicious and simple dessert.
Immediately following is a selection of apple pie recipes
ranging from simple to fanciful and from historic to contemporary.

✳ Pioneer Apple Pie

*Apple pie was a favor-
ite among early set-
tlers. Before their
orchards bore fruit,
apples were not easy
to come by. Often pies
were made with dried
apples, or sometimes
soda crackers and
spices were combined
to make a mock apple
pie. Pioneer home-
makers took pride in
their baking abilities,
and there were prob-
ably as many recipes
for apple pie as there
were pioneer wives.*

*This version, with
a whole wheat pie
crust and topping, fea-
tures the tart Jonathan
apples and pecans of
Kansas.*

PIE CRUST
½ cup whole wheat flour
½ cup unbleached white flour
⅛ teaspoon salt
⅓ cup butter, chilled
3 to 4 tablespoons ice water

FILLING
5 cups Jonathan apples (5 to 7 apples)
½ cup sugar
1 teaspoon cinnamon

TOPPING
¾ cup whole wheat flour
⅓ cup sugar
¼ teaspoon cinnamon
6 tablespoons butter, chilled
2 tablespoons pecans, ground

Pie Crust: Combine the whole wheat flour, white flour,
and salt. Cut in the butter with a pastry blender or a fork
until crumbly. Add the water a tablespoon at a time, stirring until mixture can be formed into a ball. Roll out the

dough on a lightly floured surface to ⅛-inch thickness. Fit the dough into a 9-inch pie plate.

Filling: Peel and slice the apples into a large bowl. Combine the sugar and cinnamon and stir into the sliced apples. Fill the pie shell with the apple mixture.

Topping: Combine the whole wheat flour, sugar, and cinnamon. Cut in the butter until crumbly. Stir in the nuts. Sprinkle the mixture evenly over the apples. Bake at 425 degrees for 15 minutes. Reduce heat to 350 degrees and continue baking for 35 to 40 minutes, or until the apples are tender and the topping is lightly browned.

Serves 6 to 8.

✳ Sour Cream Apple Pie

Mrs. Harold Johnson, Dwight

This rich apple pie, with a sour cream filling and a brown sugar topping, tastes somewhat like a cheesecake. Mrs. Johnson says it was served to her when she was a young girl, and she serves it to her family and friends today.

1 egg
1 cup thick sour cream
½ teaspoon vanilla extract
½ teaspoon salt
¾ cup sugar
2 tablespoons all-purpose flour
2 cups apples, finely chopped
1 unbaked 9-inch pie shell

TOPPING
½ cup brown sugar
⅓ cup all-purpose flour
¼ cup butter, chilled

In a large mixing bowl, beat the egg. Add the sour cream, vanilla, and salt, mixing well.

In a separate bowl, combine the sugar and flour. Add this to the sour cream mixture, beating well. Stir in the chopped apples.

Pour the filling into the unbaked pastry shell and bake at 450 degrees for 15 minutes. Reduce heat to 350 degrees and continue baking for 30 minutes more. Meanwhile, make the topping.

Topping: In a medium-sized bowl, combine the brown sugar and the flour. Cut in the butter with a pastry blender or a fork until the mixture is crumbly.

After the pie has baked for a total of 45 minutes, remove it from the oven and sprinkle on the topping. Return the pie to the oven and bake for 10 minutes more.

Serves 6 to 8.

✳ Old English Apple Pie

Lorraine J. Kaufman, Moundridge

"Black walnuts provided hours of enjoyment for me as a child growing up on a farm in eastern Kansas, where the walnut trees thrive along rivers and creeks," writes Lorraine Kaufman. "It was always fun to gather them in the woods on a crisp fall day, and I learned to crack them as a Sunday afternoon pastime. A few sharp blows with a hammer on the pointed (stem) end, after the hull was removed, produced the whole center piece in the shape of a 'W.' The quarters, held gently in case the hammer missed, were then easy to crack.

Black walnuts, rich in protein and fat, made a delicious snack or provided a distinctive flavor for a variety of dishes. A favorite way to use them was to combine them with fresh, crisp apples in an Old English Apple Pie."

2 eggs
1½ cups sugar
1 cup all-purpose flour
2 teaspoons baking powder
½ teaspoon salt
2 cups fresh tart apples, peeled and finely chopped
¾ cup black walnuts, chopped

In a large bowl, beat the eggs until thick and lemon colored. Add the sugar slowly and continue beating until well combined.

In a small bowl, sift the flour, baking powder, and salt together. Add the dry ingredients to the egg mixture and beat well. Add the apples and nuts, stirring until all ingredients are completely mixed.

Pour the batter into 2 well-greased 9-inch pie plates or a well-greased 13 x 9–inch baking dish. Bake at 350 degrees for 25 to 30 minutes. (This pie makes its own crust on top and bottom.) Serve with whipped cream or ice cream.

Serves 12.

✳ Sugar-free Apple Pie

Stevens County Library, Hugoton

For those who must avoid sugar in their diet, this tasty and tart apple pie is a delightful alternative.

1 6-ounce can unsweetened frozen apple juice concentrate
2 rounded tablespoons all-purpose flour
1 teaspoon cinnamon
¼ teaspoon salt
5 to 7 apples
1 tablespoon butter or margarine
nutmeg (optional)
1 unbaked 9-inch double-crust pie shell

In a small saucepan, combine the frozen apple juice, flour, cinnamon, and salt. Stir constantly over medium heat until the mixture is thick and bubbly, 3 to 5 minutes.

Peel and slice the apples and stir them into the apple juice mixture. Pour the mixture into the unbaked pie shell and dot with butter. Position the top crust over the filling, cutting slits for the steam to escape. Trim and seal the

edges. Brush the top very lightly with water and sprinkle with nutmeg, if desired.

Bake at 450 degrees for 15 minutes. Reduce heat to 350 degrees and bake for 30 minutes more.

Serves 6 to 8.

✳ Jody Pie

Joan Carey, Topeka

"There are few things in life that are perfect," says Frank, "but for most guys, it's his mother's apple pie. Meaning no disrespect to your mother, but for me, it's my mother's pie. Every time I eat some, I pity the poor soul that wasn't born into our family. Not only is this pie easy to make, but it has medicinal value as well. It can cure the pain of a little league strike-out or take the sting out of a sore arm when painting a house. Looking back, we had it so often that I realize why it's more memorable than my batting average. I recommend it highly."

PIE CRUST
1½ cups all-purpose flour
⅛ teaspoon salt
½ cup shortening or chilled butter
4 to 5 tablespoons ice water

FILLING
5 cups tart apples (5 to 7 apples)
½ cup sugar
1 teaspoon cinnamon

TOPPING
¾ cup all-purpose flour
⅓ cup sugar
½ teaspoon cinnamon
6 tablespoons butter, chilled

Pie Crust: Combine the flour and salt. Cut in the chilled butter with a pastry blender until there are only small crumbs. Add the water, a tablespoon at a time, stirring until the mixture can be formed into a ball. Roll out the dough on a lightly floured surface to ⅛-inch thickness. Fit the dough into a 9-inch pie pan and crimp the edges for decoration.

Filling: Peel and slice the apples into a large bowl. Add the sugar and cinnamon and stir until well mixed. Turn the mixture into the unbaked pie shell.

Topping: Combine the flour, sugar, and cinnamon in a bowl. With a pastry blender, cut in the butter until the mixture is crumbly. Cover the top of the pie with the mixture. Bake at 425 degrees for 15 minutes. Reduce heat to 350 degrees and continue baking for 30 to 40 minutes, until bubbly and lightly browned.

    Serves 6 to 8.

✳ Anna Lee's Banana Cream Pie with Perfect Pie Crust

Fresh dairy products are a must for making the very best cream pie. Fresh farm eggs are often available from Kansas farmers or at farmer's markets across the state.

  Jayni's mother, Anna Lee Amos, is well known among her friends for her pie-making expertise. She has perfected her pies and pie crusts over the years and has shared her secrets with her daughter. "The secret to a very 'short' crust is a little extra short-ening," she says. "It makes a lighter crust that won't get soggy if it sits for a day or two."

  We must confess, however, that we've never seen one of her pies last that long.

PERFECT PIE CRUST
1½ cups all-purpose flour
½ teaspoon salt
10 tablespoons shortening
3 to 4 tablespoons ice water

PIE FILLING
½ cup sugar
⅓ teaspoon salt
2 tablespoons cornstarch
¾ tablespoon all-purpose flour
2¼ cups whole milk
2 eggs, beaten
¾ tablespoon butter
1 teaspoon vanilla extract
1 cup bananas, sliced

TOPPING
½ cup whipping cream
¼ teaspoon vanilla extract
1 to 2 tablespoons sugar, to taste

Perfect Pie Crust: Sift the flour into a medium-sized bowl. Stir in the salt. Cut in the shortening with a pastry blender or a fork, until crumbly. Add the water a table-spoon at a time, stirring with a fork, until the mixture can be formed into a ball. Roll out the dough on a lightly floured surface to ⅛-inch thickness. Fit the dough into a 9-inch pie plate. Prick the bottom and sides of the pie shell with a fork and bake at 450 degrees for about 10 minutes, or until the crust is light gold. Do not over-brown. Cool completely before adding the filling.

Pie Filling: In a large saucepan (or a double boiler, if pre-ferred), combine the sugar, salt, cornstarch, and flour. Add the milk and eggs, stirring constantly over medium-low heat. Cook and stir until the mixture thickens, 15 to 20 minutes. Remove the pan from heat and, to remove any lumps, strain the filling into a large bowl. Stir in the butter and vanilla. Cool to room temperature.

When the filling is completely cooled, gently fold in the sliced bananas and pour into the baked pie shell. Cover and refrigerate until ready to serve.

Topping: Whip the cream with the vanilla and sugar. Spread on top of the pie and serve immediately.

Serves 6 to 8.

Variation: For coconut cream pie, omit the bananas and add ¾ cup of shredded coconut to the cooled filling. Sprinkle the whipped cream topping with 2 tablespoons lightly toasted coconut.

✳ Burnt Sugar Pie

Twila Roenne, Osborne

"In the summer of 1928 my father worked with a neighbor's threshing crew on a farm near Codell," writes Twila Roenne. *"The neighbor's wife served Burnt Sugar Pie to the crew for dessert. It was a big hit with the crew and Dad brought the recipe home for my mother. Those who cook from*

⅓ *cup sugar*
3 *cups hot milk*
⅓ *cup all-purpose flour*
½ *teaspoon salt*
1 *cup sugar*
3 *egg yolks, beaten*
1 *to 2 teaspoons vanilla extract, to taste*

MERINGUE
3 *egg whites*
¼ *teaspoon cream of tartar*
pinch of salt
½ *teaspoon vanilla extract*
¼ *cup sugar*

1 baked 9-inch pie shell

Place ⅓ cup of sugar in a saucepan over medium-high heat until it melts and turns light brown. Slowly add the hot milk, stirring until the sugar is dissolved.

In a small bowl, sift the flour, salt, and sugar together. Add slowly to the hot mixture, stirring over medium heat until it is nearly thickened, 3 to 5 minutes, taking care not to scorch. Stir a small amount of the hot mixture into the beaten egg yolks and immediately pour the egg mixture into the hot mixture. Stir constantly until the mixture thickens, 3 to 5 minutes more. Continue stirring while the mixture boils gently for about 1 minute. Remove from heat and, to remove any lumps, strain the filling into a bowl. Stir in the vanilla to taste and cool slightly.

Meringue: In a large mixing bowl, beat the egg whites until frothy. Add the cream of tartar, salt, and vanilla. Gradually blend in the sugar, a tablespoon at a time, beating until stiff peaks form.

Pour the cooled filling into the baked pie shell. Top with the meringue and bake at 400 degrees for 5 to 8 minutes, or until meringue is golden brown.

Serves 6 to 8.

✳ Cinnamon Cream Pie

Mrs. Violet Parsons, Alden

This custard pie flavored with cinnamon is an old family favorite that was first baked by Violet Parsons's mother many years ago. It is so simple that it can be assembled in minutes.

2 eggs
⅔ cup sugar
⅓ cup all-purpose flour
2 teaspoons cinnamon
1 teaspoon vanilla extract
1½ cups half and half
1 unbaked 9-inch pie shell

In a large bowl, beat the eggs and sugar together. Beat in the flour, cinnamon, and vanilla. Stir in the half and half and pour into an unbaked pie shell.

Bake at 350 degrees until the filling is slightly firm, about 45 minutes. Cool to lukewarm and serve.

Serves 6 to 8.

✳ Sweet Potato Pie

Deanna Lovejoy, Lawrence

The secret to superior sweet potato pie is using the freshest sweet potatoes. Cooking them in their jackets preserves their sweetness and makes for easier peeling, while using a food mill or potato ricer eliminates the fibrous texture of the larger sweet potatoes.

4 medium-to-large sweet potatoes
1 cup sugar
½ cup butter, softened
1 14-ounce can sweetened condensed milk
1 cup milk
6 eggs, well beaten
¼ teaspoon baking powder
1 teaspoon nutmeg
1 teaspoon cinnamon
1 teaspoon vanilla extract
2 unbaked 9-inch pie shells

Boil the well-washed sweet potatoes in their jackets in a covered pot of salted water. When tender, drain off the water and dry them by shaking the pan over the heat source for a minute or two. Remove the skins when they are cool enough to handle. Put the potatoes through a food mill or potato ricer, or mash them in a large bowl.

Mix in the sugar and butter. Add the sweetened condensed milk, milk, and eggs, mixing well after each addition. Stir in the baking powder, nutmeg, cinnamon, and vanilla, mixing well.

Pour the filling into 2 unbaked pie shells and bake at 350 degrees for 45 to 60 minutes, or until a knife inserted in the middle comes out clean and the top is nicely browned.

Serves 12 to 16.

✳ Pecan Pie

Pecan trees are native to Kansas and grow in the southeast and south-central regions. The pecans are harvested in the fall from cultivated trees. The freshest pecans make the best pies, and the addition of maple syrup makes this version an all-time favorite.

3 eggs, slightly beaten
⅔ cup sugar
⅓ teaspoon salt
¾ cup dark corn syrup
¼ cup maple syrup or maple-flavored pancake syrup
1 teaspoon vanilla extract
⅓ cup butter
1 cup fresh pecan halves
1 unbaked 9-inch pie shell

In a large bowl, combine the eggs, sugar, salt, dark corn syrup, maple syrup, and vanilla. Beat well with an electric mixer or a wire whip.

Melt the butter in a small pan over low heat. Slowly pour the melted butter into the syrup mixture, beating

well. Stir in the pecans and pour into the unbaked pie shell.

Bake at 350 degrees for 40 to 45 minutes.

Serves 6 to 8.

✳ Black Walnut Pie

Edna McGhee, Madison

The unique flavor of black walnuts adds a new twist to a pie that is otherwise similar to pecan pie. Edna McGhee says, "This pie is so rich that you can easily cut it into eight servings, but so delicious no one will want you to."

¼ cup sugar
½ cup brown sugar
1 cup light corn syrup
3 tablespoons butter or margarine
3 eggs
1 cup black walnuts, coarsely chopped
1 tablespoon sugar
1 tablespoon all-purpose flour
1 unbaked 9-inch pie shell

Combine the sugars and corn syrup in a saucepan. Stir over medium heat, just to boiling, and immediately remove from heat. Stir in the butter until melted.

In a large bowl, beat the eggs slightly. Gradually stir the syrup mixture into the eggs. Add the walnuts and stir to combine.

Combine the sugar and flour in a small bowl or cup. Sprinkle evenly over the bottom of the unbaked pie shell. Turn the walnut mixture into the pie shell.

Bake at 350 degrees for 40 to 45 minutes, or until the top is browned.

Serves 6 to 8.

✳ Pie Plant Pie

Ruth Kelley Hayden, Atwood

Ruth Kelley Hayden writes, "When I was growing up in Atwood, rhubarb was called pie plant and nearly everyone had several rhubarb plants in their garden. A spring treat was always a pie plant pie."

PIE CRUST
1½ cups all-purpose flour
½ teaspoon salt
¾ cup shortening

3½ tablespoons cold water
½ teaspoon white vinegar
1 egg, slightly beaten

PIE FILLING
3 cups fresh rhubarb, cut into 1-inch pieces
1 cup sugar
3 tablespoons all-purpose flour
⅛ teaspoon salt

2 tablespoons butter

Pie Crust: Mix the flour and salt in a large bowl. Cut in the shortening with a pastry blender or a fork until the crumbs are about the size of peas.

Combine the cold water, vinegar, and egg in a small bowl. Add to the flour mixture, stirring until the mixture can be formed into a ball. Divide the mixture in half and roll out to ⅛-inch thickness on a lightly floured surface.

With half of the dough, line a 9-inch pie plate. Use the other half for the top crust.

Pie Filling: In a large bowl, combine the rhubarb, sugar, flour, and salt.

Pour the mixture into the pie shell and dot with the butter. Top with the crust, cutting slits for the steam to escape. Trim and seal the edges.

Bake at 400 degrees for 10 minutes. Lower heat to 350 degrees and bake for an additional 30 minutes.

Serves 6 to 8.

✳ Fresh Apricot Pie with Whole Wheat Pie Crust

Hildred Schmidt, Walton

When Hildred Schmidt mentioned our search for Kansas recipes to her family, they immediately said, "Send in your apricot pie recipe!"

Hildred tells us that she created the recipe when she acquired some land with apricot trees on it. "We had an abundance of fruit and I began to look for apricot pie recipes," says Hildred. "Although we had probably two dozen recipe books, I could find only recipes using canned or dried apricots in pies. Thus, this recipe was created out of necessity and

2½ to 3 cups fresh ripe apricots, unpeeled, pitted, and sliced
¾ cup sugar
2 tablespoons apricot juice or water
1½ tablespoons frozen orange juice concentrate
3 tablespoons minute tapioca

WHOLE WHEAT PIE CRUST
¾ cup whole wheat flour
1¼ cups unbleached white flour
⅜ teaspoon salt
⅔ cup butter or margarine
5 to 7 tablespoons cold water

1 tablespoon butter or margarine
1 tablespoon milk (optional)
sugar (optional)

Place the apricots in a large bowl. Add the sugar, apricot juice or water, orange juice concentrate, and tapioca. Stir to combine and set aside.

Whole Wheat Pie Crust: Combine the flours and salt in a large bowl. Cut in the butter or margarine with a pastry

a desire to use fresh homegrown fruit."

blender or a fork until the mixture resembles small peas. Add the water a tablespoon at a time, stirring with a fork, until the mixture can be formed into a ball. Divide the dough in half and roll out to ⅛-inch thickness on a lightly floured surface. Line a 9-inch pie plate with half of the dough and use the remaining half for the top crust.

Spread 1 tablespoon of butter or margarine in the bottom of the pie shell. Pour in the apricot filling and top with the crust, cutting slits for the steam to escape. Trim and seal the edges. Brush the top lightly with milk and sprinkle with sugar, if desired.

Bake at 400 degrees for about 50 to 60 minutes, or until browned and bubbly.

Serves 6 to 8.

✳ Cherry Orchard Pie

Irene S. Vogel, Lawrence

In the summer, cherries from backyard trees or orchards can be picked, pitted, and

3 cups fresh pie cherries
½ cup cherry juice, approximately
1 cup sugar
3 tablespoons minute tapioca

put into a pie. Irene Vogel keeps unbaked cherry pies in the freezer to bake at a later time, such as for birthdays or holidays. In fact, her family has a tradition of serving her pie of homegrown cherries at Christmas dinner.

dash of salt
¼ teaspoon almond extract (optional)
1 unbaked 9-inch double-crust pie shell
3 tablespoons butter

Pit the cherries and place them in a bowl. Let them stand long enough to allow about ½ cup of juice to accumulate. Drain, reserving the juice.

In a small bowl, combine the cherry juice, sugar, tapioca, and salt. Add the almond extract, if desired. Pour half of this mixture into the unbaked pie shell. Add the cherries and top with the remaining juice mixture. Dot with butter and position the crust over the cherries, cutting slits for the steam to escape. Trim and seal the edges.

Bake at 400 degrees for 50 to 60 minutes, or until golden brown.

Serves 6 to 8.

✳ Raisin Sour Cream Pie

Mary Lou Klein, Great Bend

"This recipe originated with my maternal grandmother, Alma Jelkin," writes Mary Lou Klein. "She lived on a farm, so in spite of hard times, eggs and cream were plentiful. Raisins were cheap in those days and were a special 'store-bought' treat for her children. Grandma was noted for 'making do,' creating delicious food and beautiful handcrafted items out of seemingly nothing.

2 cups raisins
1 cup water
2 cups thick sour cream
1 tablespoon all-purpose flour
⅓ to ½ cup sugar, to taste
1 teaspoon cinnamon
¼ teaspoon nutmeg
¼ teaspoon salt
3 egg yolks, slightly beaten
1 teaspoon lemon juice or vinegar (optional)
1 baked 9-inch pie shell

MERINGUE   (optional)
3 egg whites
6 tablespoons sugar
½ teaspoon vanilla extract

This pie was a favorite of all the family and the recipe was given to me by my mother. I, in turn, have passed it down to my three daughters."

Place the raisins and water in a large saucepan. Bring the mixture to a boil over high heat. Immediately reduce heat to low and simmer until the raisins are tender and have absorbed most of the water. Remove from heat and stir in the sour cream.

In a small bowl, sift the dry ingredients together and add to the raisin mixture, mixing well. Stir in the egg yolks and cook over low heat, stirring constantly until the mixture thickens, about 5 minutes. Remove from heat and cool. (If the filling is not sour enough, add 1 teaspoon lemon juice or vinegar, if desired.)

Meringue: In a large mixing bowl, beat the egg whites until frothy. Beat in the sugar a tablespoon at a time, until the mixture is shiny and stiff peaks form. Add the vanilla and mix well.

Pour the raisin filling into the baked pie shell. Chill and serve. (If desired, top with meringue and bake at 350 degrees for 15 minutes, or until the meringue is golden brown.)

Serves 6 to 8.

✳ Mrs. Wintle's Lemon Curd Tarts

Peg Bowman, Wichita

For over sixty years, St. James Episcopal Church of Wichita has held an annual tea and bazaar to help support several charities. Peg Bowman was kind enough to send us this recipe—along with her comment that these tarts, originally served by the tea's founder Mrs. Walter

TART SHELLS

3 cups all-purpose flour
1½ teaspoons salt
1 cup shortening
5 to 6 tablespoons cold water

LEMON CURD

2 lemon rinds, grated
½ cup lemon juice
2 cups sugar
½ cup butter
4 eggs, well beaten

Wintle, are a traditional mainstay of the confections available at the tea.

Tart Shells: In a large bowl, sift the flour and salt together. Cut in the shortening with a pastry blender, until the crumbs are the size of peas. Sprinkle in the cold water, a tablespoon at a time, stirring or lightly kneading until it forms a smooth dough. Roll out the dough on a lightly floured surface to ⅛-inch thickness. Cut into 2½-inch rounds. Fit the rounds into muffin pans and prick the bottoms with a fork. Bake at 450 degrees for 10 to 12 minutes until lightly browned. Cool the tart shells before filling.

Lemon Curd: Combine the lemon rind, juice, and sugar in the top of a double boiler. Add the butter and heat over simmering water, stirring with a wooden spoon until the butter is melted. Stir in the beaten eggs and continue cooking until the mixture is thick enough to pile slightly when poured from the spoon, about 15 minutes.

Let cool slightly and fill the tart shells with the lemon curd. Serve warm or at room temperature.

Makes 4 dozen.

✳ Mincemeat Parfait Pie

Clarinda Burchill, El Dorado

Clarinda Burchill, co-owner of the Burch-Hill Dining Room, tells us that a newspaper editor in El Dorado, a devoted customer, once called her Mincemeat Parfait Pie "the ambrosia of the gods."

2 3-ounce boxes orange-flavored gelatin
1 cup boiling water
1 quart vanilla ice cream, softened slightly (butter pecan or maple nut may be used)
1 18-ounce jar mincemeat
2 baked 9-inch pie shells

In a large bowl, dissolve the orange-flavored gelatin in the boiling water, mixing well. Cool the mixture over a bowl of crushed ice, or in the refrigerator, until it begins to thicken and becomes the consistency of honey.

Whip the gelatin on high speed with an electric mixer until thick and fluffy. Turn the mixer to low speed and add the softened ice cream and mincemeat. Mix just until combined. Divide the mixture into the 2 baked pie shells, refrigerate, and chill until firm.

Serves 12 to 16.

✳ Lemon Cake Pie

Mrs. Robert G. Steele, Fort Scott

When baked, the top layer of this dessert is magically transformed into cake, and the bottom layer into lemon pie. That makes it difficult to decide if it's a cake or a pie—but easy to decide it's delicious!

2 egg yolks
1 cup sugar
2 tablespoons butter, softened
2 to 3 tablespoons lemon juice
grated rind of 1 lemon
¼ cup all-purpose flour
1 cup milk
2 egg whites
1 unbaked 9-inch pie shell

In a large mixing bowl, beat the egg yolks with the sugar until thick and lemon colored. Beat in the butter, lemon juice, and lemon rind. Beat in the flour. Add the milk, mixing well.

In a separate bowl, beat the egg whites until stiff peaks form. Fold the egg whites into the batter.

Pour the batter into the pie shell and bake at 350 degrees for 45 to 60 minutes, until the pie is set and browned on top. Cool before cutting.

Serves 6 to 8.

✳ Vinegar Cobbler

Gayla Hart Croan, Fort Scott

Early settlers and soldiers coming to the Sunflower State were limited in their fruit selections, especially during the winter months, which also limited sources of vitamin C. Vinegar was supplied to the soldiers at Fort Scott on a daily basis by the army to prevent scurvy, and pioneers used it for the same reason. This one-hundred-year-old recipe from Gayla Hart Croan's great-grandmother is a creative way to make "a daily ration of vinegar" much more palatable. The family enjoys it still on special occasions.

1 cup white or apple-cider vinegar
1½ cups water
2 cups plus 2 tablespoons sugar
2 tablespoons cornstarch
2 teaspoons cinnamon
1 tablespoon butter

DUMPLINGS
⅓ cup shortening
½ cup water
1 teaspoon baking powder
1 teaspoon salt
1 to ¼ cups all-purpose flour

Combine the vinegar, water, sugar, cornstarch, cinnamon, and butter in a large iron skillet or a 9-inch heat-proof pan. Bring the mixture to a boil over medium-high heat while making the dumplings.

Dumplings: In a mixing bowl, combine the shortening, water, baking powder, and salt. Gradually mix in as much of the flour as needed to make a fairly stiff dough.

On a lightly floured surface, roll out the dough to ½-inch thickness and cut the dumplings into 1 x 2–inch rectangles. Generously flour the dumplings to help thicken the syrup and drop them into the boiling liquid. Place the skillet or pan in the preheated oven.

Bake in a preheated 350 degree oven for about 40 minutes, or until dumplings are lightly browned.

Serves 6.

✳ Blackberry Cobbler

Blackberries grow wild in Kansas and are often found along fence rows. Those who endure the ferocity of the wild fruit's thorns claim to prefer its tartness over the sweeter cultivated variety. The berries may be eaten raw, sugared with cream, or, as in this recipe, baked in a cobbler and served warm with vanilla ice cream.

3 cups blackberries
¾ to 1 cup sugar (depending on tartness desired)
2 tablespoons all-purpose flour
¼ teaspoon cinnamon

TOPPING
1 cup all-purpose flour, sifted
3 tablespoons sugar
1½ teaspoons baking powder
¼ teaspoon cinnamon
¼ teaspoon salt
¼ cup butter
1 egg, slightly beaten
¼ cup whipping cream

Rinse the blackberries and drain well. Place the berries in a large bowl. In a small bowl, combine the sugar, flour, and cinnamon. Mix well and gently stir into the berries. Pour the berries into an 8-inch or 2-quart baking dish.

Topping: In a mixing bowl, combine the sifted flour, sugar, baking powder, cinnamon, and salt. Cut in the butter with a pastry blender or a fork, until crumbly. Stir in the egg and cream just until moistened.

Spoon the topping in 6 to 8 mounds on top of the blackberries. Bake at 400 degrees for 25 to 30 minutes, or until the topping is browned and the filling is bubbly.

Serves 6.

✳ Peaches 'n' Cream Cobbler

Nothing equals the flavor of a fresh ripe peach, and nothing brings out smiles like a peach cobbler. Its very name evokes the notion of good country cooking. This recipe

3 cups fresh peaches
1 tablespoon lemon juice
6 tablespoons sugar
1 tablespoon all-purpose flour
½ cup whipping cream

TOPPING
1 cup all-purpose flour

goes a step further by
adding cinnamon to
the topping and cream
to the peaches.

2 tablespoons sugar
½ teaspoon cinnamon
1½ teaspoons baking powder
¼ teaspoon salt
¼ cup butter, chilled
1 egg, slightly beaten
¼ cup milk

Peel and slice the peaches and place them in a large bowl. Add the lemon juice and mix well. In a small bowl, combine the sugar and flour. Add to the peaches and mix well. Gently stir in the cream. Pour the peach filling into an 8-inch baking dish. Set aside.

Topping: Sift the flour into a large bowl. Add the sugar, cinnamon, baking powder, and salt. Stir to combine. Cut in the butter with a pastry blender or a fork until the mixture is crumbly. In a small bowl, combine the egg and milk and stir into the flour mixture, just until the ingredients are combined. Drop by spoonfuls, making 9 mounds, on top of the peach filling.

Bake at 400 degrees for 30 to 35 minutes, or until the topping is browned and the filling is bubbly.

Serves 4 to 6.

All a Cake Should Be

On festive occasions, the meager corn and wheat supplies were often baked into special breads, cakes, and biscuits. Bessie Wilson recalled one such occasion near her McPherson County homestead:

> "When it was known that Mr. J. B. Jackson was to be married at Ellsworth on September 6, 1875, some of the neighbors planned a surprise for him and his bride on their return. Mother was asked to bake a cake for the affair. In consequence, we ate our bread without butter for several days in order that father might have enough to take to the store and exchange it for the amount of sugar necessary to make a cake. This he did, covering the sixteen miles on horseback. Mother's was the only cake at this important gathering, and despite the fact that she had no recipe to go by, and that she used sour milk and soda in the making, it was pronounced by those who partook as being all a bride's cake should be" (in *Pioneer Women: Voices from the Kansas Frontier*, edited by Joanna L. Stratton [New York: Simon & Schuster, 1982]).

✳ Mennonite Wedding Cake

Gorovei

Lorraine J. Kaufman, Moundridge

"Weddings were celebrated in a big way by the Swiss German Mennonite farmers of the central Kansas plains at the turn of the century," writes Lorraine Kaufman. "They brought a rich heritage of good food

¾ *cup butter*
1 *cup whipping cream*
1 *cup milk*
¾ *cup sugar*
1 *teaspoon salt*
2 *packages dry yeast*
¼ *cup warm water*
6 *egg yolks*
1 *teaspoon vanilla extract*
5 to 6 *cups all-purpose flour, sifted*

ideas with them when they immigrated in 1874. Wedding celebrations included at least one big meal, if not two or three for all the guests. While this custom has given way to a more homogeneous American pattern, some of the recipes are still favorites.

Gorovei is baked for special occasions today. Made from fresh cream, butter, and eggs, it is frosted with a boiled powdered sugar and cream icing. It is decorated with corn candy, as in bygone days, to add a festive air."

CREAM AND SUGAR ICING
1 cup sugar
¾ cup whipping cream
2 tablespoons white corn syrup
1 teaspoon vanilla extract

corn candy, for decoration

Melt the butter in a saucepan over low heat. Add the cream, milk, sugar, and salt, stirring until the sugar is dissolved. Remove from heat and pour the liquid into a large mixing bowl. Cool to lukewarm.

Dissolve the yeast in the warm water. In a small bowl, beat the egg yolks. Add the egg yolks, the vanilla, and the yeast mixture to the lukewarm liquid, beating well. Stir in 3 cups of the sifted flour. Set aside in a warm place until the mixture is bubbly, about 1 hour.

Gradually add as much of the remaining flour as needed, beating after each addition, until a soft dough is formed. Turn the dough onto a lightly floured surface and knead well, about 10 minutes.

Place the dough in a greased bowl, cover, and let rise in a warm place until doubled, about 1 hour. Punch down and let rise again until doubled.

Turn the dough onto a lightly floured surface, cover, and let stand for 10 minutes. Cut the dough into 5 to 7 equal portions, shaping each into a ball. Place each ball in a greased 8-inch pie plate, flattening and spreading the dough to make a thin cake. Cover and let each rise until nearly doubled, 45 to 60 minutes.

Bake the cakes at 300 degrees for 20 minutes. Remove the cakes from the pans and cool on racks. Frost with Cream and Sugar Icing and decorate with corn candy.

Cream and Sugar Icing: Combine the sugar, cream, and white corn syrup in a small saucepan. Cook over medium heat, stirring until the mixture reaches soft-ball stage (234 to 240 degrees). Remove from heat and add the vanilla. Beat the mixture until a soft spreading consistency is reached. Spread quickly on 2 to 4 of the cakes and top with the corn candy immediately.

This recipe will require two preparations of the icing.

Do not double the recipe, as it "sets" quickly and it is easier to work with a small amount.

Makes 5 to 7 8-inch cakes.

✳ Whole Wheat Vanilla Cake

The addition of whole wheat flour gives this cake a deliciously different flavor and texture.

¾ cup shortening
1½ cups sugar
1½ teaspoons vanilla extract
1¼ cups white cake flour
1 cup whole wheat flour
3 teaspoons baking powder
1 teaspoon salt
1 cup milk
5 egg whites

VANILLA–WHEAT GERM FROSTING
2½ cups powdered sugar
5 tablespoons butter, softened
⅛ teaspoon salt
1 teaspoon vanilla extract
3 to 4 tablespoons milk
1 tablespoon toasted wheat germ

In a large mixing bowl, cream the shortening and sugar until light and fluffy. Add the vanilla and mix well.

Sift the cake flour into a large bowl. Stir in the whole wheat flour, baking powder, and salt. Add the flour mixture to the creamed mixture alternately with the milk, beating after each addition and ending with the flour mixture.

In a separate bowl, beat the egg whites until they form stiff peaks. Gently fold the egg whites into the cake batter.

Grease and lightly flour a 13 x 9–inch baking dish. Pour the cake batter evenly into the baking dish.

Bake at 375 degrees for 30 minutes, or until an inserted toothpick comes out clean. Cool the cake completely before frosting.

Vanilla–Wheat Germ Frosting: In a medium-sized mixing bowl, combine the powdered sugar, butter, and salt. Add the vanilla and mix well. Add the milk a tablespoon at a time, mixing until a smooth, spreading consistency is reached. Frost the cake and sprinkle the wheat germ on top.

Serves 12.

✳ Coconut Buttermilk Cake with Cream Cheese–Pecan Frosting

Dolores Herd, Protection

All that is needed to accompany this rich coconut cake is a good cup of hot coffee or tea.

½ *cup butter, softened*
½ *cup shortening*
2 *cups sugar*
1 *teaspoon vanilla extract*
5 *eggs, separated*
2 *cups all-purpose flour*
1 *teaspoon baking soda*
1 *cup buttermilk*
1⅔ *cups flaked coconut*

CREAM CHEESE–PECAN FROSTING
½ *cup butter, softened*
1 8-*ounce package cream cheese, softened*
1 *teaspoon vanilla extract*
⅛ *teaspoon salt*
1 1-*pound box powdered sugar*
1 *to 3 tablespoons milk*
½ *cup pecans, ground*

In a large mixing bowl, combine the butter and shortening and beat until light and fluffy. Add the vanilla and mix well. Add the egg yolks, one at a time, beating well.

In a small bowl, sift the flour and baking soda together. Add the dry ingredients to the batter alternately with the buttermilk, ending with the dry ingredients. Mix in the coconut.

In a separate bowl, beat the egg whites until stiff peaks form and gently fold them into the batter.

Pour the batter into a greased and floured 13 x 9–inch cake pan or bundt pan. Bake at 350 degrees for 40 to 50 minutes, or until an inserted toothpick comes out clean. If using a bundt pan, let the cake cool for several minutes, remove from the pan, and cool on a wire rack.

Cream Cheese–Pecan Frosting: In a mixing bowl, combine the butter and cream cheese, mixing well. Mix in the vanilla and salt. Slowly add the powdered sugar, blending until smooth. Stir in the milk, a tablespoon at a time, until a spreading consistency is reached. Stir in the ground pecans. Frost the cake when it is completely cool.
Serves 10 to 12.

✳ Home Front Chocolate Cake

Mary Kelley Maley, Salina

Mary Kelley Maley tells us that conservation of food was a mighty weapon of the war effort on the Kansas home front during World War II. Eventually, wartime rationing meant that ration stamps as well as cash were needed to purchase fats, meats, and processed foods. Purchasing butter or lard took precious ration stamps that were needed for more nutritious foods. Hydrogenated oils and cake mixes were not perfected until after the war; consequently,

⅔ cup clarified chicken fat*
½ cup sugar
1½ cups light corn syrup
2 teaspoons vanilla extract
3 eggs
3 1-ounce squares unsweetened baking chocolate, melted
3 cups whole wheat flour
½ teaspoon baking soda
2 teaspoons baking powder
½ teaspoon salt
1¼ cups buttermilk or sour milk
frosting for a two-layer cake

In a large mixing bowl, cream the chicken fat and sugar together until fluffy. Add the syrup gradually and beat well. Add the vanilla. Add the unbeaten eggs, one at a time, beating until light after each addition. Pour in the melted chocolate and mix well.

* Clarified chicken fat is skimmed from the top of the chilled chicken broth, after boiling a chicken.

the clarified chicken fat skimmed from congealed chicken broth became the ingredient that made it possible to have a cake for the special occasions.

Mary Kelley Maley contributed her 1940s cake recipe, which uses chicken fat in place of shortening. Whole wheat flour adds a nutty flavor, and buttermilk enriches it.

Combine the dry ingredients in a separate bowl and add to the batter alternately with the buttermilk, ending with the dry ingredients.

Grease and flour 2 9-inch cake pans. Pour in the cake batter and bake at 350 degrees for 30 to 35 minutes, or until an inserted toothpick comes out clean.

Cool the cakes in the pans for 10 minutes. Remove and cool on wire racks. Frost with your favorite frosting and serve.

Serves 8 or more.

Variations: For a spice cake, omit the chocolate and add ½ teaspoon ground cloves, ½ teaspoon cinnamon, and ½ teaspoon nutmeg.

For a yellow butter cake, omit the chocolate and add 1½ teaspoons of lemon extract.

✳ Rich Chocolate Cake with Coconut-Pecan Frosting

Von Schroeder, Overland Park

This rich cake will satisfy the craving of any chocolate lover.

2½ cups all-purpose flour
2 teaspoons soda
2 teaspoons baking powder
½ cup cocoa
1 teaspoon salt
⅔ cup butter, softened
2 cups sugar
2 eggs
1 cup buttermilk
1 cup boiling water
1 teaspoon vanilla

COCONUT-PECAN FROSTING
½ cup butter or margarine
1 cup sugar
3 egg yolks, slightly beaten
1 cup evaporated milk
2 cups coconut, flaked or shredded

1 cup pecans, coarsely chopped
1 teaspoon vanilla extract

Sift the flour into a large bowl. Add the remaining dry ingredients and sift the mixture 3 times. Set aside.

In a large mixing bowl, cream the butter and sugar. Add the eggs and beat well. Add the buttermilk alternately with the dry ingredients, mixing at medium speed. Slowly beat in the boiling water. Add the vanilla and mix well.

Grease and flour 2 9-inch round baking pans, or 1 13 x 9–inch baking dish. Pour in the batter and bake at 350 degrees for 35 to 40 minutes, or until an inserted toothpick comes out clean. If using round baking pans, cool the layers for 10 minutes and remove them from the pans. Cool the cake completely before frosting.

Coconut-Pecan Frosting: In a saucepan, combine the butter, sugar, egg yolks, and evaporated milk. Cook over medium-low heat, stirring until the mixture thickens, 10 to 12 minutes. Remove from heat and add the coconut, pecans, and vanilla. Cool the frosting until it is spreadable, stirring occasionally.

Serves 8 to 12.

✳ Black Walnut Cake with Cream Cheese Frosting

Gathering native black walnuts in the fall, for use in holiday desserts, can be a family event in Kansas.

This delicious cake was a specialty of Jayni's Grandmother Grey and always a winner with her family.

½ cup shortening
⅔ cup brown sugar
2 eggs
½ teaspoon vanilla extract
2½ cups cake flour
1 cup sugar
1 teaspoon soda
1 teaspoon baking powder
¾ teaspoon salt
¾ teaspoon cinnamon
¾ teaspoon ground cloves

1¼ cups buttermilk
1 cup black walnuts, finely ground

CREAM CHEESE FROSTING
1 8-ounce package cream cheese, softened
2 tablespoons butter, softened
4 cups powdered sugar
1 teaspoon vanilla extract
1 to 3 tablespoons milk

Cream the shortening and brown sugar together in a
large mixing bowl. Add the eggs and vanilla and mix well.

Sift the flour into a large bowl. Add the remaining dry
ingredients and sift again. Add the dry ingredients to the
batter alternately with the buttermilk, mixing after each
addition and ending with the dry ingredients. Add the
black walnuts and mix well.

Grease and flour 2 8- or 9-inch cake pans. Pour in the
batter and bake at 350 degrees for 35 to 40 minutes, until
an inserted toothpick comes out clean.

Cool the cakes in their pans for 10 minutes. Remove
and cool on wire racks before frosting.

Cream Cheese Frosting: In a mixing bowl, beat the cream
cheese and butter. Add the powdered sugar and beat
until smooth. Add the vanilla, mixing well. Add milk,
a tablespoon at a time, until a spreading consistency is
reached.

Serves 8 or more.

✳ Holiday Cardinal Cake

Nancy Vogel, Hays

This white holiday cake with its mara-schino cherries is as pretty as cardinals on a Kansas snowdrift.

1 8-ounce package cream cheese, softened
1 cup butter or margarine, softened
1½ cups sugar
1½ teaspoons vanilla extract
4 eggs
2 cups all-purpose flour
1½ teaspoons baking powder
¾ cup maraschino cherries
½ cup pecans, chopped
¼ cup all-purpose flour, sifted
½ cup pecans, finely chopped (optional)
powdered sugar

In a large mixing bowl, cream together the cream cheese, butter or margarine, sugar, and vanilla. Add the eggs, one at a time, beating well after each addition.

Sift the flour and the baking powder together in a small bowl and gradually add the mixture to the cake batter. Drain the cherries, chop, and combine with the pecans and ¼ cup of flour. Fold the cherry mixture into the batter.

Grease a 10-inch bundt or tube pan and sprinkle with ½ cup finely chopped pecans, if desired. Pour the batter into the pan and bake for 1 hour and 20 minutes at 325 degrees.

Remove the cake from the oven and cool for 5 minutes. Remove from the pan. Sprinkle the top with powdered sugar.

Serves 10 to 12.

✳ Apple Cake

Freshly picked tart apples are the best choice for this simple

2 cups apples (3 to 4 medium apples)
¾ cup sugar
1½ cups all-purpose flour

apple cake. To dress it up, serve with a scoop of vanilla ice cream or a dollop of whipped cream.

1 teaspoon soda
½ teaspoon salt
1½ teaspoons allspice
½ cup English walnuts, chopped
½ cup raisins
1 egg, beaten
½ cup vegetable oil

Peel and core the apples. Chop them into ½-inch pieces and place them in a large mixing bowl. Add the sugar and mix well. Cover and let stand for 20 minutes.

In a medium-sized bowl, combine the dry ingredients, nuts, and raisins. Add the dry ingredients, the egg, and the oil to the apples, mixing well with a large spoon.

Pour the batter into a 9-inch baking dish and bake at 350 degrees for 30 to 35 minutes, until lightly browned and an inserted toothpick comes out clean.

Serves 6 to 8.

✳ Strawberry Shortcake with Vanilla Cream

It's no wonder that strawberry shortcake is a favorite in the Heartland. Wild strawberries flourish in eastern Kansas along woodland openings, roadsides, and prairies and ripen from May through July. Many people grow their own strawberries; others hand-select their berries at pick-your-own farms.

When it comes to strawberry shortcake,

SHORTCAKE
1½ cups all-purpose flour
2 teaspoons baking powder
2 tablespoons sugar
⅛ teaspoon salt
6 tablespoons butter, chilled
¼ to ½ cup half and half

VANILLA CREAM
½ cup sugar
3 tablespoons cornstarch
⅛ teaspoon salt
3 egg yolks
2¼ cups milk
2 tablespoons butter
1 teaspoon vanilla extract

*there is no substitute
for plump, red-ripe,
freshly picked berries.
This version, with rich
vanilla cream, gives
a new flair to an old
classic.*

STRAWBERRIES
1 pint fresh strawberries, stemmed
1 tablespoon sugar
1 tablespoon orange liqueur

Shortcakes: In a medium bowl combine the flour, baking powder, sugar, and salt. Cut the cold butter into the flour mixture with a pastry blender or a fork until the mixture is crumbly. Add the half and half a little at a time, stirring with a fork, until it can be formed into a ball. Knead on a lightly floured surface for 30 seconds.

Roll the dough out on a lightly floured surface to ½-inch thickness. Cut into 3- to 4-inch rounds with a cookie cutter or the rim of a wide glass.

Place the shortcakes on an ungreased cookie sheet and bake at 400 degrees for 15 minutes, or until lightly browned.

Makes 6 shortcakes.

Vanilla Cream: In a large saucepan combine the sugar, cornstarch, and salt. Add the egg yolks and stir to com-

bine. Add the milk, mixing well. Cook over medium-low heat, stirring constantly, just until the mixture thickens and begins to bubble, 12 to 15 minutes. Remove from heat and add the butter and vanilla. Pour the cream into a bowl and cool. Cover and refrigerate until well chilled.

Strawberries: Reserve 6 whole strawberries for garnish. Slice the remaining strawberries and place them in a medium-sized bowl. Sprinkle the sugar and the liqueur over the berries and stir gently. Cover and refrigerate until well chilled.

To serve, slice the shortcakes in half and place the bottom halves in individual serving bowls. Pour some of the vanilla cream over the shortcakes. Spoon the strawberries onto the cream-soaked shortcakes. Place the top halves of the shortcakes on the strawberries. Pour a spoonful of the vanilla cream over all and garnish each with a whole strawberry.

Serves 6.

Trees Were So Rare They Had Names

Immigrants arriving in Kansas soon discovered the lack of firewood. At first, gathering buffalo chips was depressing, if not degrading, for the Europeans, but this fuel proved to be clean and efficient. In *Rare Recipes and Budget Savers*, a compilation of "Hometown News" columns from the Wichita *Beacon* (Wichita: Wichita Eagle-Beacon, 1963), author Frank Good quotes a Meade County editor from 1879:

"It was comical to see how gingerly our wives handled these buffalo chips at first. They commenced by picking them up between two sticks, or with a poker. Soon they used a rag and then a corner of their apron. And now? Now it is out of the bread into the chips and back again—and not even a dust of the hands!

I was a cob picker-upper myself. My sis and I tried to keep up with that 'monster' cookstove, during harvest time, at my Uncle Charlie Deal's at Little River. A big job, we thought, but, oh, those wonderful farm dinners were something to sit up to, even if I did need a couple of catalogues under me to see above the table."

There was humor in dealing with the uniqueness of the terrain—and there was great homesickness. Many settlers found it very difficult to adjust to the lack of trees on the prairie. They were missed, not only for fuel, but also for aesthetic reasons.

Mary Furguson Darrah of eastern Kansas recalled, "Mister Hilton, a pioneer, told his wife that he was going to Little River for wood. She asked to go with him. . . . She hadn't seen a tree for two years, and when they arrived at Little River she put her arms around a tree and hugged it until she was hysterical" (in *Pioneer Women: Voices from the Kansas Frontier*, edited by Joanna L. Stratton [New York: Simon & Schuster, 1982]).

✳ Whole Wheat Gingerbread

Joan Larson Bader, Berryton

Gingerbread is an old favorite, common in earlier days because it was simple to make and ingredients such as molasses and honey were easy to come by. Today gingerbread is considered dessert, but the pioneers sometimes served it as bread with the meal.

This version, made with whole wheat flour, is delicious served warm or cold, with a dollop of whipped cream or ice cream.

1 cup molasses
¾ cup honey
¾ cup safflower oil
3 eggs
3 cups whole wheat flour
1 tablespoon baking powder
1 teaspoon salt
1½ teaspoons cinnamon
1½ teaspoons ground cloves
1 teaspoon ginger
2 cups milk

In a mixing bowl, combine the molasses, honey, oil, and eggs, beating well. In a large bowl, combine the dry ingredients and add alternately with the milk to the egg mixture, beating well after each addition.

Pour the batter into a greased 13 x 9–inch pan and bake at 350 degrees for 45 to 50 minutes, or until an inserted toothpick comes out clean.

Serves 12.

✳ Spicy Gingerbread Cupcakes with Lemon Sauce

Marilyn Eck, Bartlett

Marilyn Eck modestly writes, "This is a very good combination." The hearty ginger flavor of the cupcakes is complemented by the cheery tartness of lemon.

1⅓ cups all-purpose flour
½ cup brown sugar
½ teaspoon baking powder
½ teaspoon soda
½ teaspoon salt
¾ teaspoon cinnamon
½ teaspoon nutmeg
½ teaspoon ginger
¼ teaspoon allspice
½ cup sorghum
½ cup boiling water
½ cup shortening, butter, or margarine, softened
1 egg, well beaten

LEMON SAUCE
1 cup hot water
½ cup sugar
2 tablespoons cornstarch
dash salt
2 teaspoons lemon peel
2 tablespoons lemon juice
2 tablespoons butter

In a large bowl, combine all the dry ingredients. In a separate bowl, combine the sorghum, boiling water, and shortening, butter, or margarine. Add the egg and mix well. Pour the sorghum mixture into the dry ingredients and mix well to combine.

Spoon the batter into greased muffin tins to three-fourths full. Bake at 350 degrees about 20 minutes.

Lemon Sauce: In a saucepan, bring the water to a simmer. In a mixing bowl, combine the sugar, cornstarch, and salt. Stir a small amount of the hot water into the cornstarch mixture, then add all of the cornstarch mixture to the hot water, mixing well. Cook the sauce over medium heat, stirring constantly, until thickened.

Remove from heat, stir in the lemon peel, lemon juice, and the butter. Serve warm over the freshly baked cupcakes.

Makes 12 to 14.

✳ Pawpaw Bread

The Pawpaw, native to Kansas, is an oblong, light green fruit with a yellow flesh that tastes similar to a banana. It grows on a bush or small tree and ripens in the fall. Pawpaws were well known to the native Americans and settlers of eastern Kansas.

These days, they can still be found in the northeastern part of the state—growing on farm land or in the backyard of an older home, and occasionally for sale at farmer's markets. Pawpaws, sometimes called "Kansas Bananas," can be peeled and eaten raw or made into a delicious dessert bread.

⅓ cup shortening
¾ cup sugar
2 eggs
1¾ cups all-purpose flour
1 teaspoon baking powder
½ teaspoon baking soda
½ teaspoon salt
¼ teaspoon cinnamon
¼ teaspoon ginger

¼ teaspoon nutmeg
1 cup pawpaws (3 to 4 pawpaws)

In a mixing bowl, beat the shortening and sugar together. Add the eggs and beat well.

Sift the dry ingredients together in a large bowl and set aside. Peel and seed the pawpaws and cut them into chunks. Place the chunks in a small bowl and mash with a fork. Beat the dry ingredients into the mixture alternately with the mashed pawpaws.

Pour the batter into a greased 9 x 5 x 3–inch loaf pan. Bake at 350 degrees for 45 to 50 minutes, or until an inserted toothpick comes out clean.

Makes 1 loaf.

✳ Banana Pecan Wheat Bread

This banana bread is made with the old-fashioned goodness of real butter, wheat germ, whole wheat flour, and buttermilk. Serve it plain or toasted with butter for a breakfast treat.

½ cup butter, softened
1 cup sugar
2 eggs
1 teaspoon vanilla extract
1 teaspoon orange peel, grated
1 cup very ripe bananas, peeled and mashed
¼ cup toasted wheat germ
1¾ cups whole wheat flour
1 teaspoon soda
½ teaspoon salt
½ teaspoon nutmeg
⅓ cup buttermilk
½ cup pecans, chopped

Cream the butter and sugar together in a large mixing bowl. Add the eggs, vanilla, and orange peel and beat well. Add the bananas and wheat germ, beating until well combined.

In a medium-sized bowl, combine the wheat flour, soda, salt, and nutmeg. Add the dry ingredients to the batter alternately with the buttermilk, mixing after each addition. Stir in the pecans.

Pour the mixture into a well-greased 9 x 5 x 3–inch loaf pan. Bake at 350 degrees for 50 to 60 minutes, or until done. Cool for 5 minutes. Remove the bread from the pan and cool on a wire rack.

Makes 1 loaf.

✳ Swedish Cheesecake with Lingonberry Sauce

(Ost Kaka med Lingon)

Cindy Sears, Lawrence, and Mrs. Ernest A. (Eunice) Wall, McPherson

"By nature, Swedish people are very hospitable," writes Mrs. Eunice Wall. The holiday season is an especially favored time for entertaining, and one of the festive Swedish desserts prepared by the Swedes who settled in McPherson County is Ost Kaka med Lingon. This dessert, well known throughout central Kansas, is the final touch on the smorgasbord at the Midsummer's Day Festival in Lindsborg.

Cindy Sears provided the Ost Kaka recipe used by her family when she was growing up in Salina. Eunice Wall sent the recipe for Lingonberry Sauce she uses to top Ost Kaka. Lingonberries have been enjoyed by Swedes for generations. Mrs. Wall tells us that the small red berries grow close to the ground in clusters throughout Sweden. Once in Kansas, the Swedish immigrants cultivated their long-favored fruit here. The berries are picked in the late summer or early fall and preserved in sugar or are kept in crocks of cold water until used. They are served as an accompaniment to meats, in sauces for pancakes or desserts, or may be eaten plain with milk or cream.

Fresh lingonberries can be found in Swedish import food markets, mostly at Christmas. Lingonberry preserves are more readily found than fresh lingonberries; dilute with a little water and add a dash of lemon juice for a good substitute topping for Ost Kaka.

½ rennet tablet*
1 tablespoon cold water

*Rennet tablets are available at pharmacies or Swedish import food markets.

3 cups milk, warmed
½ cup sugar
½ cup all-purpose flour
2 eggs, beaten
2 teaspoons almond extract

LINGONBERRY SAUCE
1 quart fresh lingonberries
¾ cup water
1½ cups sugar

1 to 2 tablespoons cornstarch
¼ cup water
1 tablespoon lemon juice

In a small cup, dissolve the rennet tablet in the cold water. If it has not dissolved completely after several minutes, mash the tablet gently with the back of a small spoon.

Pour the milk into a saucepan and heat over low heat until very warm. In a large bowl, combine the sugar and flour. Slowly add half of the warm milk, stirring with a wire whip or a large spoon. Beat in the eggs until well blended. Stir in the remaining milk, dissolved rennet tablet, and almond extract.

Pour the mixture into a buttered 9-inch baking dish. Let stand for 10 minutes before baking, to thicken the custard.

Bake at 375 degrees for 45 minutes, or until the custard is set. Serve warm or chilled with Lingonberry Sauce.

Serves 8 to 10.

Lingonberry Sauce: Clean the lingonberries by removing stems; rinse and drain. In a 2-quart saucepan over medium heat, add the lingonberries, water, and sugar. Bring the mixture to a boil. In a small cup, stir the cornstarch into ¼ cup of water until smooth. Slowly pour this mixture into the sauce, stirring constantly until thickened. Reduce heat to low and cook for 2 to 3 minutes more. Remove from heat, add the lemon juice, and let the sauce cool before serving.

Makes 1 quart.

✳ Lemon Bread Pudding with Blueberry Sauce

Bread puddings are common to many cultures and consequently have become standard fare in American heritage. Long before it was appreciated as a dessert, bread pudding was presented as a first course in hard times, to lessen appetites before the main course was served. It became a family favorite when desserts, like meals, had to be determined by what ingredients were on hand. Bread puddings were once so popular that every cook had a special "pudding baking dish."

Most recipes, including this one, call for leftover stale bread to add volume and stability to the sweet custard. This easy-to-assemble recipe omits the fuss of baking the pudding in a water bath.

3 large eggs
1¼ cups sugar
¼ cup butter, softened
½ teaspoon vanilla extract
6 tablespoons lemon juice (about 2 lemons)
1 tablespoon grated lemon rind (about 1 lemon)
2 cups milk
5 cups stale white bread cubes with crust (about 8 slices)

BLUEBERRY SAUCE
2 cups fresh blueberries*
1 cup sugar
2 tablespoons cornstarch
¼ teaspoon nutmeg
pinch of salt
1 cup boiling water
3 tablespoons lemon juice

In an electric mixer, beat the eggs and sugar together until the mixture is pale yellow and smooth, about 2 to 3 minutes. Add the butter and continue beating until creamy. Stir in the vanilla, lemon juice, lemon rind, and milk.

Put the bread cubes into a buttered loaf pan and pour the egg mixture over the cubes, making sure all the cubes are well soaked in the liquid. Let the pudding mixture stand at room temperature until nearly all the liquid is absorbed by the bread, about 45 minutes.

Preheat the oven to 350 degrees. Put the pudding mixture in the oven and immediately reduce the temperature to 300 degrees. Bake for 40 minutes. The pudding should be firm and light yellow. Increase the temperature to 425

---

*A 10-ounce package of frozen blueberries may be substituted, but increase the cornstarch to 3 tablespoons and add the thawed blueberries and lemon juice at the end without returning the pan to heat.

degrees and bake for another 15 to 20 minutes until the top is raised and lightly browned.

Top with the Blueberry Sauce or simply sprinkle confectioner's sugar over the pudding and serve warm with whipped cream.

Serves 6 to 8.

Blueberry Sauce: Wash the fresh blueberries and remove any stems. Drain and set aside.

Make a flavored, simple syrup by combining the sugar, cornstarch, nutmeg, and salt in a saucepan. Gradually stir in the boiling water over medium-high heat. Bring the sauce to a boil and continue boiling, stirring constantly, for 2 minutes.

Add the fresh blueberries and return the sauce to the boil for 1 minute. Remove from heat and stir in the lemon juice. Serve hot over the bread pudding, or cool to room temperature.

Makes 2 cups.

✳ Bread Pudding with Foamy Butter Sauce

Lucille Miller, Wichita

Bread pudding recipes of the past reflected cultural variations. This one was a favorite of Lucille Miller's German aunt, which she called her German pudding recipe. However, it earned another name with the family, in honor of its serving rite. As the children giggled, Mrs. Miller's aunt traditionally brought the dessert

2 tablespoons butter, softened
3 cups dry firm bread cubes
½ cup raisins
¼ cup sugar
¼ teaspoon salt
¼ teaspoon nutmeg or mace
½ teaspoon vanilla extract
2 eggs, beaten
3½ cups milk, scalded

FOAMY BUTTER SAUCE
½ cup sugar
½ cup butter
2 teaspoons milk

*to the table while
speaking in German,
"Thou shalt eat bread
pudding with foamy
butter sauce."*

1 egg, well beaten
½ teaspoon vanilla extract

Grease a 3-quart casserole dish with the butter. Mix the bread cubes and raisins together and place them in the casserole. In a large mixing bowl, combine the sugar, salt, nutmeg or mace, vanilla, and eggs, mixing well. Add the scalded milk, beat well, and cool.

Pour the milk mixture over the bread crumbs and let stand until all the liquid is absorbed, 20 to 30 minutes. Place the casserole in a shallow pan of water. Bake at 350 degrees for 45 minutes, or until an inserted knife comes out clean. Let stand for 5 minutes before serving with the sauce.

Foamy Butter Sauce: Combine the sugar, butter, and milk. Warm in a saucepan over low heat. Just before serving, add the beaten egg and the vanilla, beating with a wire whip or an electric mixer until foamy.

Serves 8.

✳ Mexican Bread Pudding

(Capirotada)

Susie Bermudez, Lawrence

Susie Bermudez remembers the holidays as the most exciting times of her childhood in Ottawa, because her family upheld the traditions of their forebears, who came to Kansas from Mexico.

The women would always gather in the kitchen to make the traditional Mexican specialties. On New Year's Eve, the children were allowed to stay up late and help in the kitchen. The men were served first, the children next, and the women last. "At midnight everyone would hug and cry because we were together again another year and we would remember a loved one now gone," recalls Susie.

"What child could sleep after all that food and excitement!"

Susie's recipe for this Mexican-style bread pudding was used by her mother on special feast days, especially Easter. She says this dish is very popular with Mexican people and is delicious served as a dessert or as a side dish to meats.

1 cup brown sugar
2½ cups water
1 small stick of cinnamon
8 slices white bread
2 to 3 tablespoons butter, melted
½ cup raisins
1 cup apples, thinly sliced
½ cup salted peanuts, coarsely ground
½ cup cheddar cheese, shredded

Place the brown sugar, water, and cinnamon stick in a large saucepan. Bring the mixture to a boil, reduce heat to low, and simmer uncovered for 5 minutes. Remove from heat, discard the cinnamon stick, and cool slightly.

Toast the bread, brush with the melted butter, and cut it into 1-inch squares. Fold the toast, raisins, apple slices, and peanuts into the brown sugar mixture.

Butter an 8-inch baking dish and add the bread pudding mixture. Cover with foil and bake at 350 degrees for 20 minutes. Top with the shredded cheese and bake uncovered for 20 minutes more.

Serves 6.

✳ Creamy Rice Pudding

Gertrude Ward, Coffeyville

According to Gertrude Ward, rice pudding is one of the earliest Kansan desserts. The ingredients were easily available to women in frontier settlements, where inventiveness and frugality went hand in hand. The cousin to rice pudding was called "spotted pup." It was a sweetened rice,

1½ cups water
⅔ cup white rice
2 eggs, beaten
½ cup sugar
2 cups milk
1 teaspoon vanilla extract
¼ teaspoon nutmeg
¼ teaspoon salt
½ cup raisins
heavy cream (optional)

Bring the water to a boil in a medium-sized saucepan. Add the rice and return to boiling. Stir and cover. Reduce

spotted with a handful of raisins, that was a welcome treat to pioneers who crossed the Great Plains in wagon trains.

Gertrude tells us, "I'm seventy-three years old and have lived in Kansas all my life. I can remember my mother making rice pudding when I was a child."

heat to low and simmer for 14 minutes. Do not lift the cover while cooking.

In a large bowl, beat the eggs with a wire whip. Add the sugar and beat well. Pour in the milk, stirring to combine. Add the vanilla, nutmeg, salt, raisins, and the hot rice. Stir the mixture and pour into a 1½-quart casserole.

Bake at 325 degrees, stirring frequently until most of the liquid is absorbed and the pudding begins to set (about 50 to 60 minutes, or until an inserted knife comes out clean).

Serve warm or cold, with cream, if desired. Refrigerate any remaining pudding.

Serves 6.

✳ Plum Pudding

George Laughead, Jr., Dodge City

"As a child in Medicine Lodge, my grandmother, Jessie Rankin, played in Carry Nation's front yard," says George Laughead, Jr., recounting his Kansas heritage. "She married and moved to Dodge City in 1905 where my grandfather, George E. Laughead, worked in the town's first brick bank building, built around 1892. Characteristic of the time and place, he carried a gun under his vest until the 1920s."

Characteristic of their Scottish descent

1 cup suet, finely chopped
1 cup fine dry bread crumbs
1 cup dark corn syrup
2 eggs, beaten
2 cups all-purpose flour
½ cup sugar
2 teaspoons baking powder
¼ teaspoon soda
½ teaspoon nutmeg
½ teaspoon ground cloves
½ teaspoon allspice
¾ cup milk
1½ cups raisins
½ cup walnuts, coarsely chopped

FOAMY SAUCE
2 egg yolks
1 cup powdered sugar
dash of salt
1 teaspoon sherry, rum, or vanilla extract
1 cup heavy cream
2 egg whites

In a large bowl, combine the suet and the bread crumbs. Add the corn syrup and eggs, mixing well.

Sift the flour with the dry ingredients into a separate bowl. Add the dry ingredients to the suet mixture alternately with the milk, mixing after each addition. Stir in the raisins and walnuts.

Fill a well-oiled 3-pound coffee can or deep-sided baking dish with the pudding (do not fill over two-thirds full). Place the can or baking dish on a rack inside a deep kettle containing 2 inches of boiling water. Cover and cook over low heat for 2 hours, or until the pudding is slightly resistant to the touch. Replenish the water as necessary during cooking.

Foamy Sauce: In the upper part of a double boiler, beat the egg yolks with the sugar and salt until they are lemon colored. Stir in the sherry, rum, or vanilla extract and the cream. Cook over simmering water until it coats the back of a spoon, about 5 to 10 minutes. Set aside.

Whip the egg whites in a large bowl until stiff peaks form. Pour the cream and egg mixture over the egg whites, stirring with a whip until well blended.

To serve, unmold the pudding, slice, and pour the Foamy Sauce over each serving.

Serves 8.

✳ Persimmon Pudding

Theodora Dixon, Caney

*The wild persimmon is
prolific in Kansas and
can quickly take over
an unattended pas-
ture. Though ranchers
consider it a nuisance,
its tasty fruit makes it
certainly worthwhile
to leave a few sap-
lings along a fence line
or at the edge of the*

*1½ cups persimmon pulp (1½ to 2 pounds fresh
    persimmons)
1 cup all-purpose flour
½ cup sugar
¼ teaspoon baking soda
½ teaspoon cinnamon
⅛ teaspoon salt
½ cup evaporated milk
1 egg yolk
1 teaspoon vanilla extract*

woods. A good frost
in late fall will ripen
the firm and puck-
ery fruit to the soft,
sweet, orange delicacy
that resembles a little
wrinkled pumpkin.

Theodora Dixon
has a special interest
in collecting recipes
using the persimmon
—a combination of
rekindling childhood
memories and indulg-
ing in an excuse to
go to the pasture on a
crisp fall day to pick
the wild persimmon,
free for the finding.

1 tablespoon butter, melted
½ cup black or English walnuts, chopped
1 egg white
½ pint whipping cream
½ teaspoon vanilla extract
sugar, to taste (optional)

To make the persimmon pulp, wash the persimmons and lower them into a large pan of boiling water for a few seconds to scald. Remove them from the water and drain. Press the persimmons through a sieve or strainer to remove the seeds and skins. Measure 1½ cups of pulp and set aside, or cover and refrigerate until ready to use.

Sift the flour into a large bowl. Add the remaining dry ingredients and sift again.

Add the persimmon pulp, evaporated milk, egg yolk, vanilla, butter, and walnuts to the dry ingredients. Stir until well blended. In a separate bowl, beat the egg white until stiff. Gently fold the beaten egg white into the persimmon batter. Butter a 9-inch baking dish and pour in the batter.

Bake, covered, for 1 hour at 325 degrees. Remove the pan from the oven and immediately remove the cover.

In a large bowl, whip the cream with the vanilla and sugar to taste. Cover and refrigerate until ready to serve.

Serve the pudding warm or cold, topped with a dollop of whipped cream.

Serves 6 to 8.

✳ Suet Pudding with Lemon Sauce

Anna Ruth Beck, Halstead

Anna Ruth Beck re-
members having suet
pudding on cold winter
evenings. Her father
would go to the shed

1 cup boiling water
1 cup beef suet, ground
1 cup molasses
3½ cups all-purpose flour
1 teaspoon soda

where the side of beef
was hanging and cut
a roast from the frozen
meat. They would
often use the suet to
make the pudding.
  Anna Ruth's
Grandfather Weaver
brought this recipe
from Lancaster
County, Pennsylvania,
to Harvey County,
Kansas, in the 1870s.

1 teaspoon cinnamon
½ teaspoon ground cloves
½ cup raisins

LEMON SAUCE
½ cup sugar
⅛ teaspoon salt
1½ tablespoons cornstarch
1½ cups boiling water
2 tablespoons lemon juice
1 teaspoon grated lemon rind
2 tablespoons butter

In a large pan, bring the water to a boil. Remove from heat and add the ground suet and molasses.

Sift the flour into a large bowl. Add the soda, cinnamon, and ground cloves and sift again. Add the flour mixture to the suet mixture and beat until thoroughly mixed. Dust the raisins with a small amount of flour and blend into the mixture.

Grease the top pan of a large double boiler and pour the mixture into it. Cover and cook over low heat for about 2 hours. Check the bottom pan of the double boiler occasionally and add more water, if needed. Serve warm with Lemon Sauce.

Serves 6 to 8.

Lemon Sauce: In a medium saucepan, combine the sugar, salt, and cornstarch. Add the boiling water and stir to a smooth paste. Cook, stirring constantly, over medium heat until mixture is thick and bubbly. Remove from heat and stir in the lemon juice, grated lemon rind, and butter.

Makes 1½ cups.

Variation: Instead of all white flour, use 1½ cups of stone-ground whole wheat flour plus 2 cups of all-purpose flour.

✳ Lemon Ice Box Pudding

Clarinda Burchill, El Dorado

Clarinda Burchill writes that this recipe was a specialty at the Birch-Hill Dining Room in Augusta, a popular dining room in Butler County in the late 1930s and early 1940s, and in her catering business in El Dorado.

This light and cool "old-fashioned" dessert is the perfect ending to a family dinner.

3 eggs
1 cup sugar
4 to 5 tablespoons lemon juice
grated rind of 1 lemon
1 cup whipping cream
⅔ cup pecans or walnuts
1¼ cups crushed vanilla wafers, divided

In a large bowl, beat the eggs well with a wire whip or an electric mixer. Add the sugar, lemon juice, and grated lemon rind. Cook over low heat in the top of a double boiler, stirring constantly, until the mixture thickens, about 5 to 8 minutes. Pour the mixture into a large bowl and cool.

Whip the cream. Gently fold it into the lemon mixture along with the nuts.

Line an 8-inch pan with 1 cup of the vanilla wafer crumbs. Pour in the pudding and top with the remaining ¼ cup of crumbs. Cover and chill for several hours, or overnight, before serving.

Serves 8.

✳ Indian Pudding

This modern recipe for Indian pudding, made with cornmeal and flavored with spices and molasses, is nearly as elaborate as authentic Indian pudding, in which cornmeal is thickened with fowl eggs, flavored with wild berries, and seasoned with coltsfoot herb rather than salt.

½ cup stoneground cornmeal
1 cup milk
2 tablespoons sugar
⅛ teaspoon baking soda
¼ teaspoon salt
¼ teaspoon cinnamon
¼ teaspoon ginger
⅛ teaspoon nutmeg
2 tablespoons molasses
½ cup cold milk
¼ cup raisins
whipped cream, sweetened to taste

Pour the milk into a small saucepan. Slowly add the cornmeal and mix well. Place the pan over medium heat and cook, stirring constantly, until the mixture thickens and begins to boil. Remove from heat immediately. Combine the sugar, soda, salt, cinnamon, ginger, and nutmeg in a small bowl and stir into the cornmeal mixture until smooth. Add the molasses, cold milk, and raisins, and mix well.

Pour the mixture into a 1-quart baking dish. Cover tightly with aluminum foil and bake at 325 degrees for 30 minutes. Remove the foil, stir gently, and bake uncovered for 20 to 25 minutes more, or until the edges are set but the center is still moist.

Cut into wedges and serve warm or cold and top with a dollop of whipped cream.

Serves 4.

✳ Homemade Vanilla Ice Cream

Many years ago, during long prairie winters in Kansas, ice cream was made by mixing together snow, sugar, and milk. More than a frozen treat for children, it seemed miraculous: mothers took something dormant and cold from outdoors and made it sweet and wonderful.

The invention of the ice-cream maker by Nancy Johnson in 1846 turned ice cream into the smooth and rich frozen custard we know today. When the hand-cranked machines were used, homemade ice cream was a ritual and a demonstration of stamina performed by the older children. The pace of the cranking was often carefully monitored by the firm commands of a grandmother determined to produce an ice cream worthy of her homemade pie. Though electric ice-cream makers have taken over the task of cranking, homemade ice cream remains forever popular at church socials, picnics, and family gatherings.

The rich flavor and creamy texture of this gourmet-quality ice cream is the result of first preparing a simple cooked custard. The custard must then be thoroughly chilled before freezing. Served plain, it's good enough to stand on its own, but with fresh strawberries or apple pie, it is the supreme Heartland dessert.

3 cups half and half
4 egg yolks
¾ cup sugar
⅛ teaspoon salt
1½ teaspoons vanilla extract

Place the half and half in a large pan. Scald by heating over medium-high heat until hot and bubbly but not boiling. Set aside and cool to warm.

In the top of a double boiler, whisk the egg yolks, sugar, and salt together with a wire whip over low heat just until the sugar is dissolved. The water in the bottom pan of the double boiler should be simmering, not boiling.

Remove the pan from heat and add some of the warm half and half by spoonfuls, stirring constantly. Very slowly, pour a thin stream of the half and half into the egg mixture, stirring constantly. (A very slow addition of the half and half is necessary to keep the eggs from curdling.)

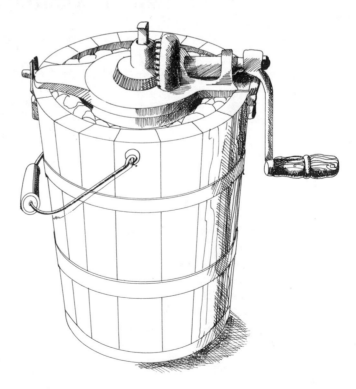

Return the pan to low heat and cook, stirring constantly with a large spoon, until the custard thickens and coats the back of a spoon, about 15 to 20 minutes.

Strain the custard to remove any lumps into a large bowl. Stir in the vanilla. Cover and refrigerate overnight before freezing.

Freeze the custard in an ice-cream freezer according to the manufacturer's directions. For best results, measure the ice and the salt according to the weather. In hot weather, layer 5 parts ice to 1 part salt in the cannister. In cool weather or in air-conditioning, layer 4 parts ice to 1 part salt. If you are using a hand-cranked machine, crank with a steady, continuous motion.

Makes 1 quart.

✳ Frozen Fruit Whip

Evelyn Hornbostel Clark, Haysville

"Every pastor's wife brings great recipes to a congregation," writes Evelyn Clark. *This recipe, originally shared with church members by Mrs. Gayle Freeberg, has been widely distributed among her admiring friends. In Haysville, you need no other introduction than "this is one of Mrs. Freeberg's recipes" to receive a positive response.*

1 cup water
1½ cups sugar
1 cup oranges, diced
1 cup canned peaches, diced and juice reserved
1 cup canned pineapple chunks, juice reserved
2 tablespoons maraschino cherries, chopped
1 cup orange juice
¼ cup lemon juice
liquid from an 8-ounce bottle of maraschino cherries

Make a simple syrup by combining the water and sugar and boiling for 2 to 3 minutes. Pour the syrup into a large container and cool to room temperature. Combine the reserved juices from the peaches and pineapple chunks to make 1 cup. Add to the syrup, with the fruit and remaining juices, mixing well.

Place the mixture in the freezer and freeze to a slush, stirring occasionally, about 6 hours. Serve while still a frozen slush.

Serves 12.

✳ Kolaches

Mildred Tacha, Jennings

Mildred Tacha tells us that Bohemians, Moravians, and other immigrants from what is now Czechoslovakia first came to the Big Timber area in Decatur County in the early 1870s. They were known for their delicious cooking, and one of their specialties was the Kolache, a rich, fruit-filled pastry. Recipes have been handed down from one generation to the next, and there are many versions.

The Tacha family was one of the original families to settle around Big Timber, and they have carried on the tradition of

2 packages dry yeast
½ cup warm water
1 cup milk
½ cup instant mashed potato flakes
¾ cup butter or margarine, softened
½ cup sugar
1 teaspoon salt
3 eggs
4½ to 5 cups all-purpose flour, divided

PRUNE FILLING
2 pounds pitted prunes
1 cup applesauce
1⅜ cups sugar
2½ tablespoons lemon juice

CHEESE FILLING
1½ cups dry cottage cheese
1 large egg, beaten
⅞ cup sugar
2 tablespoons all-purpose flour
2 teaspoons orange juice
1½ tablespoons lemon juice
½ cup raisins (optional)

CRUMB TOPPING
¼ cup sugar
1 cup all-purpose flour
⅓ cup butter

¼ cup warmed vegetable oil

In a large mixing bowl, dissolve the yeast in the warm water.

In a saucepan over low heat, heat the milk, instant potato flakes, butter or margarine, sugar, and salt to 110 degrees (lukewarm). Stir the milk mixture into the yeast mixture. Add the eggs and beat for 2 minutes. Add 2 cups of the flour and beat until smooth. Gradually stir in enough of the remaining flour to make a soft dough. Knead the dough gently, just until it can be handled. Shape the dough into a ball and place in a greased bowl. Turn once to grease the surface. Cover and let rise in a warm place until doubled in size, 1½ to 2 hours. (If you have not yet made the filling, prepare one or both of the fillings below while the dough is rising.)

After it has doubled, punch the dough down and divide it into 4 equal portions. Divide each portion into 12 pieces. Form the pieces into small balls and place them 3 inches apart on 4 lightly greased baking sheets. Cover and let rise in a warm place until doubled, 45 to 60 minutes.

Make a deep depression in the center of each ball, forming a small rim. (The dough under the depression should be quite thin or it will rise up and push the filling out.) Fill the depressions with the Prune or Cheese Filling (or canned fruit filling) and top with some of the Crumb Topping. Let rise for 45 to 60 minutes.

Bake the Kolaches at 400 degrees for 10 to 12 minutes. Before removing the Kolaches from the pans, brush the rims lightly with warmed vegetable oil. Remove from the pans and cool.

Prune Filling: Place the prunes in a saucepan and cover with a small amount of water. Simmer over low heat until tender, 15 to 20 minutes. Drain the prunes well and blend in a blender or food processor. Blend in the applesauce, sugar, and lemon juice. Cool before using.

Cheese Filling: Press the dry cottage cheese through a sieve to produce a finer texture. Place it in a saucepan and add all the remaining ingredients except the raisins. Cook over low heat, stirring constantly, until the mixture thickens, 5 to 8 minutes. If desired, simmer the raisins in a small amount of water for 5 to 10 minutes. Drain well and stir into the filling. Cool before using.

Crumb Topping: In a mixing bowl, combine the sugar and flour. Cut in the butter with a pastry blender or a fork until the mixture is crumbly.

　　　Makes 48.

✳ Almond Strudel

Isabelle Ripplinger, Lawrence

Isabelle Ripplinger, a French student studying English literature at the University of Kansas, combined the filling of a French tart called pithiviers *and the filo dough used*

1 cup almonds, finely ground
¾ cup sugar
2 small eggs, or 1 extra large egg
2 tablespoons rum or brandy
6 leaves filo dough
¾ cup butter, melted
1 to 1½ cups dry bread crumbs
confectioner's sugar

for Greek baklava to create this recipe. She sells her pastries at the Lawrence Farmers' Market.

Combine the ground almonds, sugar, egg, and rum in a mixing bowl or a food processor. Set aside.

Thaw the filo dough according to package instructions. Place one leaf of the filo on a damp cloth. Brush it very lightly with the melted butter. Sprinkle the dough with the dry bread crumbs. Place a second leaf of filo on top of the first. Brush it lightly with butter and sprinkle it with bread crumbs. Place one-third of the filling evenly along the long edge of the filo dough. Roll the filo up in the style of a jelly roll, with the aid of the cloth. Place the roll on a greased sheet pan. Brush the strudel with butter. Repeat with the remaining leaves of filo and the rest of the filling.

Bake the strudel at 400 degrees for 20 to 25 minutes, or until golden. For a nice glaze, sprinkle the strudel lightly with confectioner's sugar for the last 5 minutes of baking.

Cut the strudel while still warm, but serve at room temperature or chilled.

Makes 3 strudels, serving 9 to 12.

✳ Ocean Waves

(Listy)

Mrs. Sylvia G. Vopat, Wilson

Listy (Czech for "leaves"), Elephant Ears, or Celestial Wonders are a few of the names these light, fried pastries are known by. This recipe has been handed down in the Vopat family for more than three generations.

In more frugal times, Sylvia Vopat recalls that duck eggs were often used in

3 eggs
3 tablespoons cream
½ cup sugar
½ teaspoon salt
2½ to 3 cups all-purpose flour
oil or shortening for deep-fat frying
powdered sugar

In a large mixing bowl, beat the eggs until uniformly mixed. Beat in the cream, sugar, and salt. Gradually add the flour, stirring until the dough can be formed into a ball. On a lightly floured surface, roll out the dough to ¼-inch thickness. Cut the dough into odd or triangular shapes.

the recipe instead of chicken eggs, since the chicken eggs could be marketed. Also, vegetable oil or shortening now replaces the lard specified in the older version.

In a heavy-bottomed pan, add oil to a depth of at least 2 inches and heat to 375 degrees. Fry the dough in small batches, trying not to overcrowd the pan. Turn to brown evenly, 1 to 2 minutes. Remove the Ocean Waves with a slotted spoon and dust them with powdered sugar before serving.

Makes about 4 dozen.

✳ Peppernuts

(Pfeffernuesse)

Lorraine J. Kaufman, Moundridge

Pfeffernuesse, or peppernuts, are a traditional Christmas cookie among the Swiss German Mennonites of south-central Kansas. The custom seems to have originated when extended families gathered together to share the cooking duties and everyone pitched in to make these tiny cookies.

There are many variations on this recipe. Some make the cookies "as hard as nuts" and yield enough to be measured by the peck. The following recipe for Lorraine Kaufman's melt-in-your-mouth version makes a more manageable quantity. (However, you may

1 cup butter or margarine
1½ cups sugar
1 egg, beaten
2 tablespoons dark corn syrup
½ teaspoon anise oil*
3¼ to 3½ cups all-purpose flour
2 teaspoons baking soda
1 teaspoon cinnamon
1 teaspoon ground cloves
1 teaspoon ginger
¼ teaspoon nutmeg

In a large bowl, cream together the butter and sugar. Add the egg, syrup, and anise oil and mix well.

Sift the dry ingredients together in a large bowl. Add the dry ingredients, ¼ cup at a time, to the butter and sugar mixture, mixing well after each addition. When thoroughly mixed, cover the dough with plastic wrap and refrigerate until ready to use, for easy handling.

To shape the peppernuts, roll small portions of the dough into "pencils" about ⅓ to ½ inch in diameter. Make ⅛- to ¼-inch slices. Place the slices cut-side down on an ungreased cookie sheet. Bake at 350 degrees (325 de-

* Anise oil is available at pharmacies.

find yourself making a second batch.)

grees if using all butter) for 5 to 6 minutes, or until the peppernuts are lightly browned.

Makes 3½ quarts.

✳ Swedish Ginger Cookies

(Pepparkakor)

Mrs. Ernest A. (Eunice) Wall, McPherson

Pepparkakor is a traditional Swedish cookie similar to the gingersnap. Its spicy flavor is a perfect accompaniment to coffee, the Swedes' favorite beverage.

1 cup sugar
¼ cup butter or margarine
½ cup shortening
¼ cup molasses
1 egg
2 cups all-purpose flour
2 teaspoons soda
¼ teaspoon salt
1 teaspoon cinnamon
1 teaspoon ground ginger
½ cup sugar

In a large mixing bowl, cream the sugar, butter or margarine, and shortening together. Add the molasses and the egg, mixing well.

In a separate bowl, combine the flour, soda, salt, cinnamon, and ginger. Add the dry ingredients to the batter and mix well. Cover and chill for 1 hour.

Roll the dough into ¾-inch balls. Place ½ cup of sugar in a shallow bowl. Roll the balls in the sugar and place on a cookie sheet. Flatten each with a small glass or a smooth object. Bake at 350 degrees for 6 to 8 minutes.

Makes 5 dozen.

✳ Aunt Miranda's Sour Cream Tea Biscuits

Mrs. Harold Johnson, Dwight

James Beard reports that "the New York Dutch were probably the first to popularize 'koekjes,' baked in outdoor ovens, an oven built into the side of the fireplace, or on a griddle set over hot coals. But obviously cookies were difficult to bake until the wood-burning stove or coal-fired kitchen ranges were in general use. They became a standard item for lunch boxes and for snacks, and so constant was the demand that the cookie jar or tin was brought into fashion" (James Beard's American Cookery *[Boston and Toronto: Little, Brown and Company, 1972]).*

3 eggs
2 cups sugar
1 teaspoon vanilla extract
1 cup butter, softened
1 cup sour cream
6 cups all-purpose flour
1 teaspoon baking soda
1 teaspoon baking powder
1 teaspoon nutmeg

sugar

In a large mixing bowl, beat the eggs. Add the sugar, mixing well. Beat in the vanilla and butter, then the sour cream.

In a large bowl, combine the dry ingredients. Add the dry ingredients gradually to the creamed mixture. If the cookie dough appears too sticky to handle, cover and chill for about 1 hour.

Roll out the cookie dough to ⅛- to ¼-inch thickness between two sheets of waxed paper or on a lightly floured surface. Cut the cookies with a 2½- or 3-inch biscuit or cookie cutter. Place them on a cookie sheet and sprinkle lightly with sugar. Bake at 375 degrees 8 to 10 minutes.

Makes 5 to 6 dozen.

❋ Sorghum Chewies

Marilyn Eck, Bartlett

Marilyn Eck, whose family owns a sorghum mill in southeast Kansas, comments, "When our grandparents and great-grandparents were raising their families, sorghum was a very important staple in the diet. As we only had a vague recollection of sorghum making, we wanted to [re-] acquaint ourselves

1 cup plus 2 tablespoons sugar
3/4 cup shortening
1 egg
1/3 cup sorghum
1 teaspoon vanilla extract
2 1/4 cups all-purpose flour
3/4 teaspoon salt
1 1/2 teaspoons soda
1 cup quick-cooking rolled oats
1 6-ounce package chocolate chips
1 cup flaked coconut

In a large bowl, cream the sugar and shortening together. Add the egg, sorghum, and vanilla. Beat well.

with it and let our children see and become a part of it. Our interest grew and we sensed an enthusiasm in those around us. Sorghum making has now become a major part of our lives."

Sift the flour, salt, and soda together in a separate bowl. Add the dry ingredients to the cookie mixture, mixing well. Stir in the rolled oats, chocolate chips, and coconut. Drop the mixture from a teaspoon, 2 inches apart, onto a lightly greased cookie sheet.

Bake at 350 degrees for 12 minutes, or until lightly browned.

Makes 6 dozen.

✳ Persimmon Cookies

Theodora Dixon, Caney

At first, European immigrants considered wild persimmons too astringent to eat. They learned from the Indians that persimmons must not be picked until fall, after the first frost, when they become sweet. They are probably the last fruit of the season to ripen, long after other fruits have been harvested. This unusual fruit, found in Kansas, makes moist and delicious cookies.

1 cup persimmon pulp (about 1 pound of fresh persimmons)
½ cup butter or margarine
½ cup brown sugar
½ cup white sugar
1 egg
1 teaspoon baking soda
2 cups all-purpose flour
½ teaspoon ground cloves
½ teaspoon cinnamon
½ teaspoon nutmeg
1 cup raisins
1 cup chopped pecans

To make the persimmon pulp, wash the persimmons and lower them into a large pan of boiling water to scald for a few seconds. Remove them from the pan and drain. Press the persimmons through a sieve or strainer to remove the seeds and skins. Measure 1 cup of pulp and set aside, or refrigerate until ready to use.

In a large mixing bowl, cream the butter or margarine with the sugars. Add the egg and beat well. Stir the soda into the persimmon pulp until dissolved. Add the pulp to the creamed mixture and beat well.

In a separate bowl, combine the flour with the spices. Slowly add the flour mixture to the batter, mixing after each addition. Stir in the raisins and pecans.

Drop the batter by rounded spoonfuls onto a greased cookie sheet. Bake at 350 degrees for about 10 minutes, or until lightly browned.

Makes 5 dozen.

✳ Sugarless Wheat 'n' Fruit Cookies

This cookie contains no sugar and is sweetened naturally with coconut and dates. The flavors of these cookies seem to blend and improve with age, so make them a day or two before you plan to eat them—if that's possible!

½ cup butter, softened
1 egg
2 teaspoons vanilla extract
1 cup whole wheat flour
1 teaspoon baking powder
⅛ teaspoon salt
1 cup flaked unsweetened coconut
1 cup unsugared dates, chopped
4 teaspoons fresh grated orange peel
1 cup pecans, finely ground

Cream the butter, egg, and vanilla together in a large mixing bowl.

In a small bowl, combine the whole wheat flour, baking powder, and salt. Add the flour mixture, a little at a time, to the creamed mixture, beating after each addition.

In a medium bowl, combine the coconut, dates, orange peel, and ½ cup of the pecans. Stir into the cookie mixture.

Divide the dough in half and form into 2 logs, approximately 1½ inches in diameter. Place the remaining ½ cup of pecans on a piece of waxed paper. Roll the logs in the nuts. Wrap each log in waxed paper and chill for 1 hour.

To bake, slice the logs into ⅛-inch rounds and place them on an ungreased cookie sheet. Bake at 350 degrees for 10 to 12 minutes, until lightly browned.

Makes 5 dozen.

✳ Korny Kansas Cookies

Anyone who is fond of the flavor of corn will get a kick out of these unusual cookies.

1¼ cups yellow cornmeal
1½ cups all-purpose flour
1 cup sugar
½ teaspoon soda
½ teaspoon salt
1 cup butter, chilled
1 egg, slightly beaten
1 teaspoon vanilla extract
whole pecans

In a large mixing bowl, combine the cornmeal, flour, sugar, soda, and salt. Cut in the butter with a pastry blender or a fork until the mixture is crumbly. Add the egg and vanilla. Mix well.

Shape the dough into 1-inch balls and place 2 inches apart on a greased cookie sheet. Place a pecan atop each cookie and press down to flatten slightly.

Bake at 325 degrees for 15 to 18 minutes. Cool the cookies on the sheet for 1 minute before removing.

Makes 4 dozen.

✳ Danish Almond Creams

Pam Hansen, Lawrence

"My fondest memories of my Danish grandmother are of her warm, caring personality, her beautiful gardens, and her home-baked goodies," recalls Pam Hansen. In Pam's Danish cookie recipe, a rich almond cream is sandwiched between delicate butter pastries.

2 cups all-purpose flour
1 cup butter, slightly softened
4 teaspoons whipping cream
3 to 4 teaspoons cold water
1 egg, beaten
sugar

ALMOND CREAM
1 cup powdered sugar
¼ cup butter, softened
1 teaspoon almond extract
2 to 3 teaspoons whipping cream

In a large bowl, cut the butter into the flour with a pastry blender or a fork until the mixture is crumbly. Stir in the whipping cream. Stir in the cold water a teaspoon at a time until the dough can be formed into a ball (it should have the consistency of pie dough). Cover the dough and chill for 30 minutes.

Roll half of the dough out to ⅛-inch thickness on a lightly floured surface. Cut into rounds with a 1½-inch cookie cutter or a shot glass. Place the cookies on an ungreased cookie sheet. Repeat with the remaining dough. Brush each cookie lightly with the beaten egg and sprinkle lightly with sugar.

Bake at 350 degrees for 8 to 10 minutes, or just until the tops begin to turn golden. Remove the cookies from the cookie sheet immediately and cool completely.

Almond Cream: Place the powdered sugar in a large bowl. Blend in the butter. Add the almond extract and mix well. Add the cream a teaspoon at a time, blending until the mixture is smooth and the desired spreading consistency is reached.

Spread about ½ teaspoon of the Almond Cream on the unglazed side of a cookie. Top with the unglazed side of another cookie to form a sandwich. Cover and refrigerate if not serving right away.

Makes 4 dozen.

✳ Casserole Cookies

Mrs. Harold Johnson, Dwight

Mrs. Harold Johnson says Kansans are great on baking both casseroles and cookies, so why not Casserole Cookies? These date and coconut cookies are baked in a casserole dish, then rolled

2 eggs
1 cup sugar
1 teaspoon vanilla extract
¼ teaspoon almond extract
pinch of salt
1 cup unsugared dates, cut into small pieces
1 cup unsweetened flaked coconut
1 cup nut meats
powdered sugar

into balls and dusted with powdered sugar. They're delicious!

In a large bowl, beat the eggs and sugar together. Add the vanilla and almond flavorings and a pinch of salt, mixing well. Stir in the dates, coconut, and nuts. Turn the mixture into a greased 2-quart casserole and bake at 350 degrees for 30 minutes.

Remove from the oven and immediately beat the mixture with a wooden spoon. Cool the mixture until it can be handled. Form the mixture into 1-inch balls. Dust with powdered sugar.

Makes 4 to 5 dozen.

✳ Black Walnut Bars

The distinctive flavor of black walnuts, long appreciated by Kansas cooks, gets a boost from chocolate in these popular bars.

1¾ cups black walnuts, finely ground
2 tablespoons all-purpose flour
½ teaspoon baking powder
⅛ teaspoon salt
3 egg yolks
½ cup sugar
1 teaspoon vanilla extract
3 egg whites

CHOCOLATE FROSTING
2 tablespoons butter
1 ounce unsweetened baking chocolate
1 cup powdered sugar
⅛ teaspoon salt
½ teaspoon vanilla extract
1 to 2 tablespoons milk

2 tablespoons black walnuts, coarsely chopped

Combine the ground black walnuts with the flour, baking powder, and salt in large bowl. Set aside. In another bowl, beat the egg yolks and sugar until the mixture is thick and lemon colored. Add the vanilla and mix well. Set aside. In a large bowl, beat the egg whites until stiff peaks form. Fold the nut mixture into the egg yolk mixture. Then fold this mixture gently into the beaten egg whites.

Pour into a greased 9-inch baking dish. Bake at 350 degrees for 25 to 30 minutes. Cool completely before frosting.

Chocolate Frosting: Melt the butter and chocolate in a medium-sized pan over low heat. Remove from heat and stir in the powdered sugar and salt. Add the vanilla and mix well. Add the milk a little at a time, mixing until a smooth spreading consistency is reached. Frost and top with 2 tablespoons of chopped black walnuts. Cut into bars.

Makes 16.

✳ Heartland Cookie Bars

The tasty combination of rolled oats, wheat germ, pecans, coconut, and raisins creates a healthy bar from the Heartland.

½ cup butter, softened
¾ cup brown sugar
1 teaspoon vanilla extract
2 eggs
½ cup whole wheat flour
½ cup unbleached white flour
1 teaspoon baking powder
¼ teaspoon salt
½ cup rolled oats
¼ cup honey-crunch-style wheat germ
½ cup pecans, coarsely chopped
½ cup unsweetened coconut
½ cup raisins

In a large mixing bowl, cream the butter and the brown sugar. Add the vanilla and eggs. Mix well.

Combine the whole wheat flour, white flour, baking powder, and salt in a separate bowl. Add the dry ingredients gradually to the creamed mixture, mixing after each addition. Add the oats, wheat germ, pecans, coconut, and raisins, stirring just until combined. Spread the mixture into a greased 8-inch baking dish. Bake at 350 degrees for 25 to 30 minutes. Cool and cut into squares.

Makes 12 to 16 squares.

✳ KANSAS MENUS

KANSAS HARVEST DINNER
Corn Puffs (p. 3)
Harvest Tomato Salad (p. 296)
Home-Style Steak with Butter Crumb Dumplings (p. 70)
Corn with Anise Butter (p. 260)
No-Knead Whole Wheat Rolls (p. 338)
Apple Butter (p. 367)
Burnt Sugar Pie (p. 395)

WILD AND DOMESTIC SPECIALTIES
Morel Mushroom Turnovers (p. 8)
Nasturtium-Spinach Salad (p. 293)
Kansas Corn Chowder (p. 46)
Hunter's Pheasant with Red Wine Sauce (p. 190)
Cracked Wheat with Green Peas (p. 237)
Zucchini with Pecans (p. 279)
Applesauce (p. 370)
Honey Whole Wheat Bread (p. 321)
Sand Hill Plum Butter (p. 366)
Persimmon Pudding (p. 433)

SUNDAY DINNER IN THE HEARTLAND
Fresh Asparagus Spears with Dip (p. 3)
Wilted Lettuce (p. 291)
Roast Pork with Vegetables and Gravy (p. 127)
Peas with Fresh Mint (p. 273)
Sour Cream Beets (p. 272)
Crisp Icicle Pickles (p. 374)
Best White Bread (p. 324)
Wild Mulberry Jam (p. 367)
Classic Apple Pie (p. 386)

SWEDISH SMORGASBORD
Swedish Rye Bread (p. 333)
Fruit Soup (Frukt Soppa) (p. 59)
Herring Salad (Sill Sallad) (p. 313)
Swedish Meatballs (Köttbullar) (p. 16)

Swedish Brown Beans (Bruna Bönor) (p. 284)
Swedish Cheesecake with Lingonberry Sauce (Ost Kaka med Lingon) (p. 426)
Swedish Ginger Cookies (Pepparkakor) (p. 445)
Swedish Coffee (p. 26)

PARSON'S DINNER
Pickled Asparagus (p. 373)
Patio Corn Salad (p. 300)
Parson's Pan-Fried Chicken (p. 157)
Real Mashed Potatoes (p. 250)
Mint Glazed Carrots (p. 271)
Spring Peas with Lettuce (p. 273)
Cornmeal Rolls (p. 338)
Lemon Ice Box Pudding (p. 436)

MIDWESTERN BACKYARD BARBECUE
Grilled Mushrooms (p. 9)
Lettuce Salad with Garlic Vinaigrette (p. 290)
Beef Tenderloin Fillets with Sweet Red Pepper Stuffing (p. 77)
Baked Potatoes (p. 248)
Barbecued Sweet Corn (p. 260)
Onions with Herbs and Butter (p. 269)
Kansas-Style Honey Wheat French Bread (p. 322)
Peaches 'n Cream Cobbler (p. 408)
Homemade Vanilla Ice Cream (p. 437)

PIONEER FEAST
Black Walnut Soup (p. 57)
Sweet and Sour Cabbage Slaw (p. 304)
Baked Prairie Chicken with Corn Bread Dressing (p. 188)
Autumn Squash (p. 264)
Sourdough Potato Bread (p. 327)
Prickly Pear Jelly (p. 369)
Vinegar Cobbler (p. 407)

KANSAS ETHNIC DINNER
Vietnamese Spring Rolls (p. 13)
European Vegetable Soup (p. 49)

Italian Leg of Lamb (p. 120)
German Potato Pancakes (Kartoffelpuffer) (p. 253)
Lima Beans Brittany Style (Flageolets à la Bretonne)
   (p. 283)
Sourdough French Bread (p. 326)
Kolaches (p. 440)

✳ CONTRIBUTORS

Mrs. George (Wilma)
Ackerman, Sabetha
Lisa Albright, McLouth
Steve Albright, McLouth
Thomas Alexios,
Lawrence
Grace B. Anderson,
Lawrence
Mariellen Appleby,
Sedan
Joan Larson Bader,
Berryton
Mrs. Bettye Bartlett,
Fowler
Anna Ruth Beck,
Halstead
Mrs. Anna Benyshek,
Cuba
Susie Bermudez,
Lawrence
Louise Berning-Wendler,
Scott City
Judith Bird, Dodge City
Merle Bird, Rossville
Warren A. Bird, Dodge
City
John Bowden, Lawrence
Peg Bowman, Wichita
Patty Boyer, Lawrence
Mrs. Alice Brax,
Lindsborg
Barclay J. Brumley,
Manhattan
Clarinda Burchill, El
Dorado
Josephine Caput,
Frontenac
Joan Carey, Topeka
Elizabeth W. Carlson,
Topeka

Mrs. Cleo Carson, Erie
Evelyn Hornbostel Clark,
Haysville
Beverly J. Corcoran,
Pittsburg
David A. Gaddy Cox,
Kansas City
Eileen Cox, Lakin
Mark Creamer,
Lawrence
Gayla Hart Croan, Fort
Scott
Mrs. Lambert Dahlsten,
Lindsborg
Kittie Furbeck Dale,
Ellis
David Dary, Lawrence
Ruth Deckert, Pawnee
Rock
Nila Denton, Stockton
Rose Mary Dietz,
Hoisington
Theodora Dixon, Caney
Marilyn Eck, Bartlett
Julia Egnatic, Kansas
City
Eileen Ellenbecker,
Marysville
Michael Ellenbecker,
Lawrence
Ken C. Erickson, Garden
City
Beulah Farha, Wichita
Hazel E. Fenske, Wichita
Elton & Helen Fenton,
Bonner Springs
Marjorie Fox, Coffeyville
Leanna Galloway,
Lawrence
Dorothy Geier, Girard

Agnes Gladden, Dodge
City
Marijana Grisnik, Kansas
City
Patricia Habiger,
Spearville
Selan U. Hall, Jr.,
Lawrence
Mrs. Julia Peterson
Hampton, Oskaloosa
David Hann, Lawrence
Pam Hansen, Lawrence
Mrs. Otto (Emogene)
Harp, Marienthal
Ruth Kelley Hayden,
Atwood
Aletha Hensleigh,
Winchester
Dolores Herd, Protection
Nadine Herridge,
Oswego
Landon Hollander,
Lawrence
Barbara Holzmark,
Leawood
Mrs. Thomas Hood,
Liberal
Janice Raven Hornbostel,
Junction City
Sally Hubbard, Lyons
Mrs. Robert Jandera,
Hanover
Addie Johnson,
Hutchinson
Georgina Johnson,
Hillsboro
Mrs. Harold Johnson,
Dwight
Simone Johnson, Topeka

Mrs. Edward Kauffman, Haven
Doris Kaufman, Wichita
Lorraine J. Kaufman, Moundridge
Mary L. Kelling, Hays
Rhonda Kessler, Sawyer
Ruby Kessler, Sawyer
Kelly Kindscher, Lawrence
Mary Lou Klein, Great Bend
Mrs. Virginia Love Krey, Garden City
Harry W. Kroeger, Jr., Lawrence
Norman & Anna Marie Krusic, Frontenac
George Laughead, Jr., Dodge City
Fred Leimkuhler, Tonganoxie
Ralph & Gloria Leonhard, Berryton
Stevens County Library, Hugoton
Mrs. C. H. (Maxine) Liming, Dearing
Doris R. Loganbill, Moundridge
Kathryn Long, Edna
Deanna Lovejoy, Lawrence
Marna Lovgren, Oswego
Mary Kelley Maley, Salina
Kay Marshall, Tribune
Mrs. Larry G. (Deb) Martin, Redfield
Diana Matthews, Lawrence
Esther Fenton Mauk, Bonner Springs

Mrs. Wallace E. McClenny, Valley Falls
Edna McGhee, Madison
Lou Belle Meyer, Sylvan Grove
Ruth Meyer, Linn
Lucille Miller, Wichita
Mary Mize, Topeka
Mrs. Alice P. Morgan, Lawrence
Teresa Morgan, Roeland Park
Stephanie Swieton Mroz, Mission
Marilyn Neill, Fredonia
Marlene Neufeld, Buhler
Virginia Nordyke, Ottawa
Floyd & Becky Ott, Eudora
Judith Paisley-Brown, Dodge City
Mrs. Violet Parsons, Alden
Mary Terrill Pattie, Topeka
Karen Pendleton, Lawrence
Gladys Peterson, Lindsborg
Eunice M. Pittman, Bloom
Barney Pontious, Parsons
Jay Pruiett, Lawrence
Agnes Sabatka Reeh, Atwood
Esther Reilly, Dorrance
Isabelle Ripplinger, Lawrence
Joan Rockers, Garnett
Twila Roenne, Osborne
Ms. Terry L. Ryan, Tecumseh

Olga Saia, Frontenac
George Samskey, Jr., Kansas City
Bob Schaffer, Lawrence
Mrs. Frank (Anna) Schippers, Victoria
Eleanor Schippers, Victoria
Mrs. Jean Schmelzla, Fulton
Hildred Schmidt, Walton
Niki Schneider, Lawrence
Von Schroeder, Overland Park
Cindy Sears, Lawrence
Joyce Shafer, Ada
Kate Shreves, Overbrook
Bill Simon, Eudora
Charlene Mason Simpson, Garland
Elizabeth M. Skinner, Wichita
Flora Smith, Ottawa
Katherine Hahn Smith, Coffeyville
Ray O. Smith, Longford
Lillabelle Stahl, Burlingame
Mrs. Robert G. Steele, Fort Scott
Mrs. Albertha Sundstrom, Lindsborg
Mildred Tacha, Jennings
Marj Thompson, Hutchinson
Maxine Todd, Sedan
Kristine Leann Turner, Chanute
Irene S. Vogel, Lawrence
Nancy Vogel, Hays

Mrs. Frank G. (Marie) Vopat, Wilson

Mrs. Sylvia G. Vopat, Wilson

Lindi Ensminger Waldman, Prairie Village

Mrs. Ernest A. (Eunice) Wall, McPherson

Gertrude Ward, Coffeyville

Lanora L. Webb, Liberal

Elda Wenzel, Wichita

Shelley White, Lawrence

Sharon K. Wienck, Barnes

David Willer, Lawrence

Caroline Wittman, Topeka

Carol Kennedy Zacharias, Topeka

✳ INDEX

Ackerman, Mrs. George (Wilma) (Sabetha), 71, 75
Albright, Lisa (McLouth), 279
Albright, Steve (McLouth), 184
Alexios, Thomas (Lawrence), 120
All a Cake Should Be, 410
Almond Strudel, 442–43
Amaranth Muffins, 353
Anderson, Grace B. (Lawrence), 208
Anna Lee's Banana Cream Pie, 394–95
Appetizers, 1–2
    artichokes, baked, 4
    asparagus, fresh with dip, 3
    beverages, 25–29
    chicken wings, 12
    corn puffs, 3–4
    granola, 22–23
    guacamole quesadillas, 6
    marinated peppers, 5
    mushrooms, 7–10
    Nadjev, 15–16
    popcorn, 19–21
    prairie fire dip, 23
    soy nuts, 19
    spring rolls, 13–14
    super crunch muffins, 17
    Swedish meatballs, 16–17
    sweet macaroni, 18
    venison mincemeat pie, 10–11
Apple, 387–89

and swedes sauté, 276–77
butter, 367
cake, 418–19
pies, 386–87, 389–94
with pork, 131–32
sauce, 370
-stuffed pork tenderloin, 131–32
Appleby, Mariellen (Sedan), 64, 95
Applesauce, 370
Apricot pie, 401–2
Artichoke hearts
    baked, 4
    in risotto, 239
Asparagus
    fresh, spears with dip, 3
    mold, 309
    pickled, 373
    soup, 47–48
    spears vinaigrette, 307–8
Aspic, chicken, 310
Aunt Ida Weaver's Eggnog, 27–28
Aunt Jane's Sweet Potatoes, 257
Aunt Miranda's Sour Cream Tea Biscuits, 446
Autumn Squash, 264–65

Baby Grandma's Hot Polk Salad, 294–95
Bader, Joan Larson (Berryton), 351, 422
Baked
    artichoke hearts, 4

cornmeal dumplings, 229
ham loaf, 144–45
potatoes, 248–49
prairie chicken with corn bread dressing, 188–89
Banana
    cream pie, 394–95
    -peanut salad, 317–18
    pecan wheat bread, 425–26
Bar-B-Q Beaver, 197
Barbecue
    beaver, 197
    beef brisket, 75–76
    buffalo, 114–15
    burgers, oven, 109–10
    cheese and pepper pizza, 234–36
    chicken with hot and sweet barbecue sauce, 164–65
    chuck roast, 66–67
    rabbit, 196–97
    sweet corn, 260
    See also Grilled
Bartlett, Mrs. Bettye (Fowler), 317
Bass, 208–9
Beans
    with beef, 93–95
    black, 150–51, 299–300
    casserole, 45–46
    German baked, 285–86
    green, with new potatoes, 282
    with ham hocks, 44
    kidney (red), 300

Beans (*continued*)
  lima, 283–84
  salad, 299–300
  skillet baked, 286
  sweet and sour, 283
  Swedish brown, 284
Beaver, 197
Beck, Anna Ruth (Halstead), 338, 434
Beef, 61–63
  with beans, 93–95
  brisket, 75–76
  chili, 88–93
  flank steak, 83–84
  ground, 16–17, 93–111
  hamburgers, 107–10
  kabobs, 85–87
  London broil, 82
  prime rib, 76–77
  roast, 64–67
  round steak, 70–75
  sirloin, 84–87
  soups, 33–34, 36–38
  steaks, 80–83
  stews, 32–33, 67–69
  Swiss steak, 71–72
  tenderloin, 77–80
  veal, 118–20
Beef and Bean Dinner, 95
Beef and Cheese Chowder, 37–38
Beef Tenderloin Fillets with Sweet Red Pepper Stuffing, 77–78
Beef Tenderloin Fillets with Shallot and Parsley Butter, 79
Beefalo, 116
  chili, 117–18
  meatloaf, 117
  stew, 118
Beefaloaf, 117
Beefiesta Kabobs, 86–87

Beer-Batter Shrimp with Spicy Shrimp Sauce, 209–11
Beer-Rye Muffins, 355
Beets, 272
Benyshek, Mrs. Anna (Cuba), 153
Bermudez, Susie (Lawrence), 153, 196, 378, 430
Berning-Wendler, Louise (Scott City), 86
Best White Bread, 324–25
Better Biscuits, 349–50
Beverages
  coffee, 26–27
  eggnog, 27–28
  punch, 28–29
  wassail, 25–26
Bierocks, 100–101
Bird, Judith (Dodge City), 17, 354, 355, 356
Bird, Merle (Rossville), 12, 338
Bird, Warren A. (Dodge City), 90
Biscuits
  better, 349–50
  elegant, 350–51
  whole wheat buttermilk, 351–52
  whole wheat sesame drop, 352
Black Bean Salad, 299–300
Black Beans with Smoked Sausage and Rice, 150–51
Black walnut
  bars, 452–53
  bread, 345–46
  cake, 416–17
  pie, 399–400
  soup, 57
Blackberry Cobbler, 408

Blue Cheese Chicken Rolls, 174–75
Blueberry Muffins, 354–55
Bohne Berogge, 236–37
Bowden, John (Lawrence), 201, 234
Bowman, Peg (Wichita), 404
Boyer, Patty (Lawrence), 205, 332
Braised Beef Burgundy, 67–69
Braised Wild Duck, 193–94
Brax, Mrs. Alice (Lindsborg), 6
Bread, 319–20, 324
  banana pecan, 425–26
  black walnut, 345–46
  corn, 346–49
  Houska (Czechoslo-   Vanocka
    vakian Christmas
    bread), 334–36
  Indian fry, 345
  oatmeal, 330–31
  Polish nut, 336–37
  pumpkin yeast, 332–33
  sage, 331–32
  sourdough, 325–28
  Swedish rye, 333–34
  white, 324–25
  whole wheat, 321–24, 329–30
  See also Rolls
Bread Pudding with Foamy Butter Sauce, 429–30
Breaded Fresh Pork Tenderloin, 133
Broccoli with Lemon Cream, 279–80
Broiled Bass with Tarragon Butter, 208–9
Broiled Mushrooms with Herb Butter Stuffing, 9–10

Brown Rice Salad, 315
Brumley, Barclay J.
    (Manhattan), 104
Bruna Bönor (Swedish
    Brown Beans), 284
Buffalo, 112–14
    barbecue, 114–15
    burgundy, 115
Buffalo Chicken Wings,
    12
Bulgur Wheat Dish, 238
Burchill, Clarinda (El
    Dorado), 271, 272,
    405, 436
Burger Bean Bake, 94
Burgers
    dinner-style, 108–9
    oven barbecued, 109
    steakburgers deluxe,
    107–8
Burnt Sugar Pie, 395–96
Butter
    apple, 367
    Sand Hill plum, 366
Butter Balls in Chicken
    Broth (*Butter Glase*),
    56–57
Butter-Basted Grilled
    Chicken, 165–67
Buttered Noodles with
    Toasted Bread
    Crumbs, 220–21

Cabbage
    and brown rice casse-
    role, 240–41
    casserole, Italian, 243
    escalloped, 280–81
    rolls with creamed
    sauerkraut, 142–43
    slaw, 304–5
    See also Sauerkraut
Cake, 410
    apple, 418–19

black walnut, 416–17
coconut buttermilk,
    413–14
holiday cardinal, 418
home front chocolate,
    414–15
Mennonite wedding,
    410–12
rich chocolate, 415–16
spicy gingerbread
    cupcakes, 423–24
strawberry shortcake,
    419–21
whole wheat ginger-
    bread, 422
whole wheat vanilla,
    412–13
Calf's Liver with Sour
    Cream Sauce, 111–12
Candied Sweet Potatoes,
    257–58
Canning, 372–73
Capirotada (Mexican
    Bread Pudding),
    430–31
Capon
    grilled, 184–85
    on corn bread, 183–84
    roasted, 182–83
Caput, Josephine (Fronte-
    nac), 42, 99
Carey, Joan (Topeka), 393
Carlson, Elizabeth W.
    (Topeka), 66
Carson, Mrs. Cleo (Erie),
    301, 313
Carrots
    crunch, 380
    grilled, with leeks,
    269–70
    mint-glazed, 271
    relish, 380
    scalloped, 270–71
    with snow peas and

onions, 272
Casseroles
    cassoulet, 45–46
    cinnamon chili mac,
    92–93
    corn and oyster, 241–42
    corn with macaroni,
    262–63
    cottage cheese, 227–28
    farmer's corn, 242–43
    Italian cabbage, 243
    pork and sauerkraut,
    148–50
    savory cabbage and
    brown rice, 240–41
    tomato and brown rice,
    238–39
    vegetable, 274
Casserole Cookies, 451–
    52
Cassoulet, 45–46
Catfish
    grilled in corn husks,
    201–2
    kabobs, 203–4
    lemon grilled, 200
    Neosho River, 201
    stew, 39–40
    with horseradish sauce,
    205
    with orange and lemon
    slices, 203
Cattlemen's Prime Rib
    Special, 76–77
Charcoal-Grilled Ham
    Steaks with Hot
    Mustard Sauce,
    145–46
Cheese
    cake, 426–27
    farmer's, 381–82
    -filled noodle pockets
    (*Käse Maultaschen*),
    223–25

Cheese (*continued*)
  German (*Käse*), 382–83
  rarebit, 245
Cherry Orchard Pie, 402–3
Chicken, 155–56
  aspic, 310
  baked, 163
  barbecue, 164–65
  Bombay, 175–77
  borscht, 39
  breasts, 166–78
  with blue cheese, 174–75
  casserole, 181
  fried, 157–61, 168–69.
  grilled, 165–66
  hunter's, 172–73
  with leeks and red pepper, 166–67
  lemon pepper, 169, 175
  and macaroni casserole, 182
  with morels, 171–72
  with noodles, 179
  pie, 177–78
  roasted, with pearl onions, 162–63
  rolls, 178–79
  salad, 310–11
  smoked, 167–68
  Swiss cheese, 173–74
  with tarragon cream, 172
  wings, 12
Chicken-Fried Steak with Gravy, 72–73
Chili
  cinnamon, 91–92
  cinnamon chili mac, 92–93
  country chunky, 91
  Dodge City, 90

roundup, 88–90
  speedy beefalo, 117–18
Chorizo (Mexican Sausage), 153
Choucroute Garnie (Pork and Sauerkraut Casserole), 148–50
Chuck Wagon Bean Pot, 93–94
Chuck wagons, 87–88
Cinnamon
  chili, 91–92
  chili mac, 92–93
  cream pie, 396–97
  popcorn, 21
Clark, Evelyn Hornbostel (Haysville), 439
Classic Apple Pie, 386
Classic Beef Stew, 32–33
Cobbler
  blackberry, 408
  peaches 'n' cream, 408–9
  vinegar, 407
Coconut Buttermilk Cake, 413–14
Coffee
  marinade, 85
  Swedish, 26–27
Collard Greens and Turnips, 275
Condiments
  butters, 366–67
  Dutch honey, 372
  jams and jellies, 367–70
  relishes, 375–80
Cookies
  Aunt Miranda's Sour Cream Tea Biscuits, 446
  black walnut bars, 452–53
  casserole, 451–52

Danish almond creams, 450–51
  Heartland cookie bars, 453
  korny Kansas, 450
  peppernuts, 444–45
  persimmon, 448–49
  sorghum chewies, 447–48
  sugarless wheat 'n' fruit, 449
  Swedish ginger, 445–46
Corcoran, Beverly J. (Pittsburg), 274
Coriander Pork Chops with Red Wine, 135–36
Corn, 258–59
  with anise butter, 260–61
  barbecued, 260
  breads, 346–49
  casseroles, 261–63
  cob jelly, 368–69
  creamy, 262
  fritters, 3–4
Cornmeal
  cookies, 450
  dumplings, 229–30
  griddlecakes, 358–59
  mush, 230–31
  polenta, 106–7
  rolls, 338–39
  scrapple, 141–42
Corn Puffs, 3–4
Cottage Cheese Casserole, 227–28
Country Chunky Chili, 91
Country Pork Sausage, 151–52
Country Steak Kabobs, 85–86
Country-Fried Chicken Breasts, 168–69

Country-Style Ribs with
    Willer Barbecue
    Sauce, 139–40
Cowboy Pork Chops, 135
Cox, David A. Gaddy
    (Kansas City), 101,
    331, 345
Cox, Eileen (Lakin), 262
Cracked Wheat Salad with
    Lemon Vinaigrette,
    314–15
Cracked Wheat with Green
    Peas, 237
Cracklin' Corn Bread,
    347–48
Crappie, 207–8
Crappie Meunière, 207–8
Cream of Country Ham
    Soup, 43–44
Creamed Capon on Corn
    Bread, 183–84
Creamer, Mark (Law-
    rence), 80
Creamy Corn, 262
Creamy Rice Pudding,
    431–32
Crème Fraîche Chicken,
    170
Crisp Icicle Pickles, 374–
    75
Crispy Baked Crappie
    Fillets, 208
Crispy Oven-Fried
    Chicken, 161
Croan, Gayla Hart (Fort
    Scott), 407
Croatian Potato Salad,
    302–3
Cucumbers in sour cream,
    307
Cucumber relish, 375–76
"Cure-all" Chicken Soup,
    38–39

Curried Tuna Salad, 313–
    14
Czech Capital of Kansas,
    152
Czech Christmas Soup,
    40–41
Czech Sausage (Jaternice),
    153

Dahlsten, Mrs. Lambert
    (Lindsborg), 333
Dale, Kittie Furbeck
    (Ellis), 55, 56
Dandelion Jelly, 369–70
Danish Almond Creams,
    450–51
Dary, David (Lawrence),
    114, 115
Deckert, Ruth (Pawnee
    Rock), 367, 369
Deer steaks, 195
Deluxe Chicken and Rice
    Casserole, 181
Denton, Nila (Stockton),
    353
Desserts, 384–85
    cakes, 410–24
    cobblers, 407–9
    cookies and bars, 444–
    53
    pies, 386–87, 389–407
Dietz, Rose Mary
    (Hoisington), 304
Dilled New Potato Salad,
    303
Diner-Style Burgers,
    108–9
Dixon, Theodora (Caney),
    109, 297, 300, 433,
    448
Dodge City Chili, 90
Dopp i Grytan (Dip into
    Kettle), 33–34

Dove, 194–95
Drukla Noodles, 221
Drying fruits and vege-
    tables, 380–81
Dumplings
    cornmeal, 229–30
    potato, 228–29
    gnocchi with meat
    sauce, 65–66
Duck, 193–94
Dutch Honey, 372

Eck, Marilyn (Bartlett),
    20, 94, 133, 330, 423,
    447
Eggnog, 27–28
Egnatic, Julia (Kansas
    City), 48, 336
Eileen Ellenbecker's Roast
    Capon, 182–83
Elegant Biscuits, 350–51
Ellenbecker, Eileen
    (Marysville), 183
Ellenbecker, Michael
    (Lawrence), 182
Enchiladas, tofu-spinach,
    244–45
Erickson, Ken C. (Garden
    City), 35, 36
Escalloped Cabbage, 280–
    81
European Vegetable Soup,
    49–50

Farha, Beulah (Wichita),
    111, 238
Farmer's Cheese, 381–82
Farmer's Corn Casserole,
    242–43
Fenske, Hazel E. (Wi-
    chita), 147
Fenton, Elton and Helen
    (Bonner Springs),
    372, 380

Fish, 198–99
  bass, 208–9
  catfish, 200–205
  crappie, 207–8
  soup, 40–41
  stew, 39–40
Flageolets à la Bretonne
    (Lima Beans Brittany
    Style), 283–84
Flank Steak Mexicana, 83
Flank Steak with Onions
    and Red Wine Glaze,
    83–84
Fox, Marjorie (Coffey-
    ville), 306
Freight Train Fillets, 79–
    80
French influence, 148
French Onion Soup (Soupe
    à l'Oignon), 51–52
Fresh Apricot Pie with
    Whole Wheat Pie
    Crust, 401–2
Fresh Asparagus Soup,
    47–48
Fresh Asparagus Spears
    with Dip, 3
Fried
  frog legs, 214–15
  morel mushrooms, 7
  oatmeal, 231
  okra patty, 281–82
  pheasant, 190
  potatoes with garlic and
    onion, 252
  yellow squash, 268
Frog Legs, fried, 214–15
Frontier Chicken Salad,
    310–11
Frosted Punch, 28–29
Frozen Fruit Whip, 439
Frukt Soppa (Swedish
    Fruit Soup), 59–60

Fruit Yeast Sourdough
    Starter, 325–26

Galloway, Leanna (Law-
    rence), 275
Game, 155–56
  beaver, 197
  duck, 193–94
  dove, 194–95
  pheasant, 190–91
  prairie chicken, 188–89
  quail, 192
  rabbit, 196–97
  venison, 10–11, 195
Garlic Popcorn with
    Toasted Almonds,
    19–20
Garlic Potatoes Supreme,
    251–52
Geier, Dorothy (Girard),
    37
German
  apple pancakes, 361–62
  baked beans, 285–86
  cheese, 382–83
  potato pancakes
    (Kartoffelpuffer),
    253–54
Germans in Kansas, 222–
    23
Gladden, Agnes (Dodge
    City), 19, 316
Gnocchi with Meat Sauce
    (Gnocchi con Salsa Di
    Carne), 65–66
Gorovei (Mennonite
    Wedding Cake),
    410–12
Grain
  bulgur, 238
  cracked wheat, 237,
    314–15
  granola, 22–23

  oats, 231, 330–31,
    356–57
  See also Corn; Rice
Grampa's Favorite Soup,
    42–43
Grandmother's Corn
    Bread, 348–49
Grandmother's Pea Salad,
    301
Granola, 22–23
Great Stuffed Pumpkin
    Recipe, 102–4
Green Beans with New
    Potatoes, 282
Green Tomato Relish,
    376–77
Griddlecakes. See Pan-
    cakes
Grilled
  breast of dove with
    grapes, 194–95
  capon, 184–85
  carrots and leeks, 269–
    70
  hamsteak, 145–46
  lemon catfish, 200
  mushrooms, 9
  sweet potato sticks, 258
  See also Barbecue
Grisnik, Marijana (Kansas
    City), 15
Guacamole Quesadillas, 6

Habiger, Patricia (Spear-
    ville), 70, 238, 309,
    353
Hall, Selan U., Jr. (Law-
    rence), 281, 294
Ham
  appetizer, 15–16
  loaf, 143–45
  steak grilled with hot
    mustard sauce, 145–46

steak soup, 42–44
steak with apricot
    nectar, 146–47
Hampton, Mrs. Julia
    Peterson (Oskaloosa),
    284, 313
Hann, David (Lawrence),
    196
Hansen, Pam (Lawrence),
    450
Harp, Mrs. Otto (Emo-
    gene) (Marienthal),
    329
Harvest Honeymoon,
    69–70
Harvest Meals, 159–60
Harvest Tomato Salad, 296
Harvey, Fred, 205–7
Hayden, Ruth Kelley
    (Atwood), 400
Hazel's Delicious Quiche,
    147
Heartland Cookie Bars,
    453
Hearts of Palm Salad with
    Jalapeño Relish, 298–
    99
Hensleigh, Aletha (Win-
    chester), 158, 193
Herd, Dolores (Protec-
    tion), 413
Herridge, Nadine
    (Oswego), 201, 381
Herring Salad (Sill Sal-
    lad), 313
Holiday Cardinal Cake, 418
Hollander, Landon (Law-
    rence), 211
Holzmark, Barbara (Lea-
    wood), 67, 140
Home Front Chocolate
    Cake, 414–15
Home-Style Steak with

Butter Crumb Dump-
    lings, 70–71
Homemade Chicken and
    Noodles, 179–81
Homemade Pasta, 218
Homemade Vanilla Ice
    Cream, 437–39
Homestead Cucumber
    Relish, 375–76
Homestead Fever, 53–54
Honey Whole Wheat
    Bread, 321
Hood, Mrs. Thomas
    (Liberal), 360, 361
Hornbostel, Janice Raven
    (Junction City), 283
Hot Dog Relish, 379
Houska (Czechoslovakian
    Christmas Bread),
    334–36
Hubbard, Sally (Lyons),
    296
Hunter's Chicken (Pollo
    alla Cacciatora),
    172–73
Hunter's Pheasant with
    Red Wine Sauce,
    190–91

Ice cream, homemade,
    437–39
Indian
    fry bread, 345
    pudding, 436–37
    tacos with hot sauce,
    101–2
Indians in Kansas, 263–64
Indoor/Outdoor Ribs,
    138–39
Italian
    cabbage casserole, 243
    leg of lamb, 120–21
    meat roll, 74–75

Jalapeño Pepper Relish,
    378–79
Jam, wild mulberry, 367–
    68
Jandera, Mrs. Robert
    (Hanover), 111
Jaternice (Czech Sausage),
    153
Jefferson County Fried
    Chicken, 158–59
Jelly
    corn cob, 368–69
    dandelion, 369–70
    prickly pear, 369
Jody Pie, 393–94
Johnson, Addie (Hutchin-
    son), 59
Johnson, Georgina (Hills-
    boro), 39, 339
Johnson, Mrs. Harold
    (Dwight), 143, 390,
    446, 451
Johnson, Simone (Topeka),
    45, 148, 283

Kansas Corn Chowder,
    46–47
Kansas Menus, 455–57
Kansas-Style Honey
    Wheat French Bread,
    322–24
Kartoffelpuffer (German
    Potato Pancakes),
    253–54
Käse (German Cheese),
    382–83
Käse Maultaschen
    (Cheese-Filled
    Noodle Pockets),
    223–25
Kauffman, Mrs. Edward
    (Haven), 367

Kaufman, Doris (Wichita),
    366
Kaufman, Lorraine J.
    (Moundridge), 58,
    236, 342, 368, 380,
    391, 410, 444
Kaw Valley Potato Salad,
    302
Kelling, Mary L. (Hays),
    285
Kessler, Rhonda (Sawyer),
    165, 300
Kessler, Ruby (Sawyer),
    28
Kibba, 111
Kidney Bean Salad, 300
Kindscher, Kelly (Law-
    rence), 225, 331
Klein, Mary Lou (Great
    Bend), 403
Kolaches, 440–42
Korny Kansas Cookies,
    450
Köttbullar (Swedish
    Meatballs), 16–17
Krey, Mrs. Virginia Love
    (Garden City), 375
Kroeger, Harry W., Jr.
    (Lawrence), 10
Krusic, Norman and Anna
    Marie (Frontenac),
    18, 74, 228

Lamb
    chops with garlic and
        rosemary, 123–24
    grilled, 122
    hash, 123
    leg, Italian, 120–21
Lamb's Quarters Lasagne,
    225–26
Lasagne
    lamb's quarters, 225–
        26

spinach, 226–27
Laughead, George, Jr.
    (Dodge City), 432
Layered Vegetable Casse-
    role, 274
Leeks, and carrots, 269
Leimkuhler, Fred W.
    (Tonganoxie), 389
Lemon
    bread pudding with
        blueberry sauce,
        428–29
    cake pie, 406–7
    chicken aspic, 310
    curd tarts, 404–5
    grilled catfish, 200
    ice box pudding, 436
Lemon Pepper Chicken
    Fillets, 175
Lemon Pepper Chicken
    with Artichoke
    Hearts, 169
Leonhard, Ralph and
    Gloria (Berryton),
    116, 117
Lettuce Salad with Garlic
    Vinaigrette, 290
Lima Beans Brittany
    Style (Flageolets à la
    Bretonne), 283–84
Liming, Mrs. C. H.
    (Maxine) (Dearing),
    144
Lindsborg, 311–12
Lingonberry Sauce, 427
Listy (Ocean Waves), 443
Little Balkans, 218–19
Little Sweden, 311–12
Lobster, 213–14
Loganbill, Doris R.
    (Moundridge), 141,
    151
London Broil in Red Wine
    Marinade, 82–83

Long, Kathryn (Edna),
    308
Lou Belle's Best-Ever
    Meat Loaf, 95–96
Lovejoy, Deanna (Law-
    rence), 347, 397
Lovgren, Marna (Oswego),
    192

Macaroni and Cheese, 227
Mak Kuchen (Poppy Seed
    Rolls), 342
Maley, Mary Kelley
    (Salina), 414
Marinated
    garden salad, 297–98
    grilled lamb, 122
    herbed tomato salad,
        297
    peppers, 5
Marshall, Kay (Tribune),
    242
Martin, Mrs. Larry G.
    (Deb) (Redfield), 97
Matthews, Diana (Law-
    rence), 52
Mauk, Esther Fenton
    (Bonner Springs), 321
McClenny, Mrs. Wallace
    E. (Valley Falls), 270,
    280
McGhee, Edna (Madison),
    3, 345, 399
Meatballs
    Italian, 97–99
    Swedish, 16–17
Meatloaf
    beef, 95–97
    beefaloaf, 117
    ham, 143–45
    vegetable, 97
Mennonite Wedding Cake
    (Gorovei), 410–12
Menus, Kansas, 455–57

Meyer, Lou Belle (Sylvan
    Grove), 91, 95
Meyer, Ruth (Linn), 262
Mexican
    beef pasties, 104–5
    bread pudding (*Capiro-
        tada*), 430–31
    influence in Kansas,
        377–78
    sausage (*Chorizo*), 153–
        54
Miller, Lucille (Wichita),
    429
Mincemeat, 371
    venison pie, 10
    parfait pie, 405–6
Mint Glazed Carrots, 271
Mize, Mary (Topeka), 257
Mom's Caraway Sauer-
    kraut, 286–87
Morel Mushroom Turn-
    overs, 8–9
Morels
    fried, 7
    turnovers, 8–9
    with chicken, 171–72
Morgan, Mrs. Alice P.
    (Lawrence), 206
Morgan, Teresa (Roeland
    Park), 23, 85
Mother's Oven Steak, 71
Mroz, Stephanie Swieton
    (Mission), 307
Mrs. Wintle's Lemon Curd
    Tarts, 404–5
Muffins
    amaranth, 353
    beer rye, 355
    blueberry, 354–55
    oatmeal spice, 356–57
    strawberry-rhubarb,
        356
    sunrise, 353–54
    super crunch, 17

Mulberry jam, 367–68
Mush
    cornmeal, 230–31
    fried oatmeal, 231
Mushrooms
    broiled with herb butter,
        9–10
    grilled, 9
    morels, 7, 8–9

Nadjev (Ham Dressing
    Stuffed in Casings),
    15–16
Nasturtium-Spinach Salad,
    293–94
Neill, Marilyn (Fredonia),
    371
Neosho River Catfish, 201
Neufeld, Marlene
    (Buhler), 297
New potatoes
    with dill and butter, 255
    with green beans, 282
    salad, 303
Nicodemus, 255–56
No-Knead Wheat Rolls,
    338
Noodles
    buttered with toasted
        bread crumbs, 220–
        21
    with chicken, 179–81
    Drukla, 221
    homemade, 218
    pockets, 223–25
    See also Pasta
Nordyke, Virginia
    (Ottawa), 241
Nyponsoppa (Rose Hip
    Soup), 58–59

Oatmeal
    bread, 330–31
    fried, 231

raisin pancakes, 360–61
    spice muffins, 356–57
Ocean Waves (*Listy*),
    443–44
Ogorki ze Smietana (cu-
    cumbers in sour
    cream), 307
Okra patty, fried, 281–82
Old English Apple Pie,
    391–92
Old-Fashioned Potato
    Cakes, 250–51
One-Rise Cinnamon Rolls,
    343–45
Onion soup, 51–52
Onions with herbs and
    butter, 269
Orange Bow-Knots, 341–
    42
Ost Kaka, 426–27
Ott, Floyd and Becky
    (Eudora), 386, 389
Oven-Baked Chicken
    Tarragon, 163
Oven Barbecued Burgers,
    109
Oven Caramel Corn, 20–
    21

Paisley-Brown, Judith
    (Dodge City), 13, 35
Pancake Day, 359–60
Pancake Omelet (*Schmar-
    ren*), 362–63
Pancakes
    cornmeal, 358–59
    German apple, 361–62
    oatmeal raisin, 360–61
    potato, 253–54
    whole wheat, 357–58
    yogurt, 361
Papa Joe's Italian Meat-
    balls and Spaghetti,
    97–99

Parsley-Parsnip Soup, 52–53
Parson's Pan-Fried Chicken, 157–58
Parsons, Mrs. Violet (Alden), 372, 396
Pasta, 216–17
  buttered, 220–21
  chicken and noodles, 179–81
  Drukla, 221
  homemade, 218
  with Italian tomato sauce, 219–20
  lasagna, 225–27
  macaroni with cheese, 227
  noodle pockets, 223–25
  spaghetti with meatballs, 97–99
  sweet macaroni, 18
  See also Noodles
Patio Corn Salad, 300–301
Pattie, Mary Terrill (Topeka), 226
Pawpaw Bread, 424–25
Peaches 'n' Cream Cobbler, 408–9
Peas
  salad, 301
  snow, 272
  with fresh mint, 273
  with lettuce, 273–74
Pecan Pie, 398–99
Pendleton, Karen (Lawrence), 3, 47, 373
Pepparkakor (Swedish Ginger Cookies), 445–46
Peppered Pork Chops, 134
Peppernuts (Pfeffernuesse), 444–45
Pepperoni Pizza with Pineapple and Green

Pepper, 232–34
Perfect Deer Steaks, 195
Perfection Salad, 308–9
Persimmon cookies, 448–49
Persimmon pudding, 433–34
Peterson, Gladys (Lindsborg), 16
Pfeffernuesse (Peppernuts), 444–45
Pheasant, 190–91
Pho Tai (Vietnamese Beef and Noodle Soup), 36–37
Pickled Asparagus, 373–74
Pickles, crisp icicle, 374–75. See also Relishes; under specific food items
Pie
  Anna Lee's banana cream, 394–95
  apple, 386–94
  black walnut, 399–400
  burnt sugar, 395–96
  cherry orchard, 402–3
  chicken, 177–78
  cinnamon cream, 396–97
  fresh apricot, 401–2
  Jody, 393–94
  lemon cake, 406–7
  mincemeat parfait, 405–6
  Mrs. Wintle's lemon curd tarts, 404–5
  pecan, 398
  pie plant, 400–401
  raisin sour cream, 403–4
  rhubarb, 400–401
  shepherd, 105–6
  sweet potato, 397

venison mincemeat, 10–11
Pineapple Beets, 316–17
Pioneer Apple Pie, 389–90
Pioneer Coffee Steaks, 81–82
Pittman, Eunice M. (Bloom), 130, 341
Pizza
  barbecued, 234–36
  pepperoni, 232–34
Plum Pudding, 432–33
Polenta with Meat Sauce, 106–7
Polish Nut Bread, 336–37
Polish-Style Cucumbers in Sour Cream (Ogorki ze Smietana), 307
Polk salad, 294–95
Pollo alla Cacciatora (Hunter's Chicken), 172–73
Pommes Frites, 253
Pontious, Barney (Parsons), 195, 197
Poor Man's Soup with a Rich Man's Flavor, 55–56
Popcorn
  caramel, 20–21
  cinnamon, 21
  garlic, 19–20
Poppy Seed Roll (Mak Kuchen), 342–43
Pork, 125–26
  cabbage rolls, 142–43
  chops, 134–38
  ribs, 138–41
  roast, 127–29
  salad, spinach, 129
  sausage, 148–54
  and sauerkraut casserole (Choucroute Garnie), 148–50

scrapple, 141–42
with sweet and sour
sauce, 133–34
tenderloin, 131–33
See also Ham
Potato
baked, 248–49
cakes, 250–51
dumplings, 228–29
fried, 252, 253
mashed, 250
new, 255, 282, 303
pancakes, 253–54
salad, 302–3
scalloped, 254–55
slaw, 305
sweet, 257–58
yogurt stuffed, 249
Poultry, 155–56. *See also*
Chicken
Prairie chicken, 188–89
Prairie dog, 196
Prairie Fire Dip, 23
Preserves, 364–65. *See*
also Butters; Jams;
Jellies
Prickly Pear Jelly, 369
Prime rib, 76–77
Pruiett, Jay (Lawrence),
190, 194
Pudding
bread, 428–31
creamy rice, 431–32
Indian, 436–37
lemon ice box, 436
persimmon, 433–34
plum, 432–33
suet with lemon sauce,
434–35
Pumpkin Yeast Bread,
332–33

Quail, 192
Quiche, 147

Rabbit, 196–97
Raisin Sour Cream Pie,
403–4
Real Mashed Potatoes,
250
Reeh, Agnes Sabatka
(Atwood), 286
Reilly, Esther (Dorrance),
56, 100, 221
Relishes, 364–65
carrot, 380
green tomato, 376–77
homestead cucumber,
375–76
hot dog, 379
jalapeño pepper, 378–79
Rhubarb pie, 400–401
Ribs
country-style, 139–40
indoor/outdoor, 138–39
with kraut, 140–41
Rice
casserole, 238–41
pudding, 431–32
risotto, 99–100, 239–40
salad, 315–16
wild rice supper, 241
Rich Chocolate Cake,
415–16
Ripplinger, Isabelle
(Lawrence), 442
Risotto Milanese, 99–100
Risotto with Artichoke
Hearts, 239–40
Roast
beef, 64–67
capon, 182–83
chicken with pearl
onions, 162–63
pork, 127–29
turkey, 185–87
Rockers, Joan (Garnett), 161
Roenne, Twila (Osborne),
395

Rolls, 338–45
Rose Hip Soup (*Nypon-*
soppa), 58–59
Round Steak with Green
Peppercorn Gravy,
73–74
Roundup Chili, 88–90
Ryan, Ms. Terry L.
(Tecumseh), 343

Sage Bread, 331–32
Saia, Olga (Frontenac), 97,
243, 291
Salads, 288–89
asparagus, 307–8
banana-peanut, 317–18
bean, 299–300
beets, 316–17
chicken, 310–11
corn, 300–1
cracked wheat, 314–15
cucumber, 307
greens, 294–95
hearts of palm, 298–99
herring, 313
jellied, 308–10
lettuce, 290–92
marinated garden salad,
297–98
nasturtium-spinach,
293–94
pea, 301
polk, 294–95
potato, 302–3
rice, 315–16
sauerkraut, 306
slaw, 304–5
spinach, 129, 167–68,
292–93
tomato, 295–97
tuna, 313–14
Salt Pork, 41–42
Samskey, George, Jr.
(Kansas City), 302

Sand Hill Plum Butter, 366

Sauerkraut
  creamed, with cabbage rolls, 142–43
  salad, 306
  with caraway, 286–87
  with ribs, 140–41

Sausage
  with black beans and rice, 150–51
  cassoulet, 45–46
  casserole, 148–50
  country, 151–52
  Czech, 153
  Mexican, 153–54
  Nadjev, 15–16
  turkey apple, 188

Savory Cabbage and Brown Rice Casserole, 240–41

Savory Squash Cobbler, 265–66

Scalloped Carrots, 270–71

Scalloped Potatoes, 254–55

Scallops, 212

Schaffer, Bob (Lawrence), 79, 203

Schippers, Eleanor (Victoria), 362, 382

Schippers, Mrs. Frank (Anna) (Victoria), 223

Schmarren (Pancake Omelet), 362

Schmelzla, Mrs. Jean (Fulton), 69

Schmidt, Hildred (Walton), 50, 401

Schneider, Niki (Lawrence), 122

Schnibbelbohnen (sweet and sour beans), 283

Schroeder, Von (Overland Park), 227, 369, 415

Scrapple, 141–42

Seafood with Red Pepper Noodles, 213–14

Sears, Cindy (Lawrence), 426

Shafer, Joyce (Ada), 93, 110

Shellfish
  lobster, 213–14
  shrimp, 209–13
  scallops, 212

Shepherd Pie, 105–6

Shortcake, strawberry, 419–21

Shreves, Kate (Overbrook), 244, 352

Shrimp, 209–13
  Quantrill, 211–12

Sill Sallad (Herring Salad), 313

Simon, Bill (Eudora), 203

Simple and Delicious Apple Pie, 387

Simpson, Charlene Mason (Garland), 254

Sirloin Steak with Midwest Marinade, 84–85

Skewered Scallops with Garlic and Red Pepper, 212

Skillet Baked Beans, 286

Skinner, Elizabeth M. (Wichita), 350

Slaw
  potato, 305
  sweet and sour, 304–5

Sloppy Joes, 110

Smoked Chicken Salad with Curry Dressing, 167–8

Smothered Quail, 192

Smith, Flora (Ottawa), 160

Smith, Katherine Hahn (Coffeyville), 178

Smith, Ray O. (Longford), 113, 114

Snow Peas, Carrots, and Onions, 272

Sorghum Chewies, 447

Souffléed Turnips, 277–78

Soups, 30–31
  asparagus, 47–48
  bean with ham hocks, 44
  beef and cheese chowder, 37–38
  black walnut, 57
  butter balls in chicken broth, 56–57
  chicken borscht, 39
  corn chowder, 46–47
  cream of country ham, 43–44
  "cure-all" chicken, 38–39
  Czech Christmas, 40–41
  Dopp i Grytan (Dip into Kettle), 33–34
  French onion, 50–52
  Grampa's favorite, 42–43
  parsley-parsnip, 52–53
  poor man's soup with a rich man's flavor, 55–56
  rose hip, 58–59
  spinach, 48–49
  steak, 34
  Swedish fruit, 59–60
  vegetable, 49–51
  Vietnamese beef and noodle, 36–37

Sour cream
  apple pie, 390–91
  beets, 272

corn bread, 346–47
tea biscuits, 446
Sourdough
French bread, 326–27
potato bread, 327–28
starter, 325–26
Soybean bread, 329–30
Soy Nuts, 19
Speedy Beefalo Chili,
117–18
Spicy Gingerbread Cup-
cakes with Lemon
Sauce, 423–24
Spinach
with horseradish and
cream, 276
lasagna, 226–27
salad, 292–94
salad with pork and
pears, 129
soup, 48–49
-tofu enchiladas, 244–45
Spring Peas with Lettuce,
273–74
Squash
baked acorn, 264–65
butternut, 265–67
cobbler, 265–66
fried, yellow, 268
steamed with tomato-
basil butter, 267
zucchini, 279
Stack o' Wheats, 357–58
Stahl, Lillabelle (Burlingame), 374
Steak
flank, 83–84
on a hickory log, 80–81
round, 70–75
sirloin, 84–87
soup, 34
Swiss, 71–72
tenderloin, 77–80

Steakburgers Deluxe,
107–8
Steam-Fried Chicken,
160–61
Steamed Squash with
Tomato-Basil Butter,
267
Steele, Mrs. Robert G.
(Fort Scott), 182,
305, 406
Stevens County Library
(Hugoton), 392
Stews, 30–31
bean, 44
beef, 32–33, 67–69
beefalo, 118
catfish, 39–40
Strawberry
-rhubarb muffins, 356
shortcake with vanilla
cream, 419–21
Strawberry Hill, 14–15
Stuffed Lettuce Salad, 291
Suet Pudding with Lemon
Sauce, 434–35
Sugar-free Apple Pie,
392–93
Sugarless Wheat 'n' Fruit
Cookies, 449
Summer Salad with Citrus
Dressing, 292–93
Sundstrom, Mrs. Albertha
(Lindsborg), 33
Sunflower State Whole
Wheat Bread, 322
Sunrise Muffins, 353–54
Super Crunch Muffins, 17
Swedes, and apples, 276–
77
Swedish
brown beans (Bruna
Bönor), 284
cheesecake with lingon-

berry sauce (Ost
Kaka med Lingon),
426–27
coffee, 26–27
fruit soup (Frukt Soppa),
59–60
ginger cookies (Peppar-
kakor), 445–46
meatballs (Köttbullar),
16–17
rye bread, 333–34
Sweet and Nutty Butternut
Squash, 266–67
Sweet and Sour Cabbage
Slaw, 304–5
Sweet and Sour "Schnib-
bled" Beans (Schnib-
belbohnen), 283
Sweet Macaroni, 18
Sweet Potato
Aunt Jane's, 257
candied, 257–58
grilled sticks, 258
pie, 397
Swiss Cheese Chicken
Supreme, 173–74
Swiss Corn Casserole,
261–62
Swiss Steak, 71–72

Tacha, Mildred (Jennings),
440
Tart Potato Slaw, 305
Thompson, Marj (Hutchin-
son), 257
Todd, Maxine (Sedan), 348
Tofu-Spinach Enchiladas,
244–45
Tomato
and basil salad, 295–96
and brown rice casse-
role, 238–39
-cheese rarebit, 245

Tomato (*continued*)
  relish, 376–77
  salad, 296, 297
Traditional Roast Turkey,
  185–87
Tuna salad, 313
Turkey
  apple sausage, 188
  roast, 185–87
  with apple-tarragon
    baste, 187
Turner, Kristine Leann
  (Chanute), 65
Turnips, 275, 277–78

Veal Scallops with Mush-
  rooms and Onion,
  119–20
Veal Scallops with Tarra-
  gon Sauce, 118–19
Vegetables, 246–47
  casseroles, 238–43,
    262–63, 274
  fried, 252–53, 268,
    281–82
  greens, 275
  meat loaf, 97
  salads, 295–308
  scalloped, 254–55,
    270–71, 280–81
  soup, 50–51
  See also individual
    vegetables
Venison Mincemeat Pie,

10–11
Victoria, 23–24
Vietnamese, 35–36
  beef and noodle soup
    (*Pho Tai*), 36–37
  spring rolls, 13–14
Vinegar Cobbler, 407
Vogel, Irene S. (Law-
  rence), 302, 402
Vogel, Nancy (Hays), 25,
  102, 418
Vopat, Mrs. Frank G.
  (Marie) (Wilson), 40
Vopat, Mrs. Sylvia G.
  (Wilson), 334, 443

Waldman, Lindi Ensminger
  (Prairie Village), 213
Wall, Mrs. Ernest A.
  (Eunice) (McPher-
  son), 426, 445
Ward, Gertrude (Coffey-
  ville), 431
Wassail, 25–26
Webb, Lanora L. (Liberal),
  190
Welcome Pot Roast, 64–65
Wenzel, Elda (Wichita),
  387
Wheat in Kansas, 328–29
Whole Wheat
  biscuits, 351–52
  breads, 321–24
  gingerbread, 422

muffins, 353–54, 356–
  57
  rolls, 338
  soybean bread, 329–30
  vanilla cake, 412–13
White, Shelley (Law-
  rence), 27
Wienck, Sharon K.
  (Barnes), 261
Wild Mulberry Jam, 367–
  68
Wild Rice Club Supper,
  241
Willer, David (Lawrence),
  139
Wilson, 152
Wilted Lettuce, 291–92
Wittman, Caroline
  (Topeka), 34, 376

Yeast, sourdough starter,
  325–26
Yellow squash, fried, 268
Yogurt Pancakes, 361
Yogurt Stuffed Potatoes,
  249

Zacharias, Carol Kennedy
  (Topeka), 325, 326,
  327
Zucchini with Pecans, 279
Zwieback, 339–40